Native American Language Ideologies

Native American Language Ideologies

Beliefs, Practices, and
Struggles in Indian Country

EDITED BY PAUL V. KROSKRITY AND
MARGARET C. FIELD

The University of Arizona Press   Tucson

The University of Arizona Press
© 2009 The Arizona Board of Regents
All rights reserved

www.uapress.arizona.edu

First paperback printing 2010
ISBN 978-0-8165-2916-2 (pbk. : alk. paper)

Library of Congress Cataloging-in-Publication Data
Native American language ideologies : beliefs,
practices, and struggles in Indian country / edited
by Paul V. Kroskrity and Margaret C. Field.
p. cm.
Includes bibliographical references and index.
ISBN 978-0-8165-2719-9 (hardcover : alk. paper)
1. Indians—Languages—Social aspects.
2. Language and culture—America. 3. Ideology—
America. 4. Indians—Ethnic identity. 5. Anthropological
linguistics—America. 6. Indians—Social life and
customs. I. Kroskrity, Paul V., 1949– II. Field,
Margaret C., 1961–
PM108.N28 2009
497—dc22   2008027213

Publication of this book is made possible in part by the proceeds of a
permanent endowment created with the assistance of a Challenge
Grant from the National Endowment for the Humanities, a federal
agency.

Manufactured in the United States of America on acid-free, archival-
quality paper and processed chlorine free.

15 14 13 12 11 10   7 6 5 4 3 2

Dedicated to the memories of my father,
Sid Kroskrity, and my two "elder brothers,"
William Bright and Wick Miller.
And to Sandy, Jack, and Pat.

Contents

Part II. Language Revitalization as a Site for (Re)New(ing) Language Ideologies

Part III. Linguistic Description, Language Activism, and Reflexive Concerns

Native American Language Ideologies

CHAPTER 1

Introduction

Revealing Native American Language Ideologies

MARGARET C. FIELD AND PAUL V. KROSKRITY

The Idea of the Book

All Native American communities have experienced significant changes as a consequence of their contact with European societies and their incorporation into the nation-states of the Americas. These transformations continue today as Native American communities affirm their persistence and attempt to renew their traditions as an expression of their cultural sovereignty. Native American languages and forms of discourse, or ways of speaking, are a critical part of these processes because they provide uniquely important cultural resources for allowing communities to remake themselves, to adapt to transformed social formations, and to recontextualize traditional practices to ever-changing socioeconomic patterns.

This is an especially critical time for most Native American communities as far as their heritage languages are concerned (Zepeda and Hill 1991). In many communities highly fluent speakers are limited to a small number of elders, while in others that enjoy a larger number of people who can speak the language many bilinguals are using more English rather than the heritage language even in key arenas of language usage like language socialization. Most tribes and tribal members have become more proactive in regard to devoting time, effort, and resources to various programs of language revitalization. Heritage language maintenance and renewal programs have become a high priority for almost all tribal communities (e.g., McCarty et al. 2001; Platero 2001; Sims 2001; Yamane 2001).

But decisions about when to speak heritage and/or other languages in a community's linguistic repertoire and choices about whether to actively participate in language renewal efforts—or to assiduously avoid them—

are prompted by *beliefs and feelings about language and discourse* that are possessed by speakers and their speech communities. Beliefs and feelings about language—and those about particular languages—are indeed an acknowledged part of the processes of language shift and language death that threaten many non-state-supported languages. These beliefs and feelings, which linguistic anthropologists term "language ideologies," vary dramatically within and across Native cultural groups. Some Native American communities, for example, have inherited traditions for using language that value linguistic purism, while others perpetuate traditions that value the adoption of loanwords from neighboring languages. In some communities speakers have a long history of regarding their languages as indicators of tribal or group identity, while in other communities speakers do not regard their languages as symbolizing the group. Yet despite the cultural variation in language ideologies and their acknowledged importance to understanding language change and language contact, language ideologies have been ignored by researchers until relatively recently. With few exceptions, the dismissal of language ideologies as a kind of folk awareness of language was standard policy in both anthropology and linguistics until the past two decades. Such beliefs and feelings, according to paradigm-setting scholars like the anthropologist Franz Boas (1911) and the linguist Leonard Bloomfield (1933, 1944), were not proper objects for scientific analysis because of their presumed inaccuracy and general lack of scientific authority.

Today, however, we can effectively argue, as Michael Silverstein (1979, 1985) has done, that language ideologies are a necessary and critical part of any complete analysis of a language in a speech community. Since the 1990s a growing body of literature in anthropology and adjacent fields has emerged that has examined the importance of language ideologies as key factors in any analysis that would relate the language and discourse of any speech community to the sociocultural worlds of their speakers. Paralleling these developments in anthropology and linguistics are long-standing interests in American Indian studies on self-determination, cultural sovereignty, and more recent emphases on the "collective" perspective of tribal groups and the awareness and agency of Indian people (e.g., Champagne and Goldberg 2005; Deloria 2004).

This book, then, is devoted to understanding language ideologies and their role in the sociocultural transformations of Native American communities. Though there have been a number of edited collections of research on language ideologies (e.g., Blommaert 1999; Blommaert et al. 2003; Gal and Woolard 2001; Kroskrity 2000c; Schieffelin, Woolard, and Kroskrity 1998), this volume is the first devoted to studies of Native America. This collection samples the language ideologies of Native American communities from a variety of groups. These groups range geographically from the Canadian Yukon in the North to the Kaqchikel Mayan communities of San Antonio in Guatemala in the South. Most of the chapters deal with tribes who live in the southwestern United States (e.g., Navajo, Apache, Tewa, Hopi, San Juan Paiute); others treat Indians from the Great Plains (Arapaho, Kiowa), the Great Basin (Shoshoni), central California (Western Mono), and the Northeast (Maliseet). The authors of these chapters include members of indigenous speech communities who participate in language renewal efforts as well as several non-Native authors who know the communities they write about through extensive involvement in them and through a collaborative relationship with their members. All of these authors will provide readers with many valuable grounded studies of language ideologies in action, including those indigenous to Native communities as well as those imposed by the dominant institutions of nation-states and by language researchers themselves. Many chapters also consider the emergent interaction of indigenous and imported ideologies and the resulting effect on language beliefs, practices, and struggles in today's "Indian Country."

Introduction

Approximately a quarter of a century ago Michael Silverstein defined linguistic ideology as the "set of beliefs about language articulated by users as a rationalization or justification of perceived language structure and use" (1979:193). According to this definition, a speech community's language ideology is a conscious, or secondary, rationalization about language and its use. A community's conscious, or discursive, language ideology may reflect that speech community's understanding either of language as a code (lexicon, grammar, semantics, etc.) or of the interactional norms and expectations for language use in contexts involving speaking, such as teaching, storytelling, praying, conversation, and so on.

In the past twenty-five years the quest for an understanding of what language ideologies are and how they function within speech communities has been the focus of intensive study and debate in linguistic anthropology. Poststructural perspectives emphasizing the importance of practice in relation to structure as well as to conscious and unconscious forms of knowledge entered the debate (Bourdieu 1977; Giddens 1979), as did theories of ideological hegemony and counterhegemony (Gramsci 1971; Williams 1977). In the study of language ideologies today, as Kathryn Woolard characterizes it, "the tension between different sitings of ideology, between subjectively explicit and constructively implicit . . . versions, is a recurrent concern" (1998:6), and it is generally recognized that language ideology is an inherently plural concept. Just as speakers have multiple voices within their speaking repertoires (Bakhtin 1929, 1963), so do they have multiple ideologies of language, which are as varied and complex as the lives and daily enterprises of speech community members. Language ideologies are profitably conceived as multiple, both because of the plurality of meaningful social divisions (class, gender, clan, elites, generations, etc.) within sociocultural groups that have the potential to produce divergent perspectives expressed as indices of group membership and because of the continuous influence of nonindigenous ideologies that have influence on Native communities through their expression in its dominant institutions. Language ideologies are thus grounded in the social distribution of both indigenous social inequality and the differential impact of colonial and postcolonial contact experiences. Christopher Loether (this volume) describes the multiplicity of language ideologies that obtain for Shoshone communities and their impact on movements to revitalize their heritage language. Language activists in those communities must confront and "manipulate" both indigenous and imported language ideologies that might undermine language renewal efforts. Borrowing from Dorian (1998), Loether discusses the importation of the dominant society's "ideology of contempt," which uses a spurious social Darwinism to regard small languages as deficient and as outcompeted by superior, standardized languages supported by the federal government.

Some language ideologies are more conscious, or higher on a scale of cultural salience, than others that are less accessible to consciousness, being so much a part of everyday praxis, or practical knowledge (Giddens 1984). Following Giddens, Kroskrity (1998) has termed these two opposing ends of the continuum of awareness *discursive* and *practical* consciousness. Both are equally relevant for understanding language change, shift, and obsolescence.

The papers in this volume all derive from ethnographic studies of language use and interaction and are an exploration of language ideologies in changing Native American contexts. They discuss not only indigenous Americans' conscious language ideologies but also the often revealing relationship between such discursive beliefs about language and its use and other, more implicit realizations of language use as embedded in community practice. Starting from an understanding of language ideologies as inherently multiple, a perspective that "focuses attention on their potential conflict and contention in social space" (Kroskrity 2000:12), the contributions in this volume discuss some of the trajectories and results of such tensions on grammar, language use, the relation between language use and social identity, and emergent language ideologies themselves in Native American speech communities.

The basic fact of heterogeneity across indigenous language ideologies of the Americas is one of the main reasons for producing this book—to counter any assumptions concerning the homogeneity of American Indian cultures or of overarching "sameness" in historical experiences of contact with dominant European cultures and institutions relevant to language. In line with contemporary perspectives on language ideology, language use, and identity that emphasize that culture is never standardized or homogeneous (Bucholtz and Hall 2004a; Gonzalez 2000; Kroskrity 2000a, 2000b; Ochs 1996; Rampton 1995), the papers in this volume also illustrate how American Indian language ideologies not only are historically very different from each other but today, *even within a single community*, are typically complex, heterogeneous, contradictory, and even contentious. All of the papers in this volume focus on language ideologies in various North American and Mesoamerican indigenous communities. While most of the authors focus on Native American communities within the United States of America, Barbra A. Meek examines the Canadian Yukon, and Jennifer F. Reynolds studies Mayan communities within Guatemala.

Why Language Ideologies Now?

Why is the study of language ideologies particularly relevant to Native American communities now? There are, indeed, many reasons. These reasons may be related to the relative neglect of such "local knowledge" of languages, to their now-acknowledged powerful role in linguistic and social change, and to the complex transformations of Native American communities, which have experienced unprecedented levels of change and external cultural influence. Terming the first of the above reasons "substantive," we find in some definitions of language ideologies a focus on beliefs and feelings that were previously regarded as inappropriate objects for study by foundational anthropologists like Boas. One of the most straightforward, though insufficiently refined, definitions is that of Alan Rumsey: language ideologies are "shared bodies of commonsense notions about the nature of language in the world" (1990:346). This definition properly highlights the informal nature of most cultural models of language, but it does not problematize language ideological variation (by age, gender, class, etc.), thus promoting an overly homogeneous view of language ideologies within a cultural group. Why is this unsatisfactory? Since social and linguistic variations provide some of the dynamic forces that influence change, it is more useful to have an analytical device that captures diversity rather than one that emphasizes a static, uniformly shared culture. Used in opposition to "culture," language ideologies provide an alternative for exploring variation in ideas, ideals, and communicative practices and for understanding how their dynamic interaction plays out in linguistic and social change. One example of the analytical benefits of adopting a language ideological approach can be seen in the treatment of language beliefs and practices in the Pueblo Southwest. Whereas prior anthropological and linguistic research viewed that area's notorious emphasis on indigenous purism as due to its "linguistic conservatism" (e.g., Sherzer 1976)—a uniformist representation of Pueblo cultures that essentialized this feature of their linguistic culture—a language ideological approach (Kroskrity 1993b, 1998, 2000b) demonstrated how linguistic conservatism actually combined with several other ideals and practices modeled on the culturally salient and powerful register of "kiva speech" (te'e hiili). By carefully relating this register to the social inequality and the ceremonial erasure of intragroup divisions by class, clan, and age, through a discussion of Pueblo language ideology, "linguistic conservatism" has been better explained, resulting in an analysis that is both more probing in its exploration of the origins and ramifications of linguistic conservatism and more consistent with Native experience. While language ideological analysis can provide a more insightful and incisive analysis, it also tends to rescue important observations about the cultural diversity of language beliefs and practices that have been substantively ignored or neglected. Historically, so much attention to linguistic difference has been devoted to purely linguistic differences—differences of grammar and lexicon—that we are still just beginning to fully appreciate the diversity of language ideologies within and across communities.

Because languages are used by all people to perform so many social functions in their daily lives, language ideologies are both ubiquitous and diverse. There are local language ideologies for language socialization, for interpersonal communication, for constructing local identity, for linguistic representation, and for storytelling, to name but a comparative few loci for ideological production and metacommentary. Though language socialization studies in Native America are comparatively rare (but see Augsburger 2004; Bunte, this volume; Crago, Annahatak, and Ningiuruvik 1993; Field 1998; Meek 2001; Messing 2007; Pye 1992; Reynolds 2002; Scollon and Scollon 1981), especially given the importance and prominence of this comparative project (e.g., Ochs 1988; Schieffelin 1990; Schieffelin and Ochs 1979), studies of cultural variation in socialization practices add importantly to our understanding of how children are socialized by and to language practices. Regarding the aesthetics of interpersonal communication, Basso has described the emphasis among Western Apaches on a noncoercive, succinct verbal style in which interlocutors rely heavily on the active participation of listeners and regard an overly explicit and voluble speaker as acting "to 'smother' (*bika' nyinłkaad*) his or her audience by seeming to say, arrogantly and coercively, 'I demand that you see everything that happened, how it happened, and why it happened, exactly as I do'" (1990:153). In a study of Eskimo patterns of discourse in the English of college students at the University of Alaska, Kwachka and Basham (1990) note that Yupik and Inupiaq students' essays demonstrate a high degree of "circumspection of assertion," a traditional cultural stance linked to speaking that is retained despite language shift to English.

In many Native American communities these ideologies of communication are used in conjunction with other distinctive cultural values as resources for constructing indigenous identities in opposition to "white," Euro-American, hegemonic "others." In separate studies, for example, Basso (1979) and Trechter (2001) have demonstrated the role of such oppositions in identity construction for Western Apache and Lakhota communities, respectively. Turning to storytelling, we find many ideologized preferences in the various cultural traditions for conveying traditional narratives. In Western Pueblo storytelling, as among the Hopi and the Arizona Tewa, narrators have their long turns ratified by listeners using brief conventional expressions of their involvement (Kroskrity 1993b; Wiget 1987). For the Kiowa, "listeners are almost always being invited to participate in the storytelling itself, to add to, to comment, to interpret, and to keep the story going" (Palmer 2003:96). Other language ideologies that are important, especially in regard to language change, are those pertaining to language contact, such as those that valorize indigenous purism (Field, this volume; Kroskrity 1998) and the ownership of names, titles, ritual knowledge, and performance rights (e.g., Silverstein 2003b; Whiteley 1992). Another highly important feature of many Native American language ideologies, and one that contrasts markedly with many Euro-American folk understandings, concerns the functional role and "power" of language. Whereas "reflectionist" (Silverstein 1985) Euro-American language ideologies emphasize the denotational and referential functions of "words for things," many Native Americans possess language ideologies that view language and speech more "performatively" —as a more powerful and creative force that "makes" the natural and social worlds they inhabit. Without understanding these and other Native American language ideologies, scholars and researchers—both Native and non-Native—cannot hope to understand Native American languages and the ways speakers use them, change them, and renew them.

Other sensitizing definitions of linguistic or language ideologies have often shown a tension between emphasizing speakers' "awareness" as a form of agency and foregrounding their "embeddedness" in the social and cultural systems in which they are enveloped. In addition, these definitions also illustrate the mediating role of linguistic anthropology as an interdisciplinary field concerned with relevances of both linguistics and sociocultural anthropology, including notions about the structure and relationships of both linguistic and social systems. Silverstein's (1979:193) definition of linguistic ideologies cited earlier emphasizes the role of linguistic awareness as a condition that permits speakers to rationalize and otherwise influence a language's structure. Exhibiting a more sociocultural emphasis is Irvine's definition of language ideologies as "the cultural system of ideas about social and linguistic relationships, together with their loading of moral and political interests" (1989:255). Here language ideologies are viewed as multiple and constructed from specific political economic perspectives that, in turn, influence "the cultural ideas about language." Certainly, language ideologies are not merely those ideas that stem from the "official culture" of the ruling class but rather are a more ubiquitous set of diverse beliefs, however implicit or explicit they may be, used by speakers of all types as models for constructing linguistic performances, conducting evaluations and assessments, and otherwise engaging in communicative activity. They are beliefs about the superiority or inferiority of specific languages, such as the sentiments expressed by some missionaries and boarding school teachers of the nineteenth and early twentieth centuries that Native American languages were too primitive, too heathen, or associated with the devil (e.g., Dauenhauer and Dauenhauer 1998; House 2002). Native Americans and their languages have been influenced not only by what they and dominant society "others" thought about indigenous languages but also by what Native Americans and non-Native Americans thought about English, French, Spanish, and other "official" languages of the various nation-states in the Americas. For example, beliefs in the superiority of English, in some social Darwinist sense (Dorian 1998); sentiments behind so-called English-only legislation that English is somehow a "threatened" language (e.g., Crawford 1992; Schiffman 1996:270–75); and Euro-American language ideologies that iconically link language and nationality have all had some influence on Native American speech communities and their various language ideologies.

Native American Languages and Colonial Institutions

Given the powerful impact of colonialism on indigenous societies throughout the world (Errington 2001), it is particularly appropriate to view the institutions of the dominant society as an especially important source of hegemonic influence and to present a brief overview of them here. American Indian language ideologies share some commonalities with other indigenous speech communities due to a common history of colonization and cultural and linguistic oppression by Europeans, some of whom viewed unwritten languages as primitive and even barbaric, as specifically stated by U.S. Commissioner for Indian Affairs J. D. Atkins in 1887:

> Schools should be established, which children should be required to attend; their barbarous dialects should be blotted out and the English language substituted. . . . The object of greatest solicitude should be to break down the prejudices of tribe among the Indians; to blot out the boundary lines which divide them into distinct nations, and fuse them into one homogeneous mass. Uniformity of language will do this— nothing else will. (U.S. Congress 1868)

As this quote also reveals, some Western language ideologies also presupposed monolingualism to be the preferred state of affairs, and, as Errington found in his study of "colonial linguistics" in Oceania, "monolithic languages [were mapped] onto demarcated boundaries . . . [and were] conceived to be ethnolinguistically homogeneous groups" (2001:24). There is an immense amount of indigenous linguistic diversity in the Americas, conservatively estimated at 193 language families (Campbell 1997). The hundreds of indigenous languages spoken in the Americas, like those on other continents, were all consciously undermined by colonial regimes in educational contexts, whose goal was nothing less than total cultural and linguistic assimilation. In this volume Meek examines how the Canadian government has just in the past decade begun making serious efforts to reverse previous efforts to assimilate Aboriginal peoples, finding that "the main policy direction, pursued for more than 150 years, . . . has been wrong" (Government of Canada 1996:x, cited in Meek, this volume).

But even though many indigenous American speech communities have shared experiences as colonized peoples, from federal policies of tribal removal and relocation to forced cultural and linguistic assimilation at Bureau of Indian Affairs boarding schools, their historical and cultural experiences have also been equally divergent, including vast differences in geography and cultural adaptation to it, history, religion, social organization, and traditional attitudes toward language use. In North

America alone there were at contact possibly as many as 2,500 distinct languages (Campbell 1997) and just as many varied and complex histories of interaction with European cultures, including French-, Spanish-, and English-speaking peoples. Some American Indian cultures came into substantial contact with Europeans almost half a millennium ago, whereas others were able to retain their traditional cultures and languages well into the twentieth century, only truly coming into substantial contact with the English language with the building of roads that brought electricity, day schools, and mass media to extremely rural communities. (Contributions in this volume by Reynolds, Field, and Pamela A. Bunte discuss the recent rapid shift that is still in progress in the Mayan, Navajo, and San Juan Paiute communities, respectively.) Many indigenous communities in Mesoamerica and South America still number in the hundreds of thousands and are only now entering into the very beginning of endangered language status, as increasing numbers of children are monolingual speakers of dominant culture languages and greater numbers of indigenous peoples move from rural to urban communities (England 1998; Grinevald 1998). Large and extremely rural Native American speech communities whose languages are still relatively "safe" include Navajo, Ojibwe, Cree, and Inuktitut, all with over fifty thousand speakers as of the 1990 census (Grimes 2005; Valentine 1995). According to Krauss (1998), all the indigenous languages in the United States and Canada together currently number 211, of which 179 are currently moribund (not spoken by children). For various reasons, many of which are outlined in the contributions to this volume, even those communities whose languages are not yet considered entirely moribund may still be considered "endangered." On the other hand, Krauss also finds that thirty-two North American Indian languages *are* still spoken by children, including Yupik, Cherokee, Choctaw, Lakota-Dakota, Navajo, Western Apache, Cocopa, Yaqui, Hopi, Zuni, Havasupai-Hualapai, Jemez, Northern Tiwa, Eastern Keres, and Tohono O'odham, among others (with smaller populations of child speakers). Goddard (1996) estimates there are nine more indigenous languages spoken in Mexico that are not yet moribund. The number is probably greater in South America than in North America due to the combined factors of greater linguistic diversity as well as rurality of indigenous populations. Another factor is national pride in an indigenous identity; for example, the indigenous language Guarani, which has an estimated speaker population of approximately six million, is (together with Spanish) an official language of Paraguay (Silver and Miller 1997).

The process of language shift has frequently been described as an unconscious and monolithic process (Dorian 1989; Fishman 1991) that follows a typical and predictable pattern in every society. Romaine (1989) describes this "classic pattern" as including the stages of transitional bilingualism and diglossia, which typically may last for centuries, at least in the case of minority speech communities in Europe. This has not been the case, however, in North America, although it is often assumed to be so, as Romaine states: "In North America, Native languages have . . . undergone extreme shift since the first contact with Europeans" (1989:39). On the contrary, many rural Native American communities, such as the Navajos, found it necessary to teach English to schoolchildren until well into the 1970s (Spolsky 1978). Two of the chapters in this volume particularly take issue with top-down analytic approaches that assume invariability in the nature of social forces involved in language shift: Kroskrity focuses on the fact of individual agency on the part of speech community members and its power to effect real change in a community's language ideology, while Jeffrey D. Anderson focuses on cultural- and history-specific variation in contexts that either promote or suppress indigenous language use. Kroskrity rightly points out that most language ideological research in the past has typically highlighted the role of structure over agency, and he focuses on the individual agency and lived experience of one key actor in Western Mono language revitalization efforts. A better understanding of agency and systemic constraints on agency in relation to language ideologies and revitalization efforts may be extremely useful in understanding why academic or top-down maintenance efforts often fail, as opposed to local "grassroots" movements that are more integrated into the communities they arise in and more often succeed. (See Carter and Sealey 2000 for more discussion of social versus structural integration as applicable to sociolinguistic theory.) Collins also discusses the issue, linking agency to ideological differences between academics and indigenous communities: "As academics . . . we inhabit positions as specialists in state-certified institutions that make our statements and our silences unavoidably interest-laden" (1998:259). In this volume Amber A. Neely and Gus Palmer, Jr., pursue some of the same issues as relevant to Kiowa language revitalization efforts in Oklahoma. Bernard Perley also addresses the interplay of "agentive opportunism" and his own dual stance as both an academic and an educator involved in Maliseet language revitalization efforts. Understandably, many indigenous communities today remain deeply suspicious of any efforts involving either their people or their languages on the part of academic institutions (see also Hill 2002).

The History of Indian Education in the United States: An Overview

The history of Indian education in North America has been as unstable and contradictory as the attitude of the federal government has been over time toward the status of Native American groups in general. This schizophrenic attention to Indian education in the United States (as in other parts of the Americas) has understandably been related to the progress of language shift from indigenous languages to English (or Spanish). Although for the most part federal educational policy toward tribes commonly reflected a belief in the necessity to assimilate indigenous cultures to Western culture as rapidly as possible, often by removing children from their homes and forbidding them to speak their languages, this policy was not always the case, nor was it practiced with an equal amount of dedication in all parts of North America. A brief historical outline of federal policy toward Indian education may help illustrate this point.

During the earliest period of interaction between Europeans and Native peoples in North America, which spanned approximately 350 years, from contact in 1500 to the late nineteenth century, the education of tribes was typically left to different missionary groups, predominantly Catholic and Protestant. At this early point the choice of whether to send their children to these schools was also left up to the tribes themselves, and, not surprisingly, many tribes elected not to subject their children to Western educators, who as often as not considered play to be a sinful activity (Szasz 1988) and used corporal punishment to enforce pedagogy. During the century of treaty making between the federal government and various tribes (1778–1881), several treaties included educational provisions, and in 1802 federal money was specifically set aside for the first time "to provide Civilization among the aborigines" (Reyhner and Eder 1992). This money was divided amongst various missionary groups, and this was the arrangement until 1873.

Although religious organizations ultimately sought to convert Native Americans to Christianity in one form or another, missionary groups were by no means united in a belief in the importance of abolishing indigenous languages. Rather, many missionary groups recognized the importance of getting their message across to people in a form they could truly understand, and to this purpose it was not infrequent for educators to learn the language of the community they worked in as well as to hire successful Native students as teachers in mission schools (Reyhner and Eder 1992; Szasz 1974). Some Native cultures, most notably the Cherokees, developed writing systems for their own languages and instituted schools where their children were taught literacy in their own tongue. The Cherokees have been reported as having had extremely high literacy rates prior to their removal from their ancestral homelands to Indian country (what would later become Oklahoma) in the 1830s (Silver and Miller 1997). After their arrival in Oklahoma, the Cherokees, along with other relocated tribes, initiated their own schools, which employed a majority of locally trained Native teachers. However, the federal government closed these schools in the late 1890s (Fuchs and Havighurst 1972).

During the first half of the nineteenth century the federal government began to establish its own Indian boarding schools, which were run first under the auspices of the War Department and later under the Bureau of Indian Affairs. These schools taught Indian students manual labor skills and were dedicated to the eradication of indigenous languages along with all other vestiges of Native cultures; however, relatively few Native children attended them, and missionary groups continued to provide the bulk of Indian education for some time.

In 1867 the federal Indian Peace Commission, appointed by President Grant, called for a policy of cultural and specifically linguistic erasure:

> Through sameness of language is produced sameness of sentiment, and thought; customs and habits are molded and assimilated in the same way, and thus in process of time the differences producing trouble would have been gradually obliterated. . . . In the difference of language today lies two-thirds of our trouble. . . . Schools should be established, which children should be required to attend; their barbarous dialect should be blotted out and the English language substituted. (U.S. Congress 1868)

In 1880 the BIA issued regulations requiring that all Indian education, whether in government or missionary-run schools, must be done in English, or the schools would risk losing government funding (Prucha 1973). In spite of this threat, some missionary schools continued to employ Native teachers as well as use materials written in Native languages. (See Reyhner and Eder 1992:42–43 for specific examples drawn from various historical sources.)

By the beginning of the twentieth century, government funding of missionary schools had ended, and the BIA had twenty-five boarding schools in fifteen states serving approximately ten thousand students (Reyhner and Eder 1992; Szasz 1974), a number that was far from the total population of Indian children at the time. Compulsory attendance was reinforced by laws permitting the BIA to withhold rations and annuities from Indian families who did not send their children to school (Prucha 1973). By 1912 there were more Indian children attending public schools than BIA-run boarding and day schools, although in many rural areas boarding schools continued to be necessary due to lack of roads and transportation.

Indian education in the United States continued to deteriorate until the 1930s, when, under the direction of John Collier, a new and progressive BIA commissioner, more day schools were built, and textbooks in Native languages were again permitted. There was a greater emphasis on Indian culture in BIA schools, and an Indian preference in hiring made it possible for schools to hire bilingual teacher's aides.

Although relatively rare, bilingual teaching materials and bilingual teachers were still very much needed at this point and in some parts of the country continued to be needed up until the 1970s, as the majority of children in many rural areas were still entering school as dominant speakers of their Native languages (U.S. Congress 1969). In 1975 a revised Indian Education Act authorized funding for culturally relevant and bilingual curriculum materials. Within a decade nearly seventy American Indian bilingual education projects were being funded (McCarty 1993).

In 1966 the first tribally controlled "contract school," the Rough Rock demonstration school, was started on the Navajo Reservation; it was followed in 1969 by the first tribally controlled community college, also on the Navajo Reservation. Today both of these educational institutions teach classes in Navajo and also emphasize the importance of literacy in

Navajo. By 1988 there were sixty-five tribally controlled contract schools, and the number has continued to grow, as has the number of indigenous language programs for school-age children. With very few exceptions, today Native languages are taught as second languages to Native children. There are also twenty-eight tribally chartered colleges and three federally chartered Indian colleges across twelve states, as well as many departments of American Indian studies, all of which recognize the importance of indigenous languages. Many offer heritage language courses to local communities. The goals of heritage language courses vary, from language maintenance and indigenous literacy to language preservation and revitalization, depending on the state of the language(s) as well as local language ideologies. For ideological reasons, not all indigenous communities (especially in the Pueblo Southwest) agree about the benefits of committing their languages to written form, as Whiteley has recently argued quite eloquently: "In the transition to literacy . . . language is often flattened, secularized . . . reduced to a symbolic code largely lacking in constitutive agency" (2003:718).

Language Ideologies and Representation of Identity

The process of language shift, although completed centuries ago for some Native American speech communities (especially in the northeastern and southeastern culture areas of the United States, which, like California, are areas in which contact with Europeans was the most catastrophic), is only now taking place in others and has as much to do with indigenous language ideologies as it does with economics, sociopolitical hegemony, and geography. For example, some communities were historically bi- or multilingual, such as those along the West Coast in what is today the state of California. Before contact with Europeans, the indigenous inhabitants of California spoke somewhere between sixty and eighty languages (Silver and Miller 1997) from at least seven distinct language families (Hinton 1994), and multilingualism was commonplace. The contributions in this volume from Loether, Kroskrity, and Bunte all discuss traditional ideologies found among multilingual tribes that speak languages in regions adjacent to the Great Basin culture area. These ideologies emphasized the utilitarian nature of language(s) and historically did not link language to identity; rather, identity was linked to knowledge of cultural activities.

Hensel (1996) has made this same case for Yupik communities in Alaska. In a study of Native identity that compared Iroquoian and Algonquian peoples' public discourse, Valentine (1994) found similarly that, for Algonquian peoples, identity is most commonly linked to land and a respect for nature as a primary symbol of identity, while Iroquoian peoples view language as a more salient marker of identity.

In other parts of Native America, such as the Pueblo Southwest, language is such an important and salient marker of identity that speech communities are commonly closed to outsiders, and societal bilingualism has been (until the late twentieth century) sporadic at best (Silver and Miller 1997). Multilingualism, though more rarely societal, was common among those individuals or groups who needed to use a second language for intergroup trading and exchange, for the communication of esoteric ceremonial knowledge, or for linguistically accommodating to dominant groups. For example, Pueblo Indians who actively traded with non-Pueblo Native groups like the Comanches, Apaches, and Navajos needed to learn those languages well enough to make successful exchanges. Similarly, ceremonial elites in each pueblo were likely to have some command of neighboring Pueblo languages so that they could communicate about ritual matters (Kroskrity 1993b). We know that some Pueblos used such communication to restore ceremonies that had become defunct in their own communities. We also find multilingualism as a response to cultural dominance in the acceptance of Spanish among the Eastern Pueblos (dating from the colonial period during the sixteenth century) and, later, English throughout all the pueblos. One group, the Arizona Tewas, is the only group to experience the diaspora caused by colonial occupation and still retain its heritage language. Multilingualism was a major part of the Tewas' successful adaptation to their numerically superior Hopi hosts, and, since about 1750, the Arizona Tewas have exhibited a stable bilingualism in Hopi and Tewa (Kroskrity 1993b). In general, however, it is appropriate to see the relatively high degree of political centralization, the elaborate social organization, and the regulation of most marriage choices within most Pueblo groups (as opposed to extrapueblo intermarriage) as discouraging a norm of societal bilingualism with neighboring languages (as in Native California).

Some communities have embraced indigenous forms of literacy, whereas others have decided not to mix traditional languages with the context of modern schooling (McLaughlin 1992; Pecos and Blum-Martinez 2001; Sims 2001; Spolsky 1978). In the Pacific Northwest and parts of the adjacent Plateau culture area (Oregon and Washington), where tribes have traditionally valued wealth, status, and rank to a relatively great degree (Sapir 1949b, 1994), "words" have taken on objectual qualities, and language is now seen as a collection of words or a special kind of property (Moore 1988). In this contemporary view, which belongs most notably to these two indigenous culture areas in the Americas, languages, or what is left of them, are now considered a form of "inherited wealth" that, like other valuable property, is meant to be displayed, enhancing the legitimacy and prestige of the speaker. This is an example of what Whiteley calls the "reflexivization" of culture and language, a process brought on by globalization in which "cultural self-consciousness expands exponentially and shifts the register of significance for pre-existing cultural performances . . . especially . . . the more marked symbolic forms of cultural difference like rituals, dress, and language" (2003:715).

The process of language shift in most Native American communities is definitely not an unconscious one; instead, most community members are very aware of it. In such communities, as degree of fluency decreases, its importance as a "badge of identity" increases proportionately, and community members attain a heightened state of awareness concerning the level of fluency of other community members claiming, legitimately or otherwise, to be speakers. Community debates abound concerning what should be done to reverse language shift, but opinions and solutions vary from community to community. Complicating factors such as linguistic purism on the part of older speakers and/or linguistic insecurity on the part of younger speakers may or may not be involved. Attitudes toward codeswitching or language change may differ across communities. Several of the chapters in this book deal with these issues, among others.

Language ideological approaches view beliefs, sentiments, and practices regarding language as subject to great sociocultural variation. Traditional social categories like gender, age, and position within a social system influence views on language and speech practices, and people are likely to adopt, maintain, or modify language ideologies that reflect their sociocultural perspective and rationalize views from that vantage point. Thus, in Hill's (1998) study of Mexicano linguistic ideologies, when older Mexicano speakers in the Malinche Volcano area of central Mexico say the Mexicano equivalent of "Today there is no respect," this nostalgic view is more likely to be voiced by men. Although both genders recognize the increased "respect" once signaled by a tradition of using Nahuatl honorific registers and other polite forms, "successful" men are more likely to express this sense of linguistic deprivation of earned deference. Mexicano women, on the other hand, are more likely to express ambivalence; having seen their own lot in life improve during this same period of declining verbal "respect," some women are less enthusiastic in supporting a symbolic return to practices of former times (Hill 1998:78–79). In Kroskrity's (1998, 2000b) research on Tewa *te'e hiili* (kiva speech), he maintains that it is the social inequality of Tewa society that is partially responsible for the power of this ceremonial register through its association with a theocratic elite and with ceremonial performances that temporarily "erase" divisions by class, clan, and age and construct a unified Arizona Tewa society. In the present volume, Margaret Bender finds that Cherokee language use is seen as a marker of identity in both the Eastern and Oklahoma Cherokee communities: in both communities it is linked to Cherokee traditionalists as well as Christian cultural conservatives, and it is assumed that if someone is a serious learner of the language, he or she will ultimately act as a cultural leader of some kind. Several chapters also discuss cases of generational conflicts as an older generation valorizes traditional practices (like indigenous purism for the Navajo, as described by Field, this volume) that are not reproduced by a younger generation. In the Arapaho and Kaqchikel Mayan communities, as described by Anderson and Reynolds, respectively, we find an older generation stigmatizing the speech and speech practices (and, implicitly, the language ideologies that rationalize their greater use of nonindigenous dominant languages) of a younger generation. Given the amount of sociocultural change and the transformations of these speech communities, it is, of course, not surprising that any attempts to reproduce traditional cultural ideals and practices will be necessarily recontextualized to changing historical circumstances as partial reproductions and that members will rationalize the perspective of their generation's linguistic adaptation in the form of language ideologies of varying degrees of explication. As discussed by Irvine and Gal (2000), language ideologies that work to construct identity may exist at the level of *social activities* or *social roles* rather than among individuals within a culture. Irvine and Gal's notion of "fractal recursivity" as a semiotic process through which people construct ideological understandings of linguistic differences is crucial for understanding how it is that conflict and contradiction between language ideologies may exist even for a single individual. In other words, a single individual (within any speech community) may hold conflicting attitudes regarding a language and its use, for example, that speaking an indigenous language is crucial to one's identity as a member of that group but that one prefers one's children to be monolingual speakers of English because one perceives the dominant language as more useful for economic success (cf. Field's discussion of Navajo language ideologies, this volume). As Irvine and Gal point out, identity is produced as much through opposition and practices that promote exclusion, divergence, and differentiation as it is through cultural and linguistic homogeneity or uniformity. This perspective goes far to explain the fact of great dialectal heterogeneity in many indigenous speech communities, especially along the Pacific coast (Golla 2000).

Language ideologies are productively used by speakers as a cultural resource in the creation and representation of various social and cultural identities (e.g., nationality, ethnicity, gender, sexuality) (Bucholtz and Hall 2004a, 2004b; Trechter 1999, 2006). Language, especially shared language, has long served as the key to naturalizing the boundaries of social groups. The huge volume of scholarship on nationalism and ethnicity typically includes language as a criterial attribute. Bunte cogently observes that Southern Paiutes from San Juan have experienced ethnolinguistic repercussions as a result of their successful bid for federal recognition as a discrete group even though they live within the boundaries of the Navajo Reservation and previously lacked a language ideology that iconized their language to their ethnic identity. In part because of the role of the Southern Paiutes in boundary maintenance (Barth 1969) with surrounding Navajos, language ideologies regarding ethnolinguistic identity now emphasize the Southern Paiutes' heritage language as an expression of their identity and have moved into "discursive consciousness"— they are more self-conscious of their emblematic role in constructing their own identities in their "border zone" location (Rosaldo 1988).

In this volume several chapters examine language ideologies that relate language and tribal identity. In San Juan Paiute, Western Shoshoni, and Western Mono communities, changes have occurred that have led to a relatively recent iconization of languages to specific ethnic and tribal identities (Bunte, Loether, and Kroskrity, this volume). In these communities, factors such as a cultural emphasis on intratribal levels of organization, multilingualism, and significant levels of interethnic interaction had traditionally diminished a cultural emphasis on "the tribe" or ethnic group. But as tribes became more important units of administration and "recognition" (Silverstein 2003b) and as greater familiarity with the language ideologies of dominant institutions in the United States promoted a rethinking of language and identity relationships, ideologies that iconized language and identity in accord with those of the nation were adopted. Dealing with a comparable situation in the Canadian Yukon, Meek (this volume) explicitly demonstrates how new syncretic ideologies of language and identity were forged out of dialogues between First Nation elders, language experts, and government workers.

Thematic Concerns in This Volume

Although the chapters in this volume reveal obvious variation in attitudes toward language across American Indian communities, they also reveal some commonalities, especially in the more emergent or contemporary ideologies, which all have in common the fact that language shift is at their heart. Probably the most frequently noted of these across all the contributions in this volume is an emergent ideological process of iconization (Irvine and Gal 2000) between a language and various national, ethnic, and tribal identities (see also Nevins 2004). As Bunte, Kroskrity, Loether, and Reynolds all discuss in their contributions, this ideology of iconization is particularly new for the speech communities they work with (San Juan Paiute, Mono, Shoshone, and Mayan, respectively). All five of these communities have for centuries embraced traditional language ideologies that saw dialects as reflecting *family and kinship group*, not *tribal* or *national* identity, and that honored linguistic variety over any notions of "correctness" such as those associated with a standard or prestige dialect. Kroskrity uses the term *variationist* to refer to this egalitarian language ideology. Following Kroskrity, Loether also discusses variationist language ideology in Shoshoni country and, in particular, how the Shoshoni Language Project has aimed to manipulate it, as project members have found it to have negative consequences for their language revitalization program. Reynolds calls it a "localist ideology" and points out that contemporary Pan-Mayan iconic ideology is also an "ideology of unification" that, without identifying any Mayan varieties as more or less prestigious, views them all equally as indexical of or iconic with Mayan identity as opposed to Spanish or Guatemalan. Chapters both by Bunte and by Jule Gómez de García, Melissa Axelrod, and Jordan Lachler suggest that emergent iconizing (language and identity) ideologies are symbiotic with language revitalization efforts and are crucial to their success, as they reinforce the high level of commitment needed to make grassroots language programs work.

Bunte and Kroskrity both link emergent identity-iconizing ideologies to recent efforts to achieve federal tribal recognition, a crucial status for tribes within the borders of the United States that entitles them to Indian Health Service benefits and potential gaming revenue, among other economic benefits, and for which evidence of speaking a distinct indigenous language is a partial requirement. Both of these authors (but particularly Kroskrity, for whom the role of *agency* in changing language ideology becomes a major focus) also link emergent iconic ideology to individual agency of particular community members. In her discussion of Mayan communities Reynolds also argues that models for language shift reversal, both academic and Pan-Mayan, often undertheorize or ignore entirely the agency and power of children in the process of language shift. As sociolinguistic and language socialization research has shown, caregivers are not the only sources of input for children's developing language ideologies (Field 1998 and this volume; Hill 2002). Children as a peer group may have their own norms for interaction that may differ from those of their parents (Field 1993), although these norms may be far from conscious. Sociolinguists have likewise observed that children may be leaders in language change within speech communities (Labov 1978; Wald 1981). Children may even differ from adults in terms of the value, or linguistic allegiance, that they attach to one language or another in bi- or multilingual communities (Field 1998 and this volume; Kroskrity 1993b).

The chapters by Anderson, Reynolds, and Gómez de García, Axelrod, and Lachler also point out that emergent language ideologies in indigenous communities may also be quite transparently taken from linguistic theory. Reynolds and Gómez de García, Axelrod, and Lachler discuss how a "strong version" of Sapir and Whorf's theory of linguistic relativity is often verbalized by Mayan and southwestern indigenous language speakers but with constructive intent and results for indigenous language maintenance, as in this view heritage languages are seen as inherently superior (to English or Spanish) in descriptive power. On the other hand, it should be noted that House (2002) has made an eloquent argument to the effect that this kind of essentialism may have equally dire results for language maintenance. (See also Field, this volume, on how Irvine and Gal's [2000] notion of *erasure* is also relevant here.)

Academic language ideology may also have negative consequences for language revitalization efforts, as discussed to some extent by Anderson and Reynolds in their contributions to this volume. Anderson discusses how, in the Northern Arapaho community, a professional ideology on the part of linguists involved in language pedagogy that views language as "synchronic text-based code and lexicon" has now been internalized by Arapaho language teachers and has led to difficulties. The chapter by Reynolds examining Pan-Mayan language revitalization efforts discusses how an emergent academic ideology on the part of Pan-Mayas of national identity and unification interacts with more traditional localist or variationist language ideologies.

Reflexivity, in its more conventional anthropological sense as the effect that researchers have on their cultural representations of others (e.g., Kroskrity 2000b:32), is magnified today via the changing manner in which research is produced and appreciated within transformed and internally diverse Native American communities. Collins (1998) has already called attention to the disjuncture between members' language ideologies and those of the language professionals with whom they work. Silverstein (1998a) has suggested the need for greater awareness on the part of all linguists of the impact of their own language ideologies and language politics on those of the Native American communities in which they work. Neely and Palmer also make this point in their chapter on language ideologies related to the proliferation of Kiowa orthographies, pointing out that if a standard orthography is to be embraced, the decision must be one that is community based if it is to be accepted.

Loether writes, perhaps controversially, of the need to "manipulate" local language ideologies that obstruct language renewal efforts. Activist, even more than descriptive, linguists certainly need to understand their own language ideologies and ensure that these accord well with community perspectives with regard to setting and achieving realistic goals for language revitalization. Linguistic researchers need to examine their own ideologies as part of their "ideological clarification" (Dauenhauer and Dauenhauer 1998). This attempt to disclose the language ideologies of the researcher in order to better understand indigenous ideologies suggests an important contribution of a language ideological approach for those searching for a "decolonizing methodology" for conducting linguistic research in indigenous communities (Smith 1999:147–48). Only by becoming more aware of their own language ideologies, both those of their profession as well as those imported from the hegemonic institutions, can linguistic researchers appreciate those of indigenous communities. Perley makes this point in his chapter on Maliseet language revitalization efforts and emergent language ideologies. He takes pains to identify, analyze, and reconcile his own perspective(s) as both a member of the Maliseet community as well as an interdisciplinary academic influenced by his training in art and his involvement in Maliseet language revitalization efforts.

Some chapters discuss American Indian conceptualizations of language as a performative, dynamic entity. In her chapter examining Athabascan language ideologies in the Yukon, Canada, Meek finds that language is conceptualized as an entity "on the move," expressed in the sentiments of Yukon elders concerning the current language situation; for example, "I go by myself, no grandchildren behind me. . . . [W]e got to work hard so our grandchildren will come behind us" (Aboriginal Language Services 1991:10). This language ideology is not so far removed from that discussed by Witherspoon (1977) for Navajo speakers (whose language also belongs to the Athabascan language family) regarding the power and sentient force of language (and see House [2002] for an extended discussion of how this ideology relates to language revitalization efforts). As Silverstein (1979) has discussed, this ideology, which views language as a powerful performative force, directly conflicts with Western "reflectionist" language ideology, which views language as merely reflecting (and not affecting) an objective world "outside" of language. Neely and Palmer refer to this ideology within the Kiowa community. Especially within what they call the "discourse of tradition," they find that some Kiowa elders believe that Kiowa language should be taught only through traditional oral methods rather than through writing because "tampering" with the language "might cause something to go terribly wrong." Loether also discusses performative language ideology in Shoshoni speech communities, where he finds that people often refer to the power that language has, resulting in consequences for language use and revitalization, such as avoidance of particular words.

Finally, several of the authors here find that indigenous language ideologies link heritage languages to stylistic contexts, including religion, poetry, and storytelling. Gómez de García, Axelrod, and Lachler and Justin B. Richland report that, in the Southwest, heritage languages are preferred for describing traditional values. In his analysis of discourse from a Hopi tribal courtroom Richland describes how a Hopi advocate argues that she can explain her client's perspective, which is based on traditional Hopi values, only in the Hopi language, not in English. Richland calls this an ideology of "pragmatic relativity," as Hopi has pragmatic superiority over English for talking about things Hopi. Gómez de García, Axelrod, and Lachler discuss how many elder members of various southwestern indigenous communities (Navajo, Pueblo, and Apache) have repeatedly made statements to the effect that, for them, English lacks the descriptive and imagistic characteristics of their heritage languages. Anderson makes the same point in his chapter on Arapaho language shift, that a large part of a culture is constituted through and contained in the metaphors and cognitive imagery of its heritage language. Neely and Palmer also report that for many Kiowa people the Kiowa language is preferred for prayer.

Altogether, the chapters in this volume represent a small sampling of language ideologies to be found among indigenous peoples of the Americas. Though a more comprehensive coverage of all the Americas, one that includes representative speech communities from all culture areas and linguistic families, is a desirable and much-needed project, it would require the proportions of a large reference tome rather than those of an edited volume. At this stage, it is also appropriate to note that not all contemporary linguistic work is informed by a language ideological approach, and we hope that the present volume encourages researchers to extend this type of work to new areas and to see its relevance to more practical activities like linguistic documentation and community-based language revitalization. We especially regret the absence of contributions from indigenous speech communities in Alaska and South America, areas that are rich in a variety of Native languages, many of which are still very vibrant. But we hope this book is useful to students and researchers interested in various cultural perspectives on language ideologies, language shift, and revitalization, among other related issues, and that it encourages more work on these issues in those communities not represented here.

We fully recognize that a pioneering effort can never represent the "last word" on a particular topic. We have necessarily sought a middle ground along the dimensions of theory and method, on the one hand, and practical application, on the other. At the risk of being neither theoretical nor applied "enough" for some readers, this collection does, we feel, make a strong case for this theoretical emphasis by providing compelling case studies and advancing comparative study of language ideological processes. A widely shared feature of these studies is the focus on ideological disjunction, conflict, and change arising from the collision of indigenous and Western language beliefs and practices. Revealing language ideologies in the Native American context means disclosing the role of these beliefs and feelings in such conflicting and ongoing processes as hegemonic domination (and the reassertion of cultural sovereignty by tribes), colonization (and attempts at "decolonization" by indigenous communities), and syncretic attempts to shape practices and policies (both state government and tribal) to the evolving language ideologies of indigenous communities.

Apart from considerations of theoretical scope are the very legitimate practical concerns of indigenous communities and their concerns for language maintenance and the cultural continuity it ensures. Though we have hardly provided a "how-to" book for communities and language activists, we feel we have demonstrated the practical implications of recognizing a multiplicity of indigenous language ideologies and their impact on heritage language maintenance and renewal. In sum, we recognize that there is still much important work to be done in this area, and we hope our readers will find this volume a useful stepping-stone for further advances both in carrying forth some of the resources presented here and in addressing novel theoretical and applied problems that we have only begun to engage.

PART I

Language and Language Ideological Change

CHAPTER 2

Changing Navajo Language Ideologies and Changing Language Use

MARGARET C. FIELD

This chapter presents an overview of observations on Navajo language use throughout the twentieth century and contrasts these with contemporary observations about Navajo language use and language ideology today, in the early years of the twenty-first century. Whereas earlier work in the twentieth century by linguists and anthropologists described a comparatively conservative and homogeneous Navajo speech community, a perspective often echoed by the Navajo Nation itself today (House 2002), observations by contemporary linguists and anthropologists (Field 2001; House 2001, 2002; Schaengold 2004) have described it as emergent, heterogeneous, and even contradictory. This chapter adopts a perspective on language ideology as equally complex and dependent on the social categories of age, class, occupation, and religion (among others). I begin by reviewing some current examples of Navajo and English codemixing from naturally occurring discourse and point out that the norms for contemporary Navajo language use differ sharply from those observed and commented upon in the linguistics and anthropological literature of half a century ago. I then provide an example of actual structural change in Navajo grammar, showing how a distributive plural morpheme has come to function like an English plural morpheme. This further illustrates how previous observations on Navajo language attitudes have changed in contemporary usage. I then turn to a discussion of Navajo language ideology and consider how attributing what may be described as a relatively sudden shift in language use to a simple increase in the degree of contact with English language does not entirely explain the recent and rapid shift in Navajo language attitudes. I suggest that this change may be better understood through a consideration of heterogeneity in Navajo language ideologies and norms for language use across different segments of the

Navajo population. Following Irvine and Gal (2000), I suggest that contemporary Navajo language use and language ideologies (as in every
speech community) may be understood as a result of the interplay between various social groups (age, class, and religious affiliation, in particular) and the activities that exist within them.

Changing Language Use:
From "Resistance to Borrowing" to Codemixing

Linguists and anthropologists writing in the early 1900s shared common
observations on the conservative nature of Navajo language use. The concept of language ideology was not in use at that time, and Edward Sapir
actually attributed a conservative "psychological trait" to Athabascan languages rather than speakers (Navajo being a member of the southern
branch of Athabascan): "The Athabaskan languages of America are spoken by peoples that have had astonishingly varied cultural contacts, yet no-
where do we find that an Athabaskan dialect has borrowed at all freely from
a neighboring language. These languages have always found it easier to
create new words by compounding afresh elements to hand" (1949b:196).

At present, and in contrast to the norms of half a century ago, codemixing among bilingual speakers of Navajo and English is quite common, especially among middle-aged and younger speakers, as observed
by Young and Morgan:

> In recent years the tempo and extent of cultural borrowing have increased
> as Navajos in ever increasing numbers have gone to school or experi-
> enced life outside Navajo country. Bilingualism has grown as never be-
> fore, and there is a distinct trend on the part of bilingual speakers to mix
> the languages. The tribal council has generally insisted upon linguistic
> purity, sometimes stopping speakers in the middle of their discourse to
> insist that they speak only one language at a time, but children and
> Navajo radio announcers, as well as bilingual speakers generally tend to
> insert words and phrases from English into their Navajo discourse, espe-
> cially if the person to whom they are speaking is bilingual. (1987:7)

Codemixing by fluent Navajo speakers today generally involves mixing English nouns and adverbial phrases but not verbs into Navajo discourse. The extremely polysynthetic nature of the Navajo verb helps to

ensure this, as it is difficult for speakers who perceive verbs as a single conceptual unit to integrate English into the verb complex. The following examples illustrate this kind of codemixing, which is currently common among Navajo speakers. Most of the English nouns in the following examples have not been "Navajo-ized" in terms of phonology, either, suggesting that they should not be termed "borrowings." For example, the noun "Christmas" (in example 7) has a borrowed alternate form in Navajo (*keshmish*), but the speakers I recorded chose to use the English form instead. Examples 1–4 are drawn from one thirty-minute conversation between two Navajo-dominant bilingual speakers on the campus of the University of New Mexico, where they were both attending classes in 1997. Both of these speakers were in their midforties at the time of the recording, and Navajo is the dominant language for both of them.[1]

1. A: hai baa a'íínáá'á   last weekyéę?
      who for indef.1pl.object.drop.down week.gone
      "Whom did we [you] vote for last week?"
   B: éí t'áá níléí   absentee ballotígíí
      that just there   ballot.that one
      "just that absentee-ballot one"

That the conversation was predominantly conducted in Navajo may be observed from the fact that all of the verbs, which contain most of the grammatical information, including subject and object, as well as a wealth of other information, were in Navajo. In this example the Navajo verb "to vote" translates approximately as "to drop something down" (as a ballot into a box), illustrating the preference described by Sapir for creating new words (at least, verbs) in Navajo rather than borrowing them. The English in this example includes an adverbial phrase ("last week") and a noun phrase ("absentee ballot"), and these both show that Navajo morphology may be integrated with these parts of speech (as opposed to the verb) without any difficulty.

Example 2 is from a discussion about an economics class that both participants were taking at the time. Here many of the English expressions are nouns that are connected to the domains of school and test taking, which are relatively new contexts within Navajo culture (Deyhle 1986); this is a prototypical environment for borrowing from English (Holm, Holm, and Spolsky 1971).

2. A: Ha'at'e'ígíí   nanidayikidgo?
    what.one(s).which   thematic.distr.3subj.ask.sub
    "What in particular did they ask you [on the test]?"
  B: dikwííshįį questions . . .
       how.many
    "(I don't know) how many questions . . ."
    t'óó ahayoí, seven pages daatsí.
    many   maybe
    "A lot, maybe seven pages."
  A: ((WHISTLES))
  B: graphs, dóó, aadoo nda łahdo formulas.
       and then but also
    "Graphs and, and then but also some formulas."
    Ndi the last oneígíí . . . two pages multiple choice.
    but   one.rel
    "But the last one in particular was two pages of multiple choice."

Line 1 in example 2 contains the only verb, which contains a piece of morphology I will turn to in the next section: the Navajo distributive plural -da-. Navajo does not mark plurality on nouns but rather either encodes it in the verb stem or else uses this distributive plural morpheme, which lends a slightly different meaning. In this example it means that several questions were being asked (this will become relevant in the next section).

The next example illustrates a fairly rare kind of English–Navajo codemixing that has been termed a Navajo "auxiliary verb" construction by Canfield (1980) and Christ (1999). Typically, these constructions involve a borrowed English verb and two common Navajo verbs: "to make" or "to do." This is the only way that I have seen any English verbs borrowed into Navajo, and it is somewhat rare, at least in the speech of fluent speakers, although as Christ (personal communication) suggests, it is more frequently seen in the Navajo of younger speakers. Here the speaker is referring to a pair of moccasins he has been commissioned to make for a woman he knows.

3. B: Aadoo   ashłeehí   bich'į   show–adeeshłííł.
    Then   1p.make.imp.rel to her   1p.make.fut
    "Then I will show her the ones that I make."

The above examples have been offered as evidence to illustrate that, contrary to the observations of Sapir and other researchers of Navajo language writing in the early twentieth century, today English is frequently mixed into the discourse of fluent Navajo speakers to the extent that it may be called codemixing, that is, codeswitching within a single clause (Hill and Hill 1984). Although this form of language use has been described as devalued by researchers of Pueblo language use (Kroskrity 1993b) and is likewise considered inappropriate in more formal contexts within Navajo culture (such as political meetings), it is common now in casual conversation (for more discussion see Christ 1999).

Structural Change: From Distributive Verbal Prefix to Plural Nominal Suffix

In addition to borrowed English lexicon, ideological change is beginning to affect the Navajo language at the level of grammatical structure as well. One way in which this is occurring is in the extension of the "distributive plural" verbal prefix (seen above in example 2) to a nominal suffix, marking plurality on nouns (even English ones) in casual conversation.[2]

The following examples show the use of the distributive plural affix -da- in a way that connotes not distributive action but rather plurality of a noun phrase, and it occurs on the end of noun phrases, like an English plural s.[3] Example 4 below is from the same conversation as examples 1–3; examples 5–7 are from a bilingual speaker in the Los Angeles area.

4.
1	A: . . . (3) ha'át'eego shįį at'e ya'		. . .	i'iinííł	bich'į
2		why	maybe it.is ques.	indef.is.dropped	toward
3	holzhishgo,	níléí,			
4	season.being	there			
5	. . . (3) why is it . . . toward election time, there,				
6 →	deeyíjeehigíída,				
7	incept.3+run.rel.pl.				
8	the ones who start competing,				
9	yádałt'ígo			t'áá,	
10	themat.distr.speak.sub		just		

11   when they are speaking,
12 →   campaignda   'adeł'įgo,
13   pl. indef.distr.3p.make.sub
14   when they are campaigning,
15   . . . Hashtłíísh yee   'adzitłééhgo.
16   mud   by.them   indef.is.being.thrown
17   . . . mud is being thrown.

This example contains three tokens of the morpheme -*da*, one as a distributive plural prefix on a Navajo verb (its traditional usage) in line 9 (*yá-dałt'ígo*, "several persons are speaking") and, more interestingly, two that appear to function like the English plural nominal suffix (-*s*). In line 6 the morpheme -*da* occurs at the end of a nominalized verb, *deeyíjeehigíída*, "the ones who are competing."[4] The second noun-pluralizing usage occurs at the end of the English borrowing, "campaign," in line 12. The following examples provide additional evidence that this Navajo morpheme is beginning to function like an English plural:

5. Siiké   łeh,   gohweeh dóó cookies-da níléi   náyíídįįhgo.
   Dual.sit usually coffee and pl. there iter.we.enjoy.sub
   We usually stay home, enjoying coffee and cookies there.
6. łahdi   éíya, six months-da nahidéélgo nahasht'a łeh.
   there.at specifically   pl. iter.objs.pass.sub iter.I.fly (w/wings) usually
   I usually fly back every six months.[5]
7. Christmas doodaí Thanksgiving-da   éí   shimá   nayists'íí
                  or   pl.   anaph.   my.mom   iter.I.fly
                                                              (on a plane)
   Christmas or Thanksgivings I fly [back to] my mom again.

In examples 5–7, -*da* follows an English noun ("months-da") or a noun phrase involving English nouns ("gohweeh dóó cookies-da," "Christmas doodaí Thanksgiving-da"), even though in 5 and 6 the English nouns "cookies" and "months" are pluralized already. The verb *siiké* in example 5 contains the verb stem *ké*, "two people sit," so it's difficult to conceive of the "coffee and cookie consuming" as a distributed action (which always involves three or more participants). Clearly, -*da* does not serve as a distributive plural here. In example 6 the verb *nahidéélgo* refers to the motion of "months" as a single connected set, passing, so again the verb does not connote distributed action. In example 7 the verb *nayists'íí* refers to the flight of a single entity, so it also cannot be conceived of as distributed action. Rather, in examples 5–7 -*da* serves a pluralizing function on noun phrases that is sometimes redundant and not at all a traditional Navajo usage.

Changing Language Use, Changing Ideologies

The above examples also illustrate the fact that Navajo language ideology has changed over time to the extent that codemixing is now frequent, at least in informal conversation. Anecdotal observations concerning different Navajo attitudes toward not only codeswitching but also bilingualism may be found sprinkled throughout the anthropological literature starting as early as the 1940s:

> The striking purity of the Navajo language reflects a Navajo psychological—that is, cultural—trait of great historical importance[:] . . . [c]onservatism in language in an otherwise syncretistic culture. The highly independent spirit of the Navajo includes a definite disinclination to learn and speak the languages of other peoples. That most Navajos avoid speaking whatever English they have had to learn is familiar to Southwesterners. . . . Possibly less widely noted is the fact that the Navajo do not generally speak other native Southwestern languages. Pueblo Indians are noted linguists. . . . I have been addressed in Navajo by Acomas and Hopis . . . [but] I do not recall having heard a Navajo who has retained Navajo culture and attitudes speak any Pueblo language or anything approaching fluent Spanish. . . . Southern Utes . . . often speak fairly good English quite freely, and in general also speak either Spanish . . . or Navajo, or both; the Navajo do not speak Ute. (Reed 1944:145–46)

The noted scholar of Navajo language and culture Father Bernard Haile also came to a similar conclusion: "Pueblo contact has not influenced Navajo to a noticeable degree, while Spanish elements are comparatively few, and English elements practically none" (1941:1). W. W. Hill, writing on southwestern trading practices, offered the following anecdotal observation along similar lines: "Language barriers were of little importance, though mention was made by the Navajo that some of the Ute and Pueblo spoke Navajo and acted as interpreters. . . . [T]he Navajo, like Americans, evince little interest in any language but their own" (1948:387).

The Franciscan fathers offer the following observation on Navajo attitudes toward neighboring speech communities, which helps to explain
early-twentieth-century Navajo language ideology from a sociolinguistic
perspective: "For neighboring tribes, such as the Zuni and Hopi, the
Navajo cherish a sense of natural superiority in addition to a traditional
contempt for the latter tribe. The American, though not equal to the
Navajo in rank, is respected according to deportment, while the Mexican,
with few exceptions, comes in for a considerable share of paternalism"
(Franciscan Fathers 1910:439–40).

In the second half of the twentieth century, however, Navajo attitudes
toward English (at least) appear to have been rapidly changing. In their
1971 study of English loanwords among Navajo schoolchildren, Holm,
Holm, and Spolsky found many occurrences of English nouns and attributed this apparent increased receptivity to loanwords among Navajo
speakers to increased contact with English speakers, beginning during
World War II, when large numbers of Navajo men served in the armed
forces and others left the reservation to work in war-related industries. In
addition, they point out that, prior to the 1950s, fewer than half of Navajo
children attended school, whereas by 1955 attendance figures were closer
to 90 percent. The postwar period ushered in a period of great economic
and sociological change. Following the Meriam report of 1928, which
found that the few schools on the Navajo reservation were servicing less
than a third of school-age children (Young 1968), the Navajo Nation
began petitioning for more funding for education. In the 1950s several
federal programs were undertaken to address the need for educational
reform, including the Navajo-Hopi Long Range Rehabilitation Act, the
Special Navajo Education Program (which resulted in thousands of Navajo children being sent to off-reservation boarding schools), the Navajo
Emergency Education Program (NEEP) of 1954 (which addressed the
issue of the need for on-reservation schools), and Public Law 815, which
appropriated another $20 million for public schools on the reservation.
These "crash" programs for education understandably resulted in a simultaneous huge increase in the use of the English language, as all of the
teachers involved at this point were non-Navajo English speakers, and a
main focus of education on the reservation was the teaching of English as
a second language.

It would seem reasonable to conclude that increased contact with

English might be the reason for the increase in codemixing by Navajo speakers today. Yet it does not account for observations such as the following provided by Voegelin, Voegelin, and Schutz in their extremely thorough study of southwestern cross-cultural language use: "We know from a monographic source that some Navajo veterans of World War II reacted to Anglo-American social exclusion upon their return to the Southwest by refusing to speak English when spoken to in English. This reversion to a feigned monolingualism from demonstrated bilingualism is not necessarily restricted to returning veterans, or even to men" (1967:439).

Nor does an explanation based on increased contact alone explain the previous observations about Navajo hesitancy to adopt loanwords from other indigenous southwestern languages or from Spanish, nor does it explain all of the (often contradictory) facts about changes in Navajo language use. There is no dearth of research showing that Navajo and Pueblo peoples have been living in close proximity for centuries (Kroskrity 1982, 1993b; Schaafsma 2002) and that many other nonlinguistic aspects of Puebloan cultures have been incorporated into Navajo culture; certainly, Navajo people were exposed to various Puebloan languages to as great an extent as they have been to English (although the quality of the exposure was very different).

The influence of sociocultural factors such as the relative sizes of speech communities in contact as well as the degree of socioeconomic dominance that one speech community may be able to exert over another are important considerations for understanding language change and language shift (Dorian 1989; Thomason 2001). However, as Kroskrity (1982, 1993b) points out, especially in southwestern Native American communities these two factors alone are not enough to explain the dynamics of language contact, as language ideologies, or beliefs concerning the relationship between language and identity, or the appropriateness of specific codes in relation to specific contexts may exert powerful influences as well. As linguistic anthropologists have increasingly realized, language ideologies within a speech community as well as within a single individual are typically complex, heterogeneous, and sometimes contradictory (Irvine and Gal 2000; Kroskrity 1998, 2000c; Woolard 1998).

In his study of Yupik Eskimo identity, Hensel (1996) illustrates that the influence of a dominant culture is not homogeneous across all members of indigenous communities. Elders often cleave to traditional models of identity, whereas younger members may be more likely to internalize the dominant culture's biases and stereotypes about ethnic identity. And since language has traditionally been a crucial "badge of ethnic identity" among indigenous southwestern cultures (Kroskrity 1982), we should expect to see age variation in attitudes toward language as a symbol of identity as well. Analytical approaches that assume "ethnic absolutism" ignore the sociolinguistic relevance of social categories such as age, gender, sexual orientation, residence, occupation, interests, roles, and so on (Rampton 1995:8). For example, young people may intentionally exaggerate the differences between their own and their elders' communicative repertoires. The fallacy of the existence of top-down, culturally homogeneous ideologies, especially as related to language use, has been argued by several scholars writing on ideologies of language and identity (Briggs 1998; Gardiner 1992; Irvine and Gal 2000; Kroskrity 1998; Ochs 1996; Rampton 1995; Voloshinov 1962; Woolard 1998). Rather, these scholars argue for a model of language ideology as complex, multiplicitous, and socially constructed through the tension between cultural practice and discursive beliefs.

Language Ideologies as Inherently Multiple, Emergent, and Contentious

As Woolard (1989) reminds us, many earlier views of language and language use had an unfortunate tendency to anthropomorphize languages as actors with tendencies, and this was a mistake. Whereas earlier academic views on language and culture may have made assumptions about the homogeneity of members' attitudes and beliefs, today poststructuralist perspectives seek to deconstruct those earlier views and understand the repercussions of a "bottom-up" approach to explaining the processes of language change and language shift, among others.

Such an approach emphasizes the tension between the "subjectively explicit and constructively implicit" (Woolard 1998:6) or between conscious, discursive ideology and habitus, or practice. Irvine and Gal (2000) propose a model for understanding sociolinguistic and ideological complexity that is based on three key semiotic processes: iconicity (between a language and a culture), recursiveness (or the projection of oppositions between groups or linguistic varieties), and erasure (the process that renders some persons, activities, or sociolinguistic phenomena invisible). In the following, I use this model as a theoretical heuristic while reviewing the multiplicitous nature of language ideology within the Navajo community today.

Irvine and Gal's notion of iconicity has to do with the tendency on the part of both outsiders and insiders to essentialize or reduce the nature of "Navajo-ness" to something homogeneous and simplistic (but for slightly different perspectives on iconization of language and identity see other chapters in this volume by Gómez de García, Axelrod, and Lachler; Kroskrity; Bunte; and Richland). As House (2002) clearly illustrates in her excellent work on Navajo identity and language use, this particular semiotic process is common within the Navajo community and potentially harmful to the process of language maintenance today. For example, an insistence on the part of the Navajo Nation's tribal government and/or administrators at Dine College that homogeneity exists regarding the ability to speak the Navajo language or that there is a consensus regarding the necessity of acquiring Navajo literacy disregards the fact that many young people today do not speak the Navajo language and may feel a combination of linguistic insecurity and embarrassment that prevents them from trying to learn (or causes them to drop out of programs that require demonstration of competence in the Navajo language).

Stable diglossia, in Fishman's (1980) sense of two unrelated languages being used within separate, distinct domains (such as home versus school), has never been the case in the Navajo speech community, although this is a common assumption on the part of outsiders and even a fallacy perpetuated by some within the Navajo community who would like it to be true. Rather, in many Navajo homes, uncompartmentalized bilingualism has been the case since approximately World War II, followed by English monolingualism on the part of schoolchildren since approximately 1975. Intergenerational differences in language use are great. Middle-aged members of households are typically called on to serve as interpreters between the oldest and the youngest generations. This situation has also been described for several other southwestern languages, including Comanche (Casagrande 1954), Keres, Tiwa, and Arizona Tewa (Kroskrity 1982). These communities have in common with the Navajo a couple of historical facts. First, they were originally large enough to survive the "biological death" that wiped out many Native

American languages through rapid reduction of population (Hill 1983). Second, they have all been the victims of "imperfect transmission," or an interruption in the natural process of language socialization across generations, in conjunction with the rapid acquisition of a new language by large numbers of a population within a lifetime. For indigenous speech communities in the Southwest this interruption may uniformly be attributed to the existence of BIA boarding schools.

Irvine and Gal's second semiotic process, recursiveness, is helpful in thinking about the multiple kinds of oppositions and layerings of ideology that exist today in the Navajo community across age groups as well as other social groups. As Kroskrity (1982:58) has suggested, boarding school life created a new reference group for many young Native Americans who gained an "urban orientation" that their unschooled parents did not share. Returning Arizona Tewa students, for example, felt comfortable answering their elders' Tewa discourse in English, a sure sign of a new disparity in values attached to different codes. In the Navajo community these returning boarding school students, who today are older adults, often are heard to verbalize the sentiment that English is important as a "language to get ahead," and for this reason they want their children to be native speakers of English. Today those children often are dominant speakers of English, having only a passive (receptive) competency in Navajo at best. A crucial aspect of Irvine and Gal's recursivity is that it recognizes ideological oppositions between activities or social roles, that is, as existing at the intraindividual level rather than defining oppositions between stable social groups. This analytical perspective allows for (and makes sense of) apparent contradictions in language ideology within the Navajo community, such as the fact that many members of the same bilingual generation discussed above who want their children to be native speakers of English also share a language ideology in which Navajo is an important symbol of group solidarity (Brown and Gilman 1960). The value of bilingualism is not a foregone conclusion for many members of this generation, however, as some believe their own ability to learn English has been impaired by the fact that they also speak Navajo.

A view of Navajo language as central to group solidarity is also shared by many elder monolingual Navajo speakers (Parsons-Yazzie 1995, 1996). However, elder monolingual speakers also have their own point of view concerning Navajo language use, what Dorian (1994b) has termed "older speaker purism" (see also chapters in this volume by Anderson and Loether for further discussion of this topic). They do not approve of Navajo language change or the increasing degree of codemixing. Young adults and adolescents, on the other hand, enthusiastically embrace code-mixing and, perhaps less consciously, changes to Navajo grammar. This age group in many cultures has its own ideas about group solidarity that revolve around age as well as ethnicity. Then there are the Navajo children of today who have access to English-language media their parents never had in the form of movies, TV, magazines, and video games. As Holm and Holm (who are both educators) have put it, "In most schools and communities, Navajo does not have the 'status' that English does. The more rural and/or economically poor students in ESL programs tend to be just those who have relatively lower status in the school and community. Thus begins the vicious cycle whereby the use of Navajo in school comes to acquire low status, as Navajo is equated with rurality, poverty, and lack of 'cool' " (1995:154–55).

This language ideology is not shared by most Navajo adults.[6] In fact, it is often the exact opposite: rurality may be associated with a low annual household income, but it also often coincides with traditional religious practice, a high degree of Navajo language retention, social class differences, and, as discussed in Levy and Kunitz (1974), access to resources on the Navajo reservation.

According to Aberle (1966), class distinctions have existed in Navajo culture at least since the mid-nineteenth century, when the acquisition of livestock together with good grazing land allowed some families to increase their wealth more than others. In a more recent study Levy and Kunitz (1974) found that religious differences on the Navajo reservation tended to follow class lines. Levy and Kunitz argue that wealthier Navajos, who historically have held more livestock and grazing land, have been able to continue living a traditional pastoral lifestyle and tend to practice traditional Navajo religion, whereas poorer Navajos have had "more incentive to adopt white ways" (1974:186) and have more frequently adopted Christianity. I might add, from my own observations, that "upper-class" Navajo families also typically control access to important community economic and political resources such as school boards and/or chapter houses. Notably, the language used in Navajo Nation politics and chapter house meetings is Navajo, so the link between Navajo language and political or economic power is fairly obvious. On the other hand, some Christian Navajos, whom Levy and Kunitz identify as commonly lacking access to political and economic resources on the reservation, have been known to complain to school districts that they do not want their children learning the Navajo language because of a perceived close affiliation between Navajo language and traditional Navajo religion.

Irvine and Gal's notion of recursivity is seen in the clustering of oppositions across activities or social roles (albeit all of them Navajo) such as age, religion, lived experience, and social class. Thus, to the degree that an opposition is perceived between historically wealthy and well-connected Navajos and those who are disenfranchised in Navajo terms, this opposition is reinforced by oppositions in religion (Christian versus traditionalist) and attitudes toward the Navajo language. At the same time, this recursivity is cross-cut and further complicated by ideologies that vary (and cluster) across age groups. For example, "elder speaker purism" (regardless of religious affiliation) is linked to powerful feelings concerning Navajo identity and group solidarity and is in direct opposition to a variety of language ideologies on the part of younger Navajos, be it linguistic insecurity, an emergent identity as speakers of "Navlish," or rejection of Navajo language entirely on the part of very young children.

Finally, Irvine and Gal's third semiotic process, erasure, seen in a disregard for internal variation, is also apparent in the Navajo community (and not just attributed by linguists and anthropologists). The work of House (2002) has explored this dimension of Navajo language ideology in detail, but, to summarize here, the process of erasure is most obviously seen in assertions of the existence of community-wide bilingualism (or stable diglossia) on the part of government and academic institutions, which insist on or require a degree of Navajo fluency that many tribal members cannot meet. It is also seen in elementary school programs that choose to ignore beliefs on the part of some Navajo parents that school is not the appropriate context for Navajo language (this may be true of both traditionalists and Christians). And it is seen in the antithetical belief held by many Navajo parents that schools will manage to teach their children Navajo, so the parents don't have to.

Implications for Language Shift and/or Maintenance

That Navajo language ideologies, at least among younger speakers, are changing to allow codeswitching and codemixing may be a positive force for Navajo language maintenance. As pointed out by researchers of language shift and obsolescence (Gal 1989; Huffines 1989; Schmidt 1985), an ideology of "elder purism" may be deadly to endangered languages, whereas a certain amount of flexibility, such as in allowing codeswitching by imperfect younger speakers, can only encourage younger speakers to try to learn their heritage languages, albeit with a likely possibility of language change. The structural change discussed in the first half of this chapter is an example of such change. On the other hand, because Navajo is an extremely polysynthetic language, with a tightly integrated verb structure, it is unlikely that Navajo verb structure will change much, apart from allowing the incorporation of English verbs into "auxiliary constructions." The examples presented here all come from the conversation of fluent bilingual speakers who prefer to integrate English noun phrases into their predominantly Navajo speech. What younger, imperfect speakers of Navajo would likely do is the opposite: integrate Navajo noun phrases and discourse particles into clauses with predominantly English verbs.[7] This would not be a good strategy for Navajo language maintenance, because if younger speakers do not practice producing Navajo verbs, they will never be able to master them. Whether a tolerant attitude toward codeswitching will prove to be a force for language maintenance or language shift would appear to be very hard to predict at this point.

Conclusion

To summarize, I have tried to show that Navajo grammar and language use, described as "extremely conservative" within just the last half century, is now changing in response to use by bilingual and increasingly English-dominant speakers, many of whom not only freely borrow English nouns into Navajo but codemix as well. I have also provided evidence for a structural change in Navajo grammar involving borrowing into Navajo of an English grammatical form (plural marking on noun phrases), further illustrating how Navajo language attitudes have changed and are reflected in contemporary usage of fluent Navajo speakers. However, I also argue that this relatively sudden shift in language use and language attitudes is not adequately explained by reference to a simple increase in the degree of contact with English but may be better understood through a consideration of heterogeneity in Navajo language ideologies and norms for language use across the different social categories of age, class, occupation, and religion (among others). I have employed Irvine and Gal's (2000) model of three key semiotic processes to illustrate this point. In particular, the semiotic process Irvine and Gal call recursivity is useful for understanding how language ideologies may differ and conflict even for a single individual.

Members of the Navajo community, like all human beings, adopt multiple social roles across various contexts and in doing so may find themselves (more or less consciously) speaking English and/or Navajo to different extents. These social contexts and social roles have changed over time in response to contact with Euro-American culture, government policies such as forced assimilation through boarding schools, economic opportunities on and off the reservation, and many other forms of social change over time (see Anderson, this volume, for a discussion of how such changes have affected Arapaho language use and language ideology). I have discussed some ways in which Navajo language use and language ideologies align or oppose each other across age, class, and religious lines as well as other kinds of life experience (such as growing up in a boarding school or suffering discrimination on or off the reservation). Navajo language ideologies also vary across contexts, such as tribal council meetings, informal conversation, and playground interactions, among an infinite number of others. Some of these ideologies, especially those related to formal contexts (such as political meetings, school instruction, and religious or ceremonial contexts), may be more conscious or discursive, with proscriptive rules concerning language use (i.e., no codemixing or English at all or, alternatively, no Navajo at all). On the other hand, Navajo language ideologies may also be unconscious, unspoken, or simply implicit in social practice, especially in less formal contexts and among younger members of the speech community. Navajo people may have both types of language ideologies, and conflict between them may be difficult for individuals to resolve, as when some adult fluent speakers feel guilt over their children's lack of fluency later in life. Yet it is important to realize that there are legitimate rationalizations and ideologies on the part of parents and children for this language shift, which is increasingly the norm.

Irvine and Gal's semiotic process of recursivity explains how language ideologies that conflict across social groups (whether based on age, religion, class, or other social factors) may intensify each other. Linguistic purism on the part of elders may trigger linguistic insecurity on the part of younger, imperfect speakers, which may lead to younger speakers' refusal to speak the language and intensify language shift. On the other hand, tolerant attitudes toward language change such as the example discussed in this chapter (of the distributive plural verbal morpheme coming to function like an English plural morpheme on noun phrases), an inevitable result of language use by bicultural, bilingual younger community members, can only be helpful. The Navajo speech community is one of the largest indigenous speech communities in North America, with over 100,000 speakers, yet it is experiencing language shift. The reasons for this shift are as complex as the lived experiences of all of the Navajo people themselves and their multiple attitudes, sentiments, and beliefs regarding the Navajo language. We can only hope that the Navajo language will continue to change in response to use by future generations of Navajo people in an ever-changing world.

CHAPTER 3

Contradictions across Space-Time and Language Ideologies in Northern Arapaho Language Shift

JEFFREY D. ANDERSON

In 1878, when the federal government relocated the Northern Arapaho tribe to the Wind River Reservation in Wyoming, all of the approximately eight hundred members were fluent in their indigenous language. Most were also fluent in Plains Indian sign language, some in one or more neighboring languages, and only several in English. By 2005 less than approximately 7 percent of the more than six thousand members of the tribe remained fluent in Arapaho. As Salzmann (1998:287) confirms, language shift has progressed to what can be defined as an irreversible stage. At present all remaining fluent speakers are bilingual and members of at least the grandparental generation. The age discrepancy in fluency varies with family and individual childrearing contexts, but only several people under the age of seventy remain fluent. Today, all children acquire English as their first language. In all social domains English predominates except in educational contexts for language renewal, ceremonial speech, and occasional interaction among elders. When elders are together they sporadically switch to Arapaho but generally only for a few exchanges as a speech event unfolds. Despite concerted efforts over the past twenty-five years, language renewal programs have produced no fluent speakers among younger generation students studying it as a second language in formal educational contexts.

In the Northern Arapaho speech community the process of language shift over the past seventy years, and more recent efforts in the past three decades to reverse it, have been concomitant with a proliferation of competing and converging language ideologies. During the same history the Wind River Reservation social landscape and temporal order have changed dramatically. During my first continuous field study of 1988–94 I participated in many language and cultural education programs and was thus daily immersed in discourse articulating these ideologies. As Arapaho people talked about elements or the whole of language(s), I came to realize that the ideologies expressed were efforts to understand and resolve contradictions generated by the dramatically changing environment beyond language itself.

Older fluent speakers today comment, often with a profound sense of loss, that they have few opportunities in their daily lives to speak Arapaho with others. With modern ordering of space-time, the vast majority of elders live in nuclear or extended domestic social spaces in which they are the single speaker or only one among several fluent senior relatives. Those who participate in interviews and educational programs often mentioned to me that they looked forward to such rare times to speak the language and connect with others in their own generation.

As many observe, language shift is not just a demographic process of declining numbers of speakers but also a process of contracting "domains" of usage (Fishman 1972:440–53) or sites of cultural production (Silverstein 1998b:138). Language or speech does not, however, construct the social space and time of its use sui generis. As I explain elsewhere (Anderson 1998:51–52), domains themselves are equally constituted by the interdimensionality of time and space on a number of levels. The socially constructed spaces and time orientations in which Arapaho people live, such as ceremony, home, school, political discourse, and economic activity, have all changed significantly in history, both in the ways sites reproduce social relations internally and in the speech practices that link the domains together. Borrowing a useful term from Giddens, it is insightful to examine speech practices and reflective ideologies relative to "time-space zones" as individuals and groups move through "time-space paths" (1987:146) in daily life and trajectories of larger extension, such as the annual calendar, life cycle, and family history.

What is needed is more attention in anthropology to the way communities change their speech practices in response to constructed changes in the physical and social environment. Built environments can enhance or inhibit any social practices, whether by design or unintentionally (Lawrence and Low 1990:461). More generally, as Harvey recognizes, imposed orders of space and time are the principal apparatus of "conquest, imperial expansion, and neocolonial domination" (1990:419). Following Foucault (1984:252), it can be said that governments exert power through built forms in a process of canalization, the control of the flow and distribution of individual bodies in space. With respect to time, Munn states, "Control over time is not just a strategy of interaction; it is a medium of hierarchic power and governance" (1992:109).

Top-down-imposed orders of space and time were alien to indigenous peoples and as a whole were the primary apparatus for transforming the system of social reproduction, including language and culture. It is therefore essential to examine ways Arapaho people have tried to appropriate those structures, construct new structures, or adapt traditional ones to invent or sustain language and culture.

In Native American history, dominant ideologies and their instantiation in local space-time orientation have never been coherently hegemonic. Approaches to language ideologies must steer theory away from reified social forces or hegemony toward an understanding of competing and historically shifting ideologies, which Friedrich defines as "pragmatic ideologies" (1989:300–302), grounded in the particular, concrete practices in local, socially constructed spaces and time orientations. Rather than blending, though, Euro-American oppressive and progressive ideologies have generated enduring contradictions in a hybridized chaos unique to the space-time of reservation communities in the United States.

Wind River, like other reservations, is largely a constructed environment (Lawrence and Low 1990) always in the making and remaking, shaped by state policies that shift precipitously among competing, evolving ideologies that never congeal into a coherent or uniform system of thought qualifying as hegemony any group can embrace or resist in total. Thus, Arapaho language has shifted to English in a history in which, as Althusser recognized, "the locus of confrontation may vary according to the relation of the contradictions in the structure in dominance in any given situation" (1969:215–16). Dominant language ideologies are therefore neither wholly uniform nor explicitly durable within a speech community undergoing shift. At one level, language shift on reservations took place in a social space-time different from that of other groups, such as urban or transnational immigrant ethnic groups. State-sponsored shifting utopian models in reservation history have resulted in a local heterotopian space-time (Foucault 1986). The contradiction between utopian missions of integration and heterotopian realities of sequestration provides the material for many local language ideologies. As discussed below in more detail, Arapaho language ideologies negotiate but never resolve the contradictions between a utopian language renewal mission and the objective reality of shift as an irreversible process, between the utopian model of Euro-American education as the universalizable solution to all problems and the impoverished local political economy, and between idealized nostalgic purism within Arapaho ideologies and the proliferation of modern technologies and bureaucratic apparatuses of communication and governance.

In the relatively new study of language shift there has been a tendency to remain unreflexive about the social scientific ideological ground and spatiotemporal constructions that support it (Collins 1998:259). To borrow Phillipson's terms, models of shift are often "bedeviled by myths and binary over-simplifications" (1992:23). Today there is no permanent, closed, "us versus them" border to contest, no singular Euro-American ideology set against a singular Arapaho language ideology, and there probably never has been.

Beginning in the 1880s, for example, competing Euro-American ideologies approached the Arapaho speech community with contradictory purposes, such that repression reigned in some time-space zones, while acceptance and even valorization applied in others. In the mission boarding school at St. Stephens children were barred from speaking Arapaho in the classroom, but in chapel the priests and brothers spoke Arapaho with the aim of conversion. By the 1890s and early 1900s other Euro-Americans arrived to research the very language and culture that federal agents sought to eradicate.

Dimensions of space and time interrelate to define language ideologies in four correlative ways, which I explore in the rest of this chapter. First, competing dominant culture ideologies have imposed orders of space and time on the reservation as solutions to the "Indian problem," reflecting a range of dominant ideologies toward American Indians, from extreme racism to progressive compassion. Beginning with the first relation, as Deloria suggests, "It is debatable which factor was most important in the destruction of tribal ceremonial life: the prohibition of performances of traditional rituals by the government, or the introduction of white man's system of keeping time" (1985:18). The same statement applies if language prohibition is inserted and the effects of time for restructuring space appended. It is not enough to situate language loss and ideological frames about it in the narrow spaces, policies, or historical moments wherein Arapaho language has been openly repressed.

Second, all local language ideologies, in Friedrich's sense of "pragmatic ideologies," incorporate spatial and temporal indexicality, as it is used to both legitimize and challenge social practice. Arapaho language ideologies offer insights into the contradictions of shift, which are about competing interests in the control of local social time and space for many functions, such as constructing identity, maintaining hierarchy, securing access to resources, and solidifying social boundaries.

Third, language ideologies are situated within particular sites of linguacultural production and reproduction, such as ritual practice and schools. Arapaho language ideologies are situated in contradiction and contestation over practices in or about some social time-space zones more than others.

Fourth, prevailing Arapaho ideologies today aim to address these contradictions through self-determination, particularly through control of local space-time and in opposition to Euro-American knowledge, resources, and expertise.

Relation One: Imposed Orders of Space and Time

Throughout contact, Euro-America has specifically engineered imposed orders of spatial and temporal orientation for reservations, primarily through the state, with the manifest functions of governance, assimilation, improvement of life conditions, protection, and even progressively motivated reform while serving the latent functions of separation, exploitation, and dependency, primarily for acquiring and maintaining control of Arapaho lands and resources. Over the long duration, past policies, though suspended by the state and other dominant institutions, continue as sources of contradictions long after those policies are supposedly reversed by state action or local agency. What is past and reformed to Euro-American ideologies is thus present and real de facto to Arapaho people.

Imposed from a distance with the ideological mission of assimilation, Euro-American-designed housing, settlement patterns, building forms, scheduling, clocks, calendars, and other forms have indeed combined to attenuate the viability of Arapaho speech practices. One of the most profound changes in the history of the Arapaho language was the exile from traditional land, beginning with the Colorado gold rush of the late 1850s. Lost with relocation were taxonomies and mythopoetic connectivities coupled with natural seasonal changes, faunal behavior, floral growth, and celestial movements over the huge landscape Arapaho people once inhabited in eastern parts of what are now Colorado and Wyoming and western sections of Kansas and Nebraska.

Among fluent speakers born both before and after the reservation period, Arapaho speech practices had already experienced a number of significant internal shifts owing largely to relocation. Much of the language and knowledge once tied to horse-buffalo nomadic subsistence, place-names, and ritual traditions were lost by the first generation that spent their childhood on the reservation. The shift from nomadic hunting subsistence over 100,000 square miles of Colorado, Wyoming, and Nebraska to confinement on the reservation effected uncoupling of the language from extensive natural, historical, and cosmological knowledge. As the men and women of that generation passed away, so did many of the traditional taxonomies, images, tropes, and stories intricately tied to a broader landscape and associated paths of movement in time. Such knowledge can be reproduced only indexically in practice, a learning time-space no longer available on the reservation. Lost with this larger field have been a number of specialized jargons within Arapaho itself, such as medicine, arts, tool making, and ritual. Also lost in the early reservation period (1878–1920s) were various ritual traditions and curing practices, all with their own specialized vocabularies, mythical foundations, and oral history as conveyors of language.

After the tribe was relocated on the reservation in 1878, Arapaho language shift took place in a bounded "built environment," which Lawrence and Low define as a product of "human building activity" or a "physical alteration of the natural environment, from hearths to cities, through construction by humans" (1990:454). The same can be applied to time on reservations. Missionaries, government officials, and local Euro-American settlers constructed time orders based in ideologies for canalizing indigenous peoples' practices and thus synchronizing them with the trajectory of progress, cultural evolution, and modernization. Similarly, all constructed forms of space were imposed to reorder time. For instance, the sedentism of reservation confinement and subsequent individual landownership through allotment of lands in severalty aimed to tie Arapaho people to a new sense of time, an agrarian seasonal time of individual responsibility for private property and self-improvement through continual work. Allotment policy instituted by federal mandate, beginning in 1900 at Wind River, aimed to reshape social space-time from communal to individual nuclear family domains. Assignment of nuclear families to individual allotments of 80 or 160 acres aimed to cultivate individualism and economic self-sufficiency through agriculture. However, because most assigned allotments were not irrigated or cultivable, extended families gathered to reside on the more productive farms. In short, the government's planned agrarian individualism actually promoted extended family cooperation and with it the spatial and temporal domains for maintaining Arapaho language. Over time, allotment did tie extended families to parcels of land as a basis for cooperation as well as identity of place without precedent in the prereservation period. Eventually, these family places became a basis for contemporary factionalism articulated in part in language ideologies.

Besides the cooperative farming and gardening work, most families sought seasonal employment through sheep shearing, potato picking, lumber hauling, cowboying, and other work available through the federal agency or non-Indian employers off the reservation. Such labor required no literacy skills and little English fluency that could not be served by boarding school–educated younger people as interpreters. Arapaho continued to be the dominant language for all these activities out in the fields, on the herding trails, and in the sheep-shearing or potato-picking camps. Usually a number of families traveled to work sites together to form seasonal camps.

At the same time, any surplus of food, goods, or wages was readily shared through redistributive feasts on individual allotments. Families gathered to camp at least overnight, to sing, dance, play games, and tell stories, providing many opportunities to speak Arapaho. Economic exchange was thus encoded not just by an ethos of generosity but also by a communal connectivity for social relations accompanied by Arapaho ways of speaking. In general, the consensual-communal ethos sustained by traditional age-structured relations and various forms of ceremonial, economic, and social events provided settings for the sociocultural reproduction of the Arapaho language. Against socially fragmenting policies, though, Arapahos actively sought to sustain remaining communal spaces and times and invent new ones. Through the 1940s families continued to gather for seasonal events, such as Christmas week at the local dance hall, summer celebration events in adjacent Euro-American towns, cooperative agriculture such as herding and threshing, and various events at the missions. Leaders and elders actively cultivated and encouraged distinctly Arapaho space-time and thus identity while accepting and compartmentalizing Euro-American forms. By maintaining spatiotemporal boundaries within the reservation speech community, language shift and culture loss were somewhat effectively allayed.

While providing spatial loci for cooperation and redistribution, allotment set the course for a shift in social life from the camp to the settled extended family and anticipated a subsequent decline in social space and time for interfamilial interaction. Issues of property and the bonds between kinship and place began to move to the foreground for increasing demarcation of extended family boundaries and, among other things, cultivating the ground for contemporary competing ideologies, including those about language.

In the view of the assimilationist ideologies imposed through the mission boarding schools, beginning in the 1880s, English speech competence and literacy in particular were to link individual citizens to the larger spatiotemporal orientation of universal democratic governance and participation in a market economy. These were the utopian aims of the prohibition of Native language use in boarding schools in 1887 (Atkins 1973). Expressing a powerful contradiction, both the schools and the reservation as a whole were homologous forms of Euro-American sequestered space-time, ostensibly there to protect the occupants temporarily from the very same society into which they attempted to integrate them over the long duration (Elkin 1940:241). In response, Arapaho people developed their own English dialect and along with it a language and culture still set apart in space-time from the surrounding non-Indian world.

Regardless of local conditions, time regimen and sedentism in space were supposed to solve all "Indian problems." The mission to reorder seasonal time framed Gross's (1949) observations of Arapaho acculturation in the 1940s. His argument, which reflects a Jeffersonian model of progress, was that noneconomic or nonutilitarian "nomadism" was dysfunctional for economic development. Arapahos continued to be "nomadic," moving seasonally to ritual and social events, but they did so because of subsistence practices necessitated by reservation conditions of uneven geographical development of farmlands, not because of a cultural desire to "wander," as Gross suggests. With relocation came a shift from seasonality, which was tied to natural rhythms, to imposed systems of time, which were primarily agrarian and calendrical time systems based on Arapaho negotiations between survival and compliance.

On another level, the imposition of Euro-American-modeled domestic and public architectural forms has had a great impact on Arapaho linguistic practices and social relations. The accomplished Arapaho architect Dennis Sun Rhodes has observed in his lifetime a spatiotemporal shift from tents and log cabins in the pre–World War II era to modern multiroom houses. The latter were constructed to be homologous with architectural space and time orientation elsewhere imposed by Euro-American society, that is, with time-space zones for specific functions and boundaries for personal space. This, he suggests, has worked against the traditional respect in relations across generations and genders. In short, domestic time-space zoning creates boundaries among generations and between genders. The historical shift from tipi to modern housing has brought, according to Sun Rhodes, a loss of shared space:

> This communal space developed my worldview. I grew up to respect all my relatives. An example of interpersonal relationships between men and women that developed from this space was the practice of averting the eyes or leaving the area when the other was changing clothes. This taught a fundamental respect for one another that operated without special cubicles or walls. The communal space shaped the entire system of social norms for the tribe. (1993:42)

The communal space of the tipi, carried over into the single-room log cabin of the pre–World War II era, helped maintain interpersonal values and an interpersonal time, synchronizing rhythms with others upon which speech practices were reproduced. By contrast, Euro-American ideologies from various political positions aim to hermetically seal public versus private boundaries while filling the resulting domestic vacuum with a manufactured unifying mass media of print culture, radio, television, and cyberculture, all of which has generated a dependency on popular culture and mass consumption that, rather than unifying, in fact divides on a number of lines of social cleavage. Daily life paths of young people are now consumed by school followed by compact disc players, television, video games, DVDs, and other new technologies that offer experiences in the rapidly moving language and fashion of hypersensualized images. Perhaps more than federal government power, the dominant force in restructuring social space-time in the past thirty years has been consumer culture.

Rather than creating unity and order, constructed reservation space and time have evolved an ongoing collision of accumulated space-time forms across and within institutions. In all human history reservations have been among the greatest failures of social engineering imposed by state governance. A greater share of order in people's lives has been achieved, however transiently, more through Arapaho agency itself than through state-sponsored programs, whether progressive or assimilationist. Constancy in time must be effected locally, often with great difficulty. Euro-American models of spatial and temporal orientation at all levels have failed in general to provide a "rationally" scheduled linear life path to individuals or a functional developmental course to the tribe as a whole.

Relation Two: Language Ideologies as Indexes of Competing Interests

A second dimension of language ideologies is that, like all ideologies, they are constructed of relations in and of space-time at multiple levels beyond the situation of the utterance. For example, ideologies construct contrasts and continuities between past and present practice, recursively retrieve past material to legitimate the present, strategically position self or group in or outside of public social spaces, assert metapragmatic judgments about the movement of practice, employ life history as a gauge of present conditions, and define boundaries between community and the Euro-American world. As all ideologies vary, language ideologies diverge considerably in the range of temporal and spatial location, extension, and inclusiveness. On the one hand, language ideology can be situated indexically in and of the unfolding details of discourse, but, on the other, it can become "ideologies of language" (Woolard 1998:4), indigenous theories of the relationship between language as a whole to mythical, historical, or cosmological processes.

Some language ideologies are situated in the mythico-ritual time of Arapaho existence, some in the social indexicality of differences of identity reflected by choice of a particular lexical or grammatical form, some in the contradictions between Euro-American historicized ideologies and local Arapaho perspectives, some in acceptance or rejection of larger Pan-Indian or academic discourse and practice, and others in the local political divisions based on family and district divisions.

Prior to the reservation period, Arapaho age-structured modes of discourse and practice held sovereign control over construction and reproduction of sociocultural space and time. Arapaho society flourished in a highly integrated extensive system of practices for maintaining a shared spatiotemporal homology (Anderson 2001:91–118). Each season, stage of life, direction, epoch in mythical time, and stage in ceremonial practice was associated with one dimension in a quadripartite system. Within that homologous order, core Arapaho tropes, images, and mythical structures reproduced meaningful connectivities and stimulated the play of creativity.

As I discuss in *The Four Hills of Life* (Anderson 2001), social space was also once structured by age rank such that elders sat in positions of prominence while other age groups positioned themselves by gender and age accordingly. An age-graded system situated older men and women in control of the construction of space and the tempo of time at all levels of social practice related to life movement, including speech itself. Elders' speech performances and nonverbal communication, whether in ritual genres of prayer, storytelling, speeches, or everyday interaction, shaped consensus in the production of group and tribal ideologies for social practices of varying spatial extension and temporal duration. Elders were thus once the social clock and spatial center, orchestrating collective practice and consciousness in most domains of space and processes in time.

In speech contexts, as in ritual practice, all communication had to first turn to the oldest speaker(s) present and then be transmitted through all intermediary age levels present. All public discourse in the construction of knowledge had to be mediated by age:

"What do they remember about this place?" I would ask Tom. Tom would repeat the question to Sage in Arapaho. Sage would generally relay it, in the same tongue, to Griswold. Griswold would ponder a bit with a sort of inscrutable oriental smile, his eyelids drooping, and then answer Sage in a nearly inaudible whisper. Sage would transmit this to Tom, and Tom would translate it to me. Just why Tom didn't ask Griswold directly I don't know, except that the procedure conformed to the Indian's respect for age. The order of rank was Griswold, Sage, Tom and myself. (Toll 1962:8)

As Fowler (1982) and others recognize (Elkin 1940; Hilger 1952; Starkloff 1974), elders were once the center of all ideological production, including ideologies about language, culture, and religion. Today, elders' authority over discourse and public knowledge still holds true in some time-space zones, especially for ceremonial issues, but beyond these in an increasingly narrow range and for a shorter duration. Arapahos still approach ceremonial leaders from the most senior generation to answer questions or resolve ideological issues related to religion, culture, and language. These include various specialized roles, such as the Four Old Men for all religious matters, Sun Dance leaders, Drum leaders, and, with language renewal efforts since the early 1980s, the Arapaho Language and Culture Commission (ALCC).

Northern Arapaho tribal governance established the ALCC following linguist Zdenek Salzmann's recommendation to coordinate all language and culture education research and implementation in the various schools on the reservation. Following the model instituted on many reservations, the ALCC became a hybridized organization, mixing the traditional authority associated with age with the bureaucratic specialized functionality of a modern tribal program. Directors and members thus had to juggle two sorts of authority by maintaining a position of legitimacy over language and culture education in the eyes of the community while sustaining bureaucratic efficiency and accountability in relations with the tribal government. In the process, the ALCC became a site of competing language and cultural ideologies. Literate forms of Arapaho language became temporally enduring, objectified forms—in ways not envisaged by researchers—that elders and others found difficult to revise. The process of standardization through a literacy program set younger generation members and teachers who acquired literacy skills apart from elder, more fluent speakers. Along with the ALCC, the three schools at Ethete, St. Stephens, and Arapahoe became sites of ideological production (Silverstein 1998b:137–38), negotiating the contradiction between classroom literacy education and the localization of such sites as sequestered and specialized contexts of practice often associated with particular families or groups. (See Neely and Palmer as well as Reynolds in this volume for extended discussion of similar issues in Kiowa and Mayan speech communities, respectively.)

Today, elders recognize that their once-omnipresent authority to effect consensus and the flow of social practices has given way to competing ideologies from younger generations (see Field in this volume for a discussion of age-based competing language ideologies in the Navajo speech community) and from imposed Euro-American claims to epistemological authority (Anderson 2001:279–318). In general, elders see a social world that in traditional terms is referred to as "craziness," or in Arapaho, *hohookee-*, a foolish behavior of "moving too fast" (Fowler 1982) into situations without thinking or just running hectically from one place to another, associated with immaturity and Euro-American ways of acting and speaking. Paraphrasing what several elders explained, "When you speak English you don't have to be as careful, you can just say what you want, but with Arapaho you have to be careful, take time to think about what you are going to say." More broadly, older fluent speakers associate the loss of Arapaho language and discursive practices at large with the increasing pace of younger generations' social lives, which they see as less attuned to the Arapaho theory of slow, deliberative, and consensually ordered practices.

With increasing urgency through the 1990s, Arapahos and Euro-American social scientists involved in language renewal recognized that they were competing for space and especially time in the collective time-space paths of community members' schedules. Time is increasingly perceived, in Euro-American terms, as a scarce resource to be claimed or allocated. Language is taught in primary and secondary school grades, often accompanied by culture, history, and art, as a regular school subject confined to one period daily or only several times a week. Upon leaving school, students have few opportunities to use the language in their daily lives. After years of work to get a permanent place for Arapaho language in schools, only a single small block in the daily schedule is allocated, though Head Start and kindergarten have longer immersion sessions. I have heard many times that there is "too much competition" in the daily life paths of students, parents, and community members to expand the presence of language and culture programs. Summer language and culture enhancement programs must compete for children's and families' time with athletics, powwows, television, bingo, video games, travel, and other extracurricular school activities. The vast majority of nonfluent adults report that they would like to learn the language but simply have no opportunities in their schedules.

The reservation has also experienced a loss of permanent communal social spaces. During the early reservation period families gathered at various sites along the various rivers in recognized camps. Today the flow of life has shifted from the rivers to the roads and modern housing patterns. Still, many extended families form clusters of houses on shared housing sites or allotted lands still held in the family. Before automobile travel came to predominate, the towns and missions on the reservation were also thriving social centers of activity, from trade to work and social interaction. Today, the once-vibrant town of Arapahoe, for example, has ceased to exist, though prior to World War II it had a railway station, a hotel, several stores, and a government subagency office. Elders today recall the "old-timers" sitting around the town for hours on end talking in Arapaho accompanied by sign language. Arapahoe, along with several other camps and centers, has dissolved into an aggregate of buildings or function sites as time-space zones for specialized events in the daily and weekly cycle. In their daily life paths, people move in and out of these zones for different functions without a common gathering point or center of communication for the community or tribe.

Automobile transportation in general has accelerated the pace of social life and shifted many functions to the non-Indian towns just off the reservation. Since the 1940s this increased mobility has exacerbated the trend toward fewer and shorter communal gatherings, though most are much larger in numbers attending. For instance, it is now possible for more people to attend events for brief periods on or off the reservation and then return home without the need to camp for the duration. Even when I arrived at Wind River to begin research in 1988, there were many more campsites at the powwow grounds than there are today. Elders comment, too, that with cars and modern technology people do not stop to visit in the leisurely way they once did. While traveling from one end of the Arapaho section of the reservation to another, relatives or friends often stopped to camp at each other's homes. Despite this trend toward a hurried pace and shorter encounters, Arapaho communities and families do still come together and cohere much more than their non-Indian counterparts. Families gather for important life transitions of members; grandparents remain active in childrearing; and communities still congregate in times of crisis. However, communal spatiotemporal orientation finds itself in contradiction with a growing sense of the acceleration of movement with modernity in general (Gleick 2000) and scarcity of time affecting indigenous communities today (Smith 1982).

Implicitly or explicitly, a counterideology responds that traditional Arapaho discursive practices are simply too slow to keep up with the pace and volume of what modern governance, technology, education, economic planning, and mass popular culture impose or require. Tribal leaders and administrators can no longer rely on orally transmitted information framed by traditional discourse schema. Rather, they must pore over piles of documents, produce many themselves, and be able to translate their import to the community. One ideology for political leadership thus stresses the need for advanced formal education based on realities of new rhythms of time and constructed spaces imposed by changes in policy, economy, technology, and culture. Accordingly, the argument proceeds, traditional language use is simply not enough to keep up with modern tribal governance.

Until the 1950s restricted mobility across reservation boundaries allowed Northern Arapahos to maintain a strategy of compartmentalization, as Spicer (1954) first defined for culture contact and Gumperz (1972:230) extended to language contact, which they applied to demarcate Arapaho language and culture from imposed language, religious practices, value orientations, and other social forms (Anderson 2001:240–73; Fowler 1982:244ff.; Starkloff 1974). From early on, then, there was very little interference, hybridization, or creolization in the contact between English and Arapaho. Unlike some other Plains groups, however, the Arapahos did not as a tribe militantly defend boundaries by resisting the mission boarding schools, Christianity, assimilation policies, and English literacy. Rather, Arapahos appropriated them in a compartmentalized social space-time that remained under their control for the first half of the twentieth century. From the 1940s on, however, this process of local appropriation of control over the linguacultural boundaries began to change dramatically.

Much discussion during my field research revolved around concerns about mixing, syncretizing, or hybridizing linguacultural forms in ways inconsistent with former spatiotemporal compartmentalization. At one level, metalinguistic discourse often turns to neotraditional religious and social events that tend to mix elements from different traditions, such as peyotism, Pan-Indianism, Lakotaization, and Christianity. With respect to language, elders at times disagree about what technologies or Euro-American practices should be used for language renewal. Many of these discussions center around the question of whether or which Arapaho language and culture resources should be kept within local boundaries for local use only. One traditional elder related to me that the language could not be written down and should not be placed on the Internet because it would lose its spirit. By contrast, others argue that all technological means possible must be used to make the language available to tribal members and non-Indian scholars, who can then be drawn upon to help the cause. In all, language ideologies must negotiate the contradiction between proliferating channels of information flow across reservation borders and commitments to maintain local boundaries.

Relation Three: Language Ideologies as Indexes of Particular Spaces and Times

The third way language ideologies are related to space and temporal orientation is the location of contestation in specific sites. One site for Arapaho language ideological discourse is ritual practice. Within the Arapaho theory of practice there is a unique cultural attention to "doing things in a good/correct way" (Anderson 2001:240–73), including various genres of ritual speech performance. One ideological position emphasizes that the "language is sacred," combining both an Arapaho pragmatic purism and Pan-Indian discourse for social action. Such an ideology of sacralization is an effort to resolve contradictions of linguacultural loss by using the traditional heterotopic space-time, though it generates contradictions of its own.

The language as sacred ideology borrows from several spatiotemporal frames of reference. At one level is a unique Arapaho purism, paralleling the concerns Kroskrity (1998) identifies for Tewa ritual discourse. In all ceremony, pragmatic schemas lend temporal and spatial order to unfolding events and effect relationships among humans and between the sacred above and the human realm below. As a result of proper performance, blessings follow that move outward to the tribe and move time forward with renewed direction and purpose. Today, increasing numbers of ritual leaders and participants are nonfluent in Arapaho. One controversy revolves around the question of whether prayers and other supplications must be performed in Arapaho for the Creator to hear them and for the beneficial effects to follow. In cosmogonic time, language does indeed serve as a vertical connection between above and below and as the foundation for Arapaho identity in a mythically chartered ongoing relation to sacred beings (Dorsey and Kroeber 1997:16). During creation a council of all the people decided by consensus that Arapahos would continue to speak the original language and occupy the middle of the earth, while other peoples would move to the margins and speak different languages. The narrative continues that this is the fourth world in mythical time following the last flood and that at the end of this era, if Arapahos have died, there will be another deluge. Since "everything depends on them," there is a deep concern whether language loss is movement toward the extinction of the Arapaho people and the end of the world. Such concerns are connected to other ideologies about social changes, such as the increasing intermarriage with non-Arapahos, increasing divisions within the tribe, and the commercialization of Arapaho culture.

With such an association, the ideology of sacralization aims to galvanize community support for the language, paralleling the increasing participation since the 1970s in the Sun Dance and other ceremonies, and places boundaries on it comparable to those maintained for religion. Those involved in language renewal also often compare the limited community involvement in their programs to burgeoning community involvement since the 1970s in neotraditional revival of Arapaho ceremonies and introduced or recently invented Pan-Indian social and religious traditions. Some educators and elders even mentioned to me the idea of making language fluency a prerequisite to participation in traditional religious activities, realizing, though, that this was a less than serious proposal, given Arapaho openness and generosity toward those who want or need to participate in them.

At another level, this ideology aims to situate authority over language within the realm of ceremonial leadership as opposed to the factional vicissitudes of tribal politics. The assertion that the "language is sacred" is also influenced by a neotraditional empowerment strategy of making sacred all things and forms that remain from the past or are recently invented for ritual or just "traditional" spaces and times.

Those who dismiss the extreme language-is-sacred view stress that the Arapaho language belongs everywhere to everyone and emphasize a unique Arapaho religious pluralism grounded in contact history. Proponents of this counterideology dismiss the claims they perceive of a group or family to "own the language" in the way ritual leaders or families own rights to various positions or ceremonies. While supporters of the language-is-sacred ideology perceive their efforts as metonymically identifiable with tribal consensus and mythico-ritual continuity, opponents reduce the claim to short-term factional interests in order to appropriate power and resources. While recognizing past traditions of rights to storytelling and other ritual speech genres, they also refer to a past when the language was not under ceremonial control.

Language ideologies relating to ritual speech performance thus encapsulate a larger contradiction for Arapaho religion. On one side is an Arapaho purism of pragmatic reproduction to do things in a good or correct way as they have always been done according to chartered pragmatic schemas. On the other is the growing participation of nonfluent speakers, many of whom have not been instructed about those pragmatic schemas. There is thus an increasing scarcity of ritual leaders with the communicative competence to perform all the necessary functions, while since the 1970s the number of participants has increased significantly. As in many other indigenous communities, ideologies revolve around the contradiction between linguacultural reproduction and adaptation necessitated by increasing participation and decreasing human, material, and discursive resources.

Other sites of ideological production and contestation are those assigned to language renewal itself, such as schools, research settings, and local cultural organizations. Language renewal has been sequestered in time-space zones in the three main schools on the reservation (Arapahoe,

St. Stephens, and Wyoming Indian at Ethete), two local colleges (Wind River Tribal College and Central Wyoming College), and several offices for committees, cultural centers, and tribal government. Unless one is on staff or has family or friendship relationships with those spaces, it is difficult simply to move into such time-space zones to participate or observe. I discovered firsthand that one of the ongoing challenges is to control public discourse about those time-space zones of language and culture education. Lack of public information about programs can spawn suspicion or criticism across factional or community boundaries, at times resulting in political action within or outside the accepted channels. Language and culture programs must thus employ discursive political strategies to maintain their position and viability in tribal factional politics. This includes maintaining a base of support in participants' family and community as well as among principal tribal leaders, both religious and political.

To maintain themselves, language renewal programs have also been forced to conform to the Euro-American formal pedagogical model that requires, increasingly during the conservative shift in national educational politics, a burden of proof of success in quantifiable decontextualized knowledge addressed to a distant, centralized authority. Classroom space has been a silently and at times openly contested time-space zone, especially as Arapaho language, culture, and history have become part of the curriculum at all levels since the 1970s. During my fieldwork I participated in various educational programs at Arapahoe, St. Stephens, and Central Wyoming College. I realized there are various contradictions between Arapaho and Euro-American ideologies for the construction of educational space-time.

The aims of formal education and other social institutions have been to create a spatiotemporal break from family and real communities through sequestration of education from lived language and culture (Giddens 1987). Euro-American education presumes sequestration from home and "family culture" as a condition for the idealized life trajectory of well-scheduled learning and working life. The early mission boarding schools were explicit about this break, at times nearing total institutional control. With similar force, Euro-American formal education has long imposed a temporalization of the life trajectory it associates implicitly with future-directed enlightenment, rationality, and progress for the individual and thus for the collective. Excluded is the function of how to connect knowledge learned to local culture and language. By contrast, Arapaho teachers and students maintain a much more fluid order of time and space in educational contexts, often commenting openly that they are not running things the way non-Indian people do. Relatives and friends of participants can move into and out of learning spaces. Schedules can more readily be adjusted to address personal matters, family crises, and community events. As Philips (1989) and Pickering (2004) recognize, reservation time is negotiated intersubjectively and resists the rigidity of work-discipline, though schools find themselves on the local border of a hybridized space-time, neither completely within Euro-American scheduling regimen nor entirely constructed by "Indian Time." Accordingly, educational time-space is subject to contradictions. Too much conformity to Euro-American regimen draws criticism of "moving too fast," and insensitivity to others is often referred to as "taking over." Too much latitude can draw Euro-American and Arapaho criticism of irresponsibility.

On a broader scale, at Wind River and to some extent throughout indigenous communities the shared social spaces and temporal orientations of generations have become increasingly segregated through constructed specialized time-space zoning of schools, housing, work, and other social functions. Ideally, Euro-American educational space-time excludes age groups not specific to grade or function. For the past fifty years of shift, children have also spent increasing amounts of time in peer-specific activities, both during school and in extracurricular activities. Arapaho efforts to maintain communal multigenerational events for linguistic and cultural continuity and crisis response are still quite strong, though Arapaho language no longer prevails in those events. Regular ties between generations in the Northern Arapaho community remain much stronger compared to those in the surrounding non-Indian world, though disjunctures between generations have clearly widened in the history of shift.

Theories of language loss invoke ideologies that variously blame language prohibition by agents of assimilation, the choice to assimilate by older Arapaho generations themselves, or the insidious colonization of everyday lives by radio and television. Elders often invoke the shift to "white man's ways" from "Arapaho ways" to explain why it has become increasingly difficult to maintain Arapaho language as a system of discourse within a larger context of social practice. They refer to the increased tempo afforded by technology, such that people no longer have to go through proper steps in their actions but can "just flip a switch" and "jump in their cars and go to town" to acquire what they want.

Relation Four: Language Ideology and Self-Determination in Indian Country

Within the fourth dimension of the relationship between language ideology and space-time, the ideologies of compartmentalization, sacralization, purism, and other boundary mechanisms are encompassed by a larger mission aiming toward self-determination. This movement synthesizes academic, Arapaho, and Pan-Indian ideological models for preservation and renewal. Arapaho commitment to maintaining boundaries distancing Arapahos from both non-Indians and Eastern Shoshones has evolved throughout the reservation period but emerged in the 1990s as an effort to regain control of the local political economy and locate control of all local affairs within Arapaho social spaces and temporal orientation. The Northern Arapaho tribe has constructed and expanded an administrative center for self-determination at Ethete with satellite offices at Arapahoe on the east end of the Arapaho side of the reservation. All federal grant–funded or tribally maintained programs for housing, child welfare, resource management, and education formerly administered jointly with the Eastern Shoshone tribe have separated and moved operations from Fort Washakie to the Arapaho side of the reservation.

The same "we can do it on our own" ideology has been brought to bear on language renewal as well. This ideology combines traditional compartmentalization with contemporary and at times militant self-determination as empowerment. One extreme ideology, articulated as a preference by Salzmann (1998:287), maintains that Arapahos should keep all language and culture research and texts local and under their own control. This view parallels the ideological trajectory of many federal and private granting policies that at the outset lend full support and establish Euro-American-based spatiotemporal structures, followed by decreasing support so that local governance and knowledge bases take over within a prescribed timeline. In this view, outside non-Arapaho experts, including linguists and anthropologists, are necessary at first but unnecessary in the long run, given that educated Arapahos, traditional consultants, and local technologies will build human and material resources to implement and administer the program. Yet since Salzmann's original visit and training sessions in the early 1980s, a series of non-Indian social scientists and educators have visited the reservation to start or redirect the language renewal process, generally with the newest pedagogical method or technology in hand.

Another strand comes from militant Pan-Indian discourse about tribal education and political economy. This ideology is based on the assumption that non-Indian academics tend to commercialize and appropriate language and culture for their own profit or career advancement at the expense of local uses of knowledge. Academic approaches and appropriated texts are deemed exploitative and distorting a priori. Ironically, such a view reduces language and culture to commodity-like forms of value alienated from local social relations of control. In my experience this militant voice for academic self-determination comes mainly from a few Arapahos in formally educated younger generations connected to Pan-Indian decolonizing discourse. However, it does overlap with an Arapaho concern that non-Indian research, observation, and publishing have the potential to "take too much away" to spaces inaccessible to Arapaho people. The question of what academic research and publication provide for people locally is indeed a valid one in most instances and a question researchers in indigenous North American communities have had to address much longer and more seriously than their colleagues working elsewhere in the world where the time-space separation of fieldwork and publication is still a colonial privilege. Moreover, all such ideologies hold to the view of the reservation as a nationlike closed space for which political, economic, and cultural boundaries can be maintained by vigilant self-governance. To some extent this ideology meets resistance from the many sources of Arapaho language and culture off the reservation in published and unpublished forms and, conversely, the increasing flow of mass culture, politics, and economy onto the reservation in an unprecedented wave of change.

Opposing this contemporary "border-maintenance ideology," Arapahos have a long history of cooperation and generosity with outside researchers, exceeding that of most North American indigenous communities. Most elders and many younger participants expressed to me the view that "we can use all the help we can get." In the same vein educators and researchers recognize that traditional oral means of cultural transmission are simply no longer adequate to revitalize language and teach culture and history. Rather, they see a need to use all the technologies available.

As the self-determination ideology illustrates, all language ideologies are to some extent hybridized constructions borrowing from multiple sources. Neatly dichotomizing ideologies thus give way to complex connectivities. For example, Arapaho language ideologies involved in renewal have been shaped by anthropological and linguistic orientations to language and culture, in turn importing their own spatial and temporal constructions (Collins 1998:259). Research on the Wind River reservation began in the 1890s with James Mooney's work on the Ghost Dance and continues to the present day. The vast majority of anthropological and linguistic studies carried ideological assumptions preferencing synchronic over diachronic models, decontextualized code over speech context, and past over present language and culture as well as assumptions that the linear trajectory of time is moving irreversibly toward linguacultural loss.

As a result of this ideological barrier (Anderson 1998:63–70) the process of language shift as part of a larger history and sociocultural system has been largely uninvestigated in over a century of research about Northern Arapaho language and culture. Among many researchers who visited the Wind River Reservation from 1900 to the 1970s, only two studies documented language shift in progress, though only with rather rough descriptions of generational differences in fluency. Gross (1951) observed monolingual Arapaho fluency in the oldest two generations, as he defined them, born between 1880 and 1900 in the first twenty years of reservation history but a shift to bilingual fluency among Arapahos born between 1900 and 1920. In the fourth generation born between 1920 and 1938 he recognized some loss of lexical fluency, since for this group the meaning of some Arapaho words had to be explained to them in English. Reporting on her two field stays in 1936 and 1940, Hilger (1952:94) briefly mentions that in the domestic space only a few preschool children were monolingual in Arapaho, while school-age children fluent in English continued to speak Arapaho at home and in peer group play situations.

Since Salzmann's initiative in the early 1980s, most Arapahos involved in language renewal have adopted the traditional linguist's ideology that reduces language to a synchronic text-based code and lexicon. This ideology holds to the pedagogical practices of language learning called the Salzmann System, which has been used since the early 1980s: curricula at all levels proceed through the alphabet and word lists, followed by a few grammar exercises. Following the template of linguistic research, local research and education proceed from the phonetic to higher order structures, devoting focused attention to standardization of discrete forms as discourse flows.

Even much of the material collected by early linguistic research, including that of Salzmann, thus remains estranged from local usage and present realities. In language renewal discourse many comment that the words or constructions collected for dictionaries or in traditional narratives were in fact not often used in the everyday spatial temporal orientation of speech. Arapaho bilingual speakers are well aware of the disjuncture, often commenting that "no one would actually ever say that." Conversely, they recognize that many pragmatic forms with little lexical referential value have not been documented, such as the rich array of musical Arapaho expletives.

Augmenting Hill's (1998) study of a Nahuatl-speaking community's ideology of the loss of respect, Arapaho nostalgia about pastness encompasses several dimensions of space-time. In the various linguistic research projects in which I participated, there was also a clear ideological preference for the "real old words." Thus, in the metalinguistic discourse of interview sessions, elders often projected their memory back to past speech events of their senior generations. The Arapaho form was thus presented as part of a narrative in which a deceased ancestor used a particular term. Narrators often ended by saying, "Nobody uses that word anymore," followed by a pause in the group filled with a genuine reverence. Conversely, when younger speakers invented lexical forms or deviated from older grammar, older speakers and researchers (indigenous and nonindigenous alike) tended to dismiss that knowledge. Older speakers would comment, "No, there's an old word for that."

Paralleling Kroskrity's (1998) analysis of the multiple strands of Tewa linguistic conservatism, Arapaho ideologies combine an indigenous purism, an imposed literacy-based ideology of standardization, and social indexing of identity through codeswitching and correction. Woolard (1998:17) and others recognize that language renewal efforts often appropriate pedantic conceptions of language that are part of the same pedagogical ideology that originally contributed to the oppression of the language itself. On the other hand, indigenous purism derives from the age-framed Arapaho metapragmatics discussed above. As I elaborate in another context (Anderson 1998:93), elders at times assert their authority by "correcting" younger speakers' usage or dismissing their utterances in English. Older fluent speakers often switch from English to Arapaho to index their identity through continuity with pastness or to lower a younger nonspeaker's identity status by foregrounding discontinuity. Thus, younger speakers with various levels of Arapaho communicative competence relate that they hesitate to use their language in a public space for fear of being shamed by others. They maintain that their language and culture are just as genuinely Arapaho as older forms.

Language shift and renewal efforts have intensified reflexivity and metalinguistic discourse reflected against a genuine "pastness" tied to the identity of speakers and competitive claims for identity. Fluency as a tie to pastness has become an ideological contested ground for claims to authentic identity. As with culture, an authentic language existing outside of the present speech event is held up as an unchanging traditional standard at a distance from present social practices but one in practice that is fluid, contestable, and at times divisive.

One specific critique simply references the fact that outside models of renewal do not work, such as the Salzmann System of orthography. By the 1990s elders in the ALCC mandated that some aspects of the system be modified for easier use and that literacy instruction be curtailed, especially in kindergarten through sixth-grade curricula. As for all imposed orders, though, even if the system is designed for Arapaho linguistic and cultural self-determinacy, long after the agents depart, the structures remain enduring sources of Euro-American epistemological authority and thus resist transformation by local actors.

Younger generations often appeal to a neotraditional ideology that places their identity and authenticity in more recent and contemporary linguacultural contexts, most of which do not require Arapaho language. They find identity and social bonds in the expanding Pan-Indian cultural context of powwows, new ritual forms, and youth culture. After one class session at the community college in which we discussed Wind River history with a clear bent toward pastness, an Arapaho-Shoshone student commented, "I don't need this class to know who I am. I know who I am."

For some, "doing it on our own" requires reclaiming language and culture from its placement in formal educational space-time of sequestration, evaluation, and competition. To Arapahos who grew up in the 1960s and 1970s era of traditional revival, the language itself is now accessible only in the academic space and time of texts and classrooms. Many adults in their twenties to forties comment that they don't want to have to take a class to learn the language through literacy-based grammar and vocabulary lessons followed by assessment but just want opportunities to learn basic conversation without the burden of planned assignments, the expectation of regular attendance, and a performance evaluation. When arrangements are made for adult language classes of this sort, however, they are difficult to maintain because they are more difficult to fund with grants, all of which impose an ideological preference for demonstrating quantifiable outcomes. In general, there is considerable ideological resistance to the spatiotemporal constraints of language programs framed by the Euro-American-based pedagogical model.

Language renewal efforts and cultural education in local schools and organizations have come to depend on a complex flow of resources from public, state, and federal granting agencies, private foundations, and a tribal operating budget that dwindled throughout the 1990s. The success of language renewal efforts, which are framed by formal institutions in a standard bureaucratic genre and epistemology (see Philips 1998a), has become totally dependent on grant writing, activity reporting, and even curriculum development, all of which must comply with and even appeal to agencies and offices located hundreds of miles away. The ideology of "doing it on our own" must negotiate with grant guidelines and formal institutional policies developed supposedly through rational-scientific expertise at a distance from local contexts. Language renewal programs must not only comply with Euro-American bureaucratic ideology but also compete for scarce grant monies with other tribes. Professional grant writing, paid consultancy, workshop facilitation, and other professions have emerged to mediate between local organizations and granting institutions.

One context wherein Arapaho people retain a very strong consensual ideology for "doing it on our own" is the response to times of erupting crisis. Traditional ritual practices and associated political economy aimed to defeat hardship, redistribute resources (both spiritual and material), and move life forward in a good new direction. During reservation history Arapaho religious practices have maintained this mission and shifted in new directions to accommodate the increasing and changing personal, family, and tribal crises generated by deprivation, disease, alcohol, and other problems associated with reservation life. In ways that testify to the strength of the human spirit, funerary practices, collective ritual purification, sharing and reciprocity, and traditional practices respond as means of repairing the damage brought by crisis. In prereservation culture, suffering was discarded to the past and to memorialized places as bands moved to leave crises behind. In reservation confinement, crisis has become a constantly recurring reality in the lived social landscape, so ritual practices have responded by allowing placement of deceased persons, tragic events, and other crises within the time-space paths people must traverse on a daily basis.

One strand of Arapaho language ideology aims to activate the same curative power of Arapaho ritual crisis response to language shift. Some involved in renewal seek to generate the same sense of crisis in time and thus appeal to broad community support, to ceremonial leadership to give the community direction, and, as mentioned above, to sacralization of language. However, in this view language shift is seen as less of a crisis, largely because it is an insidious process, less immediate in time and space. Nonetheless, ceremonial leaders have been vocal about the importance of retaining the Arapaho language, and many renewal programs and projects have been stimulated by the ideology of shift as crisis.

By contrast, some members of the younger generations point out that there are many other issues affecting people's lives more immediately and critically than language shift. In the daily life paths of most families, housing, employment, health care, social services, and other concerns are more imminent than language shift. Only a very small number of career paths on the reservation require Arapaho language fluency. Thus, some of my students explained that learning their own language and culture in school would not help them get jobs or pursue a career. Arapaho language is no longer tied to economic production and exchange. At a deeper level, these students do not experience a connection between the Arapaho language and addressing the crises that plague their lives.

Automobile transportation, mass popular culture, a money economy, per capita payments, dependency on government assistance, and consumerism have ostensibly brought Arapaho people closer to Euro-American ideals of prosperity and quality of life but at the same time have contributed unprecedented sources of social fractures and personal disjunctures in the flow of time along daily life paths, life history, and family history. Crime, violence, substance abuse, suicide, and other self- and community-destructive practices generate episodic social and personal chaos. For many children, ties to family are modulated by shifts between crisis and stasis in which Arapaho language plays only a minimal, transient role in regaining or maintaining stability.

Younger Arapahos who grew up in this milieu often comment that in the tribe there is a general denial or cover-up of the very serious problems they experience. Ethnographic, ethnohistorical, and linguistic researchers past and present have summarily left these issues outside of their constructed boundaries of inquiry. When older generations explain these problems as a loss of Arapaho ways and associated rules for discourse, younger Arapahos hear only alienation from what is real in their lives on a day-to-day basis. Rather, they live in a social space-time in which neither traditional ways nor Euro-American institutional responses have been efficacious over the long duration.

In all, Arapaho language ideologies confront an array of contradictions, many of which derive from spatiotemporal orders continually imposed by Euro-American society. Throughout Arapaho history there has been an ongoing struggle between Euro-American dominance and Arapaho appropriation of local spatiotemporal orientation within the reservation and in the relationship between the reservation and distant but centralized power. At least for language in the present discussion, as Lefebvre recognizes, the dialectic always favors dominance in the long run.

Genuine self-governance has aimed to decolonize and reindigenize social space-time within reservation boundaries. While successful to some extent in reclaiming some time-space zones for local political, economic, and religious agency, language renewal has largely failed to revernacularize social space-time. To understand this in total in any one speech community requires research and analysis well beyond the limits of this chapter, though some suggestive paths for inquiry have been laid out. Clearly, interdisciplinary and open but contextualized models are needed within which a space-time approach to language revitalization must be at least one objective. All ideologies are constrained by the limits of space-time because they are inextricably within space and time. Referring to time in a statement that applies equally to space and language, Munn concludes, "How difficult to find a meta-language to conceptualize something so ordinary and apparently transparent in everyday life" (1992:116). Through language ideologies, researchers and indigenous folks continue to speak critically and creatively in such a metalanguage.

CHAPTER 4

"Language, Court, Constitution. It's All Tied Up into One"

The (Meta)pragmatics of Tradition in a Hopi Tribal Court Hearing

JUSTIN B. RICHLAND

This chapter explores how legal actors in Hopi tribal court employ a common Hopi ideology that their native language is a central feature of Hopi cultural identity and political sovereignty and do so for significant rhetorical advantage. By analyzing how, in the course of one exemplary trial proceeding, a Hopi tribal judge, lawyer, and advocate raise and challenge metapragmatic formulations framing usages of Hopi language as indexical of Hopi tradition and legitimate tribal governance practices, we gain insight into a regular feature of Hopi court proceedings, in which discourses about language and its role in expressions of Hopi cultural identity become sites for the articulation and contestation of Hopi juridicopolitical power (Richland 2005, 2007, in press). My aims are twofold. First, I respond to the ongoing debate in scholarship of American Indian law and nationalism regarding the role and (in)authenticity of tradition and cultural identity in tribal politics by proffering a discourse-oriented analysis that foregrounds the manner, meaning, and force that talk of tradition and identity has for the indigenous interlocutors themselves. In so doing I partake of a theme evident in several contributions to this volume that considers American Indian ideologies that explicitly or implicitly link language and its use to aspects of Native cultural identity (see, e.g., Bender, Neely and Palmer, Jr.). Second, by focusing on the link between metapragmatic discourses (Silverstein 1993, 1998b, 2003a) and the ideologies of language that inform them (Kroskrity 2000c; Schieffelin, Woolard, and Kroskrity 1998), I attempt to reveal the more immediate effects that explicit talk about talk can have in the agentive constitution (see Kroskrity, this volume) of sociopolitical relations accomplished by such talk—a middle ground between macrosociological forces and micro-interactional details that has only recently become the subject of anthropological research into law and legal institutions (e.g., Hirsch 1996; Matoesian 2001; Philips 1998a, 2000; Richland 2005, 2007, in press).

To properly set the stage for this analysis and these aims I offer a brief description of the sociocultural contexts within which the Hopi tribal court operates and how notions of tradition, law, and governance invoked in the court's rules and processes mirror prominent trends and debates in the scholarship on tribal law and sovereignty practices.

The Hopi Tribe and Its Courts: A Brief Description

The Hopi Reservation, established by executive order in 1882, currently occupies 2,532 square miles of aboriginal Hopi land in northeastern Arizona. Almost half of the more than ten thousand members of the Hopi tribe live on the reservation—along with more than two thousand non-tribal members—and are generally associated with and occupy one of twelve villages located on and around three mesas (U.S. Census Bureau 2000).

In many respects the full brunt of U.S. colonization did not hit the Hopi tribe until relatively recently. Among the indicia of this, perhaps most significant is the high level of Hopi fluency among adults over the age of twenty. The Hopi language is one of four subbranches of the Northern branch of the Uto-Aztecan language family (Mithun 1999). In a recent survey conducted by Northern Arizona University and the Hopi tribe, 49.3 percent of the Hopi tribal population surveyed claimed to be conversant in the Hopi language (Hopi Language Assessment Project 1997).

In sociopolitical terms the relatively late effects of U.S. domination are most evident in the fact that it has been since only the 1930s that anything like a formal tribal organization has existed among the historically autonomous Hopi villages. In 1936 the Bureau of Indian Affairs federated these villages into the Hopi tribe under a Hopi constitution written and adopted pursuant to policies of the Indian Reorganization Act (25 USCA, secs.

461–62, 464–79). A representative tribal council was also convened at that time as the sole body of tribal leadership. And it was even more recent (1972) when the tribal council passed Hopi Ordinance 21, which established a Hopi judiciary to replace the BIA's Courts of Indian Offenses operating on the reservation (Hopi Ordinance 21, secs. 1.1.1., 1.2.1, 1.3.1).

Ordinance 21 relies heavily on the procedures of Anglo-American-style adjudication in its enumeration of the operations of the Hopi tribal courts. Many of the basic processes and practices in the Hopi legal system are thus similar to the activities of U.S. state and federal courts. Generally speaking, Hopi tribal courts are adversarial: litigants submit written briefs and present oral arguments that set forth the facts of the dispute and interpret principles of law in a manner designed to advocate for a resolution favorable to each party's interests and to challenge the facts and law presented by their opponents. Litigants can present evidence through witness testimony as well as cross-examine the witnesses of their opponents. After the presentation of evidence, litigants provide closing arguments. Final decisions are made either by juries composed of members of the Hopi tribe (in criminal cases) or by judges (in civil cases and cases on appeal), and these decisions can be appealed to the Hopi Appellate Court upon a claim of legal error during the trial.

The participants in Hopi tribal court proceedings are also similar to the players in Anglo-American courts. Both Hopis and non-Hopis may sit on the Hopi judiciary; however, non-Hopis must have a law degree, while tribal members need not have such formal legal training (although some law-related experience is usually required). Litigants have the right to represent themselves or retain counsel. Counsel need not have a law degree or be a member of the tribe. Due to prohibitions of cost and location, counsel is extremely difficult for parties to retain, and though Hopi Legal Services offers some low-cost resources, parties regularly represent themselves or retain many different representatives over the course of litigation. Court clerks and bailiffs are also present for most trial proceedings, as are audiences composed of relatives of the parties, litigants waiting for their trials, and other court officials. All trials are held on the eastern side of the Hopi Reservation in the Hopi courtrooms adjacent to Hopi Police Headquarters near Keams Canyon, Arizona.

Tradition in Hopi and Other Tribal Law and Sovereignty Practices

At the same time that the Hopi tribal court employs these Anglo-American-style adversarial rules and procedures, other tribal legislation and case law require the court to give a preferential place to Hopi customs, traditions, and culture. In Resolution H-12–76 of 1976 the Hopi tribal council mandated that "in deciding matters of both substance and procedure" the tribal court must give more "weight as precedent to the . . . customs, traditions and culture of the Hopi Tribe" than to U.S. state and federal law. The Hopi Appellate Court has recently reiterated this rule, writing in *Hopi Indian Credit Association v. Thomas*, "The customs, traditions and culture of the Hopi Tribe deserve great respect in tribal courts, for even as the Hopi Tribal Council has merged laws and regulations into a form familiar to American legal scholars, the essence of our Hopi law as practiced, remain[s] distinctly Hopi" (AP. 001–84 [1996], 4).

In these efforts to strike a balance between Anglo-American-style jurisprudence and notions of Hopi custom and tradition, Hopi law mirrors the predicament that Frank Pommersheim, former chief justice of the Cheyenne River Sioux Appellate Court, describes for all American Indian tribal courts, that is, as institutions functioning "at the very edge of tribal sovereignty" (1995b:97). Given the limited "internal sovereign" status articulated for tribes in U.S. federal Indian law, tribal courts are caught between the "yoked objectives of federal deference and tribal legitimacy" (Pommersheim 1995b:97). In this position tribal courts must be seen to meet Anglo-American norms of justice that inform federal oversight of much of tribal authority while still generating a jurisprudence that "must not lose touch with the people and traditions that nourish them from below" (Pommersheim 1995b:97). It is only through measured navigation between this Scylla and Charybdis, Pommersheim explains, that any tribal court can truly contribute to a lasting and meaningful form of sovereignty for its tribal constituents.

Given that the vast majority of tribal courts currently operating in Indian Country today were created in the image of U.S. state and federal adversarial jurisprudence (Barsh 1999; Porter 1997), many tribal jurists have argued that charting such a course for legitimate tribal court operations has meant developing law that emerges more centrally from tribal customs and traditions, thus adding to rather than restricting the "cultural sovereignty" of tribal nations (see Coffey and Tsosie 2001; Tsosie 2002; Valencia-Webber 1994; Vincenti 1995). Failure to do so, many claim, results in the mere replication of Anglo-American laws and values within tribal borders, only further diminishing the sovereignty and cultural vitality that tribal nations struggle to preserve (Porter 1997). Thus, Vincenti writes, "The real battle for the preservation of traditional ways of life will be fought for the bold promontory of guiding human values. It is in that battle that tribal courts will become indispensable" (1995:137).

But at the same time that they express a value for use of Hopi custom and tradition in Hopi law, the Hopi Appellate Court justices have recognized that introducing tradition into contemporary Hopi jurisprudence is neither a simple nor a straightforward process. In the same opinion quoted above, the court wrote, "Hopi custom, traditions, and culture are often unwritten and this fact can make them more difficult to define" (AP. 001–84 [1996], 4). Such concerns regarding the semantic equivalence and translatability of tradition discourses into Anglo-style legal texts shadow concerns raised by jurists across Indian Country. For example, Jim Zion, in reflecting on his legal work in Cree, Pima, Navajo, and Blackfeet courts, speaks of the difficulties "finding Indian Common Law" as "sometimes due to language problems, sometimes to that fact that many Indians do not speak of their common law in articulated legal norms, and sometimes to constraints created by non-Indian thinking patterns" (1987:125).

For other scholars the problems of integrating culture and tradition into contemporary tribal law and politics are more explicitly political in nature (Biolsi 2001; Dombrowski 2002, 2005; Joh 2000; Miller 2001, 2005). Joh (2000) contends that the call for custom and tradition in tribal jurisprudence has more to do with articulating a cultural identity different from dominant non-Indian society than really reflecting contemporary indigenous beliefs, values, and everyday social practices. As such, she contends, tradition and related notions are "too problematic" to constitute a foundation for tribal governance and jurisprudence because they seem to necessarily invoke troubling "questions of authenticity, legitimacy, and essentialism" that are not easily answered in juridical arenas (Joh 2000:120).

Dombrowski (2001, 2002, 2005), in his analyses of the "politics of native culture" in southeastern Alaska, argues, on the other hand, that both performances of Native culture and the recognition of Native claims to aboriginal lands are cultural and political projects that are afforded and even underwritten by private industry and non-Indian government parties against whom it is normally assumed such practices are designed to resist. This is true, for example, where big business such as timber and fishing interests see their support of Native cultural sovereignty as ways to circumvent the stringent environmental protections that apply to harvesting on public Alaska lands but that don't apply to lands held by Native communities. Thus, Dombrowski writes, what is crucial to understand is the "flexibility that indigenous claims provide development advocates. As individuals and groups with claims on significant resources, but with few means (legislative or otherwise) to compel those in power to recognize their claims, indigenous groups remain a potential tool for governments and their industry allies" (2002:1067–68).

Yet despite the explicit recognition by these tribal legal practitioners and scholars that what constitutes tradition in contemporary tribal law and sovereignty practices must involve a careful consideration of their integration and relation to contemporary non-Indian legal and political operations, little work has been undertaken to examine the details by which this is accomplished in actual juridicopolitical practices (but see Richland 2005). Indeed, proponents of both sides of these debates in the context of tribal law bemoan the fact that there exist "very few studies on the operation of tribal courts" (Joh 2000:118 n. 9; see also Barsh 1999; Cooter and Fikenschter 1998).

Tribal legal scholarship on these issues can thus be furthered by analyses that grapple with the ways in which tribal actors employ notions of tradition as they actually engage each other in tribal legal discourses and, in so doing, constitute the emergent structure and practices of their contemporary tribal law. Critical questions can be pursued that consider how tradition is talked about in tribal law, by whom, and to what effects. For example, how are the issues of semantic equivalence and translatability between discourses of tradition and law—issues admitted as problematic even by proponents of tradition as law—addressed by the legal actors arguing over uses of tradition in contexts of tribal legal interactions? What precisely are the ideological presuppositions that inform such pragmatic concerns regarding the telling of tradition in court? And what political economic entailments result for tribal legal actors engaging each other in and through these legal discourses? How does making such claims for or against tradition shape a party's access to the material and symbolic resources that underlie their disputes and inform the legitimate operation of tribal legal institutions more generally?

Language Ideology and Metapragmatic Discourse

In an effort to address these questions I employ in this chapter an approach to analyzing Hopi courtroom talk that joins theories and methodologies of recent linguistic anthropological studies of language ideologies and metapragmatics (Kroskrity 2000c; Schieffelin, Woolard, and Kroskrity 1998; Silverstein 1993, 2003a) with studies in interaction-based legal discourse analysis (Atkinson and Drew 1979; Conley and O'Barr 1998, 1990; Drew 1992; Philips 1998b). It builds directly on a fundamental premise of the analysis of legal discourse that "in many vital respects, language is legal power" (Conley and O'Barr 1998:14) and a notion of language ideologies as a "means of relating [language] models and practices shared by members of a speech community to their political-economic positions and interests" (Kroskrity 2000b:3).

I argue that at the nexus between such ideologies of language and the actual instances of law talk they inform are tokens of language practices and discourses that can be generally described as "metapragmatic," insofar as they are instances of language use that have as their object the very language practices and events of which they are a part (Silverstein 1993, 2003a). As such they are metaindexical and, as Silverstein has deftly revealed in several essays, thus "have an inherently 'framing,' or 'regimenting,' or 'stipulative' character with respect to indexical phenomena" (1993:33, see also 1998b, 2003a).

Relying on these perspectives, I show, more specifically, how the advocates and judge in a property dispute hearing before the Hopi tribal court work to harness the tribal court's legal power by making multiply ordered metapragmatic claims that argue for competing "legitimacies" (Gal 1998; Swigart 2000) of Hopi or English (and, secondarily, index each proponent's authoritative "legitimacy" as a speaker of that language) as the exclusive code for conducting Hopi court proceedings. I investigate how the Hopi advocate for one party explicitly frames her request to use Hopi language in court as grounded on a need to express unique and nontranslatable meanings of Hopi tradition relevant to the dispute—what I call a metapragmatics of "relativity"—as well as a more explicitly politicized claim to a "right" to speak Hopi in court as a fundamental principle of the legitimate operation of the Hopi tribal legal system and, even further, as the very raison d'être of Hopi sovereignty.

I then show how these metapragmatic formulations are challenged by the Hopi judge and the opposing Anglo lawyer, who invoke "professional" language ideologies (Kroskrity 2000b) of "Anglo"-style adversarial jurisprudence that rely on transparent referentiality as central to the justice goals of the tribal court—claims that, at least in this hearing, presuppose sufficient semantic equivalence and translatability between Hopi and English. In so doing, an effort is made to reveal how the macrosociologically conceived tensions between Anglo-American legal norms and tribal traditions described above are invoked for microrhetorical effect by tribal court actors as they vie for control over the right to determine what is and isn't "legitimate" Hopi court authority. In this respect, their efforts echo some of the politics of authenticity and their substantial effects that Bender (this volume) discerns in the language ideologies surrounding Cherokee literacy programs in the early 1960s in various and competing ways as well as those that Neely and Palmer, Jr. (this volume), describe as informing debates surrounding Kiowa orthographic representation and language revitalization efforts.

Moreover, analyses that attend to metapragmatic phenomena afford an understanding of discursively mediated social practices that are at once "compatible with . . . the sui generis aspect of linguistic structure modeled by grammar" while also accommodating the need to "understand language use as its own order of phenomenon, . . . as being a realtime laying down or 'inscribing' of TEXT" (Silverstein 1993:34, emphasis in original). Additionally, this analysis contends that it is within this order of language use that a welter of language ideologies (and the political-economic concerns they presuppose and entail) can be immediately brought to bear by social actors agentively engaged in those practices. And much in the same way Kroskrity (this volume) argues for locating Rosalie Bethel's agency in shaping language ideologies among her Western Mono community in the actual details of her narrative discourses, this chapter thus offers an analytic approach that blurs the "overly familiar" division held by social science between the macrosociological and micro-interactional levels of sociological phenomena and the structure-agency dichotomies they tend to reinscribe (Gal 1998; Kroskrity, this volume).

Thus, by exploring how notions of tradition and Anglo-American law imbricate via these explicit metapragmatics articulated in tribal legal practice, I contend that this chapter affords an approach to understanding American Indian juridicopolitical processes that subsumes the questions regarding the (in)authenticity of tradition under investigations focusing on how tradition is invoked and made meaningful for the social actors employing them in the betwixt-and-between contexts of tribal law and sovereignty today.

Tradition and the Discourses of Hopi Courtroom Interactions

The courtroom interaction analyzed in this chapter is exemplary of a larger body of data of approximately thirty hours of audio recordings of property dispute hearings before the Hopi tribal court collected from 1995 to 2002. Property issues loom large in Hopi members' concerns about law and order in their communities. Indeed, despite other major governmental reforms written by federal agents into the 1936 Hopi Constitution, issues regarding probate and the assignment of lands were two of only four subject matter areas (along with family disputes and adoptions) reserved to the exclusive jurisdiction of what is generally referred to as the "traditional" leadership of the nine Hopi villages (By-Laws and Constitution of the Hopi Tribe, art. 3, sec. 2). This reservation of authority is still recognized today, and property disputes that come before the Hopi tribal court are heard there only because the village leaders have waived their article 3 jurisdiction.

Hopis' concerns regarding property remain deep, and a primary problem identified by tribal members regarding the resolution of property conflicts turns on difficulties they perceive in balancing claims to property based on notions of Hopi culture and tradition with the Anglo-American-style jurisprudence that they see as characterizing contemporary Hopi tribal law. Consequently, it is not surprising that discourses of culture and tradition are a frequent and recurrent feature of both the written texts and oral arguments proffered by litigants, witnesses, lawyers, and judges in Hopi property disputes.

A review of the forty-nine property cases on file with the Hopi court since 1995 reveals thirty-three that include recurrent claims by one or more legal actors regarding rights to the property at issue or requests for how the dispute should be resolved that invoke some aspect of Hopi culture and traditions. And of the twelve hearings from these cases for which audio recordings were available and reviewed, in only one did parties not argue a matter of Hopi tradition or culture.

However, to fully appreciate how notions of tradition are invoked for rhetorical significance and mediate the semiotic constitution and political economic force of contemporary Hopi jurisprudence, it is necessary to investigate precisely the pragmatics and metapragmatics by which tradition discourses are constituted and made meaningful in the face-to-face interactions that emerge over the course of Hopi courtroom proceedings. To do this I focus on the discourses that constituted one such property dispute that came before the Hopi court in 1997. The conflict in question concerned a Hopi man's attempt to move his trailer home onto lands in his village—lands he claimed were used and controlled by his maternal grandmother and that she offered to him for this purpose—despite orders from the village government and the tribal court not to do so. Prior to the man's efforts the village governor had petitioned for and received a court order prohibiting the man from moving his trailer into the village under penalty of fines and/or incarceration.

Despite the existence of this court order, the man moved his trailer onto the property in question. He justified this move by proffering an argument that follows generally recognized traditions of Hopi property inheritance by which matrilineally reckoned clans are understood as bearing the primary rights to lands under their control and where leading women of each clan have the authority to determine the proper distribution of use rights to fellow clan members (Eggan 1950; Levy 1992; Nagata 1970; Titiev 1944; but see Whiteley 1998). As such, the man argued, because the village governor was a man from a different clan, he possessed no legitimate authority to interfere with the ways in which the man's grandmother could pass land-use rights to him, her clan relative.

At the time of the trial, the man's trailer was still standing on the land in question.

Talk of Talk, Tradition, and Law in a
Hopi Property Hearing

The hearing in question was called in September 1997 after the village government filed a second lawsuit against the Hopi man for violation of the court order. A professionally trained Anglo-American male attorney from Salt Lake City, Utah, represented the village leaders. This attorney has many years of experience trying cases in state and federal courts as well as in the Hopi tribal court and for a time was head counsel for the Hopi tribal government.

The Hopi defendant was represented by a Hopi woman who possessed some training as a paralegal but had no law degree and relatively little litigation experience at the time of this hearing. The judge in this case is the longest-serving member of the Hopi judiciary, a Hopi man with twenty-eight years of experience on the Hopi bench. Though he has no law degree, he has had extensive judicial training. He is also deeply involved in the traditional practices of his village, having been initiated into the highest ceremonial order that a man in his village can attain. He is the only Hopi trial judge with such extensive experience in both Hopi traditional ceremonialism and tribal court jurisprudence.

Finally, while both the judge and the Hopi advocate speak both Hopi and English, the Anglo-American lawyer does not speak or understand Hopi.

Consider now the opening interaction to the hearing.[1] After calling the court to order and introducing the case before the court, the judge asks both parties if they have been able to work out any last-minute settlements. After the Anglo lawyer, Mr. Keith, explains that the matter is still unresolved after "numerous" attempts to do so, the judge turns to the Hopi advocate, Ms. Smith, and the following interaction transpires:

Example 1. Choosing the Code of the Hearing:
The Advocate Requests Hopi
001 Judge: Alright. Ms. Smith? . . .
003 Advoc: Your Honor, there has been no numerous attempts to
004 try to solve this matter (which is) unfortunately—
005 unfortunately why we're here. I do have a
006 request before I (can) continue to address this
007 court is that, ahm, <u>I would like to have some of</u>

oo8 this (defended) in ah Hopi, ah simply because
oo9 there are issues here that are land and
o10 tradition and board of directors and lower
o11 village and— and other people and things that are
o12 involved that I think can only be expressed
o13 my own language and in order to adequately
o14 represent my client and be able to express
o15 myself in my language to you which you also
o16 understand.
o17 Judge: I can understand English as— ah perfectly well
o18 too. . . .
o20 Advoc: Well exactly, but what I'm saying is there are
o21 issues that I feel I can only describe in Hopi
o22 because (.) w— just like now, you know
o23 *I' hapi yep— yep pu' himu* [*itam*
       TRANSLATION: This truly here— here now is something [we
o24 Lawyer: [Your
o25 =Honor, I'm gonna object to ah—
o26 Judge: Just a second. Go ahead.

In what is her very first turn at talk, following her answer to the judge's question about efforts to resolve the dispute, we see that the advocate announces an intent to request and then requests that she be allowed to "have some of this defended in ah Hopi" (lines 7–8). Then, without waiting for any reply, she provides a metapragmatic justification for it, one that argues that Hopi possesses a measure of what I call indexical "relativity," drawing on the classic Sapir-Whorf hypothesis (developed at least in part through Benjamin Whorf's analyses of Hopi language) that the unique structures and patterns of usage of different languages shape and constrain in different ways how speakers of one language experience, make sense of, and act in the world in ways distinct from those who are speakers of other languages (see, e.g., Whorf 1956).

Though not reaching the level of analytic rigor of professional versions of the language relativity thesis, the advocate makes a claim for the Hopi language (lines 7–12) as bearing a unique and nontranslatable capacity for indexing the significance of Hopi matters of "land and tradition and board of directors and lower village"—issues that she contends are present in this dispute and that, significantly, must be told by her in Hopi so that she can adequately fulfill her professional role to represent her client (lines 13–14).

But when she then appeals to the judge's own capacity to "understand" Hopi as another metapragmatic justification for using the language (line 15), the judge responds to her justifications with indirection, ignoring her claims to Hopi indexical specificity and countering only that he can understand English "perfectly well too" (lines 17–18). This prompts the advocate not only to reiterate her "indexical relativity" claims (lines 20–21: "there are issues that I feel I can only describe in Hopi") but to actually exemplify them. The Hopi statement she initiates at lines 22–23, in which the co-occurrence of the deictic demonstrative pronoun *yep* ("here") with the adverbial of presence *pu'* ("now" or "currently") and the inclusive first-person plural *itam* all suggest that she is attempting to "perform" her metapragmatic commentary on the courtroom speech event in which she, the judge, and the lawyer are currently engaging each other.

The advocate is interrupted in this effort, however, by the lawyer, who relies on a professionally sanctioned metapragmatics of courtroom interaction called "raising objections" not only to stop her current use of Hopi but also to challenge her request to use Hopi at any point later in the hearing. He then elaborates (see line 28 below):

Example 1, Continued. Choosing the Code of the Hearing:
The "Anglo" Lawyer Objects to Using Hopi
026 Judge: Just a second. Go ahead.
027 Lawyer: I'm gonna object to having any of this conducted
028 in Hopi. Ms. Smith is perfectly capable to speak
029 English and (this whole) court and ah the rules
030 of this court are in English and unless there
031 is a need— a demonstrated need ahm where someone
032 does not speak or understand Hopi ah— or— er
033 English rather, where you need to have it done in
034 Hopi ah it would be ah I think inappropriate.=It
035 would also be time-consuming to have translation
036 and lead to ah ah misunderstanding.
037 Advoc: Your Honor,=
038 Judge: Ms. Smith.

The lawyer, much like the advocate, then backs his metapragmatics with an explicit ideological rationalization that argues for English because the advocate is "perfectly capable" (line 29) of speaking it and because it is the official language of the court, being the code in which the court's rules are written. He then implicitly contests the advocate's metapragmatics of relativity by stating that it would be "inappropriate," "time consuming," and potentially confusing to use Hopi unless some party to the hearing doesn't understand English (lines 35, 36, 31–33).

Each of these claims is informed by an underlying presumption of sufficient semantic equivalence, pragmatic transparency, and translatability between Hopi and English for the purposes of this hearing. This metapragmatics is informed by ideologies of language that are grounded in Euro-American semantic-referentialist "folk" models of language as principally a system for labeling acts, events, and objects in the world in ways that are stable across contexts of use. Dominant "professional" language ideologies of Anglo-American jurisprudence build directly on this referentialist "folk" theory insofar as they presuppose that language is a transparent medium for referring to prior events and acts that are the contested facts underlying litigated disputes. This is implicit in one of the fundamental premises of Anglo-American jurisprudence, namely, that justice is achieved in the crucible of adversarial litigation because it is in the zealous prosecution of disputed claims and the interrogation of witnesses' representations of prior events that the "truth" of "what actually happened" can and will emerge in court (O'Barr 1982).

Here it is just this set of pragmatic presuppositions upon which the lawyer relies to argue that the advocate's request to speak in Hopi brings no other insight into the dispute than that which could be offered by her arguments as given in English. And, in fact, he suggests in lines 36–37 that the use of Hopi would only be an obstacle to the overarching justice goals of the court in this case; the use of Hopi, absent a "demonstrable need" based on a lack of fluency in English, would only lead to delay and confusion caused by the need to provide a translation.

Though the lawyer's statements are directed to the judge, the advocate, recognizing her institutional role in the proceeding as a ratified overhearer (Goffman 1974) with rights of response to this interaction, does not wait for the judge to reply but instead initiates her own turn, directed at the judge but oriented to the lawyer's challenges. She interjects:

Example 1, Continued. Choosing the Code of the Hearing:
The Advocate's Response, the Judge's Decision
037 Advoc: Your Honor,=
038 Judge: Ms. [Smith
039 Advoc: =[if we are going to reach any kind of
040 ah— (?), I think Mr. Keith is being ignorant to
041 the fact <u>we are Hopi and this is a Hopi court of</u>
042 <u>law the reasons why ahm things were developed</u>
043 <u>the Constitution, the Hopi Court, was for the</u>
044 <u>benefit of the Hopi people, not for the benefit</u>
045 <u>of the people who can't understand the English,</u>
046 which is why we're here. Because if we were— if
047 if the Constitution says that we're able to
048 resolve certain issues at certain levels and
049 when we can't then it goes to court, then <u>I think</u>
050 <u>we should be honoring that opportunity to</u>
051 <u>express—</u> and Hopi is my first language, English
052 <u>is my second,</u> only to keep up with the modern
053 society, the white man's language, the white
054 man's way, and to make a survival in this world.
055 But Hopi is still my primary language, Hopi is
056 still the way I express myself, I don't care
057 where I am, if I'm outside the Hopi
058 jurisdiction. <u>I think Mr. Keith needs to give us</u>
059 <u>that respect.</u>
060 Judge: We're gonna proceed with this hearing in
061 English its— I'm gonna ask this question though
062 Ms. Smith, do you have any witnesses or any
063 persons that are here today that are— are
064 parties to this action, who you can certify,
065 that do not speak or understand English language.

In this exchange the political-economic ideologies backing the advocate's metapragmatic request are now made explicit in her claims to another order of indexicality for Hopi usages (Silverstein 2003a), linking her
arguments to use the language with notions of Hopi cultural identity (line
41: "we are Hopi"), tribal sovereignty, and the legitimate practice of the
Hopi tribal courts (lines 42–43: "the reasons why . . . things were developed the Constitution, the Hopi Court"). Here her explicitly ideological

metapragmatics of cultural sovereignty are exemplary of what Irvine and
Gal call the "iconization" (2000:37) of linguistic signs as representations of
social phenomena because they claim that juridicopolitical uses of the
Hopi language are in fact the sine qua non of Hopi nationhood. (See also
Bender as well as Neely and Palmer, Jr., in this volume for descriptions of
similar notions emergent in Cherokee and Kiowa language ideologies,
respectively.) By explaining that Hopi governmental institutions and texts
were "developed . . . for the benefit of the Hopi people" (lines 42–44)
and then juxtaposing this group to those "who can't understand the English" (line 45) the advocate iconically equates the essence of Hopi self-
governance with Hopis' entitlement to the distinct juridical uses of the
Hopi language. She then ends this metapragmatics of cultural sovereignty
by announcing that she and the judge have a moral imperative (line 50:
"we should be honoring that opportunity") to speak Hopi throughout the
hearing—an imperative that, at the same time, she argues, the lawyer
ought to give these Hopis the respect of recognizing (lines 58–59).

Finally, as if safeguarding against the possibility that the judge may
agree with her opponent's position, the advocate shifts into a representation of self, portraying her own linguistic insecurity with English and the
primacy of Hopi as "still the way I express myself" (line 56). In so doing
she seems to pose herself as qualifying under her opposing counsel's
category as someone with a "demonstrated need . . . to have it done in
Hopi" (lines 31–34).

But despite the advocate's rich and sundry rationalizations for using
Hopi in the hearing, the judge, after a brief pause, baldly rejects her
request, stating without any uptake of her claims that "We're gonna proceed with this hearing in English" (lines 62–63). When he then asks her if
she represents anyone who does not speak or understand English (lines
64–67), he makes explicit that his decision constitutes a metapragmatic
alignment with the position of her opponent.

When the advocate does not produce a client or witness who isn't
proficient in English, it would seem that the issue of the choice of code
for the hearing is closed. But, as shown in examples 2, 3, and 4, the
advocate continues to employ pragmatic and metapragmatic discourses
to challenge and resist the judge's preclusion of Hopi discourse. We see
once again the variety of these moves that argue for the pragmatic superiority of Hopi over English when the advocate talks about Hopi tradi-

tions and also for an indexical inseparability between "Hopi and religion and . . . language, court, Constitution" (lines 4–5):

> Example 2. Ideologizing the Inseparability of Hopi Language and the Courts
> 001 Advoc: But I listened to the teachings of my people. I
> 002 listened to my heart. That's why these things need
> 003 to be done in Hopi. Because it goes beyond that.
> 004 You can't separate Hopi and religion and land,
> 005 language, court, Constitution. It's all tied up
> 006 into one. That's why we need special courts,
> 007 hear us in our language.

Additionally, she peppers her statements with Hopi lexical items (see example 3), which she then follows with English formulations of the term in legally relevant sentential contexts:

> Example 3. Integrating Hopi Lexical Items
> 001 Advoc: That's what Hopi's call *nukpana*, something bad. . . .
> 008 You're *nukpana* to your own people when you use—
> 009 when you use law set out for the benefit of your
> 010 people, against your own people.

It is via the framing of these metapragmatic discourses and ideologies that the advocate constitutes the argument that her client possessed a traditional right and duty to move his trailer onto the village lands in question, a right that cannot be usurped by village or court order because it is a right and duty placed on her client by his matrilineal grandmother and clan leader. Attempting to regiment these claims in the metapragmatics of relativity and cultural sovereignty is an effort on the advocate's part, I contend, to shape through ideology yet another indexical order— this time of a jural "legitimacy" (Swigart 2000) for her arguments and herself—by marking her Hopi proficiency and performances of that proficiency as iconic (Woolard and Gal 2002) of her authority in Hopi tradition, the verity of the claims she is making about tradition, and the problems of legitimacy that the Hopi court will face if it decides the case against her. And it is no coincidence that this next-order indexical "legitimacy" is generated in ideological opposition to and exclusion of English because this also works to exclude the Anglo attorney, his professional authority, and his legal arguments from contributing to the decision to be made by the Hopi judge while simultaneously appealing to and attempting to align with the judge through tradition.

In a less explicit but no less pervasive fashion, the lawyer relies repeatedly on his own set of metapragmatic discourses to exclude the advocate and challenge her arguments. Employing once again the metapragmatics of "raising objections" afforded by the rules of tribal court procedure, as shown in example 4, the lawyer challenges the advocate's efforts to establish that her client was only exercising his traditional rights and duties when he moved his trailer onto village lands and rationalizes this objection on the language-ideological grounds that witnesses' testimony to this effect is "irrelevant" to the issues to be decided by the court.

> Example 4. The "Anglo" Lawyer Objects to Tradition
> 001 Witns: Traditionally, I ask my grandmother.=
> 002 Advoc: Ok[ay.
> 003 Witns: =Y[ou know if it was okay? And who's the
> 004 Mongwi of the village.
> 005 Advoc: Okay, good. And ahm and in that traditional
> 006 aspect, what gave you reason to— to ask her
> 007 first. To d— d[o that. . . .
> 009 Lawyer: [Y— Y— Your Honor, ahm I guess
> 010 I'm going to object to this line of
> 011 questioning. Ahm I don't think it makes any
> 012 difference who he asked ahm un— unless he's got
> 013 permission from the village. Ah the fact is
> 014 that the court ordered him without—
> 015 t— t— to not to install it without permission
> 016 and— and to remove it if he had installed it
> 017 without permission. From the village
> 018 authorities. Ah, and the fact that he may or
> 019 may not have talked to his grandmother or
> 020 uncle or whoever, ahm those are not the
> 021 village authorities and so this line of
> 022 questioning is irrelevant as to whether or not
> 023 he violated the court order.

In framing such testimony as irrelevant the lawyer invokes another principle of Anglo-American evidence law, one that bears significant metapragmatic force in litigation contexts: only "relevant" witness testimony can be heard in court (Philips 1992).

Within this professional metapragmatics of relevance and objection the lawyer argues that this dispute is not about traditional duties at all but about the fact that the Hopi man acted in violation of the tribal court order when he placed his trailer on the land. But, just as the Hopi advocate does, the lawyer generates by this metapragmatics a competing and exclusive jural "legitimacy" all his own. By objecting, the lawyer iconically performs (also a next-order indexicality) his own authority as a trained lawyer and seasoned litigator, fluent in the language of adversarial courts and hence lending credence to his contention that tradition is irrelevant in this case. He also implies that the Hopi court must decide in his favor if it is to act in "legitimate" consistency with its own rules and procedures. Notably, these metapragmatics exclude the Hopi advocate while not excluding the judge and his experience and training in Anglo-American norms of jurisprudence.

Ultimately, the judge agrees with this latter point and finds that the Hopi man did violate the order of the tribal court. In response, the Hopi advocate announces her intent to appeal the decision. Then, in an unusual but telling move, the judge engages in a bit of metapragmatic rationalization of his own, reviewing his actions with regard to the use of Hopi during the hearing.

Example 5. Judicial Rationalizations for Code Choices
001 Judge: I basically said that we would conduct the
002 hearing in English, but I did allow Hopi to
003 come in. I did not totally bar the parties
004 from not using Hopi. First of all, there are no
005 rules or laws that state that we should
006 conduct the hearings in Hopi. (And) out of
007 fairness— because when I basically took
008 a poll of the parties yesterday— all the
009 parties had no problems conducting the hearing
010 in English. All the parties understood and
011 could speak English. Had I found that there
012 was a party with a problem expressing
013 themselves in English, then I would have said,

014 "Yes. We would conduct parts— parts of the
015 hearing in Hopi."

In example 5 the judge attempts to strike a balance between the advocate's metapragmatics by contending that he "did allow Hopi to come in"
(lines 2–3) and the professional metapragmatics of rule-oriented translatability espoused by the lawyer. Thus, with regard to the latter, the judge
is careful to state, "There are no rules or laws that state that we should
conduct the hearings in Hopi" (lines 4–6), and soon thereafter he contends that he would have allowed more Hopi in the proceedings had he
found that there were any parties with problems "expressing themselves
in English" (lines 11–15).

Throughout this hearing, then, we see how both of the lawyers repeatedly invoke multiple orders of competing metapragmatics to pit Hopi
tradition and Anglo-American norms of jurisprudence against each other.
In different ways each of these strategies operates by proposing to regiment a first-order indexicality linking Hopi language use and tradition or
English language use and the Anglo-style courtroom procedures and
then, at additional orders of indexicality, for the mutually exclusive, jural
"legitimacies" of each of these codes and their proponents' performative
capacities with regard to these pragmatic and normative realms.

By arguing in and for Hopi or English as the only "legitimate" code for
the court in this hearing, each side was both juxtaposing Hopi and Anglo-
American normative frameworks and indexing contentions that the judge
could rely on only one or the other when rendering a decision in this case.
And as we saw above when the judge rendered his decision, it was precisely between these now competing frames that he had to negotiate.
Insofar as he offered that decision in a manner that metapragmatically
echoed the Anglo lawyer's arguments but then attempted to insulate that
decision against appeal by rationalizing his actions toward the advocate's
use of Hopi in the court, he too relied at least in part on multiple orders of
metapragmatic regimentation to accomplish the task.

Conclusion

It is important to briefly point out what the lawyers didn't do with their
metapragmatic discourses. Significantly, neither side mounted a broader

challenge against the "legitimate" authority of the judge and the Hopi tribal court to hear the case in the first place. Indeed, as we saw in example 1, even the advocate framed her metapragmatic discourse of Hopi indexical relativity as partly grounded in the institutional demands of her role as an advocate of "her client" (lines 13–14) and later responded to the lawyer's objections in a manner consistent with that Anglo-adversarial role (lines 39–41).

Following Amsterdam and Bruner, who explain that legal actors recognize that "the illocutionary force of every truth claim made by an advocate is to plead one's cause" (2000:174), it is possible to understand the metapragmatic moves of the lawyer, the advocate, and the judge as all rhetorically calibrated to meet the institutional goals of the adversarial Hopi court and the individual goals of the legal actors and their clients to argue and resolve this dispute. This reveals an interesting irony for the arguments raised by the advocate, whose claims for Hopi tradition as pragmatically distinct from the English language and opposed to Anglo norms of law are revealed as always already metapragmatically subsumed to other pragmatic manifestations of those very same "Anglo"-style legal norms.

What is thus suggested by this analysis is something of a synthesis of the perspectives of the two sides to the debate regarding the role of tradition in tribal law and sovereignty practices. At first glance, Joh's (2000) critique of arguments regarding custom and tradition as being more about resistance to "non-Indian"-style law and politics (or even Dombrowski's [2005] claim that "Native culture" is often appropriated and manipulated by non-Indians) rather than as "authentic" portrayals of actual indigenous pasts seems equally applicable here, insofar as the Hopi advocate in this case invokes tradition in a manner framed by metapragmatics regimenting multiple orders of indexicality—first of Hopi pragmatic relativity, then of cultural sovereignty, and finally of jural legitimacy—in ways that exclude the Anglo attorney and his professional authority. But as we have also seen in this analysis, similar metapragmatic strategies are being employed by the Anglo attorney himself and for the purpose of indexing a similarly exclusive (albeit competing) order of legitimacy for himself and his arguments. In the context of this tribal court hearing, then, generating and articulating resistance, while undoubtedly being undertaken, is not a strategy solely accomplished by those legal actors with recourse to the metapragmatics of tradition but rather is a strategy pragmatically constituted and indexed by all the participants in this hearing interaction. Furthermore, it is a strategy being generated at a local level in competition for immediate material and symbolic gains that come from processes of dispute resolution in Hopi tribal court. As such, the uses of tradition here cannot be claimed to be so distant from the interests and concerns of tribal members, insofar as they are being invoked at least by some of them in an effort to secure those very interests and are being invoked and evaluated by local authorities (here the Hopi judge) for the degree to which they express "proper" justifications for approving or denying those interests in powerful ways.

Thus, while it may be the case that the pragmatics of tradition and the politics of culture may not always be about the "authentic" representation of the past practices and values of the indigenous people employing those notions, it is not entirely clear that such "authenticity" is the essential element of their efficacy as representations of the real interests and values of contemporary indigenous peoples today.

I have thus attempted in this analysis to build upon one of the abiding themes emergent across several of the contributions to this volume (see the chapters by Bender and by Neely and Palmer in particular), namely, to reveal how notions such as tradition, cultural identity, and sovereignty are ideologically fused with representations and actual instances of language use employed by tribal actors as they compete for the material and symbolic gains that come from deploying such discourses. At the heart of this analysis Hopi legal actors' metapragmatics in the context of their tribal court interactions and the language ideologies that inform them can be seen to operate as powerful strategies regimenting these micro-macro links, simultaneously shaping the character of such abstract notions and effectuating their employment for access to material and symbolic advantage in the everyday resolution of disputes. Consequently, and in much the same way that Kroskrity (this volume) is able to locate Rosalie Bethel's agency in the very details of her narrative discourses, it is via an analysis of the metapragmatic details of tribal court interaction that we can see that tribal legal actors are not passive players "caught up" in tensions between tribal traditions and Anglo-American justice but in fact active contributors to this tension, working it up in competition for the judge's favor and in expressions of that favor as well as the powerful legal outcomes this favor entails.

CHAPTER 5

English Is the Dead Language

Native Perspectives on Bilingualism

JULE GÓMEZ DE GARCÍA, MELISSA AXELROD, AND
JORDAN LACHLER

Issues of identity, cultural authenticity, power, and social structure are central to language revitalization projects in Native American communities. Even in situations of significant language shift, language remains a highly charged indicator of ethnicity for tribal populations.

All bilingual individuals have attitudes toward the two languages they speak. These attitudes reflect differing positions about the social categories that the two languages index, and they constitute ideologies of language structure and language usage. As Gal points out, "Different ideologies recognize or highlight different units of language as salient and as indicative of speakers' identities" (1998:326). The two languages available to a bilingual speaker can come to represent different aspects of the speaker's identity, and ideologies about language can reflect sociopolitical structures and roles. Hill's discussion of Mexicano speaker Don Gabriel's narrative about his son's murder is a particularly striking example. He uses Spanish to talk of the capitalist motivation for the murder but uses Mexicano to tell of his feelings of loss, to express the personal rather than the political impact of his son's death. The use of Spanish indexes Don Gabriel's "ongoing ideological resistance to a capitalist ideology" (Hill 1995:135).

As indigenous languages disappear, the number of bilingual speakers also necessarily dwindles. Each bilingual Indian has his or her story to tell of how he or she became bilingual and of the social situations each enjoyed or endured during the early language acquisition years. Individuals have stories to tell of how they learned a second or third language, whether it was English or Spanish or another Native American language.

Some stories involve institutional educational situations, including board-ing schools, public schools, and parochial schools. Other stories tell of intertribal family relationships and of informal contact learning situations. These stories reveal the attitudes that people currently have about their bilingualism and in particular about the colonial language in which they have achieved some degree of fluency.

Among Native American populations with whom we have worked, an attitude that has become particularly widespread in recent years is that English lacks the descriptive and imagistic characteristics of their Native heritage language—that English is "dead" in both a spiritual and expres-sive sense. Several of our current consultants have commented on the necessity of maintaining their ancestral language because their culture, their ceremonies, and their spiritual history and values can only be trans-ferred through the metaphors inherent in the language and through the cognitive imagery these metaphors invoke. Native participants in a round-table discussion on social, political, and economic factors in language revitalization at the 2002 Indigenous Languages Institute Symposium, "Community Voices Coming Together," in Albuquerque, New Mexico, lamented the fact that younger tribal members cannot understand impor-tant cultural lessons because they speak only English. "English," said one participant, "is a cold language. We don't see the pictures when we speak English, and we can't expect our children to see them either if we tell them about the Spirits in English." "Our Spiritual Helpers," says another, "don't understand English. This is why there are so many problems in our communities."

This chapter explores some of the possible sources for this attitude and examines the implications for language revitalization programs. The Native voices in this chapter come from four communities in New Mexico: the Sandia and Tesuque pueblos and the Navajo and Jicarilla Apache nations. The following presents a brief introduction to these four communities.

Sandia Pueblo

Sandia Pueblo is a small Native American community located on the northern boundary of the city of Albuquerque, New Mexico. It is one of nineteen pueblos located throughout the state. The Sandians are members of the Tiwa language group, the people who once dominated the area that now contains Albuquerque.

While remote tribes face many hardships and disadvantages, the Sandia Pueblo has a disadvantage that most tribes do not. All of the children of the tribe attend public or private schools, where they are a minority. The teachers do not teach and most classmates do not speak Tiwa. Remarkably, 25 percent of the pueblo members still speak Tiwa. However, because almost none of these speakers are under the age of fifty and the language is not being learned by children as their native language, Sandia Tiwa can be classified as "obsolescent." Despite these discouraging statistics, 93 percent of tribal members want to have language preservation and instruction, according to a survey we distributed in 2000 (Axelrod, Lachler, and Gómez de García 2001).

Linguistic research on Tiwa includes Brandt (1970), Harrington (1910b, 1910c), Laylin (1988), Leap (1988), Trager (1968), and Zaharlick (1974, 1977, 1980, 1981, 1982). There is a project in place to produce a dictionary of Sandia Tiwa, and classroom materials are being developed under the leadership of Sam Montoya, director of the Sandia Tiwa language program (personal communication, June 2003).

Tesuque Pueblo

Members of the Tesuque Pueblo are also committed to maintaining their language, Rio Grande Tewa. Rio Grande Tewa is spoken at six pueblos north of Santa Fe (Nambé, Tesuque, Santa Clara, San Ildefonso, San Juan, and Pojoaque) and is closely related to Arizona Tewa, spoken in Tewa Village on the Hopi Reservation in Arizona.[1] There are approximately 175 speakers at Tesuque out of a total population of around 400.

There has been more linguistic research on Tewa than on other members of the Tanoan branch of Kiowa-Tanoan. Work on Rio Grande Tewa has been done by Dozier (1949), Harrington (1910a, 1910b), Klaiman (1989, 1993), Anna Speirs (1974), and Randall Speirs (1968, 1972). There are a number of articles on Arizona Tewa by Kroskrity (e.g., 1984, 1985a, 1985b, 1992a, 1992b, 1993a).

A fairly strong language program has been developed at the pueblo with assistance from a grant from the Administration for Native Americans. According to the language program director at that time, Catherine

Vigil (personal communication, August 2003), summer programs and Master-Apprentice teams have been particularly successful. We responded to a request from the pueblo to install a Tesuque font (developed by Sean Burke in 2001) on all the school and language program computers, and, according to tribal language program staff members, work is under way to develop more classroom materials and a dictionary (Axelrod, Lachler, and Gómez de García 2001). There is also a Tewa reader (Abeyta 1984) as well as a dictionary of San Juan Tewa (Martinez 1982). In addition, a dictionary of Nambé Tewa is in progress (McKenna et al.), funded by a grant from the NSF as a password-protected, Web-based, electronic lexicon available only to Nambé Pueblo members.

The Navajo Nation

Navajo is spoken on the Navajo Reservation in northwestern New Mexico, eastern Arizona, and southern Utah. It is one of the Apachean languages, the southern branch of the Athabaskan languages of the Na-Dene family, which extends through California and Oregon, up through Canada, and into Alaska.

Navajo is perhaps the most robust of all the Na-Dene languages, yet it still must be considered an endangered language. According to Batchelder,

> since 1984 the Navajo Nation has mandated instruction in Navajo language and culture in K–12 schools within its boundaries. There was a great concern then, and this concern still exists today, that fewer and fewer members of the Nation have access to their rich cultural and linguistic heritage. Clearly there is substance to these concerns. The National Clearinghouse for Bilingual Education (1999) reports that there are 148,530 speakers of Navajo in a Nation of 250,000 to 275,000 people (statistics on the population of the Nation vary by source). The best measure of language maintenance is in children, and in this case, the figures are even more stark. A study conducted by Paul Platero of children in reservation Head Start programs in the early 1990s found that of the three-to-five-year-old children included in the study only 18 percent spoke Navajo (Watchman, 1994). Agnes Holm and Wayne Holm (1995) reported that only about half the students attending schools on the reservation still spoke Navajo. (2000:1)

"Ethnologue" reports that there are 148,530 Navajo speakers, of whom 7,616 are monolingual speakers (Grimes 2005). The number of first-language speakers among first graders has declined dramatically over the past thirty-five years or so—30 percent in 1998 versus 90 percent in 1968 (Platero 1992).

There are a great many grammatical and lexicographic studies of the Navajo language, and it may, in fact, be the best documented of any Native American language. Linguistic study of Navajo includes the pioneering dictionaries and grammars of Young and Morgan (1984, 1987; see also Young, Morgan, and Midgette 1992) as well as Young's more recent analysis of the Navajo verb (2000). Other important resources on Navajo grammar include Faltz (1998), Fernald and Platero (2000), and Young, Jelinek, and Saxon (1996).

There has also been a great deal of work done on Navajo language pedagogy (e.g., Dyc 2002; Fillerup 2000; Goossen 1995–98; Holm and Holm 1995). The language is taught at the college level at the two branches of Diné College and at the state universities of New Mexico and Arizona. Language programs are also in place in many elementary and secondary schools across the reservation, and school districts have been building archives for classroom materials for teaching the Navajo language (e.g., the San Juan School District, http://www.sanjuan.k12.ut.us/).

The Rock Point School on the Navajo Reservation is perhaps the most famous of the school programs focusing on Navajo language (Begay 2005; Holm and Holm 1995; McLaughlin 1989; Rosier and Holm 1980). At Rock Point kids come expecting that they will succeed, and they do—the Navajo program gives students pride in being Navajo and in their language and culture. Navajo language programs include having elders in the community come to give lessons in Navajo on Navajo cultural matters, Navajo-speaking aides being given salaries equal to those of teachers, frequent parent-teacher conferences, and activities such as language fairs and book-making nights, during which parents have oral language lessons while children who are learning to write work together to produce ten-to-twelve-page books that are completed and ready for families to take home with them at the end of the evening (McLaughlin 1989).

Also in Arizona is the very successful Navajo immersion program at Fort Defiance Elementary School. According to Holm and Holm, in these schools, Navajo was used in its own right, *not* just as the means to essentially English-language ends. Students were expected to continue to develop their Navajo language abilities *throughout* their school careers. Students were taught to read and write first in Navajo. They continued to read and write in Navajo after they learned to read and write in English . . . [and] conventionally Anglo content—math, social studies, science—also were taught in Navajo. (1995:3)

This emphasis on education in Navajo has been successful enough that the Navajo Nation now also requires the use of the language in its Head Start programs (Dyc 2002:613).

The Jicarilla Apache Nation

Jicarilla Apache is another of the Apachean languages. The Jicarilla Apaches are located on the Jicarilla Apache Reservation in north-central New Mexico. According to the tribe's 1995 *Language and Cultural Needs Assessment* survey, the level of language fluency is 21 percent of the population. Of those 21 percent of speakers of Jicarilla, 57 percent are fifty years old or older. The fluency levels of individuals age forty to forty-nine is 33 percent; for ages thirty to thirty-nine this figure reduces to 11 percent fluency. For individuals younger than thirty the fluency level is at 1.4 percent.

Concern for the preservation, acquisition, and maintenance of the language is just being realized as a priority for the tribe. The *Jicarilla Goals for the Year 2000* includes the following: "To maintain cultural integrity through maintenance of its traditions, language, and cultural practices so as to encourage and support our continued existence."

There are classroom materials in Jicarilla, including illustrated booklets and posters. There are also videos, tapes, and a CD with stories and histories in Jicarilla. An excellent small dictionary is available (Wilson and Vigil Martine 1996) as well as two other smaller works (Mersol 1981; Vicenti 1981) in addition to texts collected by Goddard (1911) and grammatical descriptions by Hoijer (1938a, 1938b) and Jung (1999). A larger dictionary, *Abáachi Mizaa Łáo Iłkee' Shijai: Dictionary of Jicarilla Apache* (Phone, Olson, and Martinez 2007), which we edited and which was funded by the National Science Foundation (NSF), was published in 2007. The community has also worked on developing a preschool immersion program, summer language camps, adult classes for both conversational ability and literacy, and public school programs (Axelrod et al. 1999; Gómez de García, Axelrod, and Lachler 2002; Gómez de García, Olson, and Axelrod 2002).

Explanations

The perceived coldness of English and the feeling that the Native heritage language has significant descriptive and imagistic power present interesting questions for linguists and anthropologists studying language ideologies. How did these attitudes arise? We outline three possible explanations, which we suggest are all involved in the language ideologies about bilingualism that we find in Native communities in New Mexico. These explanations concern (1) the social motivations for language learning, (2) the process of academic research into indigenous languages, and (3) morphological typology.

Social Explanations: Motivations for Language Learning

A social explanation has to do with the fact that many Native American people were forced to learn English for its instrumental value as the key that would open up doors to success, power, and social and economic equality—or at least to autonomy—in the emerging American society. This is a dominant ideology in mainstream American culture and one that has been internalized in most, if not all, minority communities. The discussion here points out how contemporary language ideologies in many Native American communities have reversed this instrumental ideology. English is no longer seen as a key to success; instead, it is the source of loss for their communities. English is now a "dead" language rather than an avenue to economic and social power.

We want to suggest here that many Native Americans, reflecting on the struggle of their communities for autonomy and for social and economic power, attribute the difficulties they've experienced to the adoption of English and the consequent loss of the heritage language. Native American community members often feel at a loss to understand how their heritage languages became endangered in their efforts to learn the dominant language. "We're starting to see that we're at this stage of language loss and shift," said a member of Tesuque Pueblo, "but not why and how we got to this stage."

Part of the difficulty for indigenous communities in this regard involves the motivation that underlay the shift to English. An instrumental motivation for learning English rests on the discourse (in the sense of Urban 1991) that English is perceived as the route to financial success. Instrumental motivation and pragmatic value are the most widespread "commonsense" and commonly used ways in our society of interpreting the value of a skill or of any other social behavior. So successful were educational and social policies in encouraging the use of English as the language of success and prestige that even the smallest children are aware of the relative values of their indigenous languages and English. An ethnographic study of ten children and their parents on the Navajo Reservation conducted by Parsons-Yazzie (1995) showed that even children who grow up in homes where parents and other relatives speak Navajo do not learn to speak the language fluently. As Holm and Holm describe it, Navajo children, "despite growing up in homes in which parents and relatives speak Navajo, acquired little or no Navajo. Even in the remote and traditional community in which Yazzie conducted her work, young children 'sense' the relatively lower utility and prestige of Navajo *even before* they enter school" (1995:10; see Field's chapter in this volume for a discussion of this language ideology on the part of Navajo children and how it conflicts with beliefs about language held by older community members).

But pragmatic or economic value is often in conflict with the spiritual and identity needs of Native American people, particularly those struggling for cultural survival. In one New Mexican community, because the tribe's eldest medicine man works for and is paid through the tribal facilities maintenance department, he is unable to be available to share his knowledge and his cultural skills with the children in the education department's preschool immersion program. Having the eldest medicine man in a community working in a maintenance department is about looking at community resources in terms of instrumental motivation rather than in terms of larger goals of reestablishing traditional cultural values; it's about making pragmatic goals rather than spiritual goals the primary focus (but see also Richland's discussion in this volume of the pragmatic value of Hopi language in Hopi tribal courts, which he describes as another type of instrumental usage).

Because in many cases the only contexts left for the use of the Native languages are in spiritual or ceremonial practices, these languages are imbued with greater power and sacred significance than English, which is used for more mundane activities. The use of the Native language becomes implicitly tied to spirituality, and English can seem like only a soulless medium of economic transaction by comparison. According to Dyc, "the tribal council at the Cochiti Pueblo of New Mexico, for example, decided in 1997 to prohibit the development of a written version of their Keresan language. . . . The language is considered sacred, and the tribal members wish to protect the religion by withholding the language from the public domain" (2002:612).

In some communities, such as the Navajo Reservation, the Native language is associated with political power as well as with spiritual practice. Among the Navajo, says Dyc, "in politics . . . Navajo remains the language of power. The language is used more consistently in chapter houses, the centers of decision making in small, rural communities. The Navajo language is also heard more often in the tribal council chambers" (2002:613). In those council meetings Navajo speakers hold the floor longer and are more effective in achieving their goals (Dyc 2002:613).

In the case of the Navajo, House claims that Navajo resistance to assimilation "has led to a cultural revitalization effort that stresses alteric strategies. The goal of this movement is to recover and communicate a proud and positive image of Navajo-ness—to Navajos themselves and to others" (2002:33). In the face of negative stereotypes about Navajo language and culture in the past, she suggests that "it is not surprising that a chief goal of a Navajo revitalization movement as a counterhegemonic project would be to reclaim a positive image of the Navajos, their culture, and their language" (House 2002:36).

Interest in asserting the importance of the Native language and culture while problematizing the adoption of English as taking tribal members farther from their roots and farther from the spirits of their ancestors is seen at Sandia Pueblo as well. Language program staff at Sandia Pueblo believe that documentation of the formal language of Sandia Pueblo is an important way to revive and strengthen cultural traditions. The reason English has had so much power to displace the indigenous language, they say, is that English is used for shopping, banking, and other aspects of daily life. "We need to change this practice," says one leader. "We need to begin talking about livestock and other animals in the Tiwa language. Tiwa has different words for wild animals, animals of the mountains, and animals of the plains. We need to start thinking again in terms of these distinctions."

Although instrumental motivation has become the convention as a strategy for encouraging language learning, many tribal members have come to feel that looking at Native language revitalization in this way is a dead end. They recognize that the long-standing focus on pragmatic incentives has led to a shift to English without the expected socioeconomic success and with a loss of the ancestral language and its ability to provide social and cultural grounding. Many communities are examining the possibility of combining pragmatic economic goals necessary for growth in their communities with a new focus on reestablishing traditional lifeways. As a language program leader at Sandia Pueblo puts it,

> We need to stimulate discussion of the environmental stewardship of the land as well as discussion of local economies, the use of fossil fuels, agriculture, and animal husbandry. We need to educate people about eating healthy and demonstrate that we can raise food animals for less money than they'd spend purchasing the same thing at the local organic market. This will open the opportunity for the pueblo to enter into this kind of community planning that will have enormous impact on both the pueblo and on the region.

This is very much in accord with Fishman's (1991) notion of the importance of "being Xish *through* Xish," or, as Fillerup puts it in discussing educational programs on the Navajo Reservation, "if we can ignite the fire of everyday life back into the language, we will no longer be racing against the clock, but instead trying to outrun the sun" (2000:34).

Lambert contrasts instrumental with integrative orientations for language learning, suggesting that an orientation is *instrumental* if "the purposes of language study reflect the more utilitarian value of linguistic achievement, such as getting ahead in one's occupation" (2003:314). An orientation is, on the other hand, *integrative* if the learner is interested in learning about or adopting cultural aspects of the second language community.

We are increasingly seeing a shift in Native communities to an integrative orientation. Silentman suggests that the Navajo language programs at Rock Point and Fort Defiance "offer examples of the interweaving of instrumental and sentimental values toward the language, in which a positive public-community attitude *and* new native language use contexts are developed. In these communities and others, the dual instrumental-sentimental role has enabled the success of Navajo language education despite the social, economic and political attractions of the dominant language" (1995:182).

Academic Research and Local Language Ideologies: Our Priceless Human Heritage

A second possible explanation for this new language ideology in which English is regarded as a dead language is that it is an epiphenomenon of linguistic and anthropological research on Native American languages. Much of this work is very enthusiastic about the metaphysical and conceptual systems implied by the morphosemantic strategies of these "exotic" languages. An obvious example of this perspective comes from Whorf, who says that "linguistics is essentially the quest of meaning. . . . [I]ts real concern is to light up the thick darkness of the language, and thereby much of the thought, the culture, and the outlook upon life of a given community, with the light of this 'golden something,' as I have heard it called, this transmuting principle of meaning" (1956:73). This notion formed the basis for his writings on the relationship of language and culture, especially with regard to the metaphysics expressed by the Hopi system of temporal and modal expression. In Whorf's work we see a clear illustration of the notion that different languages reveal different conceptual systems, a notion that has been misinterpreted and abused in subsequent years of research on Native American languages (Martin 1986; Pullum 1991).

The emphasis that anthropological linguists have placed on the exotic richness of Native languages or on their ability to express a conceptual system linked to a more harmonious or spiritual worldview represents the replacement of Native speakers' views of language use and meaning with romanticized notions of the cognitive significance of language form and style. As Lucy puts it, "Many studies in anthropology 'read' cultural beliefs directly off linguistic forms and do not seek additional evidence for the cognitive or behavioral reality of those beliefs. Studies of this type typically *presuppose* a close linkage between language and thought without concern for establishing the nature and direction(s) of influence" (1992:70). These studies can be an appropriation not only of the language but also of the significances the language has (or has had) for its speakers.

The growing awareness of the endangered status of most indigenous languages has led linguists and anthropologists to a modern-day rhetoric that contributes to this multiple appropriation. It has also been adopted, sometimes in unexpected ways, by tribal members and thus further contributes to these ideologies of English as the spiritually and culturally dead language. Hill writes: "Community language workers, speakers, and other members of local groups are both participants and overhearers in a global conversation about language endangerment in which the voices of academics and policymakers are especially prominent" (2002:119). She defines three themes within a rhetoric employed to demonstrate the worth of languages and the worth of the work of those advocating for their preservation.

The first of these is the theme of universal ownership, which attempts to establish that all languages belong to all of us, that each language is part of the totality of universal human knowledge and experience and is therefore important to all of us. The second theme is the theme of hyperbolic valorization of languages as objects or commodities, human treasures that should be guarded and saved. And the third is the theme of enumeration, or the counting of the numbers of speakers and the numbers of languages as language researchers compete for scarce financial resources. Demonstrating that a language has fewer speakers than other languages might set it in a priority position for the limited funding available from organizations more anxious to fund documentation over revitalization of a dying language.

While all of these themes represent an objectification of the languages and a distillation of their purpose as forms of communication and identity markers among speakers, it is the hyperbolic valorization theme that is most pertinent to our discussion on bilingual ideologies. Viewed in the perspective of what Grillo (1989) earlier referred to as a previous "ideology of contempt" for a language spoken by a socially dispreferred and stigmatized group, the new hyperbolic valorization is extremely attractive to native speakers of a now "treasured" language. In their search for funding and for recognition of the work that they do, linguists give exaggerated tributes to endangered languages, referring to them as "treasures," with all of the metaphorical extensions that term has. It entails the notion of financial value, and the question of what that financial value might be is begged by further use of the term *priceless* in many discussions of endangered languages. Hill quotes Hale's statement as an exemplar of this usage: "The loss of local languages . . . has meant irretrievable loss of diverse and interesting intellectual wealth, the priceless products of human mental industry" (Hale 1992:36).

A further entailment of the treasure metaphor is that treasures (and their values) are often hidden, except from those who are more discerning and appreciative of their worth than others. Those who recognize the sociovaloric worth of minority languages are indirectly commended, and, again, the treasure becomes somehow theirs as a reward, another sort of appropriation of the language away from its speakers and their linguistic needs and traditions.

Hill offers an alternative to the hyperbolic valorization rhetoric for practitioners of endangered language research: "It would be especially useful to work with speakers to show how these [fascinating linguistic] properties [of endangered languages] capture unique local understandings of the world that are deeply embedded in a way of life" (2002:129).

Roseann Willink, a native speaker and thirty-year instructor of Navajo at the University of New Mexico, talked with us about conceptual differences she sees between Navajo and English. English and Navajo, she says, don't have the same concepts. Navajo is "more precise," and in some situations Navajo is more descriptive. In some situations English might be better, particularly when a language behavior violates the sociolinguistic or discourse norms she feels apply to her as a Navajo speaker. For example, Dyc reports that

> the Navajo avoid speaking for another person or controlling the behavior of others. There is a preference for communication that does not threaten the autonomy and individuality of the other person. In personal interactions, social bonding typically precedes business matters or requests for

help. These practices are consistent with the concept of *k'é*, 'a preverbal element which refers to affective action and solidarity, encompassing such concepts as love, compassion, kindness, friendliness, generosity, and peacefulness' (Witherspoon, 1977, p. 84). The Western tradition of oral dispute and argumentative writing conflict with the non-coercive style of the Navajo. (2002:618)

Wilhelmina Phone and Maureen Olson, authors of an NSF-funded dictionary project on the Jicarilla Apache Reservation, also talk about the relationship of language, culture, and thought in their native language:

> *Mrs. P.*: When kids just speak English, their thinking is different, so they don't really understand our cultural traditions.
> *Mrs. O.*: In English it's just words, and you toss them together. But in Apache life is in everything, in the atmosphere and in the Mother Earth. It's a dynamic system. And that concept, that meaning, is in the language itself. English just names stuff, but it doesn't really talk about what that stuff is doing. Because of the verbs in Apache, you see things and think about things in a different way.

If this new rhetoric has connections to Native peoples' experience with academics, it is an interesting, perhaps unconscious, accommodation by Native people to the theme of hyperbolic valorization. Although this valorization of language as a treasure may not have originated within indigenous communities, it resonates with the needs and beliefs of community language activists, and they have worked to promote this view within the community. It is important to note here that community language activists, like the ones we work with, lead the discussion on indigenous language policy and planning both within their own communities and in conferences on language revitalization. These leaders have very often received academic degrees and have studied the works of writers like Hinton and Hale, Sapir and Whorf, and others in the college classroom. These activists, and others in the community as well, have come into contact with statements valorizing Native languages not only within the academic literature but also in applications for language program funding and on Web sites devoted to language revitalization.

We surmise that Native American language speakers who have heard, as Hill suggests, linguists' and anthropologists' ways of talking about their languages have adapted the valorization rhetoric in exactly the way that

Hill would want from endangered language advocates. According to Olson, "in Apache, life is in everything. . . . It's a dynamic system. And that concept, that meaning, is in the language itself." Olson's language, like the rest of the world, is dynamic, alive.

Olson's comment encapsulates Witherspoon's (1977, 1980) discussions of the traditional Navajo view of language. Witherspoon emphasizes the distinction between active and static and the importance of movement in Navajo language and culture. "Movement and life," he says, "seem to be inseparably related, if not equivalent. Movement is the basis of life, and life is exemplified by movement" (Witherspoon 1977:53). Language is associated with movement and life and also with creative power and control. Through language one can fashion the world in accordance with one's thoughts. According to Witherspoon, speech is an "externalization of thought" and an "extension of thought"; speech "represents marvelous evidence of the varied character and extensive capacity of thought. Moreover, speech is a reinforcement of the power of thought" (1977:31). Indeed, Witherspoon asserts that language, and particularly ritual language, "is not a mirror of reality; reality is a mirror of language" (1977:34). Witherspoon tells us that for the Navajo, language is "a primary way in which thought is projected onto reality" and that "it is through language that man acquires human status" and the ability to act and create (1980:8, 12). As Olson put it, language *is* life.

English, by contrast, "just names stuff, but it doesn't really talk about what the stuff is doing," according to Olson and other community language activists. Their own rhetorical expression of the ideology that their languages have some special descriptive power that English lacks is deeply embedded in their discussions of language revitalization. We have heard it said repeatedly in all of the communities we have visited that the Native language is *more descriptive* than is English in precisely those areas most intimately related to the social and personal identities of tribal people. This view is consonant with traditional ideologies about the relationships between language and thought and between language and creativity, and it is perhaps voiced more often in recent years because of the support this view receives from the valorization of indigenous languages found in academic writing. The relationship between academic influence and traditional language ideologies is a bidirectional one, though, and it is worth noting that there is also a great deal of academic literature devoted to the descriptive power and culturally revealing nature of Native languages, particularly, for example, in the area of place-name studies (e.g., Basso 1988, 1998; Hinton 1994) and analyses of animacy ranking (e.g., Creamer 1974; Hale 1973; Witherspoon 1977, 1980).

Speakership

There is another important issue resulting from contact with academics: a concern about the "authenticity" of speakers' use of their heritage language. When faced with the questions and microphones of academic researchers, an individual may feel the pressure of speaking for the whole community. He or she must record for the outside public and for the community that which must stand as a representation of the whole. This pressure leads to discussion among tribal members about who is a "real" speaker, who best represents the "traditional" ways, who is most articulate in his or her use of the language. Collins points out that academics as well are often heard to make these judgments about speakers: "As I worked with my first consultant, an elder whose first language was Tolowa, I was told by academic contacts that he was good but did not know the language as well as 'X' and 'Y,' who had passed away. Like some linguistic will-o'-the-wisp, the real Tolowa was always just receding on the historical horizon" (1998:264).

Willink reminded us that this pressure to speak correctly extends to intertribal situations as well as to those times when speakers meet with academics. Discussing the difficulties posed by the shift to English on the Navajo Reservation, Willink pointed out that

> what this means is that when we speak Navajo, we may stumble a little and mispronounce a syllable or two because we've been speaking mostly in English. If we're going to give a speech before elderly Navajos, even fluent younger speakers have to practice beforehand in order to be sure they'll do it right. There's a great deal of pressure to speak the language exactly right, because sometimes a small error will make the whole sentence wrong. One slight shift in tone or the use of a glottal stop, for example, and you've done it wrong. This contrasts greatly with English, where the pieces are bigger and the sounds not as close to one another, as in the suffixes of walk*ing* vs. walk*ed*. I remember a case where one woman gave a speech at the Chapter House on the Navajo reservation, and she

said something wrong. Everyone laughed and she left crying. It's particularly sensitive in interpreting, especially in legal cases of rape. It can be hard to translate without being very vulgar. In the courthouse, one might have to call for a recess in these cases. I tell my students, "You've got to practice so you don't mispronounce it and have it mean something awful!"

This concern about language correctness and speaker authenticity may well contribute to the attitude that the Native language has some mysterious essence not shared by English. It serves to reinforce a romanticized notion of the "rapier-like" character of the Native language as compared to the "blunt instrument" that is English (Lakoff 1987:325, paraphrasing Whorf).

Linguistic Typology and Language Perceptions

A third explanation for the idea that English is cold and blunt compared to the heritage language centers on the typology of polysynthetic morphology, a characteristic of many Native American languages. Prototypical polysynthetic languages have a great deal of synthesis (many morphemes per word) and a high degree of fusion (with the possibility of each morpheme representing more than one meaning and a high degree of opacity of morpheme boundaries). Polysynthetic languages tend to have affixes that may express the bulk of the semantic content of a particular verb. They typically show a wide variety of word formation processes, noun incorporation, obligatory agreement marking on the verb, elaborate marking of temporal distinctions, and elaborate noun classification systems. As Sapir says, in polysynthetic languages "a single word expresses either a simple concept or a combination of concepts so interrelated as to form a psychological unity" (1949a:82). It is possible that the rich morphological and semantic content of single words, particularly single verbs, in these languages encourages the notion that the languages themselves are more descriptive than other types of languages and that, by comparison, English is inexpressive.

Consider the following conversation from a work session in Dulce, New Mexico, between us and our Apache partners on the Jicarilla Dictionary Project.

Melissa: Ye'nees'áñda, is that one word or two?

Mrs. O.: Well, it could be either, but you can see pictures in your head better when you say it together sometimes.

Jule: You get pictures in your head when you speak Jicarilla? Do you get pictures in your head when you speak English too?

Mrs. P.: No, because I'm not so familiar with English. When you say "the dress is red," you don't see it, it's just a red dress. When you say "little red wagon," would I picture that in my head? No, because it's just a wagon. I wouldn't get a picture in my head with that in Abaachi either, because it's just a wagon. But *ch'aátso* [chief's headdress], yes—because it's important, and you'd see the eagle feathers.

Mrs. M.: In our way you picture everything you're talking about. The person you're talking to also pictures it the same way.

It would seem that "little red wagon" and *ch'aátso* (chief's headdress) are equally structurally complex (a noun phrase with adjectival modifiers versus a compound noun made up of a noun stem, *ch'aá* [hat], plus an adjective stem, *tso* [big]).

The structural demands of polysynthesis require that most complex noun phrases that are the names for things be descriptive. Consider, for example, the Jicarilla Apache word for "bicycle":

baas   *miá'iákeshdiákaá'í*   "bicycle"
baas   mi+iá#kesh+di+á+kaá+'i
wheels   it+with#foot+lex+valence+pedal+the.one
(literally, "wheels one pedals with the feet")

We found it interesting that the discussion of "pictures in the head" occurred in two very different sorts of situations. One was in the invention or explanation of terms for items relatively new to the culture such as pencil sharpeners and bicycles. In order to make the descriptive word for such things, according to our Jicarilla teammates, you need to picture it in your head so you can describe what it looks like or what it does. The second situation was in the description of important cultural items, particularly those used in the past.

Basso (1988) argues that place-names in Western Apache provide an important example of the descriptive power of that polysynthetic language. As in Jicarilla Apache, words in the Apache language spoken at Cibecue are rich in morphological structure and in evocative meaning.

Because of their inseparable connection to specific localities, placenames may be used to summon forth an enormous range of mental and emotional associations—associations of time and space, of history and events, of persons and social activities, of oneself and stages in one's life. And in their capacity to evoke, in their compact power to muster and consolidate so much of what a landscape may be taken to represent in both personal and cultural terms, placenames acquire a functional value that easily matches their utility as instruments of reference. (Basso 1988:103)

The mental imagery evoked by words that both Olson and Phone commented on in Jicarilla Apache is mentioned by Basso for Western Apache as well: "Unless Apache listeners are able to picture a physical setting for narrated events (unless, as one of my consultants said, 'your mind can travel to the place and really see it'), the events themselves will be difficult to imagine" (1988:110). Basso (1988:111) provides examples of these placenames, including the following. Notice how the combination of morphemes in this construction acts to provide a very pointed and detailed description of a particular place.

Tséligaí dah sidil

tse' + ligai	dah	sidil
rock/stone + white	above ground level	three or more form a compact cluster

(literally, "white rocks lie above in a compact cluster")

The direction of causality is unimportant, that is, whether the description causes the pictures or the pictures allow formation of the language; the important point here is that speakers believe their language and their culture are interdependent in this descriptive and dynamic process. In combining the frame (in the sense of Fillmore 1985) of culturally important things (be they old or new) with the structural complexity of the Jicarilla word, the descriptive language comes alive. Conversely, because the referent is not important in Jicarilla culture and since there is no lack of psychological commensurability between the words "little red wagon" in English and the Jicarilla equivalent, there are no mental pictures in either language.

Our language guide at Sandia Pueblo made a similar comment about the descriptiveness of his language. In this case there is an emphasis on the "formal language," the variety most endangered in the pueblo that is spoken now primarily by the eldest community members and only in ceremonial contexts. This consultant says, "The formal Sandia Tiwa language is a very beautiful one. In this form of the language, when one wants to say 'it snowed,' one says the equivalent of 'mother earth woke up this morning dressed in a white shawl.' If we lose the formal language we will lose much of the poetry that is part of our culture and embedded in the language."

Implications for Language Revitalization Programs

The aim of much current linguistic work in Native communities is to collaborate with tribal members in order to facilitate the building of a sense of community around language revitalization. We believe that the attitude that the heritage language is inherently superior in its descriptive power and inextricably linked with cultural and spiritual traditions is of great value for communities in building a sense of identity around language. (See Reynolds and Bunte, this volume, for descriptions of a similar dynamic in Pan-Mayan and Southern Paiute language revitalization and identity-building efforts, respectively.)

What many Native groups say they really want to teach is identity, and language serves as part of that identity. This is language socialization, an area that cannot be addressed solely by curriculum design, particularly not a curriculum that stresses artificial but easily evaluated constructs such as colors and numbers. This type of curriculum development is so intertwined with the principles and methods of education within the dominant culture that the larger goal of language socialization is often forgotten.

Problems related to language loss and shift in indigenous communities seem to be not only that heritage languages are no longer spoken by the younger generation and that the contexts for speaking the language within the community are diminishing but also that dominant-culture ways of addressing these challenges are being adopted. Responsibility for revitalizing languages is most commonly situated within the institutions that are constructed to mirror dominant-culture values: the schools and the tribal bureaucracy.

In discussing this issue with members of the Jicarilla Apache Tribe, bilingual teacher Maureen Olson reported that difficulties coordinating with tribal leadership can have very negative consequences for language programs in the community and in the schools. State teacher certification is also an important issue. Mrs. Wilhelmina Phone, a language specialist with over thirty years of experience writing, analyzing, and teaching her language, was disqualified from public school teaching because she had no official certification. She believes that a language program can be lost because of these issues. She spent many years working to produce language materials and lessons herself, but, without support and coordination from tribal leadership, her materials were lost, and she became too discouraged to continue.

The process of linguistic socialization begins in childhood as adults transmit important cultural information to the next generation through a range of language behaviors. Among these are sayings and stories that are themselves passed down through generations to explain social expectations and consequences. Linguistic socialization is a crucial but often overlooked component of language stabilization.

According to Ochs, every sentence in any conversation or discourse not only carries semantic and pragmatic meaning but also expresses affect: "In most arenas of daily communication, speakers convey not only information concerning some state or event but their feelings about some state or event as well, and languages will have varying structures for encoding this level of information. . . . [A]ll sentences expressed in context will have an affective component" (1986:256).

Children are socialized into the expression of affect by adult speakers of the language. They learn which emotions are expressed and which are suppressed, and they learn which expressions of these emotions are culturally appropriate. This expression of affect ranges from formulaic expressions of gratitude to expressions of grief over the death of a loved one. A child learns, in other words, the culturally appropriate forms of external expression of the most personal and internal of reactions to the world. The child is socialized through language to express his or her emotions and, in some cases, socialized through language not to feel, much less to express, particular emotions.

In the case of the bilingual individual, having dual languages is a matter of having appropriateness in and allegiance to two different cultures. Regarding the sociopsychological aspects of bilingualism and "the difficulties faced by people with dual allegiances" (Lambert 2003:318),

Anisfeld and Lambert (1961; reported in Lambert 2003:316–17) examined success in second language learning of a cultural heritage language among Jewish students in Montreal. Students "were questioned about their orientations toward learning Hebrew and their attitudes toward the Jewish culture and community, and tested for their verbal intelligence, language aptitude and achievement in the Hebrew language at the end of the school year" (Lambert 2003:316). Their results showed that attitudinal factors were an important measure of success in learning Hebrew: "The measure of a Jewish student's desire to become more acculturated in the Jewish tradition and culture was a sensitive indicator of progress in Hebrew for children from a particular district of Montreal, one where members of the Jewish sub-community were actually concerned with problems if integrating into the Jewish culture" (Lambert 2003:316). In those communities of more recent immigrants where Jewish acculturation was not an issue, "pride in being Jewish" was the factor that correlated with achievement in Hebrew (Lambert 2003:317).

Lambert also discusses one group of French American adolescents in Montreal (out of three studied) who "faced a conflict of cultural allegiances since they were ambivalent about their identity, favoring certain features of the French and other features of the American culture. Presumably because they had not resolved the conflict, they were retarded in their command of both languages when compared to the other groups" (2003:319).

One's sense of oneself as an individual and as a member of a community is shaped by one's language. It is this shaping function of language that Mrs. Phone is referring to when she says, "When kids just speak English, their thinking is different, so they don't really understand our cultural traditions."

Roseann Willink, Navajo speaker and instructor, also commented on the particular challenges faced by individuals in a bilingual setting: "Why is it hard to teach kids Navajo? Everyone around you is speaking English, and because of this it's just easier to communicate in English sometimes. A lot of interaction is done only in English, and the use of English gets to be a habit. In order to be able to use Navajo with children, we need to be constantly around it, but the situations where one uses Navajo, like with our elders, are being lost."

Conclusions

The language ideologies we have been encountering stress the descriptiveness of the heritage language and its particularly superior expressive powers with respect to cultural and spiritual matters and may well signal an acknowledgment of the critical role of the sociocultural context in work to rejuvenate the language. Woolard suggests that "ideologies of language are not about language alone. Rather, they envision and enact ties of language to identity, to aesthetics, to morality, and to epistemology. Through such linkages, they underpin not only linguistic form and use but also the very notion of the person and the social group, as well as . . . fundamental social institutions" (1998:3).

Metalinguistic commentary on the relative vibrancy and dynamism of a speaker's two languages, with its patterned and ritualistic declarations of the descriptiveness and appropriateness of one language over the other in culturally specific situations, is, we believe, a genre of discourse that admits its users into the membership of proficient speakerhood of their languages. Using terminology from Silverstein, we can understand this "English is the dead language" genre as a discursive pattern that functions in two ways, "the first, to be sure, as contextually differential characterizers of some denotatum but second as indexes of users' presumed-upon (or even would-be) relational positions in a projective social distribution of conceptual knowledge" (2004:622). Speakers perform what Maureen Olson refers to as "the habit of being Jicarilla" by using certain patterns of speech, certain ways of talking about themselves and their language. They perform what Silverstein refers to as a ritualistic dynamic figuration "of social identity come to life, interactionally activated in the here-and-now of discourse for the inter-subjective work of creating, maintaining, or transforming social relations" (2004:623).

The ability to participate in the metalanguage about a heritage language makes a speaker a true member of a social group as well as someone who is proficient enough to be able to declare what is different and better and valuable in that language. The talk and the social identity take on a reciprocal relationship. One can talk about Jicarilla in this genre of metalinguistic ritual only if one is Jicarilla. Participation in the talk both requires and allows membership and personal alignment with other speakers.

We have presented three different sources that have contributed to the development of this genre. Speakers are giving voice to the disappointment they feel with a language that has not lived up to its social and economic "promise." Work with endangered language advocates has introduced rhetorical themes that encourage and validate the valorization of their languages. And the polymorphemic structure of many Native American languages makes necessary the kind of description of referents that make these languages seem more dynamic, informative, and imagistic to their speakers. Thus, in addition to indexing speaker identity as a member of a particular linguistic community, this metalanguage "makes it be so" within the belief structures of its users. The ancestral language is the living language of the culture, and English is the dead language.

Pride in heritage, ethnicity, and identity is therefore positively correlated with successful language acquisition. Pride in language and awe at its richness encourage successful language revitalization efforts. Replacing the labels of "dying," "moribund," and "obsolescent" for Native languages with the perspective that it is English that is dead may well be a strong step forward in Native communities' work toward reestablishing the heritage language and culture as dominant.

CHAPTER 6

Visibility, Authenticity, and Insiderness in Cherokee Language Ideologies

MARGARET BENDER

Since the introduction of the term *linguistic ideology* into the scholarly discourse on language-culture relations (Silverstein 1979), a wide variety of research has demonstrated the complex connections between beliefs about language and broader sociocultural beliefs, practices, and institutions (e.g., see Gal 2005; Gal and Irvine 1995; Inoue 2004; Kroskrity 2000c; Schieffelin, Woolard, and Kroskrity 1998; Woolard 1985; Woolard and Schieffelin 1994). This chapter presents two examples of interrelationship between Cherokee language ideology and specific sociohistorical contexts involving the negotiation of community boundaries and internal structure through such ideologically driven semiotic processes as iconicity, recursiveness, and erasure (Gal and Irvine 1995). Both examples affirm the powerful ways in which language ideology can inform or frame social and economic movements and trends.

The first example comes from the Oklahoma Cherokee community of the 1960s. This community was largely created by the nineteenth-century removal of thousands of Cherokees from their homeland in the Southeast to what was then the Indian Territory. Most of the descendants of the survivors of this removal lived in the 1960s in communities throughout northeastern Oklahoma, as many still do today. There is no Cherokee reservation in Oklahoma, but there were seventy-four traditional Cherokee communities in northeastern Oklahoma in 1963 (Wahrhaftig 1969a). Though the enrolled membership of the Cherokee Nation currently stands at approximately 250,000, there were estimated to be only 9,500 Cherokees living in these seventy-four communities in 1963 (Wahrhaftig 1969a:808–10). The tribal membership has been characterized as being split between those who "took part in Cherokee life" or who were "socially Cherokee," among whom were the bulk of Cherokee speakers, and those who were "socially white" (Wahrhaftig 1969b), who were much more likely to play a role in the federally appointed tribal government and local business and politics. Of 11,500 Cherokees taking part in "Cherokee life" in 1963 (those in the 74 communities and an additional 2,000 Cherokees), 10,500 were estimated to be speakers of Cherokee (Wahrhaftig 1969a). This chapter describes how a Carnegie Corporation–funded literacy and development project was redirected by a local Cherokee community organization composed of Cherokee speakers whose members held the belief that Cherokee language and literacy were valuable in their own right rather than as components of a U.S. antipoverty agenda. This group's actions pragmatically characterized the assertion of Cherokee language into public space as a form of political resistance and as an affirmation of community survival. Furthermore, the group's actions sought to calibrate (or assert an iconic relationship between) a linguistic boundary (that between Cherokee speakers and nonspeakers) with an authentic community boundary in a recursive movement between linguistic and socioeconomic levels of community differentiation and association.

The second example is drawn from the Eastern Band of Cherokees, the North Carolina Cherokee community, of the late 1990s. This is a smaller Cherokee community, having approximately 6,300 resident enrolled members in 2006 (out of a total enrolled membership of approximately 10,000). A recent survey suggested that there were 450–500 speakers in this community in 2005–6. Seventy-two percent of these speakers were estimated to be over the age of fifty; speakers under the age of ten made up only 1 percent of this number (Heidi Altman, personal communication, September 13, 2006). The second part of this chapter describes a resurgence of interest in Cherokee language education and a flourishing of visibility of the Cherokee syllabary in the local graphic landscape in the year following the Eastern Band's establishment of a casino. In this case, a public foregrounding of the Cherokee language, especially through a proliferation of signage using the Cherokee syllabary, reveals a cultural presupposition that language is a viable medium for the transformation of resources. Economic capital flowing from outside into the community from tourism and gaming, toward which many in the community express ambivalence, is transformed into positive cultural capital in part through its expenditure in the community's graphic landscape, which in turn indexes a less visible language revitalization movement. In addition, the community's unequal distribution of certain linguistic resources at that moment in history is understood recursively as an appropriate iconic representation of a careful and limited distribution of cultural and religious knowledge and leadership, which is especially important in the context of intensive and continuous contact with outsiders.

Survival and Resistance via the Cherokee Language in Oklahoma in the 1960s

The University of Chicago administered an education-and-development-related project known as the Carnegie Project (after the funding source) among the rural Cherokee-speaking communities in northeastern Oklahoma from 1963 to 1967.[1] The project "originally was an attempt to discover how to communicate literacy from one culture to another utilizing the American Indians as a special case" (Tax and Thomas 1969:940).

Officially, the project sought to further English language literacy among Oklahoma Cherokees and other American Indians. For example, it produced *Indian Voices*, described by the project's organizers as "a monthly publication which provides information in English about Indians for Cherokee and Indians nationally. Further, it defines English as a functional vehicle and integral part of a general American Indian social movement. For Cherokee specifically, the use of English to tie the Cherokee into a broader Indian horizon helps redefine English as well as increase fluency in English" (Tax and Thomas 1969:946).

Native language literacy was to provide a gateway to the ultimate goal of English language literacy and a higher standard of living. The existence of an indigenously developed writing system for Cherokee (the Sequoyan syllabary) also made possible the testing of a particular hypothesis: that literacy in their own language and using their own orthography would make it easier for the Cherokees to become literate in English. The Cherokees were chosen for the project in part because of their nineteenth-century history of literacy and high levels of education. The project also raised the question: Why were the Cherokees so much better educated in 1870, from the point of view of the 1960s educational establishment, than they were in 1963 (Tax and Thomas 1969:943–44)? Indeed, in the late nineteenth century Cherokees in the Cherokee Nation were reported to be better educated than their non-Indian neighbors (Richard L. Allen, personal communication, September 7, 2007). The systematic undermining of this state of affairs was addressed by some of the project's participants in a U.S. Senate hearing, discussed later in this chapter.

The core activities of the project included the publication of *Indian Voices* and the *Cherokee Nation Newsletter*, which included Cherokee-language articles in the Cherokee syllabary; sociocultural and linguistic research among the Oklahoma Cherokees; the production of a Cherokee-language radio program; the creation of Cherokee literacy courses for adults and school-age children; and the production of educational materials, including the *Cherokee Primer* and numerous other Cherokee syllabary texts for use in a wide variety of social contexts—school classrooms, churches, hospitals, and so on. In March 1965 fifteen hundred copies of the *Cherokee Primer* were distributed to Cherokee speakers (Tax and Thomas 1969:948). It was hoped, in line with the project's original goals, that literacy in Cherokee might serve as a stepping-stone not only to English-language literacy but to greater success in public education and to greater social, political, and economic empowerment for Cherokees. Soon, however, it became clear that participating community members were more motivated to read Cherokee than English, requesting that the project emphasize the production of texts in the syllabary (Tax and Thomas 1969:947–48).

Many community members had originally held back from participating in what may have been perceived as a foreign project. It has been suggested that reacting to external interventions by either ignoring them or taking them over was a well-established cultural practice, not specific to the Carnegie Project (Richard A. Allen, personal communication, August 10, 2007). And indeed, Bob Thomas, field director of the project, had predicted that Cherokees would "begin to see the project's activities as new and useful additions to their culture, at which point they would take them over, displace the personnel originally responsible for them, and insist that they be done 'right'" (Wahrhaftig 1998:97). According to project staffer Al Wahrhaftig, they did just this:

> Competent Cherokee elders began to "come out of the woods." Andrew Dreadfulwater, chief of the Cherokee Seven Clans Society, a thoughtful Native intellectual (though he spoke little English) and a powerful "doctor," quietly displaced Finis Smith [the original editor] and took over the

newsletter. Jim Wolf, head of the Cherokee Four Mothers Society, consented to teach a special Cherokee literacy course to mixed classes of Cherokees and whites in the Adair County high school using the new Carnegie Project–produced primers. The notion that Cherokees might use their culture and language in new and flexible ways, and that they might even insist on a place for it within "white" institutions, had gained a foothold. Within some Cherokee communities, public opinion began to demand that the gravitation towards teaching church Sunday school in English be reversed, and talk of withdrawing from churches that insisted on substituting English for Cherokee and establishing new institutions to house religious instruction in Cherokee surfaced. (1998:97–98)

As Wahrhaftig indicates, the linguistic (and broader social) concerns of this group extended to Cherokee Christianity as well as to Cherokee medicine. In addition to being a medicinal doctor, Andrew Dreadfulwater was a deacon and pianist in a Baptist church (Richard A. Allen, personal communication, August 10, 2007). This growing assertion of the importance of linguistic sovereignty soon expanded into a "nativistic social movement" focused on such issues as child custody, landownership, and hunting (Wahrhaftig 1998:98).

With the project's support, stores in Tahlequah stepped up their hiring of Cherokee speakers, and Tahlequah and Stilwell merchants began displaying signs in syllabary. The project also provided interpreters for the annual Cherokee national holiday. This forced Cherokees and whites alike to acknowledge the existence of monolingual Cherokee speakers and the legitimacy of public usage of the Cherokee language (Tax and Thomas 1969:949).

In Oklahoma in the 1960s Cherokee language use was seen as a marker that distinguished traditionalists and Christian cultural conservatives from other members of the Cherokee Nation and from non-Indians, and it set boundaries. When some of the project affiliates formed the Five County Northeastern Oklahoma Association (later the Original Cherokee Community Organization) and began meeting to address local political issues, the use of spoken Cherokee in the meetings and the use of written Cherokee to record the minutes of the meetings limited membership, participation, and outside access to the knowledge and plans being shared (Wahrhaftig 1998). The centrality of the Cherokee language in these contexts created a kind of alternate sociopolitical universe, since in the Cherokee Nation bureaucracy Cherokee speakers (as well as cultural conservatives) were fairly unusual (Wahrhaftig 1969b, 1998). The group led a 1967 protest against a tourist attraction called Cherokee Village in Tahlequah, picketing the facility's grand opening holding signs lettered in syllabary (Five County Cherokee Organization 1968). Since the targets of the protest consisted largely of Cherokee and non-Indian nonspeakers, this usage of the syllabary functioned as a nonpropositional icon of otherness to the intended audience while functioning propositionally among the in-group.

Some non-speaking Cherokees, especially those with an interest in the local political and economic establishment, found the project troubling. The visible and audible usage of Cherokee for which the project provided a supportive context was met with resistance not only by the non-Indian local authorities but, Wahrhaftig (1998) argues, by the Cherokee Nation bureaucracy itself. The gap between the OCCO and the Cherokee Nation may in part reflect the fact that the government was still appointed rather than elected at that time, so that "the Cherokee Nation as a government was only beginning to find itself again in the 1960s" (Richard A. Allen, personal communication, August 10, 2007). It is also important to note that the Cherokee Nation was (and is now) only one of the two federally recognized Cherokee tribal governments in Oklahoma, the other being the United Keetoowah Band. Like the Cherokee Nation, the United Keetoowah Band distanced itself from the activities of the OCCO (Richard L. Allen, personal communication, September 7, 2007).

Tax and Thomas describe the opposition the project faced as coming from the "Indian affairs establishment," consisting of local politicians, industrialists, and bureaucrats (Tax and Thomas 1969:947). This group expressed its own beliefs about language, challenging the motivations, legitimacy, and content of the Cherokee-language newsletter. Ralph Keen, general business manager for the Cherokee Nation, criticized what he saw as the exclusionary tactics of the Carnegie Project and its Cherokee affiliates at the 1968 hearings of the Special Subcommittee on Indian Education of the U.S. Senate's Committee on Labor and Public Welfare. "I do have disagreement with the manner in which they work, with the people they hire, with the effect they have on the total community. . . . We see certain newspapers that are being published. We see newspapers— we don't understand all they say because they print them in Cherokee, and not very many people read Cherokee nowadays" (U.S. Congress 1969:604). It became clear that Keen's concern about language was also a political one when he continued his critique of the project by saying, "In one of the latest editions, they poked fun at the [tribal] operations" in a way he believed misrepresented the tribe (U.S. Congress 1969:604).

For the speakers associated with the Carnegie Project, use of the Cherokee language was coterminous with Cherokee identity in a purported iconicity similar to that described by Meek (this volume) among Yukon Aboriginal language speakers. Furthermore, the boundary between speakers and nonspeakers of Cherokee was asserted to be the same as the boundary between authentic Cherokee community members and non-Cherokees. In 1974 Andrew Dreadfulwater, in his role as chairman of the Original Cherokee Community Organization, made this point at a North American Indian Ecumenical Conference. "Many, many years back there was already a messenger here from God to show us how to use the things we want to use. When He first made the Indian, He made the full-blood and the language. He didn't make overseas [European] languages for the Indian. . . . If we want to change to white people, the Indian has got to do it himself. First, we could stop teaching our own language" (Dreadfulwater 1998:353–54).

Some of the most eloquent and convincing witnesses at the 1968 Senate hearings mentioned above were Cherokees who had become involved with the project. These hearings served as an arena for discussion of the state of education and, implicitly, language among American Indians. They resulted in legislation that provided financial support for bilingual education for Cherokees in Oklahoma. The testimony contained in the transcripts of the hearings speaks volumes about the relationship between literacy, on the one hand, and nationhood, autonomy, and domination, on the other, as envisioned by the Cherokee participants. It also shows how understandings of literacy can differ widely among parties in a single interaction, as they do here between the Cherokee witnesses and the U.S. senators.

The larger context of the hearings itself illustrates language ideologies in conflict. One of the purposes of the hearings from the Senate's point of view was to determine what was "wrong" with Indian education in the 1960s. Some of the explanations for low English-language proficiency and literacy among minority groups popular in the dominant culture of the time would have suggested that low education levels resulted from some deficit in the target population, a deficit that might or might not be remedied by social programs and intervention. But one of the chief things that was wrong with Indian education, according to many of the Indian witnesses at the Senate hearings, was not a deficit in Indian students or communities but the enormous communicative (not merely linguistic) gap between non-Indian teachers and school administrators and students from culturally conservative Cherokee homes. What needed fixing was not Cherokee students but the nature of the teachers—some of them must be Cherokee and some of them must be Cherokee speaking to serve the needs of children whose first language was Cherokee. The examples that follow reveal that a struggle was taking place during these hearings to define and alter relationships among culture, language, and power. As Richland illustrates in his work on language use in Hopi tribal courts (this volume), formal legal settings such as this one can provide an extremely rich field of metapragmatic language ideology for participants to draw on.

Andrew Dreadfulwater and Hiner Doublehead, his interpreter, were called to testify about the state of education for Cherokees. Questioning the witnesses was Senator Robert F. Kennedy, chairman of the special subcommittee. Dreadfulwater's presence at the hearings as a witness who would speak only in Cherokee clearly made an important political statement.

> *Doublehead*: Senator Kennedy and Senator Fannin, I am Hiner Doublehead, and I will attempt to translate for Mr. Dreadfulwater. Mr. Dreadfulwater is on my left, and he will read in Cherokee and I will attempt to translate simultaneously.
>
> *Kennedy*: I wonder what that's going to sound like.
>
> *Doublehead*: When I first come up here, I was going to talk Cherokee to you. I think you would have the same experience that the Indian child experiences when he goes into a white school.
>
> *Kennedy*: A very good point.
>
> *Doublehead*: He doesn't understand what people are talking about.
>
> *Kennedy*: Take the microphone and we will just hear from you and he can read it quietly if he likes in Cherokee, and we will at least get one of the languages.
>
> *Doublehead*: He wants to read it in Cherokee, and I will come back in English with it, sentence by sentence.

Kennedy: We just have so many witnesses, and we would like to hear from all of them, and they are Cherokees. We hate to have to cut them off at the end. You proceed the way you want. I don't want to make any Cherokee mad at me right at the moment. I have a feeling there are more of them in this room than there are of us.

Dreadfulwater (in Cherokee, with Doublehead interpreting): I am glad to have the opportunity to say a few words, but a few words here upon education will not cure the situation. (U.S. Congress 1969:565–66)

Kennedy wittingly or unwittingly reveals a chasm in experience between himself and the witnesses when he says, "I wonder what that's going to sound like." He is admitting to what is clearly one of the central points Dreadfulwater and Doublehead are trying to make: that they, not he, are forced day after day to listen to an alien language. They, not he, deal on a daily basis with the need to interpret for others and themselves in order to function in a world that only acknowledges the legitimacy of one language. However, there are limits to Kennedy's willingness to accept this testimony by experience; he would rather *hear about* suffering and alienation than be shown, be made to experience, what they are like. "Take the microphone," he says to the speaker of English. "He," the speaker of Cherokee, "can read it quietly if he likes in Cherokee." The two Cherokee men do not accept this reproduction of the very hierarchy and cultural dominance they have come to testify about. "He wants to read it in Cherokee, and I will come back in English with it, sentence by sentence," Doublehead reasserts. Notice, too, that Kennedy does not seem to acknowledge that it is Dreadfulwater, not Doublehead, who is acting as the witness. Kennedy's suggestion as to how to proceed implies that Doublehead's testimony is interchangeable with Dreadfulwater's, or at least that Doublehead must be able to deliver the gist of Dreadfulwater's message without translating it line by line. Kennedy also tries to suggest that his prioritizing of the English-language speaker is actually a respectful gesture toward all the Cherokee witnesses gathered. This is a zero-sum game, he suggests, in which the discourse of one Cherokee witness must displace another because of a temporal and linguistic structure outside the control of all involved. Doublehead and Dreadfulwater reject this argument and proceed but with the understanding that "a few words . . . will not cure the situation." These witnesses assert (and model) the metapragmatic value of speaking Cherokee in this context where the propositional content of their speech will not be understood by the officially designated audience—the senators. Their talk is valuable for its own sake, whether or not it alone solves Cherokee "educational" problems and whether or not the English-speaking audience understands it.

In the second example a difference of opinion emerges between Kennedy and Cherokee witness Louis R. Gourd about (1) when the "problem" of Cherokee education begins; (2) how much linguistic contextualization (stage setting) is necessary in order to understand it; and (3) what the appropriate linguistic channel is through which to provide that information. We see here that the inherent importance of the Cherokee presence demonstrated by Dreadfulwater's testimony extends also to Cherokee speech in English.

1 *Gourd:* I am Louis Gourd. I live in Tahlequah. I am a Cherokee Indian,

2 and my age is 73. I have always lived in Oklahoma.

3 *Kennedy:* Would you proceed? Would you give us the benefit of your ideas

4 about the problems we are facing? You have lived in Oklahoma all

5 your life, I understand.

6 *Gourd:* Yes, sir.

7 *Kennedy:* And you have worked for the Bureau of Indian Affairs?

8 *Gourd:* I have.

9 *Kennedy:* For 15 years?

10 *Gourd:* Yes.

11 *Kennedy:* And you have received a high school education; is that correct?

12 *Gourd:* Yes, sir.

13 *Kennedy:* Would you tell us about the Cherokee Tribe and what you feel are

14 the problems they are facing at the moment?

15 *Gourd:* Beginning with about just a few ideas, along about 1540,

16 Hernand[o] De Soto came along; had understood that there was gold

17 discovered in our country. He didn't pay a lot of attention to

18 Indians. He saw them. And he proceeded to find out how much

19 gold there was. Along about 1567, Juan Pardo made his way,

20 probably crossing some of the paths that De Soto crossed; and he

21 took more notes and paid more attention to the Indians as to what

22 they were doing at that time. And as time went on, their

23 findings came to light, and they were sort of up and going kind
24 of people. They were interested in things and they had a way of
25 living.
26 *Kennedy:* May I interrupt you a minute? Do you have a written
statement?
27 *Gourd:* Yes, sir. I am getting up to that.
28 *Kennedy:* I see.
29 *Gourd:* Then he also found that we had a form of government. We
had our
30 own judges. We had our own diplomats. England was bartering
31 with us for different things, and we had our own civil government
32 and a democratic form of government. And along about 1820 we had
33 a system of educating our people. In other words, we had a paper,
34 the *Cherokee Advocate*, or the *Cherokee Phoenix* as they called it
35 at different times. And so as strife increased over gold and
36 land and things of that kind, we moved.
37 Then finally it was decided by the authorities that we
38 should come to another country after we had demonstrated that we
39 could operate and maintain schools in the country where we had
40 originally lived.
41 All right. We got on the trail. We proceeded to find a
42 new country, and when we got here, the same things came with us.
43 Incidentally, in Georgia we had a way of printing the paper
44 that I just mentioned, and we had a press, and the State of
45 Georgia about four or five years ago appropriated a considerable
46 amount of money to find out where that press went; and they
47 thought they had it located, and money was not going to deter
48 them from finding out, if they could, where the press was.
49 All right. Coming on to Oklahoma, then, we proceeded,
50 through old frustrations that we experienced, to try to set up a
51 way of living again in a new country. We did. We established
52 schools. We established our courts of law, and all civil
53 activities including the setting up of schools and learning, and
54 we had a religion which we brought with us.
55 Now at first we would naturally think that we did it once,
56 we did it, and we went down, and we came here and we did it again
57 and lost it. Some of the complications of our Indian thinking is
58 peculiar to most people. We entered into a good many ways of
59 thinking, because we think that this isn't our country. We

60 didn't come from somewhere else. We were here, and going to lose
61 all these things we once had. It's a peculiar way of arriving at
62 certain conclusions. I believe that's the extent of my statement. (U.S.
     Congress 1969:541–43)

Gourd is trying to place this discussion of Cherokee educational "problems" in a much broader context than Kennedy seems prepared for. At the
same time, a metapragmatic struggle takes place over the course of this
dialogue concerning the form in which Gourd's testimony is to be delivered. Gourd starts out delivering his testimony in the form of a narrative,
beginning with those aspects of his personal background that grant him
the authority to speak (lines 1–2). Kennedy reasserts the interview structure (lines 3–4). This seems to be the main purpose for his first interruption, as he does not ask any new questions, and one of his questions even
restates information that Gourd has already provided. He succeeds in
reasserting the question-and-answer format, but notice that he does not
succeed in obtaining any new information from the witness in this manner. During the question-and-answer exchange (lines 3–11) Gourd's responses are essentially monosyllabic until Kennedy returns to a general,
open-ended question (lines 12–13) that allows Gourd to resume his narrative. He does so (line 14), and although Kennedy asks him to discuss the
problems the Cherokees are facing "at the moment," Gourd makes it clear
that this story must be heard from the beginning. There is no "moment"
here, isolable from the history of European contact with the Americas.

Having failed to define the form this linguistic encounter will take,
Kennedy seeks to set boundaries by implying a mismatch of linguistic
form and linguistic medium: "Do you have a written statement?" he says
(line 22), following the rhetorical "May I interrupt you a minute?" However, Gourd resumes the oral narrative (line 25)—he is "getting up to"
(line 23) the submission of a written statement, but that statement cannot
and will not take the place of his talk in real time.

In public forums such as these Senate hearings we have the opportunity to see linguistic and educational ideologies—and their perceived
implications for the distribution of power and resources in the United
States—surface and become mobilized in very visible ways. Gourd's
speech, for example, points us toward a long and complex history of
linkage between literacy and formal educational institutions, on the one

hand, and, variably, "civilization," "progressivism," and Cherokee nationalism, on the other. While the Senate hearings seek to link a lack of
formal educational opportunity with (as it was conceptualized at the
time) a lack of development, the Cherokee witnesses point out that they
have suffered traditionally from a lack of neither of these things, even as
defined by the U.S. Senate, and that it has been in fact the dominant
presence and violent actions of the U.S. government that have cost the
Cherokees these accomplishments. Dreadfulwater also illustrates that it
is not a linguistic or communicative deficit that is harming Cherokees
educationally; it is a mismatch between the linguistic and communicative practices and expectations of the dominant society and those of most
Cherokee-speaking people.

Both Cherokee witnesses make the point that their public talking (in
English but especially in Cherokee) is valuable for its own sake. Dreadfulwater's insertion of the Cherokee language into public U.S. discourse
against the resistance of Senator Kennedy demonstrates in a practical way
this belief in the intrinsic importance of cultural presence. This is what
the Cherokees who appropriated the Carnegie Project expressed more
generally. In the larger context of political and economic oppression,
Cherokee language use represented cultural survival, continuity, and
resistance to assimilation. The language was presupposed to be valuable
in and of itself as the medium of cultural continuity and as that cultural
continuity itself (cf. Meek, this volume).

Beginning in 1969, federal funds supported a Cherokee bilingual education program in northeastern Oklahoma (Bacon et al. 1982). This program was based in four (later reduced to two) rural Oklahoma elementary
schools serving Cherokee-speaking communities, but it also produced
materials for the wider population. This program was directed at the
Cherokee-speaking community, and its activities presumed widespread
Cherokee-language fluency in the population it served. This is made
clear by the fact that many of the publications it produced were designed
to impart literacy in a writing system (either the syllabary or a Romanized
script) to those already fluent in the spoken language. The texts produced
in these years (comic books, public health manuals, driver's education
manuals, and a variety of other texts in syllabary) contained little or no
English-language material, nor did they include phonetic "crutches" (Romanized phonetic spellings) that presumed English-language fluency.

The belief in a fluent Cherokee-speaking community and the prioritizing of that community's needs provide an important point for comparison with Eastern Cherokee ideologies and practices. A different set of experiences with outsiders and a differing sense of the appropriate role for the Cherokee language to play in relationships with the members of the dominant society are related to a distinct set of beliefs about the inherent value of public Cherokee language use among the Eastern Band of Cherokees.

Language as Transformative Medium: Eastern Cherokee Language Ideology in the Mid-1990s

Two and a half years of fieldwork on the Eastern Cherokee reservation in North Carolina in the early 1990s revealed a complex set of beliefs about the Cherokee language, particularly about its indigenously developed syllabary (Bender 2002b). As it has for much of the last century, this community was grappling with the cultural incursions and staged representations of the self that go hand in hand with cultural tourism. Language played an important role in the community's negotiation of its relationship with outsiders. In this context an interconnected set of ideologies and cultural presuppositions worked together to construct, reinforce, and justify a protective orientation toward language. These beliefs included an understanding of the Cherokee syllabary as a kind of code, a characterization of the language and writing system as elusive, and a tight linkage of the Cherokee language and writing system with Cherokee culture and insiderness. In particular, this complex set of beliefs about the Cherokee syllabary served to restrict the writing system's functional usage in the production of readable text to highly circumscribed contexts but to allow for its visibility in tourism and education. While introductory Cherokee language education was available to the community at large and even to non-Cherokees, it was generally presumed that a serious language learner was furthering the goals of either Christian or medicinal religious practice or that he or she would ultimately act as a cultural leader or specialist of some kind. This in turn meant that such serious language learning and especially literacy acquisition were carefully guarded.

Because Eastern Cherokee socioeconomic life revolved around cultural tourism, at least prior to the opening of a new casino in 1997, there was a strong need to draw a line between those dimensions of Cherokee history and culture that were permissible to share with the public—those that could be commodified and consumed by others—and those that were not. While the general fact that the syllabary exists and its simultaneous links to indigenous culture and "civilization" were highlighted in the tourist realm, meaningful text and straightforwardly communicative use of the syllabary tended to occur in specialized contexts beyond the gaze of visitors, in churches and homes. This restriction was conveyed through linguistic educational practice at all levels, the goal of which was generally to make students aware of the language and syllabary but not necessarily to produce a generalized competence (Bender 2002a). As recent scholarship has demonstrated (Blommaert, Collins, and Slembrouck 2005; Collins 1998), beliefs about appropriate methods and outcomes of language education, maintenance, and revitalization are powerful language ideologies in and of themselves. Eastern Cherokee language education in the 1990s was intended to familiarize Cherokees and non-Cherokees with the language, its history, and its writing system in a way that allowed the Cherokee language to serve as a metonym for Cherokee culture and identity. At the same time, it guarded against the inappropriate language use that might follow from a widespread, unrestricted distribution of linguistic competence.

In 1998 I returned to Cherokee for the summer to carry out a language survey and interviews about community attitudes toward language education in collaboration with the Eastern Band's Office of Cultural Resources. In the context of something of an economic boom I encountered a newly celebratory orientation toward the language and a new treatment of language as a medium with the power to transform one form of value into another.

I found that the Cherokee syllabary had grown much more visible in and around the Qualla Boundary (the Eastern Cherokee Reservation) and that attitudes toward the language had shifted. Many more syllabary signs appeared, and more language-related commodities were for sale in gift shops and circulated among community members. Two new Cherokee language curricula were introduced into the tribally run preschool program and elementary school, and a trial Cherokee language immersion Head Start class was implemented in 1998. A weekly Cherokee language program even started up on local cable television the same year.

There was also an increase in overt positive expressions of interest in Cherokee language education by community members.

Notably, all of this apparent linguistic mobilization took place in the context of a shift in the nature of local tourism. Since the opening of the casino in 1997, the community had been flooded with outsiders in search of cash and the thrill of risk taking rather than cultural education. The casino does provide entertainment, but it consists of the types more generally associated with gaming venues—country and pop bands and mainstream comedians. Some tourist dollars appeared to be shifting away from the outdoor drama about Cherokee history and similar cultural attractions. The number of tribal members working in traditional craft production or other aspects of cultural tourism had seemed to decrease, perhaps because of new employment opportunities and income from the casino, along with the declining availability of natural resources (Lisa J. Lefler, personal communication, May 31, 2007).

I argue that it was not coincidental that as one set of artifacts, practices, and institutions that represent the Eastern Band as an authentic and unique Indian community to outsiders was being overshadowed by gaming and more generic forms of entertainment, the graphic landscape of the community and the objects tourists are encouraged to purchase and take away with them were increasingly marked with the indigenous syllabary. The syllabary has always been important in Cherokee tourism because it simultaneously serves as the ultimate index of the Cherokees' standing as foremost among the Civilized Tribes (one important touristic theme), as an illustration of the difference of Indian culture from mainstream U.S. culture (another important theme), and as a metonym for its famous inventor, Sequoyah (the culture hero emergent from the story of Cherokee history told through tourism). But its assertion into public space and onto commodities became more important as other images of Cherokee Indian authenticity (like the drama and the Oconaluftee Indian Village) started to lose their audience. As the community was encroached upon by a landscape-dominating nonlocal tourist enterprise, it was important to create or reinforce protective community boundaries.

This was a pivotal moment in Cherokee history. Previously, established practices and categories overlapped new ones made possible in part by new resources. Thus, it should come as no surprise that the community's practical and ideological linguistic shifts were complex, multifaceted, and variable in 1998. For example, while Cherokee language materials were being provided to homeroom teachers for integration into the school day's regular activities, the classes specifically devoted to Cherokee language education were not yet being allotted increased time, staff, or resources. And although I saw more syllabary signs than had been the case a few years earlier, there was no evidence at the time of an increase in spoken Cherokee. As it turns out, this was partly because this wave of linguistic revitalization was in its initial stage. But it also seems that the semiotic assertion of Cherokee linguistic forms and practices into public space was important for reasons beyond a drive for ordinary linguistic proficiency.

The increased attention given to language education may also be understood as a kind of reappropriation of value from this changing tourist economy. Since it was largely the revenue from the casino that funded new educational and cultural programming in the community, these new programs provided the opportunity to transform the influx of capital from gaming and its associated tourism (a source of value toward which many in the community initially expressed negative feelings) into a form that had positive semiotic and social value.

The larger educational context in which Cherokee language education unfolds is itself complex. The seven thousand or so Cherokee residents of the Qualla Boundary are served by both tribal and public schools. Parents may choose which system their children will attend, and children frequently shift back and forth over the course of their education. It was the tribal schools (formerly run by the Bureau of Indian Affairs) that offered substantial language education programs in 1998, although the public schools offered very limited Cherokee language electives as well. The greater emphasis on Cherokee language and culture in the tribal schools is sometimes a reason given by parents for sending their children to these schools, though not many parents themselves now speak Cherokee. As indicated earlier in the chapter, 72 percent of the Eastern Band's 450–500 estimated Cherokee speakers are currently over the age of fifty.

Formal Cherokee language education among the Eastern Band may be traced back to the 1970s, when a bilingual education program was implemented in the tribal schools for a few years. Language classes were then reintroduced in the tribal schools in the late 1980s, and today children have some opportunity to study Cherokee from kindergarten through high school. Adult classes are also available through the local university and community college.

A new Cherokee language curriculum was developed and implemented in the late 1990s for the Cherokee elementary school language classroom, which students in all grades visited once per week to work exclusively on Cherokee language study. At the same time, curricular materials were introduced by the Cherokee Language Preservation Project, a separate entity, for use in homerooms and activities throughout the school. Each program relied on different fluent speakers, teachers, and pedagogical materials. Each introduced different core vocabulary and used different spelling conventions. When I asked one of the language teachers if there was ever any conflict between the two programs, he suggested the analogy of a drowning person (the student) being thrown two different types of life preservers from different boats. The differences do not greatly matter, he suggested; either or both may save the person's life.

During the summer of 1998 a survey about language education directed at parents or caregivers of preschool- and elementary school–age children was placed in the newspaper as an insert and distributed in multiple locations on the reservation such as community centers, grocery stores, and the post office. This survey was co-designed by myself and the preschool and elementary school Cherokee language educators. Of the forty-four respondents, fifteen, or 34 percent, said there was a child in their home who had heard people speaking Cherokee on a regular basis, while twenty-nine, or 66 percent, said there was not. Overall, respondents expressed extremely positive attitudes toward all Cherokee language education opportunities that were suggested in the survey for themselves and for the children in their households. Ninety-four percent said they would use Cherokee language lessons in a book, if available. Ninety-six percent said they would use Cherokee language lessons in the local, tribally run newspaper, if available. Ninety-six percent of respondents also said they would watch if the same Cherokee language lessons their children see on video at school were shown on local television.

The response was even more impressive among primary caregivers whose children had been exposed to spoken Cherokee on a regular basis. These caregivers represented a group in which Cherokee language teachers and the Office of Cultural Resources had expressed particular interest at the time: families that included speakers. Of that group of twelve caregivers from families that included speakers, 100 percent who responded to each question said they would take advantage of any and all Cherokee language-learning opportunities presented to them. One hundred percent of the target group were also interested in having their children participate in a Cherokee language immersion preschool. One hundred percent were also interested in participating in an adult Cherokee language education program specifically designed for caregivers of children who are in such an immersion program.

The more stake interviewees had in children's language education, the more likely they were to support it. Thus, primary caregivers were more likely to value language education than other respondents, and primary caregivers of children who have been exposed to spoken Cherokee were even more likely to value it.

So why were the parents who responded to the survey generally so enthusiastic about Cherokee language education? The most common reasons parents positively inclined toward Cherokee language education gave were:

1. *It will help children to understand Cherokee culture.* One said that it was a "desperate attempt" to save some of the culture via linguistic tools. Another interviewee said that the "language is dying out. We'll be left without vital heritage—songs, stories, medicine— which must be done in that language" because there are "nuances lost in translation." Another pointed out that without knowledge of the language, "people know there is a way to doctor [something] but don't know the [necessary] prayer or formula."

2. *The classes support their children's ongoing attachment to the community.* Some parents argued this point even though they did not consider Cherokee language education essential to academic learning. Speaking Cherokee, it was argued, provided a sense of belonging and accomplishment.

3. *"People have [Cherokee material in] writing at home but can't read it."* Parents also mentioned the desirability of being able to read archival material such as the *Cherokee Phoenix*, the first newspaper to be printed in the Cherokee syllabary in the nineteenth century.

4. *Knowing Cherokee will assist with genealogical research.*

5. *Formal Cherokee language education exposes children to the language.* It lets them know there is a language, whether or not they become speakers.

6. *It allows children to understand speakers.* This was given as a reason even though it was acknowledged that this was not a situation that comes up very often.

7. *It boosts self-esteem.* This was especially seen as being true in an environment where everybody else speaks Cherokee (which, interviewees admitted, was not very common).

Overall, the caregivers who responded to the survey expressed either the belief that Cherokee language education offered some practical, cultural, or psychological benefits to their children or the belief that it *should* do so—that the community should be transformed so as to create a need and value for Cherokee language use. Even some of those caregivers who argued that there was little practical need for the language at the time suggested that there were contexts in which it *should* be needed, such as social services, education, and local public events. The Cherokee case thus provides an interesting counterpoint to the Navajo example discussed by Field (this volume), in which the indigenous language is actually the language used in politics and chapter house meetings but with related linguistic ideological value varying across social groups within the Navajo Nation. Functional use of the language and writing system differ markedly across Cherokee social groups based on age, religious practice, and community leadership roles, but the language ideology reflected in the local graphic landscape and in these positive caregiver responses suggests support for universal fluency and literacy. This outpouring of positive responses is notable, and it may reflect a fairly recent phenomenon. A common belief shared with me by teachers and school administrators just five or six years earlier was that many parents were not particularly supportive of Cherokee language education. If the teachers and administrators were right about this, then there may have been a shift in attitude.

It appears that the association between the influx of revenue from the casino and language education (and education more generally) has enhanced the local value of both the gaming and educational institutions. Educational programs provided a way to redeem income from a source toward which community feelings were ambivalent, and the per capita income from the casino added a new value to education: an illustration of this is the fact that per capita checks may only be received beginning at age eighteen by those who have graduated from high school or earned a GED. Nongraduates do not begin receiving the payments until they are twenty-one. These positive associations have been furthered and mobilized by the business that runs the casino and by local politicians. For better or for worse, the state of Cherokee language education is seen as an expression of the cultural values of the current political administration. One interviewee told me specifically that the fact that the previous chief was a speaker had "created [the] value" associated with Cherokee language education. This chief created a new high-profile Office of Cultural Resources specifically to coordinate language and cultural programming.

Spending gaming money on language education and other Cherokee language programming thus transformed something *external* of questionable value into something *internal* of highly positive value and, at the same time, helped to strengthen the resources necessary for the preservation of cultural autonomy and the protection of the community from the casino's socioeconomic and symbolic incursions. The interviews and participant observation I conducted in 1998 suggested that the community supported this process of transformation by expressing enthusiasm for language education in a way it had not just five or six years earlier.

But other factors contributed to the increased value placed on Cherokee language education as well. Since the Eastern Band took over its own school system from the Bureau of Indian Affairs, community members involved in administration and teaching have assumed strengthened positions as promoters of Standard U.S. English reading and writing skills. The Eastern Band itself, among whom Cherokee language use was once characterized as a form of resistance (Gulick 1958), is thus now the local enforcer of Standard English language hegemony. It seems to make sense that the relational value of Cherokee language education and Cherokee language use more generally would change in response. While Cherokee language education may still have reflected an attempt to interject traditional content into a nontraditional setting, its meanings and its potential as an act of resistance changed because the players had changed (i.e., because the Eastern Band was now responsible for its own educational system). Rather than becoming less important as the community gained empowerment, it gained a higher profile, perhaps as a counter to the community's changing relationship to mainstream U.S. culture and institutions.

The relational value of Cherokee language education also seemed to be shifting as it grew in relative importance as a site for language learning, language speaking, exposure to and/or production of texts, and so on. Whereas in the past a Sunday school class, the household, or a kind of apprenticeship with an elder family member was the most important and effective site of language use and production, as these options became less available, the community's relative interest in and valuing of formal language education changed.

The community's growing interest in Cherokee language education may also have been linked with a more general cultural revitalization (Lefler 1996). Interest in spiritual practice beyond participation in Christian churches, such as sweat lodge ceremonies and stomp dances, was on the rise in the late 1990s. There was some local conflict over this trend, with some Cherokee Christians being critical of these activities as un-Christian or, in the case of sweat lodges especially, as non-Cherokee. The speaking of Cherokee was associated with both positions because it was valued by participants in the revitalization while at the same time associated with older devoutly Christian North Carolina Cherokees who made up the majority of the local Cherokee-speaking population. Formal language education may represent a space where the resources from these different groups can be pooled productively and where the interests of both can be represented.

There are many reasons, then, why overt expressions of support for and interest in Cherokee language education were high in the late 1990s. But the question remains: Why were the resources devoted to formal language education—teachers and time during the school day—not yet increasing at the same rate as public expressions of interest? I would suggest that while Cherokee language education was seen as being good *in principle* and, as some parents said, it was seen as good for children to know there *was* a Cherokee language, widespread and, particularly, unregulated fluency was not yet a goal. While the Sequoyan syllabary was continually presented to Cherokee elementary school children, for example, by way of artwork in the schools, posters in hallways and classrooms, and occasional classroom exercises, it was not used as the primary instructional orthography for Cherokee language education, and children were not at that time required to memorize its phonetic values or use it for reading or writing. I believe this was because gaining functional command of the language, and especially of the syllabary, continued to have the very specific connotations discussed at the beginning of this section, that is, that it is elusive and inextricably linked to Cherokee cultural contexts and religious practice, whatever new connotations may have started to overlay these. Community members at the time *expected* linguistic differentiation to be iconic of the community's limited and focused (and, from the local point of view, appropriate) distribution of cultural and religious leadership and knowledge. (See Field, this volume, on recursivity across Navajo social categories, religion, and language ideologies.)

What seems like a paradox thus may not be one in reality. Adults valued the exposure to the Cherokee language provided by Cherokee language education, but the purpose of such education may have been to reproduce locally significant categories of speakers, readers, and writers, who were religious or cultural specialists and usually mature members of the community, rather than to support a more populist language movement. In addition, there may not have been sufficient political will at that time to bring those who were the most fluent speakers of Cherokee, who might be the least likely to have high school and college degrees, into the educational and administrative positions where they could really have an impact on language education or to transform tribal institutions in such a way as to make room for alternative systems of teaching, knowledge, and authority.

The increasing visibility of Cherokee writing in the contemporary Cherokee graphic landscape involves a similar nonparadox. The signs and commodities featuring the syllabary *suggested* the communicative functionality of the syllabary, yet these were usually not being "read" in the conventional sense. People were not generally using these signs, in other words, to find or identify specific locations on the boundary. But the signs still functioned as signs in a number of important senses—as indexes of cultural authenticity, as markers of otherness for outsiders, as expressions of pride for insiders. Both the arrangement of these signs and many of the local articulated responses to Cherokee language education projected a kind of ideal world—one in which Cherokee fluency is the norm, opportunities to use the language are abundant, and the Cherokee syllabary is the orthography used in daily life—onto the world that they were simultaneously reinforcing—in which Cherokee language use was precious and relatively rare.

This account of Cherokee language ideology and related practices speaks to the situation in 1998. There has been considerable change and growth in the Cherokee language education landscape since that time, so this description, like all ethnography, must be understood as historically contingent. The same, of course, holds true for the much older picture given here of language ideology and practice among Oklahoma Cherokees. The 1991 Cherokee Nation Language and Preservation Act established both Cherokee and English as official languages of the tribe. This act states that tribal members may speak in Cherokee or English in any official tribal setting, that translation services will be provided as necessary, and that bilingual staff will be placed in tribal positions that call for extensive public contact with tribal members. In these respects the act suggests continuity with the 1960s presumption of widespread Cherokee fluency. But additional stances toward the language emerge here as well as in the act's emphasis on language promotion and maintenance through educational programs, the recognition of Cherokee-speaking elders as community teachers and role models, and the general encouragement of public language use in street and other official signs, for example. The very deliberate establishment of Cherokee language–only meetings by the Cherokee Speaker's Bureau and the creation of language immersion programs for children suggest an acknowledgment that active steps must be taken to bring together the Cherokee-speaking community (Chavez 2007). It is hoped that the speakers' community, not now seen as coterminous with the Cherokee cultural community, will expand so that these community boundaries move again toward being recursively understood as iconic of each other.

The Cherokee language was a source of positive value for both Cherokee-speaking Oklahoma Cherokees in the 1960s and the North Carolina Cherokee community in general in the 1990s. In the first case, public language use became one of several tactics intended to increase the visibility of a subordinated group and improve that group's access to rights and resources. In the second case, public language use and expressions of support for language use became ways to reaffirm a community's

Indian identity in the face of other shifts in the direction of the dominant culture, while control of linguistic resources may have continued as an important form of community protection. Sociocultural differences between the two communities—for example, in the religious landscape, in the role of tourism, and in the number of speakers—all shape and are shaped by these different orientations toward language.

PART II

Language Revitalization as a Site for (Re)New(ing) Language Ideologies

CHAPTER 7

Language Ideology and Aboriginal Language Revitalization in the Yukon, Canada

BARBRA A. MEEK

> I am extremely proud that the Government of Canada is taking steps
> to make sure these languages, which are integral to the culture and
> identities of Yukon Aboriginal people, are nurtured and promoted.
> —Minister of Canadian Heritage, the Honourable Hélène Chalifour
> Scherrer, March 2, 2004

The past twenty years have witnessed a surge of interest among Yukon
First Nations in bringing back their heritage languages as well as a significant increase in funding for such projects by the Canadian government.
Many programs at the federal and territorial levels now exist to support
projects ranging from basic research and development of teaching materials to radio and television programming. The commitment to Aboriginal language revitalization expressed by the territorial government has
also generated interest in First Nations cultures by a non-Native public, as
demonstrated by such popular events as the Commissioner's Potlatch and
the Yukon International Storytelling Festival.

What distinguishes Yukon language revitalization efforts from other
endeavors is that many of these initiatives have been jointly conceptualized and guided by government agencies, language and culture "experts,"
and Aboriginal peoples. The Canadian government (federal and territorial) has been consciously shifting its policy away from social and
political dependence of Aboriginal peoples and toward First Nations'
self-determination and self-government. This translates into an attempt
to have Aboriginal direction in government programs and services. In
language planning, this collaboration has resulted in the emergence and

institutionalization of a territory-wide language ideology. This chapter explores the development of this potentially "counterhegemonic" collaboration.

Those involved in language revitalization often consider the first step toward reversal to be the assessment of language loss. To assist in assessment Joshua Fishman created the Graded Intergenerational Disruption Scale (GIDS), a scale of linguistic degradation ranging from no intergenerational transmission to contexts where the threatened language predominates. Fishman linked government with his last two stages of disruption: Stage 2, where language X is used "in lower governmental services and mass media but not in the higher spheres of either," and Stage 1, where there is "some use of [language X] in higher level educational, occupational, governmental and media efforts (but without the additional safety provided by political independence)" (1991:105, 107). Languages at these stages are less disrupted than at any other stage. However, Fishman remarked that these "lower" and "higher" levels of government are the most closely regulated by existing regimes "because of their importance in the formation and preservation of integrative attitudes, opinions, identities and the topmost skills and statuses" (1991:106). This sentiment, and "hegemony" in general, have been central concerns of the emerging language ideological literature on dominant language ideologies (e.g., see Briggs 1998; House 2002; Kroskrity 1998, 2000c; Silverstein 1998b). This suggests that any dominant bureaucratic institution will closely monitor the incorporation of alternative voices into its programs and rhetoric, including language planning and the conceptualization of language.

The language situation in the Yukon provides an interesting case study because of the government's explicit commitment to the integration of First Nations voices, the modification of its own bureaucratic rhetoric and practices as a result, and its mandate to transfer the control of and responsibility for certain institutions, through self-governing agreements, to the First Nations. Because of this collaboration, we might predict that First Nations people in the Yukon will have had a greater influence on the ideologization of their languages and language more generally, including at "lower" and "higher" governmental levels. The final analysis will be made when the full transfer of government control, or "devolution," has occurred. What we can see as the transfers take place is evidence of

Aboriginal self-determination through the transformation of the state's discourse about Aboriginal languages.

In this chapter I examine the language ideological dimensions of the institutional changes both historically and discursively, especially through themes articulated in government publications such as legislation, program reports, evaluations, project proposals, and notes from language meetings. The first section of this chapter presents the historical precursors of language revitalization in the Yukon, culminating in the Yukon Languages Act, the creation of Aboriginal Language Services, and the Yukon Aboriginal Languages Conference. The second section describes the conference itself, the ideological themes represented in speeches by participants, and the implications of its motto, "We Are Our Language." The third section discusses the dialogic nature of these conceptualizations of language and the ways in which they build upon each other. As mentioned above, territorial and national administrators created a forum for Aboriginal people and experts to collaboratively produce a unique, Yukon-centered language revitalization approach. In studying this approach we see how the dialogic construction of a language ideology relates to the state's attempts to redistribute its power through the inclusion of Aboriginal voices and the mediated, partial transfer of institutional control.

The Historical Context of Revitalization: Policy and Programs

Early British and Canadian policies promoted the rapid assimilation of Aboriginal peoples, of "Indians." In tandem with other colonial practices elsewhere, one standard tactic for accomplishing this was through residential schooling where English-only policies predominated. In the Yukon, residential schools were instituted in the early 1900s. These schools were run by Christian religious organizations—the Anglican Church, the Baptist Church, and the Roman Catholic Church—with the mandate that "the Natives abandon their Aboriginal language, accept Christian teachings, and abide by the strict social codes of the school" (Coates 1991:202). After World War II, Aboriginal education became controlled by the government. This shift in institutional control, however, did not end the English-only policy. The eventual change in federal language and education policies materialized as a result of the French language gaining federal recognition as an official language of Canada, proposed in 1971 and then legislated in 1988 (Burnaby 1999:308; Trudel 1992). Up until this time Canada had no explicit Aboriginal language policy or program.

Aboriginal language revitalization in Canada has its origins in two political policy transformations: (1) the policy shifts in the mid- and late twentieth century that changed the legal definitions and status of Aboriginal people, and (2) several legislative acts, such as the Official Languages Act of Canada, that led to a change in the status of minority languages. (See Perley, this volume, for discussion of historical events related to Aboriginal languages on the east coast of Canada.) First Nations, as they are now called, were recognized to have legitimate claims on their traditional lands beginning in the 1970s after decades of effort by Native organizations and their supporters. This change in legal status set in motion the ongoing process of land claims settlement. Also at this time the National Indian Brotherhood (now known as the Assembly of First Nations) lobbied successfully for partial control of local schooling, which allowed for the reintroduction of traditional religion, customs, and language into educational curriculum (Burnaby 1999:306–7; Drapeau 1998:151–52). With this came an end to the church-run and government-run residential schools that had done so much to eradicate Aboriginal languages.[1]

Throughout the mid-1980s, attempts to form a national Aboriginal language policy were overshadowed by other policy changes pertaining to the status of First Nations peoples. In 1985, through what is known as Bill C-31, some of the most repressive of the remaining Indian Act–era policies were retracted, the most important regarding the definition of Indian status. Under the Indian Act individuals could lose their Indian status if they owned land, voted, married a non-Indian Canadian man, and so forth. Bill C-31 reinstated Indian status for those who had lost status under these federally defined conditions. Finally, the First Nations themselves were able to control the defining of their own membership. In conjunction with this newly official political recognition and in reaction to the Official Languages Act, the Assembly of First Nations stated, as part of its 1988 document on Aboriginal education policy, that "Aboriginal languages deserve official status within Canada, constitutional recognition, and accompanying legislative protection . . . [and that] Aboriginal language education is necessary from pre-school to post-secondary and adult education" (cited in Burnaby 1999:309–10). This was a more straightforward attempt to prompt the federal government to legislate a national policy on Aboriginal languages.

Building on the bureaucratic changes in the 1980s, the government of Canada launched a new policy of negotiating self-governing agreements with First Nations. By recognizing that First Nations were legitimate political entities within Canada and that according to a reinterpretation of the Canadian Constitution such entities have the right to exist and govern themselves, the view that Aboriginal people were wards of the state was formally erased (Indian and Northern Affairs Canada 1997). These new agreements, although not creating new, autonomous political entities, arranged for the transfer of control of programs and services— including health care, child welfare, education, housing, economic development, and lands and resources—from government agencies like the Department of Indian Affairs and Northern Development (DIAND) to the newly created First Nations. In 1996 the federal government released its five-volume report from the Royal Commission on Aboriginal Peoples. This report proposed a twenty-year agenda, with over four hundred recommendations, to redefine the relationship between Canada and the First Nations. Its central conclusion was that "the main policy direction, pursued for more than 150 years [. . .] has been wrong" (Government of Canada 1996:x). As the report states, this historical policy of assimilation was in contrast to the value Canada placed on diversity, and its failure was a testament to the "enduring sense [Aboriginal people have] of themselves as people with a unique heritage and the right to cultural continuity" (Government of Canada 1996:x). Specifically regarding language, this policy change led to the development of Aboriginal Head Start programs (which were intended to put Aboriginal languages on an equal footing with English in the preschools), outlined the intention of the government of Canada to begin providing Aboriginal language services and programs, and otherwise worked to put Aboriginal language issues at the forefront of political consideration and in the minds of Canadians at large.

Today the land claims and self-government agreements in force in the Yukon contain explicit provisions for Aboriginal languages. The Umbrella Final Agreement between the government of Canada and the Council for Yukon Indians, signed on May 29, 1993, outlines these provisions. In section 2.12.2.9 the agreement states that "each Board shall consider including in its annual budget funding to allow the Board to provide its members with cross cultural orientation and education, and other training directed to improving its members' ability to carry out their responsibilities, as well as funding for facilities to allow Board members to carry out their responsibilities in their traditional language" (Government of Yukon 1993:23). Furthermore, the Umbrella Final Agreement, under the chapter on the Heritage Board in section 13.1.1.2, states that one of its objectives is to promote the recording and preservation of traditional languages, beliefs, oral histories (including legends), and cultural knowledge of Yukon Indian people for the benefit of future generations (Government of Yukon 1993:121). The Heritage Board resolutions also call for working with Aboriginal people in the interpretation of cultural materials, proclaiming that "oral history is a valid and relevant form of research" (Government of Yukon 1993:122). Finally, regarding self-government and Aboriginal languages, the Umbrella Final Agreement states in section 24.2.0 that "language, culture, and spiritual beliefs and practices are all legitimate topics for negotiation in the ongoing settlement process" (Government of Yukon 1993:260). The First Nations may negotiate the transfer of programs and services pertaining to the "design, delivery and management of Indian language and cultural curriculum" (section 24.3.2.1, Government of Yukon 1993:261). This transference is happening now, and in the future each First Nation is expected to have direct control of these programs and services.

The current language programs in the Yukon trace their roots to the 1970s, when researchers such as John Ritter and Julie Cruikshank, working on various language projects with Yukon Native peoples, helped form the Yukon Native Languages Project. The project was officially started in 1977 and was sponsored, as it is today, by the Council of Yukon Indians, now known as the Council of Yukon First Nations (CYFN). The project itself became known as the Yukon Native Language Centre (YNLC) in 1985. Since its inception it has been involved in recruiting Native speakers for linguistic documentation and for training as Native language teachers for the public schools (Moore 2002:317). This latter goal became possible with the adoption of the Yukon Education Act in 1990 (Drapeau 1998:155; Harnum 1998:478), which opened the door for Aboriginal languages in local classrooms. YNLC also initiated a program of literacy development for First Nations peoples, most of whom were considered fluent in their ancestral language. To this end, literacy workshops were held and repeated for groups of elders from most, if not all, of the eight officially recognized Yukon Aboriginal languages. The eight official Aboriginal languages were and are Gwich'in (claimed by 211 people as their "mother tongue," or first language), Han (claimed by 131 people as their first language), Kaska (claimed by 664 people as their first language), Northern Tutchone (claimed by 1,065 people as their first language), Southern Tutchone (claimed by 404 people as their first language), Tagish (claimed by 18 people as their first language), Tlingit (claimed by 424 people as their first language), and Upper Tanana (claimed by 11 people as their first language) (Aboriginal Language Services 2004b). The impact of YNLC on Aboriginal languages was significant. For many elders, YNLC provided them with their first experiences with language preservation and revitalization work. Dozens of elders from all over the Yukon have been recorded talking, singing, and telling stories in their own languages. From such work they gained a familiarity with performing for a tape recorder or video camera, creating a new site and method for the reproduction of Aboriginal language practices.

Although YNLC was managed by the Council for Yukon First Nations and funded, ultimately, by the Yukon government, national politics would lead to another government-sponsored program for Aboriginal language revitalization. As mentioned above, in the 1980s Canada was finalizing its Official Languages Act, which provided an opportunity to raise the status of Canada's many Aboriginal tongues. The Yukon government seized the opportunity and negotiated an exclusion to the Official Languages Act that would not make French and English official languages in the Yukon. Instead, the Yukon Languages Act (1988) was adopted, creating an atmosphere in which French, English, and any Aboriginal language could be used in the legislature and elsewhere (cf. Harnum 1998:478). This act stated: "The Yukon recognizes the significance of aboriginal languages in the Yukon and wishes to take appropriate measures to preserve, develop, and enhance those languages in the Yukon" and provides that "Nothing in this Act limits the authority of the Legislative Assembly to advance the equality of status of English, French, or a Yukon aboriginal language" (Languages Act). Financial support for Yukon languages would be need based, as determined or demanded by a particular situation (cf. Burnaby 1997). As a result, the Canada-Yukon Cooperation and Funding Agreement on the Preservation, Development and Enhancement of Aboriginal Languages, a five-year language agreement between the Yukon government and the federal government, was signed on February 24, 1989. With this agreement came five years of funding, the option for renewal at the end of this period (following an evaluation), and the establishment of Aboriginal Language Services (ALS), a program within the Yukon government designed to distribute funding and provide administrative support (Gardner and Associates 1997:27). The initial period of the agreement ran from February 24, 1989, to March 31, 1993, and was funded with $4.25 million. The agreement is now in its fourth renewal. These funding agreements cite objectives like "ensuring the perpetuation, revitalization, growth and protection of Aboriginal languages," "responding to the language needs of Aboriginal communities in the Yukon" (Gardner and Associates 1997:i; Metcalfe 1997:19), and "providing public services in the Aboriginal languages of the Yukon in accordance with the Yukon Languages Act" (Metcalfe 1997:225). The funding was then used for consultation for program planning, linguistic and historical research, training of teachers, translators, and interpreters, and translation of government materials and public proceedings.

Unlike that in various other minority language communities, the scenario in the Yukon is one where the government has institutionalized the preservation and revitalization of local Aboriginal languages. Rarely do we see such a substantial commitment by a dominant regime to the language concerns of a marginalized community (cf. Burnaby 1997). Attempts to address these concerns materialized through specific programs and their guiding philosophies, to which I now turn.

"We Are Our Language"

One of the most fruitful sites for exploring language ideologies are rituals, institutional or otherwise (Silverstein 1998b; Woolard 1998). The institutional rituals for Aboriginal language revitalization in the Yukon include meetings for language planning, the evaluation of programming, and public language events. The text artifacts produced from these rituals exist in the form of meeting transcripts, curriculum materials, and government reports. ALS's text artifacts, while satisfying various institutional goals, especially the federal government's evaluation requirement (see Riles 2000), also illustrate the Yukon government's attempts at a mutually derived Aboriginal language ideology. This regimentation involves both Aboriginal and non-Aboriginal voices from within and outside of Canadian institutions, that is, the "stakeholders" in the Yukon's Aboriginal languages.[2] Over the course of several ALS funding agreements the program managers and participants reflected upon and refined their objectives and methods, bringing into discursive being for the territorial and federal governments a language ideology that was encapsulated in the program's slogan, "We Are Our Language." In this section I turn to an unpacking of this slogan through an analysis of ALS documents. The analysis shows how this seemingly simple phrase indexes multiple viewpoints and beliefs about Aboriginal languages.

The motto "We Are Our Language" did not exist initially. In the earliest reports the philosophy behind language revitalization programming can be read in what is called the Yukon Program Model. The guiding principles for this model were first articulated in the funding agreement mentioned above. In developing this approach, planning consultants researched Aboriginal cultures and language revitalization techniques published by academic experts. The primary consultant, Dr. Leslie Gardner, was a non-Native woman with a doctoral degree in psychology. Her consulting business started in 1991, specializing in evaluations and evaluation training. She lived (and lives) outside of the Yukon (in Edmonton, Alberta). Gladys Netro, a member of the Vuntut Gwich'in First Nation, and Betty Metcalfe, an Aboriginal woman living in the Yukon, assisted Dr. Gardner periodically with some of the evaluations. During the first report Ms. Metcalfe was employed by ALS as the Whitehorse office manager. In later evaluations she was employed as a consultant. In the end these consultants arrived at the following position: "The Yukon model for Aboriginal language preservation, development, maintenance and renewal was based on the fundamental principle that the people are the proper stewards of their languages. The approach to the planning and delivery of programs and services was meant to be supportive and facilitative of Aboriginal people's articulation and implementation of their self-determined objectives, directions, and choices of activities" (Metcalfe 1997:223; see also Gardner and Associates 1993:12). According to Gardner and Associates, the central idea underlying the model was the phrase,

"The people own the language" (1993:15). This philosophy was presented publicly at the 1991 territory-wide conference (see below) by the then-premier of the Yukon, Tony Penikett, who stated: "Your languages are your property. They belong to you as people, as individuals, and families, and the community" (Aboriginal Language Services 1991:26). The Yukon's preliminary stance conceptualized Aboriginal languages as property, objects that can be owned, transferred, and lost. It was the government's responsibility, then, to help Aboriginal peoples achieve their "self-determined" objective to reclaim what had been lost, both territorially and linguistically.[3] In doing so the program was to be guided by and respectful of "Aboriginal values" and cultural traditions, meaning that some conceptualization of culture would become an integral component of the ideology of Aboriginal language, both for developing methods for preserving and revitalizing Aboriginal languages and for understanding the role of Aboriginal languages in everyday life. The Yukon Model articulated this:

> Because the people own the language, the intent of the program model was to engage the people in a culturally respectful way. The cultural tradition was to provide a context for the rational program development which was to reflect Aboriginal values and orientation of Yukon First Nations. That meant that the program model would be more organic than directed, that is, the second step would flow naturally from the results of the first, rather than according to a pre-set agenda. The program model was to be intentionally indirect and meant to be enabling of natural processes, and respectful of individual autonomy so central in Aboriginal culture. (Gardner and Associates 1993:12)

This model was not only a discourse about Aboriginal languages but a statement about Aboriginal cultures as well. The model assumed that "Aboriginal culture" was homogeneous, especially in regard to respect for "individual autonomy." Furthermore, the model recognized that "issues of language are complex and affected by many socio-cultural factors, profoundly linked to identity, self-concept and world view, and inseparable from culture. Because language issues were seen to be intimately linked with cultural issues, there was a need to recognize these issues as sacred and to approach them with an attitude of caution and respect" (Gardner and Associates 1993:14).

The inclusion of culture in the understanding of language arose in part from academic resources. In drawing their conclusions, the developers of the model had sought knowledge from outside experts: It may be helpful to consider some prominent and generally accepted characteristics of native culture and particularly styles of interaction and communication in order to better understand what would be respectful and appropriate. Issues from a recent article on communication styles of Indian people may be helpful. (Gardner and Associates 1993:15)

A summary of these findings was then provided. Many of the findings mirrored old anthropological observations about "Indian personality," while others reflected generic "Indian" ideals.[4] For example, Aboriginal people are described as being respectful of others and their autonomy, viewing life and everything in it as a gift from the Creator, being responsible for the care of those gifts, and "striv[ing] for harmony with nature and fellow human beings" (Gardner and Associates 1993:16). While a discussion of the role such discourse may play in the ongoing racialization of American Indians and indigenous peoples more generally is important, this same discourse appeals to a broader audience and helps to establish their support of such ventures (see Larsen [2003] for an environmental example).

Regarding language work specifically, the model borrowed heavily from James J. Bauman's *Guide to Issues in Indian Language Retention* (1980); eleven pages of quotes were excerpted from it. The excerpts inform the reader about two evaluative tasks: characteristics for assessing Aboriginal language "health" and directions for implementing an Aboriginal language revitalization program. In contrast to this early approach to language revitalization, more recent guides incorporate the opinions, advice, and practices of both "outside" experts and community internal advocates (such as Leanne Hinton and Ken Hale's *Green Book of Language Revitalization in Practice* [2001]) and include more detailed instructions for teaching an endangered language (Hinton with Matt Vera and Nancy Steele, *How to Keep Your Language Alive* [2002]). The discursive tensions, however, between "external" experts and "internal" advocates have remained, even with the careful attention to contextual differences (Hill 2002; Hinton 2002). Thus, while government officials in the Yukon intended to encourage First Nations' language reclamation, the inception of this transition began with "expert" texts authored outside of

First Nations' communities and discourses. These "expert" texts, quoted in early ALS documents, then reinforced a conceptualization of language as synonymous with cultural difference and foregrounded the concept of identity.

These expert sources also implicated elders as key resource people, integral to the maintenance and transmission of Aboriginal traditions and to a successful language revitalization program: "They are the source of the enduring wisdom contained in uniquely Aboriginal values and ways of seeing and being in the world. In many areas, the Elders have been the leaders in their communities for years. . . . The most effective involvement has Elders setting direction and policy, as well as acting in the traditional role of teachers and spiritual leaders" (Metcalfe 1997:36).

Through such statements, Aboriginal language and culture became equated with specialized forms of knowledge, or unique "ways of seeing the world," such that elders, the traditional "teachers and spiritual leaders," were positioned as the most legitimate authorities on Yukon Aboriginal language and culture (see Cruikshank 1990; McClellan 2001; Meek 2007; Moore 2002; Nadasdy 2003).[5] When the time came for the first public territory-wide consensus-building event, elders were given a privileged position such that their concerns about language and culture predominated.

Held in 1991, the Yukon Aboriginal Languages Conference brought together elders from all over the Yukon and provided a forum for them and any other stakeholder and Yukon citizen, First Nations or otherwise, who wished to speak. A report of the conference was published as the *Voices of the Talking Circle Report* (Aboriginal Language Services 1991). These voices, while emanating from various stakeholders, indicate the amount of mutual influence involved in the standardization of a Yukon language ideology. ALS, as the producer of the report, organized the statements of participating elders into a set of "issues" corresponding to major goals and themes of its program. To elucidate the ways in which Aboriginal concepts inform these broad institutional proclamations, three ideological themes organize my discussion.

The first of these ideological themes is the idea that language directly indexes identity, a semiotic relationship described by Gal and Irvine (1995) as iconicity or as a process of iconicization (Irvine and Gal 2000). This "language as identity" theme appeared throughout several of the

ALS documents, most explicitly in the phrase "Language, culture and identity are inseparable" (Aboriginal Language Services 1991:29). For some, this meant that Aboriginal languages can never disappear as long as Aboriginal peoples survive. Tlingit elder Pete Sidney expressed this as follows: "Another thing I dislike hearing about is that we lost, we lost our heritage, we lost our language. Let's examine that for a minute. What is language? Where does it come from? . . . [L]anguage is a gift of the Creator for the purpose of communication and any gift of the Creator you as well as myself know that it can never deteriorate. . . . [A]ll we have to do is dust it off" (Aboriginal Language Services 1991:11).

Along with several of the above statements, Sidney's comment illustrates a conceptualization of language as innate and central to Aboriginal identity (see also Lena Johnson's quote below). While not all participants expressed this view, many of the elders subscribed to some variety of linguistic essentialism.[6] Other First Nations people elaborated on this "language as identity" idea by describing language as the primary means for creating and maintaining relationships and for understanding one's ancestral history. Consider the following statements made by elders at this conference: "God created us to be Indian people, to speak our language, to keep our relationship, like we did a long time ago" (Lena Johnson, in Aboriginal Language Services 1991:11); "Education is very good for kids now days, but we still have to learn our culture, our language. We have to know who we are, and we have a string tied through everyone of us, we're related somehow, so this is why we respect each other" (Dora Wedge, in Aboriginal Language Services 1991:13). With respect to Aboriginality in general, Johnny Abel, a Gwich'in speaker, said, "The time has come for First Nations people to do something positive for us. The time has come for us to preserve and keep alive the use of our mother tongues. By doing this, we bring alive our cultural heritage, our self-identity, and most important our self-dignity and sense of value of ourselves as a people" (Aboriginal Language Services 1991:26).

Moving beyond individual issues of identity, statements also related identity and language to group solidarity and self-government: "As we talk about this self-government, I think it is a part of it that we try to do today [at the language conference]. I'm glad to see that we are doing this whole Yukon get-together to make a strong stand for our rights and for our future. I believe our kids will work hard to try to get back to pick up some of our language again" (Roddy Blackjack, Sr., Northern Tutchone elder, in Aboriginal Language Services 1991:19).

Comparable views were also in print elsewhere: "Indian unity, what some people call self-government, must be held together by the native languages. If you call yourself Indian and you want Indian self-government then you should conduct your business in the Indian language" (First Nations parent, quoted in Tlen 1986:30). Several other chapters in this volume (Bunte, Field and Kroskrity, Kroskrity, and Richland) make similar observations concerning an emergent iconization of indigenous language with tribal and cultural sovereignty.

The second ideological theme is the idea that language use is linked to place, such that "the home and community must be the primary basis and location for language preservation, development and enhancement efforts" (Aboriginal Language Services 1991:30). In the elders' statements from the conference the contrast between "home" and "bush" contexts is reproduced.

> Let's turn back from where we are right now, even ourselves, let's turn back to our language and start speaking our language to our kids at home. . . . Let's help the Indian instructor by talking our language, only our language, when they get home. (Tommy McGinty, Northern Tutchone elder, in Aboriginal Language Services 1991:17)

> You know I think the best way to teach . . . we all take bunch of boys out, out in the bush for month, just talk Indian to them, how to do work, cut wood, bring wood, bring water, all sit down there Indian way, but that the only way they gonna catch on fast. (Stanley Jonathan, Northern Tutchone elder, in Aboriginal Language Services 1991:17)

Such statements connected particular places with Aboriginal language use, emphasizing the need to locate language learning within culturally relevant contexts and practices. Such commentary also alluded to historical practices pertaining to language development. This subsequently led to a concern with revitalizing historical "cultural" practices as a means for restoring Aboriginal languages.

This raises the final theme, the conceptualization of language as dynamic. The following statements illustrate this conceptual dimension through their emphasis on language as interaction and interaction as socially constructive, where language itself becomes linked to reiterable social events and movement through time and space (Anderson, this volume, deconstructs this concept at length with relevance to the Arapaho community). For example, one Aboriginal person noted that "people in the communities have to get together regularly to build up their identity so they can all understand who they are, and where they may be going in life" (cited in Tlen 1986:31). Similarly, Ida Lowe commented, "Those of us who are Elders, we have to remember to tell our children and our grandchildren, to give them history of our culture because we cannot go forwards unless we find, unless we can see our tracks from behind. We have to know our roots. . . . [Children] can't go forward unless they know their roots" (Aboriginal Language Services 1991:16).

Annie Ned, a Southern Tutchone elder, reflected this in her own assessment of the contemporary language situation: "I go by myself, no grandchildren behind me. . . . [W]e got to work hard so our grandchildren will come behind us" (Aboriginal Language Services 1991:10). Such statements emphasized the processual nature of language—language as the primary means for learning about one's (Aboriginal) self. The frequent use of journey or travel (movement) metaphors also contributed to the dynamic or processual representation of language. Language becomes a practice that "brings alive" past practices and value. Note that this bureaucratically mediated perception of language as dynamic and processual in nature is different from that noted in other Athabascan communities, including Apache (Gómez de García, Axelrod, and Lachler, this volume) and Navajo (Witherspoon 1977), where language is conceptualized as a dynamic entity that has agency and power of its own.

All of these statements represent Aboriginal language as essential to Aboriginal identity and to the establishment of the linkages that bind people together: "our relatives," "our heritage" is founded upon "our language." Hence, the emergent themes of the conference, as expressed in the proceedings, meaningfully fill out the slogan "We Are Our Language."[7] This slogan as well as many of the statements articulated at the 1991 conference have been integrated into subsequent government texts and have also been voiced by local language advocates. This conceptual convergence has resulted in what could be called ideological syncretism (cf. Hill 1999), occasions where disparate ideas about language are synthesized. The next section shows the resulting dialogic emergence of a Yukon-specific language ideology.

The Dialogic Emergence of a Yukon Language Ideology

We examined above the historical events leading up to the emergence of an Aboriginally mediated language ideology. The effects of that mediation are evidenced not only by the inclusion of Aboriginal voices in government documents but in the subtle linguistic shifts appearing in later bureaucratic discourse. This section discusses some of these shifts, arguing that these transformations reflect a territory-wide repositioning of control in which Aboriginal people are increasingly able to voice and to have heard their own conceptualizations of language as well as to influence government practices.

One example of this bureaucratic change is in the expression of linguistic possession in terms of the object and the distribution of ownership. While the government initially represented Aboriginal languages as the property of Aboriginal peoples, more recent government statements have shifted the object of ownership from "language" to "responsibility." In conjunction with this change in object has been a change in the possessive pronoun from "your" to "our." Now Aboriginal language preservation and revitalization are the responsibility of all Yukon citizens, First Nations or otherwise (Aboriginal Language Services 2004b); "your" loss becomes "our" loss. The first-person plural possessive pronoun has also undergone a corresponding semantic shift from an exclusive "our" to an inclusive "our." Initial statements by government officials referred to Aboriginal languages as "your," the property and responsibility of First Nations people. In later publications this became "our," indexing an isomorphic relationship between speakers and identities. Since then, the referent of "our" has expanded to include all Yukon citizens.

As with these early possessive constructions, previous statements about Aboriginal language also perpetuated an isomorphism between cultures, peoples, and languages. Consider the following statement, where the author portrayed language as intimately involved in the transmission of sociocultural knowledge, an understanding that "aboriginal people know . . . intuitively": "Language is the vehicle of culture. The way we share culture and pass it on to the young is deeply interwoven with the ideas expressed in our language. Aboriginal people know this intuitively" (Aboriginal Language Services 1991:1).

In contrast to this representation, later statements have expanded on this singular correspondence between peoples and languages by emphasizing the locality of Aboriginal languages and their importance to the territory as a whole: "If even one language is lost Yukoners will either directly or indirectly experience it, as an entire world view will be lost; stories will remain untold; ancient knowledge about the world will become inaccessible; and the Yukon will become less culturally and linguistically diverse" (Aboriginal Language Services 2004b:133).

Along with situating Aboriginal languages as an integral part of the Yukon, the bureaucratic discourse has extended the representation of Aboriginal language from a naturalized dimension of Aboriginal identity to a counterhegemonic, democratic image of the Yukon Territory, "a place whereby all peoples have equal rights and equal access to the cultures and languages that are Indigenous to them and integral to their very well-being as individuals and as a community" (Aboriginal Language Services 2004b:136).

Along with this spatial dimension, the conceptualization of language as dynamic has also influenced government statements. This influence is evidenced by report titles such as *Walking the Talk*, *Marking the Trail*, *Telling the Story*, and *Working Together to Pass It On*. Each of these titles emphasizes movement through space and time. The most recent report, *Sharing the Gift of Language*, again reproduces this image.

Several other ideological changes are emerging as well, one of which I will touch on only briefly here due to the limitations of space. Subsequent government documents have expanded the linguistic image through the diversification of the linguistic field in terms of both languages and speakers. Initial reports and statements imagined a singular correspondence between languages and peoples and identified elders as "experts." Recent documents have recognized the multitude of dialects ("8 languages with many dialects," Aboriginal Language Services 2004b:12) and have begun to include diagrams tabulating the number of speakers of each dialect (Aboriginal Language Services 2004b). These reports have also begun to acknowledge the range of linguistic expertise available within communities, noting that "language expertise resides in more than one place" (Aboriginal Language Services 2004a:28). As part of the reconceptualization of language as dynamic, the image of knowledge itself has emerged as variable and shifting.

Much of the analytic challenge of these texts results from discursive overlapping or recursion across text artifacts, an aspect of bureaucratic textual traditions (Riles 2000). A stream of reiterations and paraphrases courses through all of the ALS documents. Because of such intertextual borrowings and repetitions, determining original authorship or chronological beginnings became difficult. What was discoverable, however, were the ideological nuances framing these bureaucratic statements and the "dialogic emergence" (Tedlock and Mannheim 1995) of a territorial language ideology. The government rhetoric was transformed by the different and often more theorized conceptualizations of (Aboriginal) language offered by First Nations participants. Through these multivocal, multiauthored events, several ideas about language emerged, from language being "a gift from the Creator" and "your property" to language being "a vehicle of culture." Through the intentional inclusion of Aboriginal voices in the text-based discourses about Aboriginal languages, a gradual expansion of the ideological repertoire has occurred, naturalized through the phrase "We Are Our Language."

Accompanying these transformations is the transference of state control to the individual First Nations. For Aboriginal languages this transference appears in the reduction of ALS staff, such that previous ALS employees are now employed by their own First Nations in the distribution of ALS funds, which primarily go to support First Nation language initiatives, and in the organizational structure of ALS, where the majority of current employees are of First Nations ancestry. Additionally, the advisory board, which controls the direction of ALS, is composed predominantly of First Nations elders and other senior First Nations people. In this context the dialogic construction of an Aboriginal language ideology corresponds with the state's desire to reorganize its power, indexing the transformation of both the voice and the dominion of the state.

Conclusion

Research on language ideologies in Aboriginal North America frequently has examined American Indian languages and ideologies against a backdrop of dominant colonial languages and ideologies and vice versa (e.g., see Collins 1998, 2003; House 2002; Whiteley 2003; see also Dorian 1998; Errington 2003). Since this research has focused on contrasting and discordant ideological perspectives, it has not been as concerned with indigenous language revitalization efforts as a collaborative institutional process informed by both Aboriginal and non-Aboriginal voices. Likewise, language ideological research concerned with institutional processes has focused frequently on the production and maintenance of a regime's or state's dominance in relation to particular ideological constructions (e.g., Spitulnik 1998a, 1998b; see also Heller and Martin-Jones 2001). This chapter expands on this work by showing how dominant ideologies and state control can be transformed through the inclusion of Aboriginal voices. When provided with opportunities for government involvement, as with the territory-wide Aboriginal languages conference, indigenous peoples can transform the hegemony of the neocolonial regime.

First Nations people have affected the government's ideological project at various ritualized moments—legislation, meetings (conferences), documentation—such that the emerging language ideology has been dialogically constructed across all stakeholders' discourses, Aboriginal and non-Aboriginal, expert and nonexpert alike. The resulting conceptualization of language acknowledges its status as both essence and process, as thing and event. While all levels of government may be tightly regulated and resistant to change, as Fishman notes, this emergent syncretic ideological field in the Yukon suggests that there are moments at which institutional control, though monitored, is malleable. At these moments social change and ideological restructuring can happen. (See also the chapters by Kroskrity and Perley in this volume for more discussion of the role of agency by indigenous language activists in effecting change in language ideology and to further language revitalization.)

Currently, one of the most apparent examples of this ideological transformation is in language education. Until recently, Yukon Aboriginal language education practices predominantly decontextualized the linguistic code, emphasizing grammatical structure and lexical items over that of communicative competence or performance (Meek 2001). One change has been pedagogical, from talking about language as a disconnected object to teaching language as a contextually grounded practice. "Being that the main purpose of language is to provide a method of communicating in a world in which it was created from, the culture and the heritage should be learned alongside that of the language" (Aboriginal Language Services 2004a:27). Putting into practice this sentiment, many language workshops and some public classrooms now incorporate culturally relevant activities as part of the learning experience. This re-contextualization both encourages language use in the educational set-ting and illustrates the various opportunities and topics available for con-versing in an Aboriginal language beyond the classroom.

As the devolution of government programs occurs, the next step will be to find out to what extent First Nations people have influenced the dominant language ideology emerging in the Yukon by comparing the government rhetoric of the First Nations with that of the dominant re-gime. This additional step will begin to address a question raised by Gal about the process through which language ideologies become "natu-ralized" and dominant, "if only temporarily and partially" (1998:321). However, sentiments of community members are never as coherently solidified as the rhetorics of governments, nor are they evaluative in the same way. While most of the people I spoke with or interviewed were generally supportive of Kaska language projects and viewed them as successful (though not necessarily in terms of reversing language shift), they expressed a range of concerns not easily compartmentalized into a singular language ideology. Several people made statements about the practicality of learning and speaking Kaska in relation to economic and educational opportunities. Some people remarked upon the historical, aesthetic, and intellectual value of maintaining Kaska, while others were concerned with the effect speaking Kaska might have on children's ability to speak English (in a normative style). Parents in particular expressed this concern along with a preference for their children to take French in school rather than Kaska, a preference having real consequences.

After having volunteered for several months in one of two Kaska lan-guage classrooms at the elementary school, I came to recognize and know all of the students, from kindergarten through fifth grade. It was apparent that the older grades had fewer and fewer students. On one day in particu-lar, after realizing that one of the students was no longer coming to class, I asked the remaining students about this "missing" person. I was told by one of his classmates that he had switched to French because "he says [it] gives him better education, prepares him better for high school." The student who switched was the son of one of the people involved in Kaska language revitalization but also someone who was a fluent Kaska speaker. Along with finding French to be more useful academically (a sentiment expressed by adults), this student may have also been bored by the Kaska curriculum, a curriculum that remained the same year after year.

Obviously, more changes are needed, but will they be enough? Will educational recontextualizations help to reverse language shift? Will ideological transformations have any effect? The answer for some researchers (e.g., Dauenhauer and Dauenhauer 1998) has been negative. Language reversal entails processes of acquisition and practice, both of which are complex and relatively understudied phenomena. To reverse language shift requires a deeper understanding of these processes. Transforming ideas about language(s) and educational conventions is only part of the overall process. Certainly, changing curriculum in order to enhance children's developing competencies rather than stifling them with the same information at each grade level would promote increased language use, or at least increased knowledge, and at the same time contribute to imagining a language as academically useful. While in the end working together to promote and create such changes may not be enough to reverse language shift (much of the literature and my own experiences seem to suggest that languages that are already extinct or near extinction may have a better chance of revival than those that are in the process of disappearing), such collaborations can certainly empower indigenous peoples, indigenous languages, and processes of revitalization.

CHAPTER 8

"You Keep Not Listening with Your Ears!"

Language Ideologies, Language Socialization, and Paiute Identity

PAMELA A. BUNTE

Language shift and language loss are never simple processes. This chapter is about the changing conditions that can lead to language shift as well as to language revitalization. Specifically, I examine one such case where an essentialized or iconized link (Irvine and Gal 2000) between language and identity developed over the last two decades of the twentieth century. I consider what this linking of language and identity, coupled with traditional socialization ideologies and practices, contributes to language shift. At the same time, I look at how the linguistic indexing of identity and those same socialization beliefs may play a positive role in the group's present revitalization process.

The San Juan Southern Paiute Tribe, the easternmost of ten Southern Paiute tribes, is located in Arizona and Utah in two small areas on the western part of the Navajo Reservation. The San Juan Paiutes are traditionally Southern Paiute speaking, but they also have a long history of multilingualism. Living at the border of Southern Paiute territory, San Juan Paiutes had historically interacted with members of the adjacent tribes, such as the Havasupai and the Hopi to their south (Bunte and Franklin 1987:22, 42–51). Although this interaction led to some intermarriages and multilingualism, the San Juans' experience with the Navajos who began arriving in the second half of the nineteenth century was qualitatively different. Navajos settled over large parts of what had been undisputed Paiute land, and by the early decades of the twentieth century Navajos were living all around San Juan Paiute settlements on what had become part of the Navajo reservation. For most of the twentieth century the community language remained Paiute despite the tribe's small size, multilingualism, and small number of speakers, although most adult San

Juan Paiutes had by necessity attained varying degrees of fluency in Navajo, the lingua franca on the reservation.

By the 1980s the tribe consisted of between six and nine extended families that were Paiute speaking and five or six more peripheral Paiute families who through particular historical circumstances had become Navajo speaking. Federally recognized only in 1990 with 192 members, the San Juan Southern Paiute Tribe was unique at that time as the only one of the ten Southern Paiute tribes where a number of families still used Paiute as an everyday language and where some children were still speaking Paiute. Presently, however, even among Paiute-speaking families, language practice is changing, and most members of the youngest generation no longer speak Paiute. Although most of the children in the Paiute-speaking families do not actively speak Paiute, many understand a great deal of the Paiute spoken around them.

Outside forces such as schooling and, more recently, the tribe's economic and political dealings with English-speaking institutions have been important forces behind the changing language use (Bunte and Franklin 2001), but San Juan Paiutes' own understandings of and responses to these "forces" have played a role in the emerging linguistic landscape. As Woolard notes, "it is through the interpretive filter of beliefs about language, cognition, and social relations that political and economic events have an effect on language maintenance and shift" (1998:16; see also Mertz 1989:109).

A number of San Juan Southern Paiute families had kept their language as a language of daily use through many adverse situations into the 1980s (Bunte and Franklin 1987). This fostered the strong conviction among Paiute-speaking elders that they would never lose their language. The San Juan elders told stories about how the children and many of the adults of other Paiute groups could only speak English. In telling these stories they showed that they believed they were different from the other Southern Paiute tribes because they had kept their language. However, they did not single out language as a part of identity or identify it as the only or main thing that differentiated groups from each other.

This was true in the critical relationship between the San Juan Paiutes and the local Navajos as well. Although being Paiute was also clearly differentiated from being Navajo, this distinction was not based on language. Intermarriages between San Juan Paiutes and local Navajos have taken place for over one hundred years; nevertheless, most of the known unions have not led to replacement of the Paiute language or culture with Navajo language or culture for either the adults or children involved. Rather, the in-marrying spouse has tended to learn Paiute. However, among two or three families, particular historical circumstances have led to a shift to Navajo language and culture.

In the same way that speaking Paiute was a taken-for-granted part of everyday life for most San Juan Southern Paiutes, other Paiute practices, both everyday behavior and rituals, were not especially marked. No hard distinctions were made between the members of Paiute-speaking families and Paiutes who participated more in Navajo language and culture. While developing the official San Juan Paiute tribal roll during the early 1980s, tribal elders insisted on the inclusion of these Navajo-speaking families. One elderly Navajo-speaking woman who was very involved in the federal recognition process was fiercely proud of her Paiute background. While telling the story of her family and explaining the historical circumstances that led her and her sisters to speak only Navajo, she commented, "We don't even talk in our own language, but we're still Paiutes" (Bunte and Franklin, unpublished fieldnotes). Although she had never spoken Paiute, she still thought of Paiute, not Navajo, as her "own language."

Around 1990 the tribe's fight for federal recognition and land produced moments crucial to the tribal members' evolving perception of their Paiute identity. When, in 1990, the Navajos' attorneys tried in the U.S. Court for the District of Arizona to discredit the Paiute claims in the Navajo-Hopi-Paiute land claims case *Masayesva v. Zah v. James* by saying that the San Juan Paiutes were really Navajos, Judge Earl Carroll told them to stop wasting his time: he had seen many Navajos, and the Paiute Blue Lee, who had testified in Paiute, definitely did not act like the Navajos Carroll knew. Another witness in the land claims case, Angel Whiskers, demonstrated his Paiute identity by highlighting his Paiute language.[1] Paiute was Angel's first language, but he had spoken only Navajo since childhood, despite living in a Paiute-speaking household in which his wife and children spoke to him entirely in Paiute. Nevertheless, at the trial he surprised everybody by speaking Paiute. Angel astutely seized the moment and presented himself as having an authentic Paiute identity as a Paiute speaker. Enacted as a situational political act, this event has been repeated in narrative form over the years. Although the import of the story is "how Angel got one over the Navajos," implied as well is a model of iconized (Irvine and Gal 2000) linkage between language and identity. There are other similar stories about other Paiutes concerning their ability to reactivate language later in life. By 1990, being Paiute and speaking Paiute (or perhaps being able to speak Paiute) had become seen by many—at least in marked public contexts—as one and the same.

The language employed by the younger members of Paiute-speaking families had begun to shift to English by the mid- to late 1980s. These changing practices, however, were taking place in a uniquely Paiute cultural context. Although in many Paiute-speaking families the language spoken by the younger members had changed, other aspects of language practice had not. That is, children were still learning to interact in San Juan Paiute–appropriate ways, but they were doing so in English.

Ironically, the shift in language practice was taking place just at the time when many Paiutes had begun to see being Paiute and speaking Paiute as essentially linked. Since speaking Paiute had—if anything— become culturally more salient, why was it primarily language that was changing? And, indeed, how had the linkage of language and identity come to be experienced as iconized? This was a change in San Juan Paiutes' previous conceptions of language that, like the Western Monos' conceptions (Kroskrity 1999, 2002, this volume), emphasized the practical or utilitarian nature of language. To understand the context in which this change happened we need to examine aspects of Paiute language ideology.

First, San Juan Paiute caregivers believe that children will eventually learn the proper way to behave if they are taught it in Paiute. San Juan Paiute elders have told me that caregivers' previous words of instruction come when needed later in life—that the words will come to the child or adult "on the wind," as it were. San Juan elder Matsik told me, "That's how it was with me—my mother's words came to me on the wind." In addition, San Juan caregivers believe that the acts of listening and hearing (as well as observing) are the basis for learning. It is not expected necessarily that the child act on the knowledge immediately. It will be used—that is, produced or activated—later when needed. The emphasis in Paiute socialization is on the attainment of the knowledge, not the immediate production of it.

Second, San Juan caregivers believe in the need to respect every person's autonomous self. Paiutes believe you cannot make anyone, even a toddler, do anything. You can give advice, but you cannot expect the person to use it immediately. Similarly, Susan Philips notes that among the Warm Springs Indians "people exert little interactional control over one another": they "may try to verbally convince others to take particular actions, try to 'give them advice,' or 'make them listen'" (1983:66), but, like the San Juan Paiutes, Warm Spring adults do not punish children if they do not take the adults' advice. Paiutes also say that you cannot speak for anyone else or speculate about what another person may be thinking. During my dissertation research with the Kaibab Paiutes I asked my consultant's daughter whether she thought her mom might need to go to the store, because if she did, I would come back to the village to pick her up. She responded, "You have to ask her." When I then said, "I can't ask her; she's not here," the daughter again responded, "You have to ask her." Then I finally understood that my question was simply culturally inappropriate, since I had been trying to make the daughter tell me what her mom was thinking.

In the rest of this chapter I address the question of why it is primarily language use that is changing. I examine how the San Juan Southern Paiute language ideologies described above intersect with the linguistic indexing of identity and how that has, in turn, affected language maintenance (see Irvine and Gal 2000; Kroskrity 1998; Silverstein 1998b; Woolard 1998).[2] In particular, I examine two aspects of San Juan language ideology: (1) the efficacy of verbal instructions for teaching proper interactive behavior and etiquette; and (2) the autonomy of the individual, or how one can instruct an autonomous child. The research analyzed here has emerged from my long-term engagement with the community, beginning in 1980 and continuing through 2007—approximately two and a half years of cumulative fieldwork. During that twenty-seven-year period I saw children of the community grow into the parenting generation and witnessed the beginnings of a potential language shift toward English. The parents of those now-grown-up children, recognizing the increasing role of English, requested that I conduct research that would involve video-taping storytelling and other socialization routines—performed in Paiute —that would provide a valuable resource for a community that needed materials to support its language revitalization efforts. What is especially remarkable in the Paiute case is the way generational difference in heritage language fluency did not provide an obstacle to unified community acceptance of the need for language revitalization. Unlike the Mayan community, where the young are "blamed" for language shift (Reynolds, this volume), or the Arapaho and Shoshone communities, where "elder purism" inhibited intergenerational transmission and healthy and adaptive language change (Anderson and Loether, this volume), the San Juan Paiute community used its generational differences to effectively assign productive roles in community-based language renewal efforts.

The Efficacy of Verbal Instructions

Most adult San Juan Paiutes who are fluent in Paiute speak to their children at times in Paiute and at other times in English, and most children, if they respond, respond in English to speech in either language.[3] Caregivers—even non-English speakers—rarely if ever insist that children respond in Paiute. Caregivers will, however, tell children that they "should speak Paiute" (*nʉngwʉampaxaxwano*).[4] Many San Juan Paiutes believe that the most efficacious way for a caregiver to teach proper interactive behavior and etiquette is to give informal verbal suggestions in everyday interactions as well as formal verbal instructions at life crisis rituals, such as the menarche and first childbirth rituals (Bunte 2000; Bunte and Franklin 1987; Franklin and Bunte 1996). These words of instruction will be reactivated, that is, "heard," when a child needs them later in life.[5] Listening or having one's ears open is a persistent theme in Paiute socialization talk. Philips (1983:64–66) talks about a similar conception, and she notes that Warm Spring Indians give more emphasis "to the child's receptive linguistic competence than to productive competence" (1983:50). We see the consequences of this language ideology among the San Juan Paiutes over and over again in adults' socialization interactions with children. In the following case the grandmother, Na'aintsits Wʉn, and aunt, Mukwiv, of a five-year-old girl, Tataats, were cooking on an outdoor fire when Tataats, with her two cousins' help, started her own fire near her grandmother's. The grandmother and aunt appeared worried that she might burn herself or perhaps disturb their cooking. The following interaction actually took place over a period of more than thirty minutes, but I give here a selection of the caregivers' instructions to Tataats and her cousins and the caregivers' comments concerning Tataats's fire making. These comments were interspersed by Paiute conversation between the adults about recent events and practical comments dealing with the cooking process.

Example 1. Tataats (T) with Grandma Na'aintsits Wʉn (N) and
Aunt Mukwiv (M)
M: *No, just leave it there.*[6] [said to T]
   Leave it there.

. . .

N: kach, kaxuts.=
   No, Grandchild [daughter's child]. [said to T]
N: =//no, no, no, no. [said to T]
M: //no, no, no.// [said to T] *Just leave it there.*=
N: = It's going to burn the tokoav. It's going to burn.
   It's going to burn the meat. *It's going to burn.* [said to T]

. . .

M: kwiya'aiva' tøtsivʉam
   You might burn your hair. [said to T]

. . .

N: Don't play with the kunats.   kwiya'aiva'a. (1)
   Don't play with the fire.   You might burn. [said to T]
N: kwiya'ita'a ich. (.o)
   This could burn you [literally: smoke-die-impersonal this=nom].[7]
   pakankʉ. pakankʉ kwara' (1)
   It hurts. It hurts really. [said to T]
N: kwikaiyʉuk, mar anikanangum hai (4)
   It's smoking, that one you're doing! [said to all the children]
   Kuuak, Tataats. (7)
Bury it [the fire], T. [said to T]
N: kwashʉt'uivaniyangum,
[I]'m going to burn you (pl) [(or better) "You (pl) will get cooked"]
[cooked/ripe-causative-future-2pl=obl, literally: (Someone?) will have
you (pl) cooked],

kachungum nana kachava'k
because you (pl) keep not listening[listen=redup-fut-neg-sub]
                    nakavavakungum.
                    with your ears [ears-at-obl-
                    your (pl)]. [said to all the
                    children]

. . .

N: avaxania' ichu kwitsiking? pagrandmaxaipu grandma kaimi
avaxanixaipɹ (1)
This shadehouse you might burn, late *grandma's, Grandma* Kaimi's,
former shadehouse. [said to T]

N: kunaix tuh kwai manga pukanik (1)
That one keeps on bothering the fire [N said to M talking laterally
about T]

N: kwiyaiva' aikano You're going to burn your hand!
You might burn, I said! *You're going to burn your hand!* [said to T]

. . .

N: kaxutsin kwiya'iva'
Grandchild, you might get burned! [said to T]

. . .

N: hee kach, hit'aiyumino. *Never listen.*
Hey, no! [You] were told! *Never listen.* [said to T]

. . .

N: Tataatsilas,[8] kach nukava' im
Little Tataats, you don't listen. [said to T]

. . .

N: kwat'ivania'm
[I]'m going to burn you (s). [(or better) "You (s) will get cooked"]
[literally: (I/someone?) will have you cooked]
                    mama,
                    with that,
                                        anixu'm. (1)
                                        if you do that. [said to T]

M: manixuxwang, paaiy avaatuxw chami'
When she keeps doing that, pour water on top of it. [M said to N
talking laterally about T]

. . .

N: Tataats! paiya'k ara'ava.
Tataats! It should be left (alone).

In this segment note that the grandmother, Na'aintsits Wʉn, and the aunt, Mukwiv, hinted, warned, and threatened mainly in Paiute, some in English, while Tataats and her cousins calmly ignored them and continued playing with the fire. This was a typical San Juan Paiute socialization interaction. I have observed many similar interactions where caregivers appear to be trying to get a child either to do or not to do something. A close analysis of the forms the adults were using to the children indicates that although it was delivered loudly, the verbal force was generally indirect and morphologically hedged, helping explain the children's reaction to the directives. In fact, the only bare directives to the children were the English and Paiute imperatives "Leave it," "Don't play with [the fire]," and "Kuuak [Bury it]." Even these bare imperatives when used by native Paiute speakers do not have the force that native English speakers would expect.[9] The Paiute imperative "Kuuak" produced the only glimmer that the children were indeed listening—one of the cousins sprinkled a little sand onto the fire in a half-hearted manner. The phrase "kwashʉt'uivaniyangum" was translated by a participant in the interaction as a threat to burn the children: "I will burn you (pl)." However, since it is softened by the agent being literally left unspecified in Paiute, it may better be translated as a warning: "You'll get cooked." What the adults were actually doing in this example was trying to persuade the children to decide through the medium of listening themselves to act differently, to not play with the fire—at least not where they were potentially interfering with the cooking.

The Autonomy of the Individual

Caregivers virtually never make a child do what they are telling him or her to do. In fact, since San Juan Paiutes believe that all individuals, even the youngest toddlers, have an autonomous self, only such noncoercive instructions or words of advice are felt to be effective. They believe that a child has to make the decision to do the behavior himself or herself. Caregivers sometimes try to get very young children to behave in certain ways by having them verbalize and internalize the negative consequences of their actions. Thus, in the following example, twenty-eight-month-old Shʉshʉʉxʉts has been gagging on large mouthfuls of spaghetti, leading

Piki, his uncle, and Kwis, his grandmother, to provide a model of exactly what he should say to himself.

> Example 2. Shushuuxuts (Sh), twenty-eight months, with Grandma
> Kwis (K) and Uncle Piki (P)
> P: "kachumoniap," ai.
> Say, "Don't do that." [Said to Shushuuxuts]
> K: "kachumoniap," ai.
>   Say, "Don't do that." [Said to Shushuuxuts]
> Sh: kachumoniap.
>   Don't do that.
> K: pikwi'ivan
>   I might choke. [Said to Shushuuxuts]
> Sh: pikwi'ivan.
>   I might choke.
> K: "pikwi'ivan," ai.
>   Say, "I might choke." [Said to Shushuuxuts]
> Sh: pikwi'ivan.
>   I might choke.
> K: "kachumoniap," ai.
>   Say, "Don't do that." [Said to Shushuuxuts]
> Sh: pikwi'ivan.
>   I might choke.

Notice that both the utterances "Say, 'Don't do that'" and "Say, 'I might choke'" might seem pragmatically odd to someone from a Euro-American background. I know that I would have told my children, "Don't do that! You might choke!" Instead, Paiute caregivers' corresponding utterances index the action as coming from the child himself. Shushuuxuts was taught to tell himself "Don't do that" and "I might choke." Rather than expecting others to tell him what to do, he was learning to internalize self-discipline (cf. Vygotsky 1986). This is not surprising, considering that Paiutes emphasize the role of individual autonomy. Note, too, that after two repeated utterances of "I might choke" Kwis returned to "Say, 'Don't do that.'" Although Kwis appeared by her prompt to expect Sai to repeat "Don't do that," Shushuuxuts's response of "I might choke" was also appropriate and demonstrates a beginning internalization of why he should not take big mouthfuls. It also demonstrates that he was listening.

With children older than about three years, however, Paiute caregivers do not model instructions for them to repeat; rather, the caregivers just expect these children to listen and observe.

Although to outsiders San Juan children do not always appear to be paying attention (see Philips 1983:50), they do listen, they do learn, and they usually end up being very helpful and respectful when they get older. Older children take an important role in watching younger children, for example, and are quite responsible helping with daily activities. Two years after the interaction about the fire, Tataats—at seven years old—was now seen by her grandmothers in the interaction below as a helpful, respectful young girl. In the following interaction Tataats's grandmother and her grandmother's sister (both grandmothers to Tataats) praised her helpfulness.

> Example 3. Tataats (T) sits on the couch between her two grandmothers, Na'aintsits Wʉn (N) and Mantsikw (M), in their house, and Mantsikw praises Tataats's helpfulness
> M: T cleaned the house across. (1)
>   She vacuumed. (1)
>   Cleaned up the living room. (3)
>   She's really helpful to her mom. (.0)
> N: She even made her own bed.=
> T: =[giggle]

Linguistic Indexing of Identity

What all this means is that Paiute children from Paiute-speaking families are instructed in traditional Paiute ways and usually end up acting in Paiute-appropriate ways because they have listened and observed. In everyday interactions the caregivers' and the children's goals are generally to get something done: the house cleaned, the dinner cooked, visitors greeted, and so on. In these cases people tend to notice whether the event was successfully concluded and whether the children behaved appropriately for their age. Thus, where the language of the family—or even just of the children—is English rather than Paiute in an interaction, mostly nobody notices. These moments provide occasions when languages can begin to shift almost imperceptibly. There are several possible ways that are not mutually exclusive to understand what is happening here.

1. Since the children generally have behaved appropriately, caregivers tend to categorize the children as having Paiute identity and erase the parts of the behavior that do not fit in, such as that they're not speaking Paiute (Irvine and Gal 2000:38).
2. Everyday language choices tend to go unmarked.
3. Paiute ideology emphasizes listening, hearing, and observing, not immediate production of cultural behavior. Although most San Juan children do not now actively speak Paiute, some of these children demonstrate their knowledge of Paiute by responding to Paiute requests or questions either by performing the activity requested or by responding correctly, albeit in English. Caregivers, therefore, may feel that these children are Paiute speakers or at least potential Paiute speakers.

As San Juan Paiutes belong to a small tribe (now about 255 members) and have been surrounded by Navajo speakers for more than a century, language has always been a distinguishing marker of the group for outsiders. For the Paiutes themselves language was taken for granted, since a core group of families had continued to use Paiute as the home, work, and political language of the tribe. When dealing with outsiders, however, Paiute language was used to index Paiute identity. At some point in the early to mid-1990s two factors converged that made salient (at least intermittently) the language used in interaction between Paiute tribal members. The first factor was the emerging view that the Paiute language was an essential part of an authentic Paiute identity. As Paiute speaking is also associated with Paiute ways of interacting, socialization of youngsters, and traditional worldview and religion, the Paiute language has shifted for some Paiute speakers from one of simply indexing Paiute identity to one where Paiute speaking has become revalorized as emblematic of a distinct social and moral character and of a person who behaves in morally appropriate ways—an instance of Silverstein's (1998a:130–34) second-order indexicality. In Irvine and Gal's (2000:37) terms the relationship between language and identity is viewed by some of the San Juan community iconically rather than simply indexically. Irvine and Gal note that "by picking out qualities supposedly shared by the social image and the linguistic image, the ideological representation—itself a sign—binds them together in a linkage that appears to be inherent" (2000:37). Thus, Paiute speakers seem to consider individuals who speak Paiute to possess the qualities that a Paiute-speaking individual would traditionally have had, and they understand such iconized linkages to be intrinsic or essential.

The second factor encouraging the belief that the Paiute language was essential to Paiute identity was the related development of various linguistic projects taking place in the community, including, by 1995, discussion of possible Paiute language programs. These revitalization-maintenance programs were spurred on by the developing linguistic essentialism or iconization coupled with a beginning awareness that children were not speaking much Paiute.

At least by the late 1990s the marking of language choice was taking place sporadically in everyday situations and perhaps more consistently in formal public contexts. With regard to everyday household interactions, I have heard caregivers tell their children that they should speak Paiute. These rare moments when the focus turns on the language itself are not especially predictable—although I was, of course, present the times I heard it, and my presence may have triggered it. When they told their children to speak Paiute, generally nothing changed in the interaction; I cannot remember ever hearing a child start talking Paiute when told to do so. I also do not think anyone expected them to. For Paiutes the words are there to be gathered or re-collected when needed.

Public interactions, in contrast to everyday ones, are more politicized, more apt to be conscious performances, and, lately, more likely to focus on language. In most public contexts (and this has been true at least since 1980) Paiute is the first language spoken. It is then translated as needed into English, rarely into Navajo. As there are several Paiute-speaking community members whose comprehension of English appears to be minimal, the use of Paiute could be thought of as just a practical necessity.[10] However, Paiute is frequently used when it is not actually necessary for comprehension. In addition, when there is a public forum and Paiute is not used, I have heard grumbling—"We're Paiute, so they should say it in Paiute." Another example of the politicization of the Paiute language and its linkage with Paiute identity took place in 2001 at a workshop on language revitalization when, during a break, a Paiute-speaking man confronted a tribal employee who was from one of the Navajo-speaking Paiute families. The Paiute-speaking man told the other tribal member that since he did not speak Paiute he was not Paiute and should leave the language workshop.[11] Although iconizing the link between language and identity did not create these preexisting divisions in the tribe, it has helped provide a terminology and framing ideology for such situational politics.

In other communities where languages are endangered there are adults who heard the language as children, mastered the language as adults, and taught it in language programs (Alexandra Jaffe, personal communication, 2003), all of which requires a high level of commitment. Such a level of commitment may be easier to develop if community members feel that speaking the endangered language is an essential element of their identity. If that is the case, the Paiute situation has several helpful elements.

1. Fluent adult speakers of Paiute have ideologically iconized Paiute language to their Paiute identity.
2. There are still a number of Paiute speakers of different ages.
3. There are English-dominant children presently being raised hearing Paiute speech, some of which is directed at them. These children and young adults demonstrate comprehension of Paiute interaction and could—if motivated—become speakers and activate their knowledge at a later date.
4. Paiute language socialization ideology supports such a belief: when parents, grandparents, aunts, and uncles say, "You should speak Paiute," they do not expect the addressee to perform right then. It is up to individuals to make the decision whether and when to speak Paiute.

What, then, will happen with the San Juan Paiute language is an important question and one that only the San Juan people will be able to answer. Nevertheless, there are some encouraging signs. The San Juan tribal council, which in the 1990s and early 2000s was composed primarily of Paiute speakers, including one monolingual Paiute speaker, applied for and received a couple of language grants, including an Administration for Native Americans Planning Grant. The tribe is also working on a project that includes immersion summer camps. Compared to many other North American tribes, the San Juan Paiute community, with its core of fluent speakers, is in a good position to reverse the current trend of language loss.[12] However, as we have seen, the current situation does not appear to be producing many new speakers.

In November 2001, as part of the planning grant, Leanne Hinton and Nancy Steele conducted a language revitalization workshop at the Paiute Health Department in Tuba City. In this workshop Hinton and Steele demonstrated their oral communication–based methodology, including the well-known Master-Apprentice Program (Hinton 2001b), and provided many examples of how it could be used flexibly to work in the San Juan situation. They emphasized, in particular, how caregivers could get children to respond in the Native language. An incident at the workshop itself demonstrated the potential success of this strategy. After I turned off the videotape at a break during the last day of the workshop, I observed one caregiver, Tsanna, interacting with her four-and-a-half-year-old nephew, Shushuuxuts, by this time a bilingual Paiute/English speaker. He wanted some food and asked for it in English, but she ignored him until he asked in Paiute. I turned the video recorder back on and got the rest of the interaction on tape.

> Example 4. Tsanna (Ts) with her nephew Shushuuxuts
> Ts: impara'ai? (3) impara'ai ich?=
>   What is it? What is this?
> Sh: =[shrugs] (1) [Ts continues
>   holding the piece of food and
>   looking at S]
>
> Sh: tokoav ala'ai. (.0)
>   It's meat.
> Ts: tokoav ara'ai. =
>   It's meat.
> Sh:=   =tokoav ala'ai. (.0)
>   It's meat.
> Sh: káruts.[13] (1)
>   Carrot.
> Ts: káruts. [holding up a carrot] (.0)
>   Carrot.
> Sh: káruts.
>   Carrot.

In this example as well as in the action that preceded it we see Tsanna using strategies she had just been hearing about and observing in the workshop demonstrations and exercises. Although Tsanna had, in fact, used similar (but not exactly the same) strategies with Shushuuxuts when he was much younger, I had not seen her use them with him for the previous year and a half. I think that the reason this workshop "worked" at least for her was that Hinton and Steele selected strategies compatible with San Juan language practices and ideology to demonstrate. They circumvented the problem of verbal instructions for autonomy by giving Paiute speakers specific strategies that got their children speaking Paiute by making them *want* to do so. They did this by demonstrating—with the help of a Paiute child—the use of untranslated Karuk, a Northern Californian language spoken by Nancy Steele, who was demonstrating the immersion method of the Master-Apprentice Program in play settings and in a participatory storytelling session. They also explained and modeled using the Native language for various everyday and special activities. This latter strategy is most likely to work well when the activities are ones in which the children are excited to participate.

The interaction between Tsanna and Shushuuxuts was especially significant, I felt, because Tsanna had been skeptical about the efficacy of language-teaching methodologies that had been presented at a previous language revitalization workshop she had attended. She had been worried, in particular, about how one could *make* children *not* speak English —a goal she felt was impossible.

A related challenge is for people to recognize that language loss is taking place in spite of young people behaving properly as Paiutes and in spite of caregivers' instructions to their children that they should speak Paiute. After the workshop described above, Paiute speakers expressed concern that their language would be lost if they could not get the younger generations actually speaking. They already were aware that they needed to speak Paiute to the children but at the workshop seemed to begin to appreciate that it was important to get their children responding in Paiute as well.

Although Tsanna, like other tribal elders, believes strongly that Paiute children should be able to make the decision about what language to speak in a given situation, she wants Paiute to continue to be spoken and had been raising Shushuuxuts in a Paiute-speaking household. Prior to this workshop Tsanna and others thought the only solution was to do what Tsanna was doing with Shushuuxuts. Although it *is* probably the best solution, there are two major problems. First, at some point even in this "best practices" scenario the children would start answering in English (indeed, as we saw above, even Shushuuxuts tried to interact in English).

Figure 8.1. Paiute children playing together and talking to Pamela Bunte near Hidden Springs, Arizona, in 2002.

Second, although a number of households had attempted to speak primarily in Paiute, only one was able to sustain the practice. Therefore, having more realistic alternative strategies that would promote Paiute speaking was seen as important. This workshop was crucial because it made people aware that, even though non-Paiute-speaking children may decide to speak Paiute later in life, the future of the Paiute language would be much more secure if they could set up situations where children would more likely speak the language while they were young. Also, there were multiple ways of doing this that could be compatible with Paiute ideologies of socialization.

At this point the future of the Paiute language is unclear. As Hinton reviewed with the group that they should "leave English behind," an interesting interaction took place.

Example 5. As Hinton (LH) speaks, one woman, Mantsikw (M), leans
out and loudly tells her sister, Na'aintsits Wᵾn, to *listen*
LH: *The first point would be to try not to use English with*
　　　　　　your=
M:　　　　　　　　　　　　　　*=Listen to that N!=*
All:　　　　　　　　　　　　　　　　　　　　=[laughter and
　　　　　　　　　　　　　　　　　　　　overlapping Paiute talk]

When Mantsikw told her sister to listen, everybody laughed because
everyone knew that although Na'aintsits Wᵾn is semifluent in English,
she speaks it a great deal of the time with her grandchildren. I think it was
also funny to the group because of the use of the word "listen." Usually
used with children in socialization talk, here the concept was being used
with an adult, one of the socializers. In addition, she said it in English
and not in Paiute, even though she was emphasizing the need to "leave
English behind."[14]

Although this example illustrates some of the challenges faced by the
community, San Juan Paiutes believe that if Paiutes who "know" Paiute—
even if they are nonspeakers—want to speak Paiute, those words will
come to them when they need them. In addition to the case of Angel
Whiskers, there are other precedents for this happening. A Kaibab Paiute
man who used to visit the San Juan had reactivated or regathered the
language that he had as a child and additionally became the song leader
at funerals, and I have seen a young San Juan Paiute man work hard at
reactivating his childhood Paiute speaking.

The San Juan Paiute people, like people in other communities, are
juggling multiple language ideologies, some of which are or seem contradictory (Kulick 1998; Madumulla, Bertoncini, and Blommaert 1999). Indeed, in some cases it is the same people who both believe that the words
(i.e., the language) will come on the wind to be reactivated and that it
might be necessary to set up programs in which the language is taught.
The San Juan Paiute people who hold both beliefs do not seem to feel
conflicted—they are just pragmatically hedging their bets and planning
programs that will get their young people speaking Paiute now rather than
leaving everything to the very real possibility of later words arriving on
the wind.

CHAPTER 9

Embodying the Reversal of Language Shift

Agency, Incorporation, and Language Ideological Change in the Western Mono Community of Central California

PAUL V. KROSKRITY

As Edward Sapir once observed, "Our natural interest in human behavior seems always to vacillate between what is imputed to the culture of the group as a whole and what is imputed to the psychic organization of the individual himself" (1934:408). As a foundational figure for both the Americanist tradition in linguistics and for the field of linguistic anthropology, Sapir realized early on the difficulty and delicacy of achieving that analytical balance between perspectives that emphasize the formative forces of society and culture, on the one hand, and those that highlight individuals and their own psychological imperatives for shaping their worlds of experience, on the other. In this chapter I want to suggest that the wisdom of acknowledging these levels of "warp" and "weft"—if I may extend the imagery of weaving to the ongoing creation of a social fabric—is relevant to language ideological studies of Native American communities and may restore a balance between appreciating the powerful roles of political economic forces and the agency of individual Native American social actors (Deloria 2004).

When Michael Silverstein first defined linguistic ideologies as "sets of beliefs about language articulated by users as a rationalization or justification of perceived language structure and use" (1979:193), he did so not merely to acknowledge the existence of such folk beliefs about language but to demonstrate both their potential and actual potency (as in changes involving the early-nineteenth-century loss of "thou" from non-Quaker English speech and the late-twentieth-century removal of the generic "he" from American English) to transform those structures. The comparatively short history of language ideological theorizing thus originates with an emphasis on speakers' awareness of language and the transformative potential of this consciousness as a form of agency. This is especially noteworthy because most of this research, in its emphasis on symbolic domination, dominant language ideologies, and the socioeconomic foundations for speakers' perspectives on language, typically highlights "structure" rather than "agency." But while such an emphasis on structure is often appropriate and even overdue, given preferences in many forms of linguistic research to construct language as an apolitical object (Kroskrity 2000b, 2004), failure to admit "agency" as an analytical factor robs language ideological research of crucial tools for understanding both language ideological variation and diachronic change.

In this chapter I want to briefly explore some ways in which a contrapuntal emphasis on agency might serve to illuminate processes of language ideological change and begin to redress what Carter and Sealey (2000) describe as the imbalanced treatment of structure and agency. While the scholarly literature on this subject in sociocultural anthropology appropriately problematizes agency in social life by locating it at many different levels of organization, in this chapter I want to deploy Laura Ahearn's "provisional" definition of agency as "the socioculturally mediated capacity to act" (2001:112) as a means of briefly exploring the agency of one member of the Western Mono community of central California. More explicitly, my objective here is to examine two expressions of agency embodied by the Western Mono elder Rosalie Bethel, who until a stroke in 2001 could easily be regarded as her community's leading language activist.[1] I want to read aspects of her agency from two distinct and complementary types of data. One of these sources is life history narratives (Langness and Frank 1981) and their emphasis on "turnings" (Mandelbaum 1973) or experiences of transformation.[2] Complementing this more phenomenological perspective, a close analysis of a brief but important interactional strip of a narrative performance provides an opportunity for microanalysis comparable to the kinds of conversational analyses regularly conducted by anthropologists and sociologists.

This juxtaposition of diverse sources enables an analysis of the types of agency exhibited by an elder and language activist. Here I focus on activities that have either produced language ideological change or resulted in overt action designed to reverse the language shift (to English) that now severely threatens the Western Mono language in such central California towns as North Fork, Auberry, and Dunlop. In both sources I emphasize an especially robust agency that is something more than merely a "capacity to act"; it is rather an awareness leading to the transformation of selves and systems. By reflecting on these instances of noncompliance to language shift and death, I hope to use these "meditations in an emergency" to suggest both the importance of agency in language ideological research and the need for its typological refinement in this context.[3]

Intrinsic and Imposed Relevances for the Western Mono Community

Today Western Mono is an endangered language spoken by members of the Mono community in various central California towns. In communities like North Fork, Auberry, Dunlop, and Sycamore live about fifteen hundred Mono Indian people (Spier 1978). Within this dispersed community there are approximately forty-one highly fluent speakers and perhaps as many as two hundred people with some knowledge of the language (Hinton 1994:27–31).[4] Almost all the highly fluent speakers are sixty-five years of age or older. Western Mono, closely related to languages like Northern Paiute and Shoshoni, is in the Numic branch of the Uto-Aztecan language family.

But Western Mono's status as an endangered language is surely attributable not to its family tree but rather to the hegemonic influence of Spanish and Euro-American invasions. A more comprehensive reconstruction of the indigenous (precontact) local language ideologies as well as a more complete treatment of the impact of these colonial influences in shaping language ideologies in contemporary Western Mono communities are beyond the scope of this chapter and provided elsewhere (Kroskrity 1999, 2002). Nevertheless, it is important to mention three interrelated precolonial language ideological patterns of use as well as the linguistic discrimination of the colonial period as preparatory background for understanding both Rosalie Bethel and her performance of an innovative yet rather traditional coyote story. The three precolonial language ideologies that can be reconstructed as dominant (Kroskrity 1998) are syncretism, variationism, and utilitarianism. Syncretism is a value on linguistic borrowing from neighboring languages that characterized

many California Indian groups (Silver and Miller 1997). One manifestation of syncretism is the high number of loanwords that have entered
Western Mono through the interaction of its community members with
those of neighboring speech communities like the Yokuts and Southern
Sierra Miwoks (e.g., Kroskrity and Reinhardt 1984; Loether 1997). Intertribal relations between these groups often included intermarriage and
multilingualism. This cultural emphasis on hybridity and linguistic pluralism provided no foundation for an indigenous language ideological
"iconization" (Irvine and Gal 2000) between a specific language and
corresponding ethnic identity.

This absence of iconization contrasts markedly with the Euro-
American pattern of "linguistic nationalism" as described by Anderson
(1983; Silverstein 1996:127).[5] Associated with many of these European
nationalist programs is the emphasis on a single standardized national
language that becomes emblematic of a shared national identity for its
citizens. But in contrast to standardizing linguistic regimes that either
seek to eliminate or supplant variation due to region, ethnicity, class, and
so on, Western Mono communities have promoted a language ideology of
variationism in which dialectal variation is not hierarchized but is instead
naturalized as the expected outcome of family and individual differences.
This emphasis has historically valorized such forms of variation even to
the point of honoring family and individual differences rather than adopting a singular or orthodox vision of what is linguistically correct or socio-
linguistically prescribed (Kroskrity 2002). A contemporary reflex of this is
that many Monos still explain cultural differences within their group by
appealing to regional, family, and individual variation (e.g., Gaylen Lee's
[1998] account of Western Mono cultural variation) rather than to a more
correct or authoritative vision of traditional Mono language and culture.
Certainly, many Western Mono people privately view their family's cultural practices as especially authoritative, but they publicly acknowledge
and valorize considerable variation. Variationism as a language ideology
is likely the product of retaining a Great Basin or Numic value on speech
variation founded on the decentralized and relatively nonhierarchical
sociopolitical structures of their ancestral communities.

In addition, members of the community also emphasized the utilitarian nature of language—language as a tool or a technology. When the
Mono community experienced language shift from Mono to English

early in the twentieth century, many parents felt it was inappropriate to teach their native language to their children when it appeared that economic change was necessitating increasingly more use of English. Several of the oldest members of the community reported that their parents refused to teach them their ancestral languages and rationalized this choice by describing their children as *kumasa-tika*, "bread eaters," who would no longer need a language associated with hunting and gathering and acorn-processing activities (like Mono) but would instead require English as the language of the emerging cash economy.[6] In its emphasis on economic adaptation and its "erasure" (Irvine and Gal 2000) of other functions involving cultural transmission and the maintenance of group identity, utilitarianism promoted a rather voluntary view of the language shift to English that swept through Western Mono communities. This more traditional view of languages as tools as well as the linguistic discrimination faced by Mono people in the schools and promoted by the federal and state governments played a role in reducing the number of speakers who would pass their language of heritage on to younger generations.

Though ethnocidal educational policies did much to link Mono and other indigenous languages to a "stigmatized ethnic identity" (often an important factor in cases of language shift, as in Dorian's [1981] study of East Sutherland Gaelic, Gal's [1979] research on Hungarian speakers in the Austrian community of Oberwart, and Kulick's [1992] examination of Gapun language shift), such practices did not and could not dictate English as the language of the home. The utilitarian view of language that associates it with technoeconomic strategies prompted many multilingual parents to make English the language of the home because of its enhanced utility in a continually more encompassing cash economy.

Today the language shift is almost complete in that English now performs virtually all the functions once performed by Western Mono. The one domain in which Mono language and song persist is in Native religious activities, where Mono is strongly preferred. But the lack of a vital ancestral language has not led to a collapse of the Western Mono community. In their view Mono people are such not by virtue of speaking an ancestral language but by participating in Native activities, including festivals and funerals, and by assisting their family and friends within the group. The language is viewed as a significant cultural resource but not any more so than a knowledge of basket making or plant use. This, at least, was the state of affairs when I began the UCLA Mono Language Project in 1980 and began conducting workshops with community members during which we, at the request of Rosalie Bethel, produced a dictionary of Western Mono designed for community members (Bethel et al. 1984).

But three interrelated developments seem to signal a new day for the Mono language as a symbol of Mono cultural identity. Its incorporation in language and culture programs in the schools, its symbolic role in the battle for federal recognition, and the Native American Languages Acts of 1990 and 1992 all promote a rethinking of local linkages between a language of heritage and an ethnic identity. It is now fashionable for Mono people to call themselves Nium, using the Native self-designation as a loanword into local English.[7] Local schools have used a combination of federal funds and local monies to create Mono language and culture classes for all students. These classes are not designed to restore fluency to the community but rather to familiarize Mono and other children with important cultural vocabulary (kin terms, food names, place-names) and linguistic routines (greetings and closings). These terms are explicitly linked to Mono culture and identity and represent curriculum innovations designed to improve the self-image of Indian students. Students who receive these lessons certainly receive from their early classroom experience a message very different from the one experienced by Rosalie Bethel and her generation.

On another front, Western Monos have been one of many California Indian tribes to seek federal recognition. The rigorous criteria that must be met by candidates for recognition do not explicitly mention languages, but they do mention the need to demonstrate maintenance of cultural continuity. Thus, even a partial reversal of language shift in the direction of the indigenous language, even if it approximates the limited goals of so-called language and culture language renewal programs, represents a development of great personal and political significance for many members of the Western Mono community. While under the present policies of hegemonic institutions such as schools and government agencies that have clearly reversed practices of discrimination, encouraged participation in language revitalization activities, and explicitly inscribed the linkage of Mono language and identity, many Monos have clearly revised the traditional absence of an iconized (Irvine and Gal 2000) relationship between language and identity that was once manifested in the formerly dominant indigenous language ideologies like utilitarianism and syncretism. For them the now-dominant language ideology of the nation-state, one that explicitly links language and identity, has "trickled down" into local consciousness. But some individuals anticipated this process because they were preadapted much earlier for this correlation of language and identity by their own personal experience. Rosalie Bethel is such a person.

Rosalie Bethel: The Incorporated History of a Language Activist

For one central member of this community and the narrator of the story "Coyote Races the Little Mole," this rebirth of interest in Mono language and culture was not rekindled in the more generous climate of language ideological change (from "above") within the past three decades but rather in one that had been burning brightly for many previous decades. Though a comprehensive treatment of how Rosalie Bethel's life experience, her "incorporated history" (Bourdieu 1990:66), prepared her for her current role as both a champion for language renewal and a proponent of language ideological change must await a more comprehensive lingual life history (Kroskrity 1993a), here I observe several biographical details that permitted Rosalie Bethel to personally anticipate certain ideological changes that were to sweep through Mono communities at a later date.

One of the important details concerns Rosalie's early childhood experience of language and identity both within her own home and in her early school experience. Her mother, Annie Wenz, was a relatively monolingual Mono woman from the North Fork band, but her father was a German immigrant who came to California initially as a mason who expected to find work after the great San Francisco earthquake had leveled much of the city. Despite linguistic differences that were never bridged, Rosalie's parents maintained a stable household in which Rosalie prospered in her early childhood years. Though her father was a good provider for the family, he became intolerant of his wife and daughter's participation in indigenous cultural activities shortly before he abandoned them altogether. As a mixed-blood child in a family in which cultural differences regularly contended and conflicted, Rosalie early on experienced a social world in which languages were iconized (Irvine and Gal 2000) to cultural identities. While other Mono children experienced a more syncretic or hybridizing approach to cultural differences within and outside their homes, Rosalie's experience was one of polarization, of having to choose between mutually exclusive identities rather than adopt a hybridized identity. Her father, after divorcing his wife, further attempted to remove Rosalie from additional Native influence by placing her in a mission orphanage rather than in the custody of her own mother.

> My father tried to make me stop speaking Mono and going to events with other Mono people. He even tried to stop me from talking to my mother but I refused. When I would not go away with him and leave my mother, he brought me to the Mission and told them my mother was "unfit" to take care of me because she was an Indian. So they kept me there and only once in a while could I see my mother when they let her visit me. When I was lonely and had nobody to talk to I spoke Mono to myself at night to remind me of her so I would not be so sad. (Rosalie Bethel, personal communication)

This mission experience as well as her early experience in public schools confirmed for Rosalie the apparent incompatibility of "Indian" and "white" as she was subjected to teachings and practices that clearly stigmatized indigenous cultures and languages and attempted to expunge them from the children. The stigma of being "Indian," as Rosalie Bethel still recalls, was so polluting that non-Indian children were encouraged to use sticks rather than directly touch or hold hands with Indian children in the course of classroom and general school activities. But whereas Rosalie's mixed-blood status and her indigenous cultural orientation denied her the status of being "white," they did not pose any problems for her acceptance in the Mono community. Since local criteria for inclusion were long on cultural requirements and exceedingly short on genetic purity, Rosalie was consistently acknowledged as a member because of her fluency in the language and her vast storehouse of Mono cultural knowledge, which she continued to learn as an adult from cultural leaders in the community even after the death of her mother. These elders were willing to converse with a relatively young woman who spoke Mono so well and who seemed so interested in the cultural details of gathering plants, dispensing Native medicines, and performing important ritual events.

Rosalie's successful resistance to the attempted socialization to stigmatized status by both the mission and public elementary schools was supported by many elders within the Mono community, by her attending Sherman Indian School in Riverside, California, and by her successful adoption of the role of a culture broker in which she mediated between the Mono community and the dominant Euro-American society. Rosalie Bethel has always credited many Western Mono elders for sharing their cultural knowledge with her and encouraging her to learn as much as she could about the Mono culture.[8] Rosalie's association with the elders while she was young was partially their attempt to compensate for the disruptive influence of her non-Native father and his attempts to tear her away from her maternal culture. She described the situation: "Many of our people looked out for me because they knew my father had sort of abandoned us. Children usually get lots of help from their father and his family and since I didn't have that kind of help many folks stepped in to give me a hand when I was growing up."

While Rosalie was secure in her Mono identity, her attendance at Sherman Indian School in Riverside, California, proved to be an experience that only fortified this identity rather than diminished it. Ironically, while such vocational schools were designed in accord with assimilationist philosophies to impart skills and values that would prepare students for the bottom-rung jobs in a capitalist economy, Rosalie found that meeting other young women from a variety of other California Indian communities actually enhanced her sense of being a Native American and sparked her additional interest and determination to know more about her own indigenous heritage.

> You know they taught us to cook and clean house, I guess we were being trained to be maids. But I was never much good at it! All that work and in a short while all that dust and mess, it just comes right back! But what I really liked was getting to meet so many other Indian women about my age. They seemed to come from everywhere—there were Chukchansis and Mojaves, Paiutes and Cahuillas. We seemed to have so much in common with each other and we sure got along real well. Some of those girls knew things about their own ways of doing things that I didn't know about mine. So right then I made up my mind to go back to North Fork and learn everything I could about my people.

When Rosalie did return to her home community, it was not to practice the domestic skills that she had learned at school but rather to learn more about her culture and to begin to play a role as an important mediator between her community and the institutions of the dominant society. One of her earliest experiences in this regard was her service as a translator for the linguist Sydney Lamb, who performed his dissertation research in North Fork using the largely monolingual Lucy Kinsman, a North Fork Mono, as his principal consultant. Though Lamb's (1957) dissertation had a highly circumscribed focus on phonology and morphology, as was typical of the Bloomfieldian structuralist period in which he worked, his work provided a kind of breakthrough experience for Rosalie Bethel.

Before I did that work with Sydney Lamb and Mrs. Kinsman I think I really took my [Mono] language for granted. I could tell by the questions he was asking and the answers she was giving that there was a lot of patterning to our language. Hearing those designs in our language made me even more interested in it and made me more aware that not many people were learning these things. I think it also made me think about linguists as very talented people but it also helped me to understand that our language was special. It had its own sounds and ways of saying things and I came to appreciate the need for working to make sure that we can save this language for our people, for our children especially.

In my first year of teaching at UCLA in 1979 a niece of Rosalie Bethel who was completing a graduate degree in film studies contacted me. She told me that her aunt wanted to meet me because she was interested in working with a linguist who wanted to help her document the Mono language. It is clear that she took this work seriously, even though she lacked any formal training in linguistics, for when I first met her in 1980 she had compiled two shoeboxes full of index cards, each containing a Mono vocabulary item. For the next twenty years she was the central figure of the community-based UCLA Mono Language Project, which would ultimately produce a descriptive grammar, a dictionary (Bethel et al. 1984), and even a CD-ROM (Kroskrity 2002; Kroskrity, Bethel, and Reynolds 2002).

Even in this highly abbreviated form, this brief sketch surely suggests the biographical experiences that would be responsible for Rosalie's own language ideological reformulation of Mono utilitarianism. For her the Mono language was more than just a reference guide to plant names and gathering strategies; it was inextricably connected with issues of identity. For her the ancestral language, which linked her to her mother and maternal culture, became deeply connected with her personal and cultural identity as a Mono person, with a means, as she put it, "for knowing who we are" (Kroskrity, Bethel, and Reynolds 2002). While the agency of Rosalie Bethel's innovation of iconizing language and identity suggests the importance of individuals as loci for language ideological change, it may also open this study up to critiques of Western preoccupation with "atomic" individualism (Ortner 1996). But a perspective informed by an individual's "incorporated history" is necessarily an account of a person's confrontation with the imposed relevances of his or her social world. Even highly salient forms of agency involved in "heroic" transformation of self and system are clearly social products. Thus, Rosalie Bethel's rethinking of culturally available ways of linking language and identity is not the result of some private meditation but rather the outcome of an imposed agenda that intruded upon her early on and required her to problematize notions of language and identity that others in her community could more easily take for granted.

Rosalie Bethel's Recontextualization of "Coyote Races the Little Mole": Embodied Ideologies in Performance

In addition to reading forms of agency from the narratives of life history data, it is useful to see them manifested in interaction. Since Rosalie was both the main consultant for the Mono Language Project as well as its local organizational representative, she took on a dual responsibility on the evening of January 5, 1993, both by attempting to provide a model narrative and by calling together a meeting of the North Fork Mono "academy"—elders whose specialized knowledge of Mono culture (e.g., Lee 1998), including history, basket making, language, and plant technology (Goode 1992), earned them the status of expert within and often outside of their local community.

On the agenda that evening was the topic of orthography and the formatting and presentational aspects of a new version of the *Practical Dictionary of Western Mono*. What the participants were somewhat unpre-

Figure 9.1. Rosalie Bethel tosses a superheated rock out of her cooking basket as she prepares acorn dumplings for attendees to the UCLA Mono Language Workshop held in July 1981. The digitized photo is part of a background screen from the interactive CD-ROM *Taitaduhaan: Western Mono Ways of Speaking*.

pared for was a plan presented by Rosalie Bethel to lead by example in the offering of stories and songs, which could be recorded. As the last couple of invited experts entered and took their seats, I noticed that Rosalie's greetings were becoming more mechanical and that her responses to my conversation conveyed a distraction. As I noticed her becoming almost meditatively preoccupied and then reengaging with a smile on her face and that special gleam in her eyes, I suddenly remembered her flair for the dramatic, and I plunged my hands into the camera bag at my feet.

Just as I grabbed my SONY 8 mm camera, Rosalie, without introduction, burst into the narrative "Coyote Races the Little Mole."[9] While both textual and interactive levels of analysis warrant full treatments in their own right, my goal here is to focus on only two emergent features of performance as expressions of agency in her recontextualization of the story. The features of the performance that receive analytical attention are (1) Rosalie's general orientation to an imagined audience reachable through the video camera (as revealed by visual analysis of her nonverbal behavior) and (2) her inclusion of an explanatory section in a story for which all previous versions show no comparable explication.

The first of these recontextualizing moves is manifested in eye contact and body orientation. Though body orientation, gesture, and facial expression are a part of all performed "oral traditions" as well as conversational storytelling in general, these bodily practices are especially important in the analysis of this narrative event. A close analysis of the videotaped performance reveals that when Rosalie narrates the story, she does not orient to the audience of Native experts present in the physical setting but rather to the unseen, "imagined" audience represented by the video camera. Her marked lack of eye contact with a copresent audience is actually a form of avoidance, which itself provides an important detail that might be variously understood as a metacommunicative recontextualization cue or a performance key (Bauman 1975; Gumperz 1982; Hymes 1981). At this level, the near-complete lack of eye contact actively signals that this performance is not primarily aimed at the copresent audience but is to be evaluated as a kind of pedagogical discourse directed at those who need either language instruction or narrative explication. When this metacommunicative level is recognized, we see that Rosalie's lack of interest in establishing a mutual gaze with any of her copresent audience members is not an embodiment of inattention to them but rather a respectful gesture that conveys critical information as to how the whole performance should be interpreted.

This second recontextualizing move adds unusual explanatory material, as indicated in example 2 below. In all previously recorded versions of the story—those performed both for researchers who were part of the Mono Language Project "team" and for her close Mono-speaking friends in the community—no such section exists. A sentence like example 1, which is the sixty-first sentence of the performed narrative, would often have served as the concluding sentence. Such a practice is consistent with an older traditional strategy of requiring very active participation by the hearer to supply unstated cultural knowledge and to make culturally appropriate inferences.

Example 1.
Onnoho yaisi onno na-ponaa-kU.
Then and then PAS-win-NOM:OBL[10]
'And then (he knew) he was beaten.'

But in this performance the story ends with an explanatory section.

Example 2. Explanatory coda to "Coyote Races the Little Mole"

2 RB: [Uhu mɨyu-tsi' (.) [nihi tɨsumiya-daa-pI].
       [((leans forward))[((leans back, low volume))
       that mole-DIM very think-HAB-COMPL
       'That little mole had been very thoughtful.'

3   Uhu mɨyu-tsi' ti-poso'o-hotU yaduha-s ihi sunawi-t.
       that mole-DIM own-friend-with talk-SUB he thought
       'That little mole had talked with his friends and planned it.'

4   "Hɨ-bo' 'a-wiya'! ['a-inee-s, ɨɨ-bo' iga-gaa-wai."
       [((gestures to pick something up))
       you-EMPH IMP-go, him-say-SUB you-EMPH enter-go-FUT.
       "When he says, 'Go!' you enter (the burrow)."

5   "Taaqwa yaisi iya [sɨmɨ'-a a-na-wadiqa-qwee-dugu
       [((begins to move hand as if placing))]
       We: INCL and there one-OBL it-PAS-finish-LOC-through
       "And another one, across the finish line
            "[a-dɨgɨ'i-wai.
            [((places imaginary mole))
            him-place-FUT.
            we will place."

6   "Mowahu yaisi isa' pitihuu-gaa-wai-s ɨɨ-bo',
           [Nii tɨ-wusu'a-t' inee-wai.
       [((throws up hands in abbreviated replay of celebration))]
       Now and coyote arrive-go-FUT-SUB you-EMPH
           'I it-win' say-FUT.
       "And now just as Coyote approaches (the finish), 'I won!' you say."

7   ["Taaqwa-bo' nasimi-tU mɨyu simi'i-nisU [sunawi-di.
       [((looks left, panning head)) [((looks right))
       We: INCL-EMPH all-SUBJ mole one-like appear-PROG.
       "We moles all [look alike."

8   "Qadu'u yaisi uhu isa' [sutabihi-dɨ.
       [((looks over to left, flips her hand up))

NEG and that coyote know-can-TNS
"And that Coyote cannot [figure it out."
9 [Uwamaqahuu ti-ponaa-t.
   [(((Facing right and ending with a nod to camera))
   In:this:way it-win-TNS
   'That's how it was won.'
10 Audience Member: ano'otU [barely audible]
                      enough
                   'That's all.'
11 RB: [Onno [a-na-wadiqa-nU.]
        [(((brief head movement without mutual gaze to left))
        [(((looking directly at camera))
        then its-PAS-finish-NOM
        'Then, it's finished.'

In Richard Bauman's (1986) well-known study of Texas storyteller Ed Bell's different performances of the same tall tale, Bauman found that Bell's narratives to professional, in-group audiences tended to lack the detail and elaboration that characterized his performances to relatively anonymous and noncocultural audiences. But Bethel's telling of this same narrative, identical in all other aspects, to this in-group actually includes key explanatory material left unexplicated in the other versions. Either hearers must know from the more traditional form of the story that a team of moles (and not a single, exceptionally fast mole) defeats Coyote, or they are left to wonder, like Coyote himself, how someone with such comparatively long legs could lose to one so much smaller.

So why tell knowledgeable audience members something they already know? Rosalie's performance is, in part, to an imagined Mono speech community that includes some members who may have acquired the linguistic skills to understand her narrative but who nevertheless lack the cultural familiarity and access to a narrative-external explanatory discourse. Thus, her story is recontextualized to a new audience that does not already bring a large stock of cultural and linguistic knowledge to her telling of the narrative, to an imagined audience now learning its language and culture of heritage from her through this new media technology.

But though Rosalie physically orients to this imaginary audience (as previously mentioned), it is important to remember that she has not completely forgotten her immediate audience—this is apparent in her nod to me to stop recording, in her preference for later self-concluding the narrative as a display of authority, and in her postnarrative framing (unrecorded) in which she retrospectively frames her performed narrative as a cultural model that can be given to young people through an appropriate educational technology and thereby assist in the now widely valued project of "saving" the Mono language and culture. Thus, just as the audiences of this performance are multiple, so too are the narrator's motives: teaching and entertaining through traditional narratives, promoting the ancestral language, manifesting cultural identity, displaying cultural and linguistic authority, and providing an exemplary performance of a novel pedagogical discourse expressed in the indigenous language.

As for agency in this performance, one can find it in many forms and at many levels. Among these there is the agency of the performer of verbal art, invoking cultural frames and inviting audience evaluation (Bauman 1975). There is the agency of telling any narrative, "personal" or "traditional" (to use a conventional but false dichotomy), and of encoding it in the Mono language. There is the agency of recontextualizing a narrative, especially in the innovative form offered by Bethel above, in order to make a performance that especially fits the audience and setting. There is the agency associated with Rosalie Bethel exercising her preference to close her own story, (as in example 2, line 11). But my goal here is not to find an omnipresent agency, a mantra parallel to the caricature of Foucault that finds "power, power, everywhere," or to affirm what Alessandro Duranti (2004a) eloquently termed "the inevitability of agency." Rather, my objective in this chapter is to explore some of the more promising connections between agency and language ideologies that might be revealed when we closely attend to the language ideologies embodied by individual speakers with distinct lingual life histories. Regarding "ideological awareness," the focus on Rosalie Bethel's "incorporated history" (Bourdieu 1990:66) has provided a case study that suggests some of the factors that make uncritical acceptance of dominant ideologies problematic. It also prompts some members to change or improvise forms of action that may, as in the case of Mono language ideologies regarding language and identity, anticipate more general acceptance in the community at a later date. Even in its abbreviated form here this sketch of an aspect of Rosalie Bethel's lingual life history provides some insights into the appreciation of "linguistic individuals" that offers an alternative to their being treated as merely a distinctive array of linguistic styles (e.g., Johnstone 1996).

Regarding language ideologies read from interaction as well as from interactional data, I also have suggested the importance of recognizing a particularly robust agency associated with the goal of transformative change. In the case of this retelling of a Coyote story, Bethel modeled a novel pedagogical discourse in an attempt to persuade other elders to do likewise as part of the current movement to revitalize and renew Western Mono language and culture. She collaboratively, with my partially informed assistance, produced a video-recorded performance designed for nonpresent audiences. Though apparently spontaneous in its abrupt and apparent lack of introductory framing, this "modeling" performance by Rosalie Bethel requires some interpretive unpacking in regard to its intentionality. It is useful to clarify that on the basis of conversations with Rosalie just prior to the meeting I was aware that she had prepared something to present to the group, something designed to encourage participation either in more immediate recordings for the Mono Language Project or in later, comparable efforts designed to present aspects of Mono language and culture to younger Mono learners. I thought she would use the meeting to encourage other elders to assist in a project aimed at recording heritage language narratives. Given the widespread use of English in the community, I expected her message to be delivered in English. Instead she chose to lead by example. One problem with describing her performance as a kind of "modeling" is the potential for overclaiming intentionality, for viewing it as totalizing consciousness of all aspects of performance. But certainly her performance is selectively intentional—she knows what she wants to achieve, but she relies on her intuitions as a performer to "select" the interactional means of making her performance into a demonstration. As such, the interactional means of recontextualizing the story and conveying the pedagogical "model" was more an "emergent" aspect of performance (Bauman 1975; Williams 1977) than a self-conscious act.

Though transformative in its intent to introduce a new discursive form for an audience, the practice of providing a tangible example rather than merely talking about the "proposed" model is highly in accord with local language ideologies that emphasize the utilitarian side of language and that assume very actively engaged listeners who can figure it out themselves without potentially offensive explication. Thus, even bold innovative moves—like the recontextualization detailed above—are often presented in more culturally familiar frames. The other elders were surprised by Rosalie Bethel's performance, but they were hardly shocked by it, and many would later speak approvingly of its general message.

While the comparatively petite forms of agency associated with practical consciousness and language ideological drift will always remain an important focus of research that acknowledges the relatively quiet power of language ideologies, we cannot disregard the more self-conscious and discursively aware forms of agency that represent more salient attempts to change the self and its role in the system in part by challenging typically uncontested ideologies. Only through better understanding of both agencies, robust and petite, and the further exploration of the analytical terrain between them will it be possible to fully understand language ideologies as dynamic social processes.[11]

Conclusions: Reflections on Agency and Language Ideologies

Given the rather wide range of definitions and analytical proposals regarding agency that have emerged from recent sociocultural research on agency (e.g., Ahearn 2001; Comaroff and Comaroff 1997; Karp 1986; Ortner 1996) and given the limited scope of the present chapter, I restrict my discussion to three intersecting dimensions that strike me—on the basis of research just discussed—as potentially very significant areas of mutual concern to students of agency and of language ideological processes. The first of these is the dimension of awareness, ranging from something like embodied practices with only a "practical consciousness," on the one hand, to explicitly intentional and discursively conscious, on the other. Rosalie Bethel's explicit plan to do a "demonstration performance" exemplifies the latter, while her personal innovation of an iconization of language and identity better approximates the former. Though such differential awareness clearly has implications for how agency will be expressed, with self-consciousness more closely correlated with modes of presentation and reception that enjoy some cultural currency, it need not be viewed as a determining factor in attempts at transformative change or in distinguishing such robust change from mere reproduction. In other words, discursive consciousness—the capacity to be so aware of some aspect of one's language (either use or structure) that one can verbalize about it—need not be viewed as the prerequisite of transformative change but rather as the necessary condition of a relevant metalanguage or of an explicit strategy for promoting change. Also relevant here is the foundational observation of language ideological research (e.g., Silverstein 1981) that not all aspects of language structure and use are equally available to members' awareness and ideological processing. Many discourse phenomena routinely fly beneath the language ideological radar of speakers (e.g., Kroskrity 1997; Scollon and Scollon 1981).[12] In my discussion above, Rosalie Bethel's partial awareness of her demonstration performance suggests the strategic innovation of a discourse form that often resists awareness as well as a general lack of awareness of the actual performance details that "key" that performance. She was very aware of text editing involving the addition of the explanatory coda yet selectively unaware of how she had used gaze avoidance in her storytelling to metacommunicate the existence of another, largely nonpresent audience.

The second dimension invokes a continuum between social transformation and social reproduction. As in the performance of routine social forms and norms, most social activities consist of action that is simultaneously creatively innovative and mere social reproduction. Rosalie Bethel's recontextualized Coyote story is certainly no exception. We could say that she merely reproduces local language ideologies regarding the cultural prescriptions concerning time (evening) and season (winter) for telling traditional stories. But she does syncretically transform the structure of her story to include an elaborated code–like, pedagogical discourse–type explication. Similarly, her life history also suggests that while she merely reproduced many local language ideologies (like utilitarianism and variationism) that were dominant in the indigenous community with which she identified, the extraordinary circumstances of her early experience of language and identity strongly predisposed her to problematize local notions and innovate a more personally meaningful language ideology involving the iconization of language and identity. The fact that her move to this position, unlike the more recent moves of the majority of Mono community members, was not modeled or scaffolded by hegemonic institutions of the state does not rob these others of their agency. It merely recognizes the greater agency required of those who innovate and often stand relatively alone, waiting for others to align. Creating a useful distinction, Karp (1986:137) reserves "agency" for such "effective" action, preferring to use the term "actor" for those persons whose action is clearly more the product of orienting to existing rules.

The final dimension of agency that is useful to discuss here is that of consequentiality—the influence on self and others. In the performance data we can usefully distinguish between those consequences that more closely approximate her objectives as a performer—her production of a demonstration story and her relatively effective appeal to other elders for greater involvement—and certain consequences. In this performance the unintended consequences included the fact that her recorded images would later be digitized and incorporated into *Taitaduhaan: Western Mono Ways of Speaking* (Kroskrity, Bethel, and Reynolds 2002)—a multimedia CD-ROM currently being used by members of the Mono community in their language revitalization efforts. Another observation about consequentiality that emerges more from the life history data than from the performance concerns the impact of influence. Rosalie Bethel's life history strongly suggests that individuals concerned with changing language ideologies can often be more successful in influencing themselves rather than others. Her life history shows many decisions that consistently demonstrate her iconization of language and identity well before the current conversion to the stance that is promoted by hegemonic institutions. Regarding the influence on language ideological change innovated by individuals on others in their community, it is also wise to indicate that such influences cannot be fairly judged by results alone, since dominant language ideologies associated with state-supported languages often wield a powerful influence (Dorian 1998), and many indigenous communities contain a variety of voices that speak against any change that would promote indigenous languages in any way (e.g., Dauenhauer and Dauenhauer 1998; House 2002). Given such powerful and contending forces, individual innovators—the language activists themselves—may influence others' thoughtful reception only to have a possibly more overt influence checked by these other competing factors. In other words, influence, like agency itself, must be contextually assessed.

I would like to conclude this chapter with both a cautionary statement and an exhortation regarding the study of agency and, perhaps more specifically, individual agency. There is, of course, no need to limit a discussion of the language ideological implications of agency to individual agency, since there is already a substantial literature in sociocultural anthropology that would locate it elsewhere (Ahearn 2001:112–18). The present discussion is thus restricted to the limited data at hand. But in this context it is useful to observe the danger of reifying individuals or of indulging the personalist bias of Euro-American culture in representing individuals as heroic figures immune to the pressures of socioeconomic systems. Even in these abbreviated vignettes presented here I think I have suggested ways to construct individuals as responsive to such political economic contexts and to locate their agency against this background, but the weighting of structure and agency is certainly subject to a range of interpretations. Finally (the promised exhortation), an appropriate end-point of this chapter is the importance of this work to viewing not only the language ideological processes that underlie change but also the way attending to language ideologies at this level permits an appreciation of the multiple voices within a society. As Hymes has instructively observed, "One way to think about a society is in terms of the voices it has and might have" (1979:44).

PART III

Linguistic Description, Language Activism, and Reflexive Concerns

CHAPTER 10

Shaming the Shift Generation

Intersecting Ideologies of Family and Linguistic Revitalization in Guatemala

JENNIFER F. REYNOLDS

During one late afternoon in August 1994 the teacher of an adult Kaqchikel literacy class sponsored by the Academia de Lenguas Mayas de Guatemala (Mayan Languages Academy of Guatemala, or ALMG), a prominent and autonomous Maya organization devoted to the standardization and modernization of Mayan languages, assigned the following parable to be read aloud and discussed for its cultural significance to Kaqchikel Mayas. "Man Kach'oke' (Katz'uye')" (Don't Sit Down [Sit Down]) is one among a collection of parables in a pamphlet entitled *Ri Na'oj: Maya K'aslemal—Maya Ch'ab'äl* (The Belief: Maya Way of Life—Mayan Language):

> Man kach'oke' pa ruch'okolb'äl jun ti ri'j winäq,
> roma chanin nisaqïr ri rusumal awi'.

> Don't sit down upon the chair of an elder,
> or else your hair quickly will turn white.

Juana Mactzul Batz authored the text, which was published by the Linguistic Institute/PRODIPMA, Universidad Rafael Landívar (URL). Rafael Landívar is one of the few Ladino (non-Indian, i.e., people of European or mixed ancestry) institutions in Guatemala to employ influential Maya leaders and linguists, members of a Pan-Maya social movement whose primary mission is to revive and revitalize Guatemala's twenty-one Mayan languages (England 2003; Warren 1998).[1] While "Man Kach'oke'" is first and foremost a pedagogical text, it is also a Pan-Maya ideological response to the perceived increasing numbers of Spanish monolingual Maya children. In the 1990s Pan-Mayas felt compelled to concentrate and consolidate their strategies in reversing language shift by politicizing domestic spheres of language use. In what follows I examine how Pan-Mayas' language ideologies enmesh culturally salient ideologies of familial authority and respect in their macro- and microstruggles to secure the future for their communities in an "unstable place" (Greenhouse, Mertz, and Warren 2002).

Classroom discussion over the form and content of that parable occurred almost a decade ago, but Pan-Maya texts like "Man Kach'oke'" resonate even more now that Guatemala has entered the "postwar" phase of its history. Since ex-president Álvaro Arzú signed the peace accords in 1996, representatives of the Maya movement, like other previously excluded sectors, have been allowed to participate as interlocutors in public forums on how to achieve peace and democracy in a country that, since its independence from Spain and especially after the U.S.–assisted military coup d'état of 1954, had only known military forms of governance and a thirty-six-year civil war turned genocidal project. In addressing the question of how to democratize a society that has relied upon a "culture of violence," many sectors, including representatives of Maya organizations, acknowledged that one begins with reforming the institution of "the family."[2] Despite many different contending constructions of what this Guatemalan family should look like, "the family" has become a metonym for a democratic nation-state. For example, in the national media the authoritarian state was likened to an adult, male-dominated household. *Prensa Libre*'s opinion columnist, Maíces (a.k.a. Carlos Aldana Mendoza), wrote on March 12, 1998, "Adults (parents) have the right to control, dominate, and *order* (in the most militaristic sense of the word) children to blindly and acritically obey." He argued that the new construction of family (i.e., a liberal democratic family) would engender "a community of people" and that democratizing society begins at home, where parents would exercise authority, not authoritarianism. Additional alternative visions of the family also reflected positions held by the Religious Right, universal rights advocates, and cultural rights activists. Pan-Mayas' cultural politics intervened in these debates with the demand to create a Maya nation concerned with preserving family practices according to *una Cosmovisión Maya* (a Maya Cosmology), making domestic language use an issue of identity politics and reintroducing literacy in Mayan languages via adult literacy courses (Brown 1998c).[3]

First, I provide a brief history of Pan-Mayas' participation within the greater Maya social movement in order to situate it within the politics of culture currently being fought over linguistic terrain. Of considerable importance to this history is the role that past and present North American linguists and sociolinguists have played in characterizing Guatemala's linguistic diversity and theorizing language shift. Pan-Mayas have combined North American experts' theories and analyses of language shift with their indigenous insider knowledge of typical Maya familial relations in order to "shame" young families and youths into speaking or learning to speak Mayan languages.[4] The efficacy of these strategies, evidenced in the parable "Man Kach'oke'" and its subsequent reinterpretation within an adult literacy course, are examined to illustrate how Pan-Maya ideologies of family, respect, and language at times mischaracterize family intergenerational dynamics and the functional distribution and interpretation of language socialization practices. This chapter thus contributes to an ongoing dialogue between North American scholars and their Pan-Maya counterparts to find constructive ways to appeal to geographically mobile Mayas and restless youths by generating "effective cross-class and cross-generation connections at the very moment when stratification within Maya communities is growing and marked in novel ways" (Warren 1998:204).[5]

Pan-Maya Activism: Pre- and Postconflict Guatemala

Pan-Maya language activism and the greater Maya cultural movement of which it is a part are currently being led by a group of Maya intellectuals. Many of the objectives of the movement revolve around the creation of a unique Maya nation (Cojtí Cuxil 1996; Warren 1992, 1998) defined by the principles of self-determination, cultural and linguistic pride, an abstract, translocal ethnicity, and "the belief that a rejuvenated Mayan culture can peacefully lead Guatemala into a truly culturally pluralist future" (Brown 1998c:156). Brown (1998c), citing Fischer (1992), argues that the Pan-Maya cultural approach to politics has allowed the movement to flourish during turbulent political times and has effectively created a new space for political expression and activism that empowers Mayas to reject hegemonic Ladino representations that denigrate or negate Mayan languages and cultures. Obvious examples of this are how most Guatemalans, including

Mayas, may still refer to Mayan languages using the pejorative terms *dialecto* (dialect) and *lengua* (tongue) as if Mayan languages were un-grammatical and undeserving of the *idioma* (language) status attributed to *castellano* (the Spanish language).

Guatemalan critics of Pan-Mayanism during the 1990s tried to under-mine the movement by arguing that Pan-Maya leadership and its "Maya fundamentalism" were nothing but an elite construction that misrepre-sented the interests of the "real" Maya rural majority. (See Warren [1998] for an in-depth discussion of opponents' critiques of Pan-Mayanism.) They contended that Pan-Mayas were inauthentic representatives, mem-bers of an urban, educated minority, some of whom were not fluent in a Mayan language (Brown 1998c). North American supporters dismissed this critique by underscoring the fact that there was variation within the movement, and although there were some who participated in princi-pally academic forums, there were plenty of Pan-Mayas working in ap-plied settings at all societal levels (Warren 1998).

Mayanists themselves refuted criticisms of opponents on the Right and Left as examples of the same old Ladino politics of assimilation. They maintained that both groups in their respective nationalist projects have historically viewed Mayas as the "Indian problem," traditional obstacles on the paved road toward modern progress (Cojtí Cuxil 1996; Smith 1990). Even in cases when other Mayas have viewed the movement as politically ineffective or in cases where local language communities feel the politics of Pan-Mayanism to be too restrictive (Little 2004), there is some evidence to suggest that core ideas generated by the movement are being dissemi-nated at large to the Maya population (England 2003; French 2001).

Pan-Maya counterhegemonic discourses of the late 1980s and early 1990s advocated a strategic cultural essentialism that emphasized cultural continuity in accordance with a Maya Cosmology as well as underscored active forms of indigenous resistance to cultural changes. Pan-Maya dis-courses on the traditional family held children and youths responsible for rejecting "outside" influences, solely respecting the old ways of their elders and ancestors (Fisher 1999; Fisher and Brown 1996; Warren 1992, 1998; Watanabe 2000). This placed pressure on children and youths to display deference to elders and parents, speak an ancestral language in addition to Spanish, and, in the case of girls, wear handwoven Maya clothing (Otzoy 1996).

Pan-Mayas' politics of cultural difference also have been coupled with the "science" of structural-functional linguistics and seek to reverse "divide and conquer" colonial and postcolonial language policies (Brown 1998c; England 1996, 2003; French 2003; Maxwell 1996; Reynolds 1997; Warren 1998). They thus reject a language ideology of variationism (Kroskrity, this volume). Pan-Mayas adhere to the linguistic relativity hypothesis, producing rich descriptive and prescriptive grammars that have revealed many of the structural complexities specific to each Mayan language. Moreover, these linguists provide technical support and promote standard written versions of each language (England 1996, 2003; Maxwell 1996). Some have even coined Maya neologisms to purge Spanish loanwords from usage (Pakal B'alam 1994). They have created Maya nongovernmental organizations (NGOs) for conducting linguistic research and publishing results, routinely sponsored language and culture workshops and conferences in both Ladino and Maya communities, and even taught university-level courses in linguistics, sociolinguistics, and bilingual education to train the next generations of Pan-Maya linguists. In all of these contexts Pan-Mayas communicated two distinct but nevertheless interdependent language ideologies: an ideology of "iconization" (Irvine and Gal 2000; cf. Kroskrity, this volume, and Bunte, this volume) and an ideology of unification.[6] The first language ideology refers to the semiotic tendency to transform Mayan languages into emblems (i.e., icons) of Maya ethnic identities and the concept that the adoption and implementation of standard varieties of each language will facilitate the creation of a Pan-Maya ethnonational identity, reflected in their coined expression *qawinaq* (our people). The concept of *qawinaq* directly challenges highland groups' primary identification with their local municipality (Tax 1937) and local dialect. The second language ideology of unification is aimed at reconfiguring localist language ideologies in order to stop dialectal fragmentation and the tendency for locals to identify their dialects as radically different forms or separate languages altogether (Mateo Toledo 2000; Sis Ib'oy 2000). Together these language ideologies work in concert to celebrate Maya ethnic unity in its diversity while maintaining a critical stance vis-à-vis the social processes that undermine Mayan languages and, by extension, the cultural identities of their speakers.

While Pan-Mayas have been especially cognizant of how ancestral languages are testimony of a rich precolonial history, they also acknowledge that these languages remain viable cultural resources for the reproduction of modern Mayas' cultures today. In other words, while the Maya ethno-nationalist project has reified Mayan languages for the purpose of "scheduling emblematic identity-displays" in the politics of recognition (Silverstein 2003b:538), these languages are in fact still viable codes, primary vehicles for everyday communication within a majority of highland Maya towns. This heightened linguistic awareness is in part a product of recent dramatic historical changes that have made a cultural movement (as opposed to an overtly political movement) a proactive response to the current situation wherein many linguistic communities are experiencing unprecedented levels of unstable bilingualism and language shift from Maya monolingual to Spanish monolingual. The present situation stands in stark contrast to the centuries-long history of Maya monolingualism.

It is widely believed that from the colonial era up until the 1970s most Maya municipal towns and hamlets remained predominantly Maya monolingual; in the case of towns located within the borderlands between Mayan language communities a continuum of competency across the various codes existed. Individuals who could be considered bilingual in monolingual towns were a few Mayan leaders and Ladinos who occupied local government posts or operated businesses and achieved functional bilingualism, serving as cultural and linguistic "brokers." Only towns like San Antonio Aguas Calientes, located in close proximity to Ladino centers of power, achieved a relatively stable Maya-Spanish bilingualism. Antonero men and women could boast of bilingual competency in Spanish and Kaqchikel.[7]

Scholars have attributed the survival of Maya monolingual communities to the legacy of Spanish colonial linguistic and legal policies (Brown 1998a; Garzon 1998c; Hill and Monaghan 1987). Garzon (1998c) writes that Spanish colonial linguistic policy followed a strict separation of Spanish and Indian speech communities and reflected a Spanish ideology of reconquest founded upon ethnic and religious purism. The Spanish Crown, moreover, was concerned with the rapid assimilation of Mayas to Spanish customs and beliefs. This entailed centralizing dispersed indigenous populations into nucleated towns (reducciones) typical of Spanish social organization and converting them to Christianity. The most efficient way to do so was for missionaries to interact with the Indian populations via Mayan languages. These missionaries took the study of Mayan languages very seriously. The earliest descriptive grammars of Ch'orti', Kaqchikel, K'ichee', Mam, Poqomam, Poqomchi', Tz'utujil, and Yukateko date back to the seventeenth and eighteenth centuries and were written by members of the religious orders of the Spanish Crown. Thus, it can be argued that the earliest roots of Mayan linguistics were intertwined with a colonial history of religious conversion.

Interest in Mayan linguistics was rekindled in the twentieth century, this time by a Protestant missionary, W. Cameron Townsend, founder of the Summer Institute of Linguistics (SIL). French writes that the goals of the SIL's U.S. missionary-linguists and their grammatical analysis of Mayan languages, which emphasized perceptual sameness with the Spanish language, dovetailed with the Guatemalan national project to "assimilate native speakers of Mayan languages into the Guatemalan national imagined community and the Christian faith through Spanish" (2003:484). These linguistic and political practices of assimilation were first challenged by Maya activists as early as the 1940s, when two different Maya groups, the Convención de Maestros Indígenas (Convention of Indigenous Teachers) and the Academia de la Lengua Maya Ki-ché (Academy of the K'ichee' Mayan Language, or ALMK) contested the way in which the state-backed SIL had devised an orthography to facilitate religious conversion and linguistic assimilation (French 2003; cf. Neely and Palmer, Jr., this volume). Mayas' linguistic activism did not become a force, however, until the 1970s and 1980s. In 1972 the Proyecto Lingüístico Francisco Marroquín (PLFM) was formed by secular North American linguists to train the first generation of Mayas to become native professional linguists. By 1975 PLFM had become the first autonomous Maya NGO devoted to Maya linguistic self-determination. (See French [2003] for a more in-depth discussion of the PLFM's history and influence in shaping Mayan linguistics as practiced by contemporary Maya linguist-activists.) Since then several generations of linguists have been trained at the PLFM or at Oxlajuuj Keej Maya' Ajtz'iib' (OKMA) or have had their university education sponsored by the ALMG; they have formed their own groups while maintaining professional collaborations with secular North American linguists.

Pan-Mayanism as it is practiced today must also be understood within a context of institutionalized state violence and genocide (Oficina de Derechos Humanos del Arzobispado de Guatemala 1998; Recovery of

Historical Memory Project 1999). The era known as *la Violencia* (the Violence) spanned the years 1978–85, when the military regimes of Gen. Lucas García (1978–82), Gen. Efraín Ríos Montt (1982–83), and Gen. Mejía Víctores (1983–85) turned the decades-long war against guerrilla leftist groups into a genocidal project that systematically and disproportionately targeted indigenous communities populating the western highland regions. The 1970s generation of PLFM Maya linguists were forced into hiding for fear of being targeted, as many teachers and educated Mayas were. Some went into exile, while others moved to different Indian communities where the military presence was less oppressive (Burns 1993; Manz 2004; Montejo 1987; Thompson 2001; Wellmeier 1998). Those who remained in Guatemala experienced firsthand the effects of displacement, the militarization of daily life, and linguistic assimilation.

As indicated previously, Mayas for diverse reasons began to incorporate more Spanish into their daily lives. For example, Rigoberta Menchú in her 1984 *testimonio* noted that she (as well as other catechists of liberation theology and trade union organizations) adopted Spanish to use as a weapon in solidarity with other *compañeros* (comrades) against those who attacked her people. Several Pan-Maya activists of this generation take a less radical stance than Menchú. They shared with me that Spanish simply provided a common code through which Indians from differing speech communities could bridge linguistic barriers. Speaking Spanish was not viewed as the source of the problem per se; instead, the problem was the way in which it was accorded greater societal value than Mayan languages were. Kay Warren (1998) reports that many Kaqchikel Maya activist families from San Andrés Semetabaj switched to speaking Spanish primarily because they feared that soldiers from the base stationed at nearby Sololá would accuse them of plotting against the military when they spoke in Kaqchikel. Ironically, they spoke Spanish in order to avoid being targeted as participants in subversive activities.

This trend has not reversed itself since the end of the Violence in the late 1980s, and many Maya linguists worry that although the physical extermination of Indian peoples appears to have ended, the educational policies and practices of "ethnolinguistic genocide" have not (Cojtí Cuxil 1990). Once linguist-activists reemerged on the national scene they resumed pursuit of their goal to professionalize and politicize the practice of linguistics in Guatemala and articulated the aforementioned language

ideologies of unification and iconization. Kaqchikel Mayas have disproportionately comprised the rank and file of linguist-activists, although this
is changing, since many of the ALMG's scholarships are intended to train
linguists from other linguistic regions. Their efforts have resulted in the
creation of a Pan-Maya social movement, one that seeks to secure the
future of their languages by ensuring that there are future generations of
Mayan language speakers.

Raising Our Own Linguistic Consciousness: Anthropological Linguists and Linguistic Anthropologists on Language Revitalization

During the last decade within linguistic anthropology the topics of language revitalization, reversing language shift, language advocacy, and
language rights for "endangered languages" have allowed professionals
from all three of the subdisciplinary paradigms outlined by Duranti
(2003) (anthropological linguistics, ethnography of communication and
sociolinguistics, and language ideology) to come together to share expertise and express rather discordant views from our respective research endeavors.[8] This productive explosion of individual and collective edited
publications as well as conference panels devoted to the subject has led
senior scholars like Joshua Fishman (2002) to marvel: "What a difference
40 years make."[9]

Fishman (1991) and the edited collection of Hale et al. (1992) appearing
in *Language* raised the issue that the work of anthropological linguistics
and language planning does not occur in a political vacuum. Social scientists are frequently asked to assume the role of advocate and be responsive
to the needs of particular culture revitalization movements (Hinton 1994,
2001c:240). This requires moving beyond producing descriptive grammars
and dictionaries to envisioning new kinds of applied projects.

Silverstein (1998a), however, has raised some important challenges to
the dual role that anthropological linguists play as scientists and advocates.
First of all, he observes that though linguists may have sophisticated
knowledge of linguistic form, they tend to have impoverished theories of
learning and to lack expertise in curriculum design for educational contexts. His most vociferous critique, however, reveals that the structur-
alizing linguistics of many anthropological linguistic projects are at a

theoretical loss when faced with how to analyze the globalizing processes that produce changes within language communities. Often their neo-Whorfian, purist models of language as grammar inadvertently facilitate a process already problematically labeled "language death," "language loss," or "language interference." Silverstein finally argues that anthropological linguists are ill equipped to theorize or tackle interventions within local language communities especially because many of the functional domains of language usage in a community no longer exist. He calls for linguists to become self-aware of the norms of their own language ideologies and politics before they plan interventions in a language community. This critique is well taken, but it does not leave anthropological linguists with much of a leg to stand on, especially if the anthropological linguistic project is being led by native linguists, as is the case in Guatemala.

Current North American scholarship has heeded Silverstein's call and started to engage in a self-reflexive critique of how our own expert rhetorics may be interpreted by the communities we seek to serve (England 2003; Errington 2003; Hill 2002; Whiteley 2003). It has also critically interrogated the large-scale global transformations that are giving rise to identity movements, increasing sociopolitical and cultural fragmentation, and an international regimentation of languages with a dominant elite English emblematic of a transnational cosmopolitan identity (Friedman 2003; Silverstein 2003b). Surprisingly, Fishman's (1991) model of reversing language shift has, with a few exceptions (cf. Henze and Davis 1999), received relatively little critical attention from language ideology scholars. I now engage in a much-needed critical examination of the utility and limits of adopting the reversing language shift (RLS) model.

Fishman's lifework concerns language shift, language maintenance, and ethnonational social movements. Fishman and his students have moved beyond early U.S. ethnological salvage approaches, devoted principally to the documentation of so-called disappearing cultures and languages, toward theorizing how to support cultural and linguistic continuity. Fishman coined the concept of language shift, a phenomenon whereby a bilingual speech community can become monolingual when one of its languages becomes dominant due to the perceived social, economic, or political authority accorded its speakers. He also devised a language-planning model to assist in RLS, and although it presupposes that these movements take place in liberal democratic states, indigenous activism in postdictatorial states has followed many of the strategies outlined in his model. Hinton (2001c) has recently modified the RLS model to better suit the needs of grassroots groups, which are more typical of revitalization efforts in the United States.

Fishman's RLS model problematically relies on a functionalist rendering of the world into social spheres. It is divided into eight stages that ostensibly can be tailored to fit the particular needs of any revitalization movement. The model is further divided into "weaker" and "stronger" stages of intervention. Weaker interventions (Stages 5–8) are conceived of as types of grassroots organizing that can be achieved by small groups with limited resources. These interventions include measures to reassemble the language-culture model by seeking archival linguistic and ethnographic materials (Stage 8); tapping into elderly populations' knowledge of tradition and reviving ritual domains of language use (Stage 7); the creation of a community based on an extended fictive kin model devoted to reinforcing language and culture (Stage 6); and the reinforcement of family language socialization in the ancestral language (Stage 5). In places where the "traditional family" has eroded, Fishman notes that community services that endorse the principles of the RLS movement need to be in place to lend support to families. Strong interventions include Stages 1–4 and involve making fundamental changes at the local and national levels in the spheres of education, politics, social services, and the media. He cautions small movements against undertaking strong interventions when there is no base support. Hinton (2001b) additionally notes that the RLS model has historically worked best for national indigenous languages where there was not a lot of linguistic diversity.

Fishman's (1991) central concern is that for a societal-based RLS movement to be successful, it must achieve intergenerational language transmission first at the levels of family and community. The RLS model, however, paints only in broad strokes how to reverse language shift. His approach to language socialization is undertheorized and resembles a unilinear model of linguistic and social development; the child is a tabula rasa upon which adults must inscribe cultural knowledge and language. Given that his model calls for a recovery of traditional family practices in liberal democratic societies, it is fair to assume that women (either mothers or grandmothers) shoulder the burden of "transmitting" culture and language to the next generation.

Fishman also adopts a self-help discourse to urge ethnic minority movements forward despite the daunting tasks they face. Some of the suggestions named require RLS advocates to assume a rather paternalistic point of view vis-à-vis the populations they seek to serve. For example, rather than frame members of shift generations as understandably or creatively responding to dramatic changes in their social and living conditions, the RLS model positions them as part of the problem—people responsible for the erosion of traditional family values. To counter this problem Fishman suggests that RLS movements must provide educational support for these families, which he views as lacking in both parental skills and cultural knowledge. Adoption of a deficit model seems counterproductive, given that some generations became shift generations in response to hegemonic subtractive educational policies.

The deficit roots of an RLS model were made especially apparent to me in 1998 while I was teaching a class on sociolinguistics—ethnography of communication to a group of the next generation of Pan-Maya linguists at the URL. One of my Q'eqchi' students submitted a set of field notes that followed a strict set of categories designed by a Maya NGO, his place of employment during the work week. This coding rubric assessed whether or not heads of households could be categorized as members of a shift generation and, second, what kind of intervention would be most appropriate given the socioeconomic circumstances of the village. The NGO had subscribed to a version of Fishman's RLS model, capitalizing on a metaphor of shaming heads of household into a critical linguistic consciousness—a consciousness that they were perceived to be lacking. In the remaining sections I examine discordant adult Maya perspectives on a "shaming the shift" approach to reversing language shift and suggest other voices that also need to be heard and entertained lest Pan-Mayas contribute to widening the generational gap even further in the postwar era.

Shaming the Shift Generation: Politicizing Domestic Spheres of Language Usage vis-à-vis Adult Literacy Classes

While Pan-Mayas have been quite successful at politicizing the current regimentation of languages at a national level, they have thus far been less successful in politicizing domestic spheres of language usage. (See Meek in this volume for a comparative case study where Yukon indigenous activists have successfully challenged and transformed postcolonial language ideologies and policies.) To date, they have done so by adopting culturally appropriate, intergenerational shaming strategies that highlight transgressions of appropriate and respectful behavior in Maya towns and households. These verbal disciplinary strategies resonate with family language socialization practices of respect and are predicated on the generative logic of Maya Cosmology defined by discerning unity in diversity (Fischer 1999; Montejo 2005). According to the ethnographic canon, in Maya Cosmology households are believed to function according to the principles of interdependence with autonomy, where the interdependent roles of a diverse family composition re-create the collectivity (i.e., the family) (Rogoff 2003; see Bunte in this volume for an examination of similar language socialization practices among the San Juan Paiutes). This cosmological model of family is crosscut by two dimensions of respect. The first dimension of respect is relational: the amount of deference and respect one gives and receives depends upon one's place within a gendered and age-graded hierarchy (Watanabe 2000).[10] The second dimension of respect is individual: everyone is entitled to have his or her autonomy respected (Gaskins 1999). In practice, a natural tension between the two dimensions of respect exists, though activists often privileged the first dimension over the second. Shaming the shift generation requires disciplining younger family members into respecting tradition and accommodating elders by speaking to them in an ancestral language. It has been the predominant strategy and metaphor to politicize domestic language use in extended family households.

As Mayas make up a majority population in Guatemala and activist resources are limited, Pan-Mayas have had to engage in a type of cost-benefit analysis along the following lines to assess within which communities efforts to reverse language shift might have the greatest success. They decided to concentrate their efforts in the largest Mayan language communities where there were still anywhere from tens of thousands to a hundred thousand speakers. This signified that salvage projects like the Itzaj revitalization project, where there were only a few dozen living speakers, were not a top priority (Hofling 1996). Additionally, given that many of the key activists were Kaqchikel speakers, they had the manpower and resources already in place to launch an RLS initiative in several Kaqchikel highland towns.

Pan-Mayas relied on the work of North American sociolinguists to help assess the degree to which language shift toward Spanish mono-lingualism was occurring. These scholars have established that shift is occurring across a range of places, from those that have always been easily accessible to Ladino Spanish-speaking centers, like the villages nestled in the Quinizilapa Valley (one of which is San Antonio Aguas Calientes) (Brown 1998b), to those that have become more accessible in recent years, like San Juan Comalapa (Garzon 1998a), to those that remain rather isolated, such as San Marcos la Laguna (Richards 1998). Kaqchikel towns that were assessed as already in advanced stages of shift, like those in the Quinizilapa Valley, and had no Pan-Maya family in residence were written off as lost causes. Similarly, towns that were still relatively iso-lated were seen as less urgent. Thus, large municipalities like San Juan Comalapa, Tecpán, and San Andrés Semetabaj became key sites for Pan-Maya initiatives.

Many of the attitudes identified as contributing to language shift re-volve around members of the shift generation's traumatic experiences at school as well as beliefs that their children will not succeed in school if they are fluent in a Mayan language. Other ideologies relate to parents' presuppositions that children will naturally pick up the language on their own or, alternatively, that a conscious exposure to both codes will only result in imperfect acquisition of both languages.

The adult literacy program was conceived of as a key intervention aimed at the shift generation. In 1994 Pan-Mayas launched the program within the Kaqchikel linguistic region. These fledgling literacy classes were an alternative educational space, one designed to resocialize Maya adults to valorize and use a standard written version of Kaqchikel as well as to increase respect for elders and their traditional knowledge within the community. These courses also provided important vocational train-ing. There was a real need for instructors trained in reading and writing Kaqchikel for the new bilingual schools. The resocialization and training combined were to contribute to a growing number of public intellectuals who could serve as bilingual model speakers and who especially valorized the use of Kaqchikel at home and in public settings (Brown 1998c).

Kaqchikel adult literacy courses also served as a litmus test to estimate the public's degree of interest and the feasibility of launching similar programs within the other language communities. Within two years these classes were all but abandoned. Attendance was chronically low, and despite students' favorable assessments of the courses (Brown 1998c), Pan-Maya strategies changed in favor of funding scholarships for promising bilingual students to obtain the equivalent of a bachelor's degree in linguistics, sociolinguistics, or bilingual education. While these literacy courses are for the time being no longer a top priority, they provided a discursive site to allow for "webs of interlocution" (Taylor 1989) within which dialogue between speakers of local Kaqchikel varieties could take place.[11] Of particular interest to the current discussion is how students responded to the model of family and ideology of respect promoted in these literacy classes. I now return to the multiple interpretations of that text.

From a purely textual standpoint, "Man Kach'oke'" simultaneously represents a moral, pedagogical, and ideological text, one that in microcosm reveals how Pan-Maya linguists' ideologies of family and respect intersect with language ideology. It is a moral text, a parable for cultural interpretation, instructing children to not usurp an elder's proper place within the traditional extended family. It references one of a host of locally salient cultural practices that enact an ideology of respect and family interdependence defined by an age-graded hierarchy. It is also a pedagogical text used to facilitate adults' Kaqchikel literacy acquisition. It was read immediately after students mastered the ALMG's standard Kaqchikel orthography. Finally, it is an ideological text expressing a greater Pan-Maya political goal, namely, to foster a critical linguistic consciousness by encouraging Maya bilingual students, people who could be members of a shift generation (i.e., bilingual parents who speak a Mayan language with elders but Spanish with their children), to take texts like these home and read them to their children, thereby making intergenerational use of Kaqchikel a priority (Brown 1998b, 1998c; Garzon 1998b, 1998c).[12]

On the afternoon during which this text was first analyzed by the class, those in attendance included the teacher, three male students in their midthirties, and me, an anthropologist. This was a normal day in that we constituted the core group of participants who attended class twice a week; class discussion would take place in both Spanish and Kaqchikel. The teacher passed out the text and informed us that these were our copies to keep and share with our families at home. He then asked the student to my right to lead the activity by reading aloud the first parable. I was second in line and had to read "Man Kach'oke'." After I dutifully complied with his request, the teacher initiated the discussion by generalizing the moral of the story to encompass all copresent same-aged peers. The transcript below represents the discussion that immediately ensued.[13]

In lines 1–3 of the first transcript excerpt the teacher declares that the text instructs all of us to be respectful. After one of the students acknowledges this initial paraphrase of the story, the teacher privileges a more narrow interpretation, indexically invoking the Pan-Maya cosmological family model of respect according to an age-graded hierarchy. Children are not social equals to adults, and, by extension, we cannot compare ourselves to our elders (lines 5–7).

Example 1. Transcript, "Idea Cristiana" (Christian Belief), August 1994. Primary interlocutors: teacher, student. Others in attendance: three students, including researcher.

1	Teacher:	sí pues	Yes indeed
2		es para que:::	it is so tha:::t
3		que seamos respetuosos, verda?=	that we be respectful, right?
4	Student:	=a::h=	=a::h=
5	Teacher:	=es como dice aquí que= que:	it is like it says here that tha:t
6		(0.3)	
7		que en primer lugar no podemos comparar a	in the first place, we can't compare ourselves, y'know in
		nosotros digamos en caso de niños con con con un adulto verd[a	this instance, children with with with an adult, ri[ght.
8	Student:	[sí pues.	[Yes, indeed

At this juncture in the discussion one of the students self-selects to align himself with the teacher's moral analysis of the story but also takes advantage of the opportunity to append an analogical story of his own, one that reflects Christian doctrine. The student prefaces his narrative with a reported speech, hearsay evidential *dice que* (it is said that) in line 9 that calls upon all the illocutionary force that the transposition of common knowledge onto the current narrative event entails (Haviland 1996). After the teacher acknowledges the student's preface as staking a claim to tell a story in line 17, the student proceeds to narrate the story of when the angel Lucifer attempted to assume a status to which he was not entitled and was consequently punished for his actions (lines 18–39). The student narrates in a deliberate, dramatic manner, emphatically underscoring the immorality of the intentional act by referring to Lucifer as Satan (line 22), even before he had fallen from a state of grace within the temporal frame of the narrative.

9	Student:	dice que:: digamos esto::,	it is said tha::t y'know thi:::s
10		(0.2)	
11		esta idea?	thi:::s belief
12		(0.8)	
13		digamos los e:::h	y'know the e:::h
14		(1.3)	
15		coincide con la idea, (0.2) cristiana.	coincides with the *Christian* belief
16		(0.8)	
17	Teacher:	Mh	mh
18	Student:	que a—existe digamos cu::ando,	that a—it exists y'know whe:::::n
19		(0.4)	
20		dice que:	it is said tha::::t
21		(1.0)	
22		Satanás::?	Satan
23		(1.0)	
24		*quisó* digamos decir	*wanted* y'know we would say,
		sentarse en e—(.) el trono del (.) del Dios Santísimo	to seat himself on uh the throne of the Beloved Father
25		(0.8)	
26		y:: le fue *mal.* pues cuando él quiso hacer eso.	an:::d it went bad for him, indeed, when he wanted to do that
27		(0.4)	
28		porque él quisó superarse	because he wanted to be greater than

29	(1.0)	
30	este:: digamos este: < Diós	u::::h y'know u:h < God
31	(0.4)	
32	sentarse en el trono que sólo a él le corresponde	to seat himself on the throne that only corresponds to Him.
33	(0.4)	
34	tonce de ahí digamos eh coincide con la idea?	then in this way y'know, eh it coincides with the belief
35	porque eso sí me lo contaron a mí (eso[me decía a mí ????)	because that yes/indeed is what they told me (??[?)
36 Teacher:	[mm	[mm

The story underscores the sin of pride, the desire to usurp a position to which one is not entitled; this is what damns both the actor and the action. The full weight of the consequences, however, is never relayed to the teacher and other audience members. Instead, the student underscores the parallel story lines, bringing into stark relief how Pan-Maya moral texts do not reflect a culturally unique perspective on human morality. In other words, the student imbues a cultural text with sacred Christian authority by remarking on the shared underlying principles. This comparison poses a subtle challenge to those of the Pan-Maya movement who would seek to stake a claim to an expressly Kaqchikel Maya worldview and cultural practice that rejects the history of colonial relations between Maya communities and the Catholic Church. In line 40, however, the teacher acknowledges the analogy, noting that it is indeed a comparable narrative. He thereby implicitly validates the student's interpretation and, by extension, his authority to also lay claim to a Christian identity.

After the teacher ratifies the student's comparison, the student, in a reciprocal fashion, recognizes the authority in the Kaqchikel parable and relates it to his own personal experience growing up. It is here when he finally reveals the consequences for sitting on the throne of God—or, as the case may have it, for sitting in his father's place. A lashing awaited him and his siblings (lines 43–47).

37 Student: eso es (.) la misma idea   that is (.) the same
              porque así hizo es   belief because that way he
              ma:ligno cuando él quisó   became malign when he
              °sentarse en el trono de   wanted °to sit on the
              Dios.°   throne of God.°
38   (0.2)
39   (??) pero tiene esa (0.2)   (??) but it has that
              idea=   belief.
40 Teacher: =sí pues esa (0.2)   yes indeed that (0.2) that
              compara eso verd[a   compares, it's tr[ue.
41 Student: [compara eso.   [That's comparable.
42   (0.2)
43   como ustedes lo dicen   Like you-all say
44   (1.0)
45   y cuando no tendríamos a   and when we wouldn't have
              buenas de un (0.2)   (been) good, with a (0.2)
              chicotazo teníamos que   lashing we would have
              levantar (dar lugar a)   gotten up (to make room
              °(nuestro) papá¿°   °for) (our) dad.°
46   (1.0)
47   y eso mimos idea, °(??)°   and that same belief,
              (0.4) °al menos:[:: (??)°   °(??)° (0.4) °at [least°
48 Teacher: [SÍ PUES o   [YES INDEED,
              sea que   in other words
              (.) hay ideas e bastante   (.) there are beliefs that
              buenas verda   are quite good, right
49   que que no hay que   that that should not be
              perder?   lost.

It is after this last contribution, one that stands in stark contrast to
the consequences of the parable (where one's hair turns gray), that the
teacher acknowledges the story as a whole and attempts to take command
once again of the conversational floor with an emphatic "YES INDEED"
(line 48). He generalizes that there are things (i.e., beliefs and practices)
that are good and should not be lost, but he does not specify which
dimensions of these beliefs and practices are good and should be preserved (lines 48 and 49). In so doing, the teacher glosses over a striking

difference vis-à-vis the way the moral of the story in the Pan-Maya text ends and the way the story of the Christianized Maya family enforces patriarchal respect.

What is also striking about the parable and the student's reinterpretation of it is that a Pan-Maya model of family relations as well as a Christian model reflect an adult-centric perspective. Children are not social equals to adults and as such do not merit the same kinds of enactments of respect. This position, however, is only a partial construal of a Maya Cosmology model of family defined by the dual dimensions of respect. Respect for an individual's autonomy, where the child is also understood to be an individual, is omitted. This undercuts many familial practices of respect.

It has been my experience over the years working with families who were educators, farmers, artisans, and venders from both San Juan Comalapa and San Antonio Aguas Calientes that parents and other caregivers struggle to achieve both dimensions of "respect." Families where the father overzealously interprets his role as "the patriarch" are unhappy, and women and their children often escape to spend more time within the mother's family's household compound. For the most part, children and youth, when not in school (which does adopt a system of same-age cohorts reminiscent of U.S. public schools), are active and welcomed participants in public and ritual events. There is usually a range of musical genres and activities to cater to the tastes of different generations—in addition to a live marimba band playing the traditional Maya *son*, towns also invite popular national bands or hire a DJ to play all the latest genres, from *tropical*, *romántica*, and *banda* to *reggaeton*.

Within households, children and youth also experience tremendous freedom of movement and action. Adults never plan or direct activities to keep children preoccupied. Instead, children are actively incorporated into household reproduction as caregivers and laborers, even at very young ages, as long as their participation is not disruptive of the collective (Gaskins 1999). On occasions where children and youth do get into serious trouble or place themselves in a potentially harmful situation, caregivers prefer to shame, to tease, to use bald imperatives, or even to use indirection before they resort to corporal forms of punishment (Reynolds 2002).

While the student's personal story assumes that the Pan-Maya text endorses a patriarch's right to rule his family with an "iron fist," this is not an accurate construal of the Pan-Maya text.[14] However, the student makes it resonate with what he asserts to be his generation's experience of traditional Maya family practices, though it may not be a position he entirely endorses. In fact, in a second story that is too long to be included here, the student describes how his individual ability, that of being a talented speech-maker (a *cholanel*), placed him in the untenable position of being a relatively young person who had to lead a group of elders in a ceremonial context in which they would have to symbolically raise him up over them as receptacle of ritual knowledge. In so doing, he acknowledges that young people, because of their individual interests and abilities, can also be active participants in ritual as well as other cultural productions. He highlights memories from his own personal biography that illustrate how elders and fathers do not always make the wisest of choices and that they too are capable of betraying their children and, consequently, tradition.

Implications: On Bridging versus Widening the Generation Gap

It is humbling to consider just what Mayas from Guatemala have had to survive and overcome over the past several decades. The courage, tenacity, and devotion that Pan-Maya linguist-activists and their *paisanos* (fellow citizens, at both the municipal and national levels) have demonstrated in staking a claim to their home-places, which historically have been subsumed within a hostile racist state, should inspire other indigenous activists everywhere to persevere in their own social movements in search of recognition, self-determination, and justice. I only hope that the critical examination presented thus far of both the triumphs and limitations of Pan-Maya counterhegemonic practices as reflected in language ideologies of iconization, unification, and the adoption of Fishman's RLS model is true to the longstanding spirit of collaboration and dialogue between North American secular linguists and Maya linguist-activists. The fact that many activists have chosen ancestral Mayan languages as one of the primary vehicles through which they imagine a peaceful, multiethnic, and plurilingual society speaks to the powerful role that ideologies of language play in mediating between ever-emergent linguistic and social forms.

In the early 1990s, when I first suggested that a reflexive examination of our activist language ideologies was important, senior Mayanists did not initially agree that such an exercise was necessary. By the late 1990s Pan-Mayan linguists had reversed this opinion; they realized that in the current sociopolitical order the more profound resistance to Pan-Mayan ideas was not coming from above but from below. In a series of panel presentations in both national and international venues they began to tackle the issue of how conflicts between ethnonationalist and localist language ideologies had the potential to undermine the greater goals of Pan-Mayanism. Missing from this discussion, however, is an awareness of how ideologies of language intersect in manifold ways with other kinds of ideological practices of exclusion and belonging. This additional issue also must be addressed in their continuing struggle to ensure a peaceful Guatemala. I devote the closing paragraphs of this essay to begin the process of teasing apart some of the complex dimensions of this issue.

Renowned anthropologist Kay Warren, reflecting on ideological cleavages that have emerged between and within historical generations of activist families in Guatemala, emphasizes that it is always the generation of elders that fears betrayal: "When a younger set of elders is about to replace another, there is a combination of anger at a new betrayal and peaceful resignation in the face of cosmic cycles of rebirth through destruction" (1998:192). In so doing, she inadvertently privileges all elders' perspectives at the expense of the young. Fishman's RLS model for linguist-activists, however, intentionally does so. Elders' knowledge is considered of the utmost value for grassroots organizing (recall Stage 7), and in many social contexts rightly so. The problem, however, is that children and youths are depicted as nothing but a tabula rasa or, even worse, beings in need of cultural reprogramming. Loether (this volume) notes that if reversing language shift is to be successful, children and youth need to become agents in their own socialization into ancestral language use and experience ownership of their language as a living resource. The idea that children and youths could espouse collectivist ideals and be active participants in community practices of cultural production or that elders might have adopted destructive and exploitative social practices reinvented as

"tradition" is never entertained. For example, what would the consequences be to an RLS movement in a postdictatorial state if the kind of
fictive-kin model adopted by the community (Stage 6) was nothing but
another version of an authoritarian, patriarchal one? This is a serious and
potential outcome that must be considered, especially in sociopolitical
contexts where state violence and authoritarianism historically have predominated. Given the complexity of issues that many indigenous communities face during the age of globalization, greater care and more sophisticated social analyses are in order. It is not simply a matter that youths and
children are disrespectful and need to be shamed into respecting tradition, nor is it the case that parents from the shift generation are solely
to blame.

We need to seriously examine the role that intersecting ideologies of
family, language(s), and nation play in mediating *and* even mystifying
social relations and structural inequalities (see Bunte, this volume). For
example, Little (2004) has noted that while most Mayas in local language
communities like San Antonio Aguas Calientes do not disagree with the
basic tenets of Pan-Maya politics, they have found that the movement
does not address chronic underemployment and poor access to health
care and that the ethnolinguistic emphasis is often too rigid to respond to
political struggles at the municipal level. He writes about how artisans and
other Maya entrepreneurs, many of whom hail from San Antonio Aguas
Calientes, have had to wage a different kind of identity politics as participants within the disjunctive cultural and economic flows of global
tourism. Being a quick-witted, savvy entrepreneur is of the utmost importance, especially for women and children. People's concern was not cen-
tered on Spanish language acquisition at the expense of the local variety
of Kaqchikel; rather, people espoused a more utilitarian language ideology embodied in social practice (Kroskrity, this volume; Reynolds 2002).
Kaqchikel continued to indicate a place-based identity, one that distinguished residents from other competitors from different Kaqchikel highland towns. Spanish was the lingua franca of most economic exchanges
between Antoneros and their foreign clients, although many also had
functional command of how to conduct transactions in English, German,
Italian, and Japanese. The code that holds the greatest cultural capital in a
global political economy is English, reflecting Silverstein's observation
that in the restructuring global order certain metropolitan centers are

being passed over for others, so that in rural places like Mexico and Guatemala "'Indian' people with aspirations to significant mobility are not abandoning local languages at this point only for a Mexico City–standardized Spanish. They are doing so for English, standardized via broadcast Americana or through at least seasonal work-related presence in Los Angeles, Chicago, New York or slightly lower-tiered metropolitan areas" (2003b:550). The emerging body of ethnography on Maya in the diaspora suggests that this is indeed the case. The regimentation of codes (and their speakers) within a Guatemalan context must thus be understood within the disjunctive global flows of capital, media images, and laborers (Appadurai 1996).

In the early postwar era, what has been painfully clear to youthful Antonero venders and service workers (people not lacking in a political or linguistic consciousness) when they watched the number of tourists dwindle as the crime rate soared is that they would not necessarily be able to reproduce the family sociocultural order at home *and* enjoy the respect accorded to elders as they aged during highly unstable socioeconomic times. They saw their choices as extremely limited and felt increasingly forced to migrate elsewhere in search of the capricious promises offered but rarely attained within the global marketplace. While this trend of out-migration from Guatemala to Mexico and the United States started in the mid-1980s as a consequence of *la Violencia*, the numbers of youth migrating from all across Guatemala have even increased due in part to the neoliberal economic policies and structural adjustments that lock Guatemala in cycles of debt and dependency. The labor of these youths abroad sustains their families and communities back home. Manz (2004) cites a 2003 MIF/IDB report that Guatemalans residing in the United States sent $1.7 billion in remittances back to Guatemala. This number dwarfed both the figures reflecting U.S. foreign aid as well as other sources of national revenue. "The amount sent in remittances by July 2002 ($781.4 million) had already surpassed revenues obtained from coffee, sugar, bananas, and cardamom combined ($631.15 million)" (Manz 2004:241). Thus, it is ironic that in shaming a shift generation and singling out Spanish monolingual children as indices of cultural and linguistic loss, Pan-Mayas attempt to reinscribe national boundaries during an era when national borders are increasingly deterritorialized in the transnational flow of labor and capital.

Another danger that Pan-Mayas face is in inadvertently contributing to nationally circulating modern discourses on children as being "at risk," which marks a particular historical moment in the era of late capitalism within which children are increasingly subjected to more restrictive social policies and cultural practices that exacerbate already difficult circumstances (Boyden 1997; Scheper-Hughes and Sargent 1998; Stephens 1995).[15] In a climate where "at risk" discourses scapegoat children and youth for Guatemala's deteriorating social conditions, including unemployment/underemployment, poverty, and crime, families and communities often respond by turning their gaze inward, patrolling what had previously been porous, blurred boundaries between ethnolinguistic and "genderational" groups (Berkley 2001). As long as Mayan languages are the primary iconized signifiers of one's right to claim an indigenous identity, Spanish monolingual children and youth who were not raised speaking a Mayan language will be precluded from claiming equal membership in the movement. In fact, places like San Antonio Aguas Calientes that have been described as going through rapid language shift (Brown 1998b) are often written off by Pan-Mayas as lost communities. Instead, what is called for is recognition that communities like these are more concerned with reconstructing families and lives in a global neoliberal order where there is only a fine line between discipline and abuse and where excessive displays of force may index an unstable social order in which control is tenuously maintained by a head of household or head of state just as it is by Guatemala's current president. For these reasons and many others, our linguist-activist ideologies of language, both in Guatemala and in the United States, need to keep pace with the highly mobile and diverse group of youths who are not content to accept any group's version of "tradition"—especially if it does not accurately reflect and interrogate the shifting and increasingly unequal social fields that shape their life chances and futures.

CHAPTER 11

Language Revitalization and the Manipulation of Language Ideologies
A Shoshoni Case Study

CHRISTOPHER LOETHER

Within the last century the study of Native American languages has transformed from a descriptive and "salvage" phase to a more applied phase, in which maintenance and revitalization of the languages have become major focuses. In many revitalization programs an important factor in the success of language revitalization efforts has been community members' ideas about their language, including the social meanings that speakers attach to their language and the accepted roles of usage of the language within the Native culture and the larger Euro-American society. The acceptance or rejection of language revitalization efforts may depend more on a community's beliefs and feelings about language than on seemingly more substantive issues regarding language structure or the practical concerns of implementation. Today these folk-level concepts, beliefs, and feelings are understood as "language ideologies" (Silverstein 1979).

Native communities, of course, are hardly monolithic entities, as many studies in this volume demonstrate (e.g., Anderson, Reynolds, and Neely and Palmer). They exhibit multiple and contradictory language ideologies that may impede the success of a revitalization project. Richard and Nora Marks Dauenhauer, a husband and wife linguistic team, address this very issue in their discussion of Tlingit revitalization efforts and the need for what they call "prior ideological clarification" when they note that "certainly in Alaska, and probably throughout the United States and Canada, Native American individuals and communities are plagued and haunted with anxieties, insecurities, and hesitations about the value of their indigenous language and culture" (1998:62–63). Addressing and resolving these insecurities typically involves raising community awareness about the impact of colonial and hegemonic language ideologies on local thinking about language and communication. It also involves recognition of indigenous beliefs and practices regarding the heritage language. This process of both decolonizing imposed concepts and locating a foundation of indigenous beliefs and feelings that will support language renewal efforts I call the "manipulation" of language ideologies at the individual, family, and community levels. My perspective is that of a linguistic anthropologist who has served tribally based language renewal efforts for about two decades. Based on that experience, I contend that a community-based program of language ideological manipulation is a necessary, critical, and ongoing activity in any successful effort to engage in a program of language renewal.

One area in the language revitalization process that can be especially problematic for a community is the selection of an orthography and a standardized form of the language for teaching purposes (Neely and Palmer, this volume). In many cases, the lack of a strategy to deal with multiple and conflicting language ideologies has thwarted sincere and potentially successful efforts at language revitalization. Darrel Kipp, the cofounder and director of the Piegan Institute of the Blackfoot Nation, a very successful immersion school in Browning, Montana, expresses the frustration of an indigenous activist with such ideological variation and contestation: "You do not ask permission to use your language, to work with it, to revitalize it. . . . You don't change the entire community. . . . [Y]ou work with the people who want you to work with them" (2000:6).

In this chapter I look at how one Native American community's language ideologies have affected language revitalization efforts. I first examine the current situation of the Shoshoni language and then focus on Shoshoni speakers on the Fort Hall Indian Reservation of southeastern Idaho and the role their language ideologies have played in language revitalization efforts. Next I describe the Shoshoni Language Project at Idaho State University (ISU), located eight miles south of Fort Hall, and how it has affected language ideologies among Shoshoni speakers throughout Shoshoni country. Afterward I examine how particular language ideologies have been and can be manipulated by language activists and language revitalization specialists, focusing again on the efforts of the Shoshoni Language Project.

The Shoshoni

In precontact times the Shoshoni were spread from Death Valley in eastern California through Nevada, Utah, Idaho, and Wyoming, spilling over into the western Great Plains, and from Alberta, Canada, in the north to Chihuahua, Mexico, in the south. Today the Shoshoni are divided by anthropologists into three groups that correspond roughly to the three different environmental adaptations of the prehistoric Shoshoni. The Western Shoshoni of Nevada and western Utah lived traditionally within a Great Basin cultural context. The Northern Shoshoni of Idaho and northern Utah shared Great Basin cultural traits with the Western Shoshoni and Columbia River Plateau cultural traits with other tribes such as the Nez Perce. The Eastern Shoshoni of Wyoming adapted much more than the others to a Great Plains way of life. The Comanches are a group of Eastern Shoshoni who moved into the southern Great Plains in the early 1700s and developed a Plains cultural orientation there.

The Shoshoni language, along with Tümpisa (or Panamint) Shoshoni and Comanche, is a member of the central Numic branch of the Uto-Aztecan language family, which is widely spread throughout western North America, stretching from the Salmon River of central Idaho to El Salvador in Central America. The Shoshoni language today is spoken primarily in Nevada, Idaho, and Wyoming, with smaller numbers of speakers in Oregon, Utah, and California. Although there are no reliable census figures for the number of speakers, I estimate that there are approximately five thousand speakers of the language out of a total Shoshoni population of roughly twelve thousand persons.[1]

The Fort Hall Indian Reservation in southeastern Idaho consists of 544,000 acres and is home to both the Shoshoni and Bannock Indians, but almost 90 percent of enrolled tribal members are Shoshoni or part Shoshoni. There are approximately three thousand Shoshoni currently living on the reservation, and perhaps as many as a thousand are fluent speakers of the language, with approximately fifty speakers of Bannock among those who claim Bannock ancestry. The speakers' ages, however, are not evenly spread throughout the population, with the majority of fluent speakers being fifty years of age or older. Some children are still learning Shoshoni as their first language, but they make up less than 5 percent of the population under eighteen years of age.

The reasons for the increasing obsolescence of the Shoshoni language are numerous and complex. Shoshoni has suffered many of the same problems that confront Native American languages throughout the United States: (1) no standardized form that can be used when teaching second language learners; (2) no officially sanctioned and promoted orthography; (3) lack of written classroom materials either for first language speaker literacy or for second language learners; (4) little or no support for language programs in the schools or in the community (this can include lack of tribal support of the language); (5) shrinking domains of use; (6) negative criticisms by some community members directed toward other speakers involved in teaching the language; (7) speakers who are critical rather than supportive of novice learners; (8) intense and sustained discrimination and subordination of the language by Anglo-American society; and (9) the hegemonic domination, both symbolically and economically, of the heritage language by English.

One interesting aspect of the sociolinguistic situation at Fort Hall is that, despite the ever-dwindling number of speakers of Shoshoni, most of the "dialects" have remained intact and are still easily recognized and identified by speakers, since families from different areas of Idaho and Utah, speaking slightly variant forms of the language, were settled on different parts of the reservation and continue to live in the same areas today. Native speakers estimate that there are twenty-four different recognizable dialects or ways of speaking, all of which are tied to particular families and their original home territories. Therefore, in place of social dialects based on socioeconomic status, ethnicity, or religion, Shoshoni has what can be termed "band-centered" or "family-centered" dialects, where a speaker's family ties are easily identified by his or her speech.

The presence of so many family-centered dialects within such a small, concentrated area also presents a problem when teaching the language to second language learners, since there is no single form that is considered "standard." This presents a unique challenge to language teachers, who need to stress the importance of all dialects when teaching the language and must also be careful to point out significant dialect differences to students where appropriate. This also puts an extra burden on the language learner, who must often learn two or three different words for a single term in English. Routinely exposed to multiple dialects even within her own kin group, Drusilla Gould, codirector of the Shoshoni

Language Project and longtime teacher of the language, had a typical childhood: "When I spoke to my mother I spoke in the Lemhi dialect, and when I spoke to my father I spoke in the Wind River dialect" (personal communication, 2000).

While the lack of an official standardized form may be the norm for many Native American languages, the situation of Shoshoni is extreme in terms of Shoshoni rejection of any prestige forms or of efforts to impose one particular form to be used universally as a standard among all speakers. As the linguist Wick Miller observed concerning Shoshoni dialects: "The prevailing attitude toward language is casual and pedestrian. Language is a tool to be used for communication. Differences in verbal skills are recognized, but are not highly valued. . . . Lack of social stratification meant lack of social dialects, and left little chance for a prestige dialect to develop" (1970:32, 34).

The Shoshoni belief in the importance of family autonomy in areas such as language usage has been an important factor in determining what measures are attainable in language revitalization efforts among the Shoshoni. This is also one language ideology that can easily be traced to the traditional culture of the Shoshoni.

Shoshoni political and social organization was traditionally at the band level, and many interactions today still reflect this informal type of social structure through the importance of "family ties," especially in regard to tribal politics. Today the Shoshoni are physically scattered across five western states on fifteen different Indian reservations and Indian "colonies" or small parcels of Indian land located next to or within a town (see table 11.1). On some of these reservations and colonies the Shoshoni compose the majority, while on others they are a minority. The geographical spread of speakers and replication of tribal governments decentralize decision making by tribal governments, including such linguistic choices as the selection of an official orthography. This also has meant fewer resources for each reservation. Often various reservations spend valuable time and resources on projects that have already been done elsewhere rather than sharing with one another to minimize such wasteful replication. Although there has been an annual conference of Shoshoni language educators and speakers for some years now, they have not moved as a group in the direction of forming a languagewide academy to deal

TABLE 11.1. Shoshoni Reservations and Colonies

Reservation/Colony and Location	Main Tribe(s)
Battle Mountain Colony, Nevada	Western Shoshoni
Duck Valley Res., Nevada/Idaho	Western Shoshoni, Northern Paiute
Elko Colony, Nevada	Western Shoshoni
Ely Colony, Nevada	Western Shoshoni
Fallon Colony, Nevada	Western Shoshoni, Northern Paiute
Fallon Res., Nevada	Western Shoshoni, Northern Paiute
Fort Hall Res., Idaho	Northern Shoshoni, Bannock
Fort McDermitt Res., Nevada/Oregon	Western Shoshoni, Northern Paiute
Goshute Res., Nevada/Utah	Goshute Shoshoni*
Odgers Ranch, Nevada	Western Shoshoni
Reno-Sparks Colony, Nevada	Western Shoshoni, Washoe, N. Paiute
Ruby Valley, Nevada	Western Shoshoni
Wells Colony, Nevada	Western Shoshoni
Wind River Res., Wyoming	Eastern Shoshoni, Arapaho
Yomba Res., Nevada	Western Shoshoni

* The name Goshute Shoshoni refers to the group of Western Shoshoni living in the Great Salt Lake Desert on the Nevada-Utah border.

with issues such as creating an official orthography or standardizing the language. This has also meant that very few language materials can be shared among the different reservations, since each reservation wants its local way of speaking reflected in the materials it uses locally.

Shoshoni Language Ideologies

Though earlier studies of Shoshoni "language attitudes" may lack an emphasis on awareness (e.g., discursive versus practical consciousness and positioned interest available in a language ideological perspective [Kroskrity 2004]), Miller (1970) approximated an ideological analysis in his discussion of eight factors of traditional Shoshoni culture that influenced the community's linguistic beliefs and language practices.

The first five factors listed by Miller are clearly related to one another as factors affecting a child's learning of and socialization into the language. The first five factors are (1) considerable mobility; (2) extremely low population density; (3) no bounded speech communities, only interlocking ones; (4) only a small number of people involved in a child's language socialization, including the lack of a peer group; and (5) a great amount of linguistic diversity within the small number of speakers a child interacts with.

The last three factors all relate to the formation of dialectal and register differences in the language: (6) there is a lack of social stratification within Shoshoni society, which means there are no social dialects in the language (Miller obviously did not recognize family-centered dialects as a type of social dialect); (7) attitudes about the language are casual and concern its use as a tool of communication, therefore styles and registers of the language are weakly developed; and (8) no dialects (including one's own) are considered superior, and all ways of speaking are accepted equally by other speakers.

Among Shoshoni speakers at Fort Hall today, the number of those involved in a child's language socialization into Shoshoni is still small but for different reasons: there are now only a very limited number of people who still can and will speak Shoshoni, especially to a child. If there is not an older person in the household, such as a grandparent who insists on speaking the language with others, the child may never or only rarely be exposed to the language. This has generally been the pattern for the majority of today's young fluent speakers of the language. Many of them were raised by grandparents, a long-established pattern in Shoshoni culture (see Gould and Loether 2002:59–61). Today many children continue to learn the language without any corresponding peer group because they lack friends outside their immediate family who are speakers of the language in the same age range. This pattern of practice clearly has had an effect on these children's ideological perceptions of and beliefs about the limitations of their native language and may explain why so many young speakers have felt unable to express themselves adequately in their own language. This feeling can lead them to switch to English, which they perceive to be a more worldly and prestigious language. Shoshoni-speaking children today are still exposed to many dialectal differences among the speakers they encounter. Since Shoshoni people continue to travel frequently, especially to other Shoshoni communities, one can hear speakers of Western and Eastern Shoshoni as well as the local Northern Shoshoni dialects at Fort Hall.

Fort Hall Language Ideologies

Many of the language ideologies I have encountered at Fort Hall are also related to Miller's (1970) eight factors noted above. These language ideologies can be grouped differently using different criteria, such as positive ideologies (those that promote language revitalization) versus negative ideologies (those that impede it), contemporary ideologies versus traditional ideologies, speakers' ideologies versus nonspeakers' ideologies, and indigenous Shoshoni ideologies versus those ideologies that Shoshoni people have adopted from the larger Anglo-American society. I briefly discuss those language ideologies adopted from Anglo-Americans first.

Nancy Dorian, in her article "Western Language Ideologies and Small Language Prospects" (1998:12), discusses a quartet of language ideologies, brought to North America by European colonists and immigrants, that have negatively impacted Native languages. While I would contend that all have had some influence on Shoshoni speakers, I will limit myself to two especially pernicious types: the ideology of contempt and a belief in a linguistic form of social Darwinism.

According to Dorian (1998:9), the ideology of contempt derives from the European belief that every nation-state should have a single standardized language that has prestige over all local forms of speech. The speech of any subordinated group is therefore unworthy of promotion. Younger speakers of Shoshoni have told me that their language is of no practical value except for speaking with their grandparents and therefore does not warrant revitalization efforts. The second language ideology, a linguistic version of social Darwinism, amounts to "a correlation between adaptive and expressive capacity in a language and that language's survival and spread" (Dorian 1998:10). Languages that experience political success as "national" languages are therefore attributed a structural superiority to the "inferior" languages of subordinated groups. Many speakers of Shoshoni accordingly exhibit a defeatist attitude, telling me that there is no reason to try to save the language, since it no longer can be used to talk about everything, as in the old days, and since it no longer confers fitness to survive in the contemporary world.

There are two other language ideologies that I have seen displayed by speakers of Shoshoni at Fort Hall that correspond to other cultural attributes identified by Miller (1970:34). The first can be called "utilitarianism," which is the idea that a language is merely a tool for communication, devoid of any necessary emotional or cultural value. Kroskrity (this volume) describes a similar language ideology as indigenous to the Western Mono of central California, a group that is closely related to the Shoshoni linguistically but not culturally. Shoshoni speakers with this language ideology tend to use whichever language is more convenient for a particular situation, and in most cases that language is English. Today many Shoshoni, especially younger speakers, do not view their heritage language as a vehicle of identity or even as a distinctive cultural resource.

Another language ideology related to Miller's analysis of the sociocultural foundations of Shoshoni verbal culture may be termed "variationism" following Kroskrity (this volume). Variationism is defined as a system in which dialectal variation, usually based on family differences, is considered the expected norm. This is reflected in the Shoshoni belief that no one dialect is better than any other, since each is emblematic of a particular family or former band territory. This ideology works against the imposition of any one dialect as a standard. This ideology is manifested in many language classrooms when parents object to their children being taught a dialect of Shoshoni other than their family's own. The lack of any clearly developed sense of "formal" versus "casual" speech among the Shoshoni works against any one dialect being perceived as more "aesthetically pleasing," "pure," or prestigious (Miller 1970:34).

Another widespread language ideology present among the Fort Hall Shoshoni resembles one that Dauenhauer and Dauenhauer have termed the "genetic fallacy" (1998:84) in their work on Tlingit revitalization. This is, of course, not a culturally distinctive belief, since the "naturalization" of language acquisition, as if essential to the cultural member by birth, is nearly universal. The genetic fallacy is the assumption that a person's ancestral or heritage language is genetically easier to learn than other languages or even that it is innate and that a person should, therefore, not have to study or expend any effort in order to learn it. I have seen many a student of Shoshoni ancestry fail in the Shoshoni language classes taught at ISU because of this ideology. One negative consequence of this belief is that students who fail to learn their ancestral language when they try may suffer feelings of inferiority and lack of confidence, which in turn may cause them to withdraw from participation in other cultural activities. As Dauenhauer and Dauenhauer write: "In reality, many people are afraid of the traditional language. It is alien, unknown, and difficult to learn. It can be a constant reminder of a deficiency and a nagging threat to one's image of cultural competence" (1998:65).

Another important language ideology mentioned by Dauenhauer and Dauenhauer is the idea that, unlike other languages, Indian languages do not change over time and are spoken by the elders today virtually the same as they have always been spoken. Dauenhauer and Dauenhauer (1998:74) describe this ideology among the Tlingit. This is also a common idea that I have heard expressed numerous times by Shoshoni people, both speakers and nonspeakers of the language. This particular belief can impede any corpus planning if the changes proposed are seen by certain speakers as something the ancestors would not have approved of. This particular language ideology, like programs of purism more generally (Dorian 1998), can "freeze" a language into a certain stage that may jeopardize certain revitalization efforts, such as coining new terms or simplifying certain phonemic or grammatical processes for second language learners.[2]

There are two important indigenous ideologies in Shoshoni communities that have not received significant scholarly attention. One is the belief in the power that the language contains. There are certain words that are more powerful than others, and some of them may not even be said in front of people who can speak the language. One class of such words is the names of mountains and other geographical features. Many Shoshoni believe that if someone mentions the name of a mountain or geological feature within hearing range of it, that person can cause great harm.

A final language ideology I wish to mention is one that is best embodied by my colleague Drusilla Gould and her family. This is the idea that if a speaker takes care of the language and respects it, it will take care of that speaker. This is something one of Gould's grandmothers told her as she was growing up. When she first went to school she did not speak English, and her mother sat with her for the first year, translating both language and culture for her to ease her transition to Anglo-American culture. She has done the same for her own children, who also spoke only Shoshoni when they first entered school. It was also one of her grandmothers who first told Gould to learn to write down the Shoshoni language. This may be one of the most important language ideologies in motivating her tireless revitalization work on behalf of the language.

The Shoshoni Language Project at Idaho State University

Since 1989 the Shoshoni Language Project at ISU has implemented a number of strategies geared toward strengthening the Shoshoni language. Beginning in 1995, we began teaching elementary and intermediate Shoshoni language classes, which students can take to fulfill their general education foreign language requirement for the College of Arts and Sciences. Out of a general student body of just under 13,000 students at ISU, there are approximately 205 Native students, of which no more than 80 are enrolled members from Fort Hall. Most of the Shoshoni students at ISU are not speakers of the language, although every semester there are usually two or three young fluent speakers in the Shoshoni language classes out of a total of fifteen to twenty students. From the outset we have included younger speakers of the language in the project, encouraging them to get other speakers excited about the language. Drusilla Gould has been an excellent bridge between the Shoshoni community and the academic community at ISU, and her family is highly respected at Fort Hall because of the strength of the language within the family. Our ability to work as a team, united in our goals for the Shoshoni language, has given the project a steady direction and stability that many projects lack because of in-fighting or high turnover of personnel.

The main goals of the Shoshoni Language Project are the following: (1) to teach the language using a pedagogically sound method based on culturally appropriate schemata; (2) to raise the visibility of the language at Fort Hall and in the surrounding nonreservation communities; (3) to provide written materials in Shoshoni at different levels for people to read, from fluent speakers to beginning language learners; (4) to encourage people to write new genres in Shoshoni, such as science, history, book reviews, and current events; (5) to encourage young people to take possession of the language and to feel that they have a role to play in the future of the language; (6) to increase the number of domains in which the language is used; (7) to coin new terms that are acceptable to other speakers of the language; and (8) to increase the prestige of the language overall.

Figure 11.1. Drusilla Gould giving the keynote address (in Shoshoni) at the 2006 Great Basin Languages Conference, Reno-Sparks Indian Colony, Nevada.

Since its inception the Shoshoni Language Project has produced many language-learning materials that are currently being used in primary and secondary schools throughout Shoshoni country. We have also trained personnel from other reservations on how to produce quality language materials in the local dialect they will be teaching. We have participated in Shoshoni language conferences involving both speakers and language teachers and have made our expertise available to local public schools, giving workshops for local primary and secondary teachers on Shoshoni language and culture. The Shoshoni Language Project has also produced a homepage and online Shoshoni dictionary (http:// www.shoshonidictionary.com), which includes different levels of writing, from simple stories for beginners to traditional myths told by tribal elders, some general linguistic information, and a collection of poetry and other original writings in Shoshoni. We encourage all our students who learn to read and write in Shoshoni to teach any of their relatives who speak Shoshoni how to read and write, and we encourage everyone to write in Shoshoni. This has led to the commercial publication of a collection of bilingual poetry by one of our former students (Edmo 2002).

We also encourage students to put the language to immediate use, such as doing their shopping on the reservation in Shoshoni or conducting their business in the language when at the tribal post office. This is meant to increase the domains of use for the language. Today people feel it is odd to hear Shoshoni at the tribal grocery story or post office or casino, even though many of the workers at these places are speakers of the language. As our work has become more visible, this has led to a change in attitudes among the Fort Hall Shoshoni that has allowed ISU to begin teaching evening language classes on the reservation designed specifically for tribal members. This shows how a partnership between an academic institution and a Native American community can be very successful and fruitful for all concerned if there is trust and real concern for the feelings and opinions of tribal members and a sense of ownership by all involved.

The existence of multiple orthographies for Shoshoni has been an issue.[3] We teach our students that since there are two widely used orthographies, they are best served by learning both of them. However, some Shoshoni people feel it is inappropriate to write down the language, especially because of the power of some words. We tell these people that writing gives words a power of their own and allows the words to speak through time. We try to show them how they can hear their ancestors' voices through writing down what they have said and how this can preserve their voices for future generations.

Today there are no areas of modern tribal life at Fort Hall, whether religious, social, or political, that call for the exclusive use of Shoshoni. If the language is used at a religious ceremonial, it is because the members of the family hosting the event are speakers, not because the language is integral to any part of the ceremonial. As the number of domains in which Shoshoni can be used has shrunk, the motivation for young people has decreased accordingly either to learn the language or, if they already are speakers, to continue using the language and passing it on to their offspring. The language ideologies of younger tribal members, whether speakers or not, are of course crucial to the health of any minority language, and processes of language death are strongly associated with speakers' denigration of their own heritage languages. Reynolds (this volume) discusses the implications for language revitalization efforts when language activists ignore the language ideologies of younger speakers.

Finally, many young Shoshoni clearly have assimilated the ideas of the dominant Anglo-American society concerning the importance of the cash economy to one's own material well-being, leaving very little place for traditional culture or the language, even though this Anglo-American worldview is in opposition to traditional Shoshoni values. This is why revitalization activists need to be more attentive to the very real economic needs of minority language speakers, especially younger speakers, who are often much less stable financially. Language revitalization programs need to help tribes create economic incentives for learning and maintaining the language if speakers are to have the economic means and moral support they need to successfully raise the next generation in the language. Economic empowerment of speakers leads to symbolic empowerment of the language. Symbolic empowerment of the language leads to an increase in people learning the language, which increases economic opportunities for teachers and speakers of the language. Today Fort Hall has an unemployment rate many times higher than that of the surrounding communities. Until the Shoshone-Bannock Tribes can find some way of increasing their bottom line and the overall affluence of their tribal members, the language will probably continue to rank below such issues as housing, health, and education on the tribal government's agenda.

Manipulating Language Ideologies

How does a language activist with the goal of language revitalization in his or her community actually manipulate language ideology in order to facilitate the language revitalization process? The activist must first identify those language ideologies that can prevent successful outcomes and then decide the best method to change these attitudes. In this section I look at some language ideologies that can be stumbling blocks and how best to deal with them.

In the area of teaching the language the community must come to value those resources and methods that professionals such as linguists and educational specialists can offer. Accepting their expertise can save a community wasted time and effort. The community must see education as a tool for empowerment of the language and value the role it can play, especially in the education of the next generation of speakers. On the other hand, those of us in academia must recognize that a community's goals and even its definitions of language are often different from our own (Collins 1992). Academics and community language activists must learn to work together in a nurturing, trusting relationship in which each shares his or her own strengths. Non-Native academics must also remember that we are ethically bound to teach community language activists what we know, since they are the rightful heirs of the wealth of knowledge that their ancestors, in partnership with anthropologists and linguists, have preserved for posterity.

Anglo-American society has succeeded in destroying any symbolic value that Native languages may have had, and now it is up to tribal communities and tribal governments to reinvest their language with this lost symbolic "capital." The question arises, How does a community go about doing this? The answer is, simply, through the manipulation of the language ideologies of that community: by changing people's beliefs and ideas about the language. This is why one of the eight goals of the Shoshoni Language Project is to increase the language's prestige. This can be done by offering language classes in the local nonreservation schools, making the language more visible at public tribal events such as pow-wows, and creating rewards for using the language, especially for using the language in new and creative ways such as plays, novels, and poems.

There are a number of areas that most Native American language revitalization projects in the United States need to address in one form or another. The five most important areas are listed below:

1. Increase the domains of use for the language within the tribal society or local community.
2. Promote literacy of the language among speakers and produce written materials in the language at different levels (from beginners to fluent speakers), appealing to different interests.
3. Form some official body to control developments within the language such as decisions concerning orthography, certifying fluent speakers of the language, coining new terms, promoting a reference grammar and dictionary for both speakers and learners of the

language, and so on. This should ideally be done at the tribal or intertribal level. If this is not possible, then the speakers, teachers, and language activists should take on these responsibilities themselves through the creation of a language academy or institute.

4. Create job opportunities for speakers of the language, including language teachers, translators, and writers of educational curricular materials. This, of course, depends on creating economic opportunities for tribal members in general but also involves the creation of scholarships and grants for Native speakers to attend college and the creation of more jobs for Native language specialists within academia.

5. Create rewards for speaking the language through either contests in the language or recognition of speakers at some sort of language-centered event. This will also encourage young people to be creative with the language and may produce future writers in the language. These events can be sponsored either by the tribe or through the schools and other educational institutions.

Conclusion

In this chapter I have discussed a variety of language ideologies that I have observed among the Fort Hall Shoshoni. Here I want to assess their potential for manipulation by language activists. Those language ideologies that are clearly the product of colonial and hegemonic forces can be changed through education, but the general Anglo-American society needs to be educated as well. This has slowly occurred over the last few decades, but there still exist many negative stereotypes about Indian people, Indian cultures, and especially Indian languages out there in the popular culture that are continually reified and perpetuated in the media.

Utilitarianism is a language ideology that can be changed through the reinvestment of the language with a sense of symbolic capital. This can happen if the language receives new prestige value or if the speech community of the language is redefined in a positive manner. Ideally, Shoshoni should become the language of a group of people who use it on a daily basis, even if only in a limited number of domains to start. These can be expanded as time goes on.

The genetic fallacy and the belief that Indian languages are different from all other languages can be changed through education, especially in Shoshoni language classes, where manipulating these language ideologies can really make a difference in a student's success or failure in learning his or her ancestral language. The similarity of all languages with one another in certain areas, including Indian languages, can be stressed not only to second language learners but also to Native speakers in literacy classes, where they can be encouraged to experiment with the language by writing in new genres such as personal diaries, news articles, and family histories.

Another ideology that can be manipulated is elder purism, or the ideas and beliefs of elderly speakers and the role they can play through either negative or constructive criticism. Native American cultures generally have great respect for elders. Because of this, many young speakers of Indian languages find it difficult to go against their elders' wishes. This may also affect how they view their own language. Older speakers, through their words and actions, can often prevent younger speakers from taking possession of the language or feeling that they have a stake in the language.[4] This feeling of possession or ownership is important if speakers are to continue using the language in the future and to pass it on to the next generation. (See Reynolds, this volume, for a discussion of elder pressure on youth and the importance of accepting young speakers' version of "tradition" in Maya communities of Guatemala.) Everything possible must be done to make young speakers feel a deep connection with their language. But this is not enough, as Dauenhauer and Dauenhauer warn: "Ownership is only half of the traditional equation; the other half is stewardship and transmission to the next generation and to the grandchildren" (1998:91).

Joshua Fishman states that only if a language is being actively passed on to the next generation will language revitalization, or "reversing language shift," succeed (1991:398–99). But unless there is a place to use the language (outside of the home or school) and a reason to use it (economic or symbolic capital), the language will remain threatened with each new generation. As a means of avoiding both the threat of extinction and extinction itself, manipulation of language ideologies will provide Native American communities with a critical resource for controlling their linguistic destinies.

CHAPTER 12

Contingencies of Emergence

Planning Maliseet Language Ideologies

BERNARD C. PERLEY

In this chapter I explore some contingencies that determine trajectories for Maliseet language ideologies, which I define in a very broad sense, following Williams as "representations, whether explicit or implicit, that construe the intersection of language and human beings in a social world" (cited in Woolard 1998:3). There are many possible contingencies, but I focus on agency, opportunity, and site. I argue that the emergence of language ideologies is contingent upon an agent and/or agents taking advantage of opportunities to initiate ideological changes from sites of opportunity. I will *re-present* the changes in the development of one Maliseet language project as it reflects reorientations in ideological intent. However, before I state the language ideology parameters of my analysis I must confess that I am fully implicated in the planning of emergent Maliseet language ideologies as both a Native and an anthropologist. Hence, in addition to analyzing the process of ideological transformation I must also include a reflexive consideration of my dual role as Native and anthropologist. I begin by stating that the term "Maliseet" is the term that has been used to describe the Aboriginal peoples who live in the St. John River Valley in New Brunswick, Canada. I prefer the ethnonym Wəlastəkwıyək, People of the Goodly (or Beautiful) River, but I am compelled by the precedence of historical and literary representation to use "Maliseet." Now I follow with an anecdote to situate my involvement in planning Maliseet language ideologies.

Situating Partial Perspectives

My only memory of my first day of school was of me sitting in the front seat of the school bus with tears running down both of my cheeks. The bus driver was sitting in the driver's seat. He was turned in my direction, and I vaguely remember the expression on his face as one of benign frustration. His mouth was moving and words were coming out, but I only remember them as a jumble of sounds. My first language was Maliseet, and I found myself in an alien world where *my native language failed me*.

I share my recollection of that critical moment when my taken-for-granted lived experience was rendered irrelevant and meaningless to indicate how, as a six year old, I learned the hard lessons of an English language ethnocidal symbolic domination and its associated language ideological erasures (Irvine and Gal 2000) of Native American languages and their attendant ideologies.[1] Since that first day of school I have been grappling with the consequences of that domination and those erasures. Today, as a Native anthropologist, I find myself entangled in ideological tugs-of-war between my "professional socialization and the selective attention to language and communication that it entailed" (Kroskrity 2000a:342) and my "Native" socialization and the selective attention to language and communication that it entailed. Kroskrity's critical analysis of the Santa Clara Tewa anthropologist Edward P. Dozier's degree of "insider" status in Arizona Tewa is a cautionary tale for Native anthropologists. How do we as anthropologists and Native anthropologists evaluate the analytical benefits of "insider" status a self-described Native anthropologist purportedly enjoys?[2] As Kroskrity points out in his analysis, Dozier did not enjoy the reflexive options available to Native anthropologists in today's experimental moment but was compelled to work within "linguistic standards of anthropological authentication" (2000a:355). Furthermore, he did not have the range of situated perspectives from "halfie," that is, mixed-blood, anthropologists (Abu-Lughod 1991) to Native anthropologists (Limón 1991) from which to work. In our current age of ethnographic experimentality I wonder, as a Native anthropologist, what kinds of "deafening" (Kroskrity 2000a:357) I am subject to as I work within the constraints of my profession. I recognize the limitations of both sides of my ideological tugs-of-war and find some comfort in the idea that "perhaps all cultural members can be usefully construed as partial members" (Kroskrity 2000a:343). I construe "partial members," in both senses of "incomplete" and/or "biased," as a useful strategy for anthropologists and Natives alike. If we conceive of cultural members as "partial members," then we too can be partial participants in our self-assigned target culture, be it anthropology "culture" or "Native" culture. I accept partiality as a presupposition for analysis from both perspectives as Native and as anthropologist. We cannot know the *whole of culture* as partial members, nor can we be *all members* in any culture. Both perspectives are constrained by the situated knowledge (Haraway 1991) of particular ethnographers writing ethnographies of the particular (Abu-Lughod 1991), be they whole, halfie, or Native. Both perspectives are also constrained by the endemic incompleteness of analytical data as well as the biases of ideological stances.

As a partial member of anthropology and Tobique First Nation it is my responsibility to share some "partial truths" (Clifford 1986) that inform the following discussion.[3] First, Maliseet was my first language, but today I have rudimentary speaking ability and better-than-rudimentary comprehension. Second, I was born on the reservation but have lived off of the reservation for most of my life. Third, I did three years of fieldwork in Tobique First Nation as well as Moh-Sos School as an observer and classroom assistant and returned to finish my Ph.D. at Harvard University. Fourth, I do have family and friends on the reservation, but I don't know all sixteen hundred members of the community. Fifth, I continue to enjoy cooperation and collaboration in my anthropological work from the community despite not residing there. These are just some of the partial truths that are contributing factors in how I situate myself in Maliseet language ideology emergence.

Contingencies of Emergent Language Ideology

As I stated above, I argue that emergent language ideologies are contingent upon many factors, but for this chapter I focus on agency, opportunity, and site. By agency I mean the purposive acts initiated by language advocates to achieve their goals vis-à-vis language ideologies. By opportunity I mean the perceived openings in the intersections of socioeconomic-political structures in which agents may act. And by site I mean the specific sites and/or situations from which agents may initiate their activities with the intent of achieving their goals (Inoue 2004; Kroskrity 2000c; Silverstein 1998b). These three factors are, in turn, contingent upon interdiscursivity and intertextuality. I use interdiscursivity to describe the interdevelopmental discourses various agents have had with one another across temporal frames and between disparate sites (Bauman 2005:146).[4] I use intertextuality to describe the process of incorporating multiple textual forms together in order to enact pragmatic and metapragmatic goals (Hill 2005:113; Irvine 2004:105). The interaction between these two sets of contingencies will be explored in two parts. In part 1 I re-present the development of one particular language exercise from my fieldwork at Tobique First Nation to serve as a Maliseet language exercise. In part 2 I describe how I am currently transforming the above project. Before discussing the development and transformation of these two projects I must contextualize them in the sociopolitical-economic milieu of Canada.

Contextualizing Language Ideology Emergence

Articulating language ideology "as a socio-theoretical frame of analysis" intended to denaturalize anthropological "compartmentalization and re-ification of communicative social practices" (Woolard 1998:4) has the practical benefit of bridging linguistic and social theories. Such analyses require going beyond defining language ideology as the "set of beliefs about language articulated by users as rationalization or justification of perceived language structure and use" (Silverstein 1979:193). This defini-tion is useful for identifying speaker perceptions of language structure and language use, but it needs to be expanded to permit analysis of the pragmatic goals of heritage language advocates and heritage language communities. Therefore, supplementing the above definition to include "representations, whether explicit or implicit, that construe the intersec-tion of language and human beings in a social world" (Williams, cited in Woolard 1998:3) contextualizes these pragmatic goals as situated (Inuoe 2004:1) metapragmatic discourses whose contingency is loaded with cre-ative potential for purposive emergence of ideologies. To understand the potential for Maliseet language agents to manipulate the dominant cul-ture's language ideologies we must first examine how they are temporally and ideologically situated.

A Collision of Language Ideologies

It has been predicted that within the next decade Maliseet is one of many Aboriginal languages in Canada that could become extinct. As I indicated above, I was placed in an environment that systematically eradicated domains of Maliseet language practice. Two generations of Maliseet children at Tobique First Nation in New Brunswick, Canada, have also been denied the opportunity to acquire and use Maliseet as a first language. The civilizing and assimilatory processes described by Field and Kroskrity in the introduction to this volume are similar but not identical in Canada. I present here a selective and abbreviated history of critical events and ideologies that were instrumental in Aboriginal language endangerment and subsequent language advocacy. (See also Meek, this volume, for a discussion of historical events leading up to the present status of Aboriginal languages in the Yukon Territory.)

The decade of the sixties was an ideologically explosive period in Canada. The Trudeau government was trying to implement its "unity" ideology, while influential French leaders were consolidating support for "distinct society" status in order to protect their language and culture. At the same time, the Trudeau "unity" government planned to eliminate the category "Indian" for all government departments and services in its ill-advised white paper of 1969. The tensions of the sixties spilled into the seventies and were still debated in the terms of the Charter of Rights and Freedoms and the Constitution Act of 1982. This did not appease the French leadership, and the passage of the Constitution Act without French input angered French Canadians. By the late eighties the discussions had moved to constitutional debates that led to the Meech Lake Accord of 1990.

The year 1990 was pivotal for both the French and the Aboriginal First Nations of Canada.[5] First, the Meech Lake Accord—a constitutional referendum to address French concerns—was based on the "two founding peoples" ideology, which left the Aboriginal First Nations out of the dialogue. This angered the Aboriginal leadership, and they organized an effort to block the accord from legislative acceptance in the province of Manitoba. Elijah Harper, a member of the Legislative Assembly and Aboriginal leader, consulted with other Aboriginal leaders as well as political scholars on the best methods available to block the accord. He successfully delayed the vote by holding an eagle feather and simply shaking his head "no" when he was asked if the assembly consented to vote on the accord. This simple act was highly publicized across Canada and created political solidarity for Canada's Aboriginal First Nations. The accord was defeated, but the Aboriginal peoples did not have time to celebrate.

The second critical event of that summer of 1990 was the internationally embarrassing armed standoff between over two thousand of Canada's armed forces and thirty Mohawk warriors in the municipality of Oka, Québec. The standoff was the result of centuries-old antagonisms between the French, the English, and the Iroquois peoples over landownership. In the spring of 1990 the municipality of Oka decided to develop a nine-hole golf course into an eighteen-hole golf course by expanding into adjacent parkland. The Mohawks in the area argued that the land was a sacred burial ground and could not be violated; they then built barricades on the roads leading into the park to prevent any development. The municipality ordered bulldozer operators to take down the barricades, but they were unable to do so. The Mohawks were armed. The Sûreté de Québec was called in, shots were fired, and one Québec officer was killed. The situation escalated into the embarrassing spectacle of an armed standoff. Many Aboriginal and non-Aboriginal peoples showed their concern for the welfare of the Mohawk warriors by establishing peace camps in the vicinity of Oka. Non-Aboriginal demonstrations were televised and showed the ugliness of racism in Canada.

With the politics of exclusion (Perley 2006:208) in the Meech Lake Accord debates and the Oka crisis fresh in their minds, Canada's Aboriginal First Nations felt they were under assault by Canada's French and English peoples. The Oka crisis ended but was not satisfactorily resolved. New constitutional debates were initiated to include Aboriginal leadership. The Canadian government initiated a royal commission to look into Aboriginal grievances. Despite governmental attempts to resolve all grievances, the end result was the failure of the second constitutional referendum, known as the Charlottetown Accord, the subsequent failure of the Québec referendum for secession, and the resultant lack of confidence in the leadership of the French, the English, and the Aboriginal First Nations. It was in this ideologically charged climate that I found myself doing fieldwork at Tobique First Nation.

Tobique First Nation is the largest of five Maliseet reservations in New Brunswick. The population at the time of my fieldwork was fifteen hundred. Mah-Sos School is the only school on the reservation; it supports kindergarten through grade six. Most of the teachers are Maliseet. There were about ninety students attending the school. About another hundred students were attending the off-reservation non-Maliseet elementary, middle, and high schools. When I arrived to do my fieldwork the chief had just implemented a Native language class by hiring a university graduate trained in elementary education to teach the class. During this time another member of the community was organizing meetings to solicit support for a Maliseet immersion program. Yet another group was organizing a Maori-inspired "language nest" language immersion meeting in one of the community homes. There was a general awareness of the purported endangerment and/or imminent extinction of the Maliseet language. The Native language teacher was also aware of the state of the language and was developing language exercises to forestall Maliseet language extinction.[6]

Maliseet Interdiscursivity and Intertextuality

The Native language teacher started teaching the Maliseet language to the students at Mah-Sos School on Tobique First Nation using an oral-based pedagogy. Her decision was based on her own experience of how she learned the language. If she learned Maliseet orally, then the students would also learn Maliseet orally. The teacher's approach to teaching the Maliseet language would change, as would her ideas and beliefs about Maliseet language in the classroom. The following is a partial history of some of the changes in a Maliseet language classroom and, more specifically, in one language exercise. The changes from the inception of the exercise to its final form also reflect ideological changes that emerged from opportunistic linkages of interdiscursive events that occurred in several "official" sites over a period of three years. The complete history of the development of the Maliseet language exercise is complex and resists easy representation, so I offer my partial history of the exercise. I identify three significant stages of ideological transformation. The first stage was the teacher's exposure to additional ideologies of language instruction and her subsequent initialization of the project. The second stage implicated me as the classroom assistant providing my artistic visual representations of the Maliseet texts in the project. The third stage of the project involved the recruitment of an elder to provide "expert" consultation for the final translation of the text. In each stage of the process the principal agent, the Native language teacher, took advantage of opportunities to have conversations with multiple language advocates at different sites and at different times.

Nolosweltom and Interdiscursivity

In the first six weeks of the first year of teaching the Maliseet language class the teacher concentrated on an oral-based pedagogy. She would not allow any writing or reading in the class. As stated above, her rationale for using an oral-based pedagogy was that "Maliseet is an oral language. I learned the language orally and I will teach the language orally." After six weeks the teacher decided to test the students on what they had retained. The results were abysmal. The teacher then shifted from an oral-based pedagogy to a text-based pedagogy. Her new reasoning was that having to write and read Maliseet offered better methods for the students to retain the language by allowing them to take their work home and practice studying and speaking the language with their parents and grandparents. At the end of the following six weeks the students showed some improvement in Maliseet retention rates.

As the teacher became more committed to the text-based pedagogy she sought additional training in language instruction. She enrolled in immersion training classes at an area university and was introduced to new ideas and new language advocates. The ideas that were presented came from Maori, Hawaiian, and Mohawk language immersion programs. One key advocate she was introduced to was a Mohawk language immersion teacher who provided an opportunity for the Maliseet language teacher to visit the Mohawk immersion school. It was that experience that would inspire the Maliseet language teacher to initiate the "thanksgiving prayer" project.

As part of her coursework in Maliseet immersion training, the Native language teacher visited the Mohawk immersion school at Kahnawake Reserve, Québec. By her account she was impressed with the school's approach and was eager to learn from its example. She obtained a colorful and nicely illustrated Mohawk thanksgiving prayer book.[7] The teacher had observed the Mohawk students reciting the prayer in the classroom and was so impressed that she wanted to develop a similar prayer of thanksgiving for the Maliseet students. The teacher showed me the Mohawk book and said that we were going to make our own thanksgiving prayer book. She conceived of the "prayer" as distinct from a Judeo-Christian prayer: "It is not a prayer to icons like in the Catholic Church but a prayer for the gifts from nature, love, and community. It was a whole way of life." She wanted the children to learn "patience" because "the prayer has many words," but she also wanted them to learn the "Native perspective" about living in the world, "like the Indians in the past—before the white man came." The teacher explained that the students needed to know about the important plants "like fiddle-heads." The teacher then provided her own translation. The end result was the booklet *Nolosweltom* (I Give Thanks).

Nolosweltom and Intertextuality

The project was ready for the next stage. The teacher hired an artist to provide illustrations for the Maliseet text. She gave the artist the Maliseet text and explained to the artist the goal of providing the students with a Maliseet text with Maliseet illustrations from cover to cover. The artist came and went for the next few weeks. Fortunately for the teacher, a deadline had been imposed upon the project. The artist had a limited time frame in which to produce the drawings. When the deadline arrived the artist gave the teacher his unfinished illustrations in a manila folder. The teacher was disappointed with the illustrations because of their incompleteness and considered the illustration project over. She tossed the folder aside. I picked up the folder and told her I would work on the illustrations over the weekend.

I understood the general goal of the project as creating a series of full-color images that would illustrate the semantic specificity of each line of the Maliseet thanksgiving prayer. The previous artist used Pan-Indian motifs as well as generalized flora and fauna for each line of the prayer. I took over the responsibility to produce the illustrations, and I recalled the teacher's intent to create a prayer that recalled the Native way of life before the white man. I understood and appreciated her intentions, but I decided to make my illustrations for the prayer Maliseet specific by making all the images correspond to the local landscape. Doing so would valorize local knowledge and experience while adding a greater degree of "Maliseetness" to the project. I accomplished this goal by creating illustrations that represented specific places on the reservation as well as specifically local flora and fauna. All the illustrations could then be located in the immediate landscape as well as in the immediate experience of the community. Even though I admired the beauty of the Mohawk version, I felt it was indexically too general. While it is possible to interpret the Maliseet textual version as equally ambiguous, I wanted to disambiguate the Maliseet version by providing specific locales and items. My rationale was to provide the Maliseet text with a visual "text" that is both iconic and indexical. My intended goal was the intertextual reinforcement of "Maliseetness" through visual representation along with textual representation.

Nolosweltom and Metalinguistic Emergence

The third stage of development of the project transpired while I was back at the university finishing my dissertation. When I left the Native language classroom the teacher hired another assistant. However, the assistant was much more than an assistant. She was an elder fluent in both English and Maliseet. She was given the job as the Native language consulting elder.[8] It was only fitting that she would become the classroom assistant, since she was the elder who was the primary consultant on Maliseet grammar and vocabulary for both the teacher and myself. At this point I must make a confession—the elder happens to be my mother. She had already been unofficially involved with the classroom while I was assisting the teacher. Once I returned to the university she became officially involved with classroom language instruction. The teacher could benefit directly from my mother's knowledge of the Maliseet language as the two of them reviewed previously "completed" teaching materials and subsequently revised them. The revisions were often stated in terms of corrections in grammar, semantics, and spelling. *Nolosweltom* was one such project.

During one of my visits to the reservation and the Maliseet language classroom the teacher and the elder showed me their revised *Nolosweltom*. The graphic images were the same, and much of the text was the same. But there were changes. The most significant change was the title of the book. It was no longer *Nolosweltom* (I Give Thanks). It had become *Wəlasweltəmwakən* (An Expression of Thanks). The rationale given for this change was expressed as a way of introducing the children to the traditional community values by collectively giving thanks to the gifts from Mother Earth. Furthermore, the shift from the first person was extended to the first line of the prayer. Originally, the first line was also the title of the prayer: "Nolosweltom" (I give thanks). In the new version it reads "Wəlasweltəmohtine" (Let us give thanks).

In addition to the title change, there were changes in the text. For example, one line from *Nolosweltom* reads "Woliwon samakwon psi tec wen kississmo" (Thank you, water, so that everyone can drink). In the revised edition the line now reads "Wəliwən ciw samakwan matehc wen kətəwəhsmiw" (Thank you for the water so that no one will be thirsty). The difference between the two has been explained as more accurately reflecting Maliseet meaning and intention. These changes also reflect the metalinguistic discourses the teacher and the elder had as they considered how to properly represent the Maliseet language both orthographically and semantically. In turn, their concern for proper representation was directly attributed to their desire to ensure that the students were learning "proper" Maliseet. This was an important consideration because the students would take their Maliseet language exercises home and read them to their parents and grandparents.

Nolosweltom and the Contingencies of Emergence

The above representation of the transformation of the *Nolosweltom* project into *Wəlasweltəmwakən* is necessarily partial—as in incomplete and selective. As I argued above, Maliseet language ideology emergence is contingent upon agency, opportunity, and site. I highlighted three key transformations to illustrate that in each transformation there were new agents engaged in determining, through interdiscursive practice, the potential for manifesting Maliseet language ideology at that particular moment. In the first stage the language agents were the Native language teacher, the chief of Tobique First Nation, and the Mohawk immersion teachers. In the second stage the agents for change were the teacher, the first artist, and I. The third stage placed the teacher and the consulting elder as the primary agents for modifying the existing manifestation of *Nolosweltom* from the earlier interdiscursive engagements. In each of the stages the agents saw opportunities to modify presupposed (Gal 2005:24) ideological stances to reflect metalinguistic articulations of emergent interdiscursivities and intertextualities. In the first stage the teacher took advantage of the opportunity (1) to teach the Native language class, (2) to take the immersion training classes, (3) to visit the Mohawk immersion school, (4) to initiate a new project and enlist the help of skilled assistants, and (5) to turn those efforts into a Maliseet language book and Maliseet language practice. On the other hand, I took advantage of (1) my anthropology training to study language maintenance processes, (2) my Native heritage to gain entry to the Native language classroom, and (3) my art, architecture, and anthropology training to incorporate language with landscape. The consulting elder took advantage of the opportunity to participate first as an unofficial consultant in the "proper" representation of the Maliseet language and second as an official consultant to modify, represent, and subsequently help regiment the Maliseet language. Finally, each transformative event also indicates the sitedness/situatedness of agentive opportunism. (See also Kroskrity's discussion of "robust agency" in this volume for more on how the individual agency of language activists can result in language ideological change and efforts to reverse language shift.) Each metadiscursive and metalinguistic event occurred in an official site and context. In the above examples the "official" sites (Silverstein 1998b) were Mah-Sos School, the universities, and the Mohawk immersion school. The official contexts were educational institutions supported by local authorities such as the Mohawk Reserve, Tobique First Nation, and the area university. The confluence of agency, opportunity, and site made it possible for the various language agents to act upon their anticipations of emergent Maliseet language ideologies.

Planning Emergence:
From Interdiscursivity to Intertextuality

In this section of the chapter I focus on the transformations I am currently planning to the Wəlasweltəmwakən project. The planned transformations arise from my linking of interdiscursive events from my partial membership in the cultures of the anthropologist and the Native. My goal for the transformation of the above project is to repatriate cultural sovereignty as well as to reinscribe the Maliseet language into the landscape.

As a Native of Tobique First Nation, what do I believe about the Maliseet language? Personally, I believe I lost a rich and beautiful way of understanding and expressing my understanding of the world when I lost the ability to speak and understand Maliseet. Why do I believe that? From my English-dominant perspective I believe my elders and my elder brothers speak Maliseet with greater expressiveness than when they speak English. Their jovial, their solemn, and their reverent Maliseet discourses are often punctuated with a sympathetic comment like "Gee, Bern, too bad you don't understand Maliseet. It's funnier [or more sympathetic or more spiritual] in Maliseet." I like to believe that there are moments, with the little I do comprehend and speak, when I can glimpse the world from the Maliseet perspective. I don't have the space here to discuss whether I am experiencing a willful false consciousness.

As an anthropologist, what do I believe about the Maliseet language? I believe that if the community does not actively participate in speaking Maliseet in all social domains throughout the day, then Maliseet as spoken at Tobique First Nation will cease to exist. I believe that community members will lose a distinctive aspect of their identity as Wəlastəkwiyək, People of the Goodly River. I also believe, despite the odds, that there is potential for revitalizing Maliseet at Tobique First Nation. That is why I have been planning my Wəlastəkwi cosmogenesis project.

The cosmogenesis project seeks to resist and reverse the fractal recursivity of dominant English and French cultural erasures of Aboriginal difference. The Maliseet title of the project was and continues to be *Nolosweltom*. The principal audience for the project is the Maliseet community at Tobique First Nation. Additional audiences include other Maliseet First Nations and any other self-selected audiences who choose to engage the project in any of its manifestations.

What kinds of ideological emergence am I expecting from the project? I hope the project will elicit community repatriation of our cultural sovereignty. (For more on this topic see Field and Kroskrity, this volume.) What exactly does that mean? By manifesting language, landscape, and oral tradition into multiple intertextual indexes, I hope to "enregister" (Silverstein, cited in Hill 2005:114) transformative metadiscourses that the community can readily accept as Wəlastəkwi for the direct indexical goal of promoting language revitalization and the indirect indexical goal of promoting and repatriating Maliseet cultural sovereignty. How do I anticipate all this will work?

The original *Nolosweltom* project was a small booklet first described as

a prayer of thanksgiving. As mentioned above, I provided the illustrations
for each line of the prayer. I designed each illustration to anchor each
respective line to the immediate landscape so that the children and the
adults would recognize the prayer as Maliseet. The project expressed a
spiritual component of respect and gratitude for the gifts of Mother Earth.
For the cosmogenesis project I have included Maliseet oral traditions as
a source for making the landscape connection address Maliseet "deep
time" (Perley 2002, 2006:189). I chose to "locate" the center point of the
prayer on the Tobique Rock. The Tobique Rock in Maliseet myth is a
giant rock that was tossed by the Maliseet culture hero Kaluskup a distance of forty kilometers in an effort to strike Kwapit, the giant beaver. In
Maliseet reality the Tobique Rock is currently submerged by the Tobique
and St. John rivers at the point where the rivers meet. The Tobique Rock
serves as my *axis mundi*, centering deep time, the past, the present, and
the future. From this point of axis each line of the prayer is uttered
in twelve points on the compass. The first line must be spoken while
facing east.

At present, the project consists of many sketches, Maliseet texts in revision, a master plan, and one recording of Wəlasweltəmwakən. The next
phase of the project will consist of a series of twelve painted and mixed-
media canvases, each four feet wide and six feet six inches tall. The canvases will be arranged in a thirty-foot (plus or minus) circle along the
cardinal points with two interstitial canvases at thirty-degree intervals.
Each canvas will incorporate the text of the prayer, a medicine-wheel/
compass indicator, a representation of the Tobique landscape as viewed
from the Tobique Rock along its particular compass heading, a small
Wəlastəkwi traditional-style birch-bark scratching, an abstracted representation of the original *Nolosweltom* illustration, and a collage/mixed-media
background uniting all panels in a continuous landscape horizon. Each
panel will correspond to a specific line of the prayer and will have an audio
of a Tobique First Nation community member saying the line in Maliseet.
I plan to have twelve members of the community contribute their voices to
the project. The center of the project will have a graphic representation of
the Tobique Rock. The viewer/audience will be able to view and hear the
project from the translocalized and transtemporalized mythical Tobique
Rock. Standing at the center of the array of paintings will "laminate"

(Gal 2005:29) temporalities (Inuoe 2004; Irvine 2004), intertextualizations (Bauman 2005:146; Irvine 2004), and interdiscursive (Bauman 2005:146) ideologies.

The metapragmatic and ideological heart of this project is cosmo-genesis. It is a cultural self-making that repatriates the oral traditions from non-Maliseet storytellers, academics/critics, folklorists, and other purported experts on American Indian oral traditions. It also repatriates the Maliseet language from non-Maliseet experts, advocates, and critics; repatriates Maliseet claims to landscape; and resists the fractal recursivity of dominant cultural erasures in order to reinscribe "deep time," past, present, and emergent Maliseet language ideologies in all their complex interdiscursivities and intertextualities.

The pragmatic and ideological heart of this project is *Nolosweltom*, an intertextual augmentation of the earlier Maliseet language exercise. The pragmatic goal is to enregister new presuppositions of value for the Maliseet language in order to encourage the community of Tobique First Nation to maintain and revitalize the Maliseet language before it be-comes, like the Tobique Rock, submerged under dominant language erasures.

Cosmogenesis or Obituary?

I began this chapter with a personal anecdote in which I described the Maliseet language as having failed me. Approximately six years have passed since I participated in the *Nolosweltom* project at Mah-Sos School. My Maliseet language skills have not improved, despite the best possible conditions for learning the language. The consulting elder, my mother, would be the ideal teacher. My elder brothers would also be important teachers. During the summer of 2007 I visited my mother and had a conversation with her and my older brother about how little Maliseet I had been able to learn over the last ten years. As I was describing my frustration to them I had a heart-sinking realization that I might never be able to speak Maliseet again. The willful false consciousness I mentioned above was exposed as exactly that—willful false consciousness. I came to grips with the fact that *I failed my native language.* I say this because I feel I played a complicit part in the silencing of my language. Although it may be argued that my failure to acquire Maliseet occurred through no fault of mine, given the assimilatory forces at play, I feel that I did have access to very skilled speakers, and I could have done more to reacquire Maliseet.

How does this revelation affect the cosmogenesis project? If my attempts to enregister new presuppositions of value for the Maliseet language fail as my attempt to be a fluent Maliseet speaker have failed, then state-supported ethnocidal practices and dominant language ideological erasures will have erased Aboriginal difference at Tobique First Nation.[9] Instead of a Wəlastəkwi cosmogenesis, the project will be a grand and beautiful obituary for the language.

However, I am determined to complete the cosmogenesis project. I am counting on the contingencies of emergence to provide opportunities to reorient Maliseet language ideologies toward maintenance and revitalization. As a Native and as an anthropologist I embrace both of my partial memberships in both cultures. The cosmogenesis project is a product of my partial membership. Yet I am not satisfied with partial membership in either culture. I am a full member of both cultures. I have been socialized by both cultures to have a selective attention to language and communication together with their particular situated and partial perspectives. The convergence of two full memberships permits me to go beyond analysis by enlisting analysis to assist me in manipulating contingencies of emergence so that Wəlastəkwi cosmogenesis can be much more than an obituary. As the term suggests, it is the beginning.

CHAPTER 13

Which Way Is the Kiowa Way?

Orthography Choices, Ideologies,
and Language Renewal

AMBER A. NEELY AND GUS PALMER, JR.

Ideological representations of community and self are central to orthography development for Native American language revitalization and education, but this has not always been the case. The purpose of orthography development for Native American languages has shifted through time. After first contact it was seen as a matter of importance for translating texts in order to spread Christianity. Increasingly, assimilation became part of the colonial agenda, particularly for Protestant missionaries and government agents. From the mid-twentieth century on, the focus has been increasingly on documentation and finally on use of writing for teaching and revitalizing indigenous languages. This trajectory has not been a smooth one but has been pushed and pulled by attitudes toward indigenous languages both without and within.

Attitudes and policies about Native American languages are enmeshed within larger public spheres, which can be seen as Foucauldian discourses, or public arenas through which different agents with particular goals promote ideologies that compete for authority.[1] These ideologies can be seen as sets of ideas that work together as a whole about who should make decisions, how decisions should be enforced, and so forth. Ideologies can be professed or unconscious yet exhibited in people's actions, or they may be worked into part of a social infrastructure as practices, traditions, or laws. Kroskrity explores this function of language ideologies that "mediate between social structures and forms of talk" (2000b:21), linking social experience and language forms. A general definition of language ideologies is "representations, whether explicit or implicit, that construe the intersection of language and human beings in the world" (Woolard 1998:3). These intersections fall within a number of different domains and take place within various discourses; as Christina Eire (1998:173) remarks, these discourses are not completely separate from each other but can be interwoven in different ways. The discourse on politics within American society has in the past interacted with the discourse on pedagogy to the extent that an ideology about what and how Native American children should learn resulted for many in boarding school experiences that even today affect how these children as adults view their languages (see Crawford 1997; Linn et al. 2003). Although policies finally exist to support the teaching and promotion of Native American languages in schools and communities, many ideologies discussed here are hold-overs from that period, including language purism and linguistic social Darwinism, such as that illustrated by the English-Only movement.

In this chapter we address these issues in a larger context and then in a more specific case study. We first take a moment to examine discourses and language ideologies surrounding the role of orthography standardiza-tion in language revitalization efforts. Thereafter we build upon this back-ground in examining the situation of Kiowa, a Native American language of Oklahoma. Multiple Kiowa orthographies exist, and new ones are con-tinuously being created, a state we call *heterographia*, a term coined by Sean O'Neill.[2] In using this term we extend Mikhail Bakhtin's (1987:263) concept of *heteroglossia*, defined as a multitude of voices from different contexts to writing. Heterographia represents a situation in which one language is approached via multiple writing systems. There are multiple systems taught, while others are created in situations where students are encouraged to spell out sounds in whatever personal system seems best to them. We delineate key factors contributing to the continuing hetero-graphic state of the Kiowa language, including historical and linguistic circumstances as well as language ideologies grounded within various discourses. We then examine the constraints this state poses for language renewal efforts in the community. By weighing these factors, we present a framework for considering whether or not orthographic standardization is the best action for groups in similar circumstances, taking careful note of possible repercussions and various sociopolitical factors that could affect language renewal in the community.[3]

Orthography in Language Renewal:
The Practical and the Problematic

The usefulness of writing in language revitalization is not a straight-forward assumption, as the proliferation of literature on the topic demonstrates (Baraby 2003; Bennett et al. 1999; Biava 1990; Bielenburg 1999; Dauenhauer and Dauenhauer 1998; Hinton 2001c). Writing a language reflects concerns from discourses on politics as well as pedagogy, and there are important ideological and practical considerations to this issue. Some emphasize the impracticality of completely avoiding literacy as well as the positive social effects of indigenous language literacy (Bielenburg 1999; Spolsky and Irvine 1982). Many efforts assume literacy as a prerequisite for effective language renewal and emphasize the language as a resource as opposed to a problem or a right (Bernard 1992, 1997; Hornberger 1997). But adoption of Euro-American language ideologies regarding the proper methods of language pedagogy (through the context of school, using written methods) has led to disappointments in many communities (Anonby 1997; Cowell 2002; Greymorning 1997).

An intensified focus on oral language learning in American Indian communities has been inspired by both Joshua Fishman's (1991) insistence that revitalization needs to focus on reinstating intergenerational mother tongue transmission and the promise of Master-Apprentice approaches (Hinton 2002).[4] The success of projects that emphasize immersion learning and oral production over writing, including the Maori and Hawaiian language nests (Stiles 1997) and the Cherokee immersion preschools in Tahlequah, Oklahoma, is quite encouraging (Mary S. Linn, personal communication). In many American Indian communities there have also been a number of ideological objections to writing Native languages down. These objections include beliefs that some aspects of culture are too sacred to be written and that literacy is not a traditional educational technology as well as a desire to avoid further exploitation of Native languages (Adley-SantaMaria 1997; Brandt 1981; Pecos and Blum-Martinez 2001).

However, the reality is that certain prerequisites must be met in order to teach a language through oral means alone. For example, a language program needs fluent speakers of teaching age who have been trained as teachers as well. In communities where these resources are not available it may be unrealistic to avoid the use of writing completely (see Dauenhauer and Dauenhauer [1998] on the difference between natural and artificial learning situations). In public school circumstances it may be nearly impossible to avoid writing altogether. Ken Hale (2001:227) delineates five different types of immersion contexts, and only the first degree (learning at home) avoids writing to any large extent. Leanne Hinton also discusses the interdependence of writing and language education: "Language pedagogy depends in part on the written word: even if oral approaches are stressed and native literacy is not being taught, teachers might depend on a writing system in their language to be able to create lesson plans and curriculum" (Hinton and Hale 2001a:240).

Many tribes face the challenge of having very few fluent speakers and must fall back on early written documentation. The "Breath of Life, Silent No More" workshop held in California supports language learners who must rely upon written records when there are no more speakers of their heritage languages (Hinton and Ahlers 1999). Other tribes who have been working to reconstruct or "reawaken" their languages based upon written sources include the Pequot and the Miami, who have had a significant degree of success (Daly 2002).

The balance between oral and written production and comprehension in language learning is examined in detail by Bennett et al., who determine that there is "a place for writing in preserving oral languages" (1999:86). Based on the experiences of the Hupa community, they give practical advice in the form of a checklist and focus on the use of writing as a memory aid in oral acquisition and to add to language organization skills (Bennett et al. 1999:86). Many tribes also have "post-literacy" projects such as the multimedia dictionary and CD-ROM for the Western Mono language community described by Kroskrity (2002). These types of media are examples of how literacy and technology can help provide motivation for language learners as well as speakers by enlarging the number of domains for language use (Hornberger 1997). Increasingly, young Native American scholars emphasize appropriation of technology for Native empowerment and the reclaiming and reinventing of literary traditions (see Bernard 1992; Donaldson 1998:46–47; Lyons 2000).

Orthography Standardization Benefits and Challenges

When the language is being taught in institutions like high schools and universities, writing cannot be avoided, and neither can the question of standardization of orthography. While it often is combined with oral methods of instruction, writing is the expected means of measuring progress. The Native American language instructors at the University of Oklahoma support standardization of writing method or orthography, as it has been their experience that without literacy use, second language instruction is nil. It is especially crucial when instructors are not fluent in their heritage language.[5] In the case of Cherokee, Creek, and Choctaw (which are also taught at OU) standardization has already occurred at the tribal level, so instructors are free to concentrate on the development of teaching materials, pedagogical methods, and instruction. The Parker McKenzie writing system is used in the Kiowa language course at OU, and the instructors note that those who enroll generally do not display much resistance to the new writing system. One might say that most college students have been conditioned to learn in a formal instructional setting, so that when they enroll in a course they expect to use literacy and will be less likely to question the writing system as instructed.

Teaching American Indian languages to students, Indian and non-Indian alike, is easier for university instructors than it is for those in community class settings at the level of local community language revitalization efforts due to various language ideologies, which will be explored in more detail below. Language planners and committee members need to think about who will be using the orthography and how writing fits into the larger scale of efforts to reverse language shift. If the orthography is to be only a memory aid for the primarily oral language learner, then standardization is really not as important. The question of the relationship between orthographic standardization and language teaching and renewal has been called a "thorny" problem (Frawley, Hill, and Munro 2002a; Hinton 2001a).[6] Linguists starting with Kenneth Pike have long realized that perfect one-to-one phonetic representation is only important in the context of linguistic research and that "the purpose of an orthography is not to represent all the sounds of a language" but merely to be representative enough to be useful for speakers and learners (Francis and

Reyhner 2002:218). Employing an orthography similar to that of a dominant language may cause confusion that can be a real barrier to language teaching (Gudschinsky 1973:117). Using (English) orthographic conventions with which language learners are already familiar can also cause confusion in reproduction of the target language's phonemes.

Pedagogical wisdom holds that a one-to-one phonemic correspondence and a one-word, one-form spelling system are easier for language learners to internalize. These types of "professional language ideologies," found within the discourse on pedagogy, can be at cross-purposes with communities' own understandings and valuations of language, creativity, and syncretism (Collins 1998; Kroskrity 2002). However, a value on individual creativity can become problematic in a formal classroom context, as Innu students have found: "Continuous groping and frequent disparities in spelling habits on the part of the teachers are readily noticed by students and entail considerable disillusionment" (Baraby 2003:203). Among students themselves, an inability to read one's own notes intensifies frustration and feelings of despondency. In addition, when languages with complex phonemic inventories are undergoing language attrition (losing phonemic distinctions), accurate spelling is crucial for proper pronunciation to be learned (Dauenhauer and Dauenhauer 1998).

Other considerations linked to orthography choice involve a writing system's symbolic value, which may tie into discourses of politics and the relationship of a language and its speakers to the world at large. As Crook, Hinton, and Stinson note, "the development of writing systems is necessarily affected by social values to at least as great an extent as the values of pragmatics or linguistic economy" (1976:1). Symbolic value can be attached to a writing system both through the history of its development and through its relation or similarity to dominant cultures' orthographies. Both of these types of connections can have repercussions for the degree of ownership, representativeness, and effectiveness people ascribe to a script (Eire 2002:240). There can be both positive and negative effects to any choice of orthography. Luykx (2004:150) examines the problematic nature of orthographic standardization in Quechua, noting that using a system based on historically accurate Quechua that does not match current linguistic practice can be detrimental to the language's status as well as to pronunciation. Dauenhauer and Dauenhauer, in their discussion of Tlingit literacy, indicate that endless discussion about changing the writing system "offers a convenient opportunity to procrastinate or postpone learning to read and write in the existing standard" (1998:87). Loether (this volume) considers orthography choice to be a particularly problematic part of corpus planning. He also asserts that avoidance of such troubling issues can be a handicap for language revitalization; a strategy must be devised to deal with incompatible language ideologies. Baraby (2003:198) notes that it took speakers of Innu languages more than twenty-five years to adopt a standard orthography, as a number of communities already had writing systems for their various dialects, and they did not want to move to a system that they felt was less representative for them.

Kiowa Orthographic Choices

The Kiowa situation is particularly illustrative of the effects of "extended discussion" regarding orthography. Despite the fact that many orthographies have been developed over the years, many of them by Kiowa speakers themselves, none of these systems has gained widespread acceptance beyond the bounds of one school or group. Three systems have the longest-running periods of usage: (1) the Parker McKenzie (PMK) system, used at the University of Oklahoma since 1992; (2) the Alecia Gonzales (AG) system, an English-based orthography used at Anadarko High School since 1990; and (3) the Summer Institute of Linguistics (SIL) system, used in the hymnal booklet published in the 1960s. Taken historically, all three systems have been of perhaps equal use but tend to be limited in geographic scope. Still, since both the AG and the PMK systems are used in universities, it is fair to say they have more worldwide implications, especially since the SIL system is no longer actively taught.

Some Kiowa educators avoid choosing an orthography altogether, promoting use of a personal "phonetic" system, where language learners use English orthographic conventions to spell Kiowa words however seems best to the student, a heterographic situation. So although centripetal forces bind the community together, including an overarching concern for preservation of Kiowa language and culture, differing orthographic conventions interfere with potential cooperation between different groups of Kiowa language learners. In the next section we examine more closely the state of the Kiowa language and current revitalization efforts.

Kiowa Language: Assessing Endangerment and Resources

Kiowa is spoken in southwestern Oklahoma, mainly in Kiowa and Caddo counties (figure 13.1). As is the case for most Oklahoma tribes today, the Kiowa Tribe does not possess a reservation. Instead, many Kiowa people live in small towns or on lands that were part of family allotments, scattered among their non-Indian neighbors, and all children attend public schools together. These arrangements were made by the Jerome Commission in 1901, which forced the breakup of all reservations within the borders of the soon-to-be state of Oklahoma, including the Kiowa-Comanche-Apache Reservation. The Kiowa Tribe has approximately eleven thousand members, according to the 2005 tribal rolls. The actual number of fluent speakers is less easily discerned. There has been no systematic language status survey. Estimates range from four hundred to a mere handful, but our best guess seems to be between ten and twenty truly fluent speakers. Somewhere between fifty and two hundred people are able to converse to a degree, but some of these operate through employing phrases memorized verbatim (see table 13.1). Today, the locus of language learning is predominantly in schools. Opportunities to hear extended exchanges of spoken Kiowa are limited, and cultural events such as powwows, church events (including Native American Church meetings), and perhaps family reunions are the best opportunities to hear Kiowa spoken.[7] The language is no longer being learned by children as a first language; very little if any intergenerational mother tongue transmission is taking place. The majority of speakers are above the age of sixty, and elders do not often get or always make use of opportunities to converse in Kiowa.

The number, age, and location of speakers indicates that in terms of Fishman's (1991:88–90) Graded Intergenerational Disruption Scale (GIDS), Kiowa is somewhere between Stage 7 (socially integrated, ethnolinguistically active speakers, but beyond child-bearing age) and Stage 8 (few speakers, mostly socially isolated elders) of language shift. This is the stage of greatest endangerment, during which documentation and individual types of language learning are most appropriate. Despite this assessment, there are activities of Kiowa revitalization that pertain to Stage 5 ("extra-communal reinforcement of literacy" in Kiowa), including the teaching of Kiowa combined with literacy-based testing in public

TABLE 13.1. Estimates for Approximate Age and Number of Speakers.

	Est. Number of Speakers	Age Range of Speakers
General	~300, Range 40–500	Mostly 60+
Able to tell stories	~10, Range 5–20	60–70+
Conversational	~100, Range 50–200	50+
Can interact with formulaic phrases	200–300*	40+*
Understands	200–500	40+
Speaks a few words	~500	Most of remaining older Kiowa, kids from certain schools

*This number would likely be increased if students (Kiowa and non-Kiowa) of the Kiowa classes at OU were included.

Note: Compiled estimates from five knowledgeable community members circa April–May 2005. A systematic survey has yet to be completed.

schools and use of Kiowa at intertribal powwows. Yet the community does not actually have the resources to sustain these efforts; there are no advanced classes (except those at OU), and few at the powwows actually understand what is being said. Importantly, while Kiowa still fulfills important religious and ceremonial functions, it is no longer being spoken in most homes (a requirement of Stage 6, necessary to approach Stage 5). Stage 6 ("intergenerational, informal oralcy" [Fishman 1990:95]) is the key for language revitalization efforts, as this is the stage in which intergenerational mother tongue transmission is functional. According to Fishman's model of reversing language shift, this is the stage that must be reattained if a language is to have any hope of long-term revival and survival.

Since at least the mid-1970s there has been continued interest in teaching the language within the Kiowa community. Most Kiowa language advocates and teachers feel that writing is an important tool in language learning, although there are those in the community who disagree, preferring a focus on oral means of transmission. For the most part, teaching of Kiowa occurs in schools (on four levels: elementary, middle school, high school, and university) and organized classes. Kiowa is being taught in at least five different geographical areas, both within and outside traditional Kiowa geographic borders (see table 13.2), including three for children or young adults as well as a few community classes for adults. All

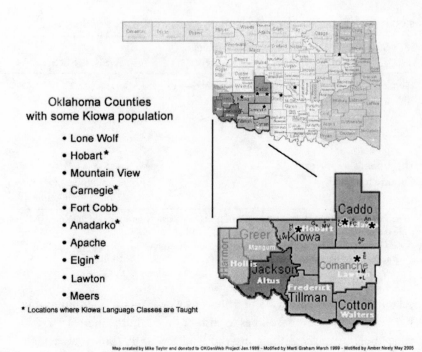

Oklahoma Counties
with some Kiowa population

- Lone Wolf
- Hobart*
- Mountain View
- Carnegie*
- Fort Cobb
- Anadarko*
- Apache
- Elgin*
- Lawton
- Meers

* Locations where Kiowa Language Classes are Taught

Map created by Mike Taylor and donated to OKGenWeb Project Jan.1999 - Modified by Marti Graham March 1999 - Modified by Amber Neely May 2005

Figure 13.1. Locations of Kiowa language classes in Oklahoma.

of the instructors utilize some form of writing in their efforts, most in combination with oral instruction.

Community efforts include language classes or group meetings from western to northeastern Oklahoma. These efforts are not centrally coordinated, and every class has its own materials, methodology, and writing system. A further challenge for cooperation is that these areas are all at some distance from each other. As shown in figure 13.1, the two closest teaching sites are Carnegie and Anadarko, separated by a thirty-to-forty-minute drive. To our knowledge there have been no successful attempts to bring language teachers together to discuss materials and methodologies.

A particularly rousing challenge is in regard to language-learning opportunities for tribal members who are spread across the country. Between the 1950s and 1970s many Kiowa people seeking jobs and economic advancement moved or in some cases were relocated (through programs sponsored by the federal government) to large cities as far away

TABLE 13.2. Places Where Kiowa Is Taught, by Location and System.

Place Taught	Level	Age Group	Writing System Utilized	Frequency of meetings (usage)
Anadarko—Public School	High School	14–18 yrs	System I	3 classes, daily
Chickasha—USAO	College/University	18 and up	System I	1 class, 1x weekly
Norman—OU	University	18 and up	PMK system	4 classes, 3x weekly
Elgin—Public School	Jr. High/High School	12–18 yrs	System VI	2 classes, weekly
Carnegie—ALC	Adults/Any Level	Adults	System IV	1 class, 1x weekly
Tulsa—UT	Adults/Any Level	Adults/Families	System II	1 class, 1x weekly
Carnegie—Public School	Elementary	5–10 yrs	System V	2x a month

USAO = University of Science and Arts of Oklahoma; OU = Oklahoma University; ALC = Adult Learning Center; UT = University of Tulsa.
Note: Based on interactions with elder Kiowa community members between April and October 2005. Systems are in descending order according to frequency of use.

as Chicago and Los Angeles. There are few materials available for self-paced learning: two tapes, one a "sampler" and the other a tale (Russell 1991), and two recordings of hymns, one with a lyrics booklet (Kotay, Lassiter, and Wendt 2002) and one with the book *The Jesus Road* (Lassiter, Ellis, and Kotay 1999). A new addition is a series of storybooks for small children by Alecia Gonzales that comes with a CD recording of the stories and color illustrations by budding young Kiowa artists. The majority of other written materials are most useful only when combined with personal instruction by a fluent speaker. This includes the course packets used at the University of Oklahoma and the textbook used at the University of Arts and Sciences in Chickasha and Anadarko High School (Gonzales 2000).

Since the language is already being taught in schools, a common orthography (with or without being officially sanctioned) could hasten the progress of revitalization efforts. Materials could be shared, providing more resources for teachers and opportunities to build upon previous stages of language learning. A shared system would also help provide more functions and domains for use of Kiowa, emphasized by Fishman as a key step in language revitalization (1991:338). Functions of long-distance communication such as letter writing, distance learning, and newsletters would also be facilitated by use of a shared writing system. A usable dictionary would be a welcome addition, and a pedagogical grammar could ease the burden of teachers.[8] Still, there are some good reasons why these developments have not yet occurred.

Writing Kiowa Sounds: Past and Present

The first attempt to write the Kiowa language in a systematic way was John Harrington's work in the 1920s. Harrington worked with his own system, loosely based upon the Americanist phonetic alphabet. His vocabulary remains to date the only large-scale published collection of Kiowa words.[9] Kiowa speaker and self-taught linguist Parker McKenzie worked with Harrington in his younger years and became a renowned linguist in his own right, receiving an honorary doctorate from the University of Colorado in 1990. McKenzie's writing system (PMK) constitutes one of two major types of writing systems in use today (see tables 13.2 and 13.3). The PMK system was designed with teaching, description, and ease of use in mind, based on the typewriter keyboard and the one-sound-to-one-phoneme principle to a large extent. McKenzie was determined to make Kiowa a written language. In his introduction to a manuscript titled "Essential Elements of the Kiowa Language" (n.d.), he wrote:

> The decision to write my native language came during my twentieth birth year, for Kiowa had been an unwritten language through the centuries. I resolved to write it some day, and that that day would be when I shall have devised and perfected the key for writing it. Finding a simplified system, however, was most baffling, and it was a prolonged process, particularly so for one lacking a sound educational background and even the first rudiments in the science of languages.[10]

The other most commonly used form of orthography we call *transphonic* (and there are a variety of related systems), which indicates their major goal: to *trans*fer literacy skills from one language to another. Many of these systems are inspired by or similar to the system designed by students and teachers at the Summer Institute of Linguistics about four decades ago. The development of the SIL system, a phonemic system based on English orthography, involved a number of people from the Kiowa community. The product of this collaboration was a book of original

TABLE 13.3. Examples of Various Kiowa Writing Systems.

	"Come here"	"one"	"man"
IPA	èm ą̀·	pá·gɔ̀	k'yą'·hị'
Harrington	'ęim-'H	pH̄'-gα	kyH̄-hị'H
PMK	èm á:	fá:gàu	qá:hị̱
Transphonic			
System I	Aim ahn	p'ah gaw	kxai-hehn
System II	Aim ahn	pah gaw	keanh hēenh
System III	Aim-An	pah-gaw	k'yah-h[ee]h
System IV	Aim-an	phah-gaw	k'yah-heen

IPA = International Phonetic Alphabet; PMK = Parker McKenzie writing system.

Christian hymns still used in the community today.[11] These English-based systems are sometimes called *phonetic*, although *phonic* is a more accurate description, as they are based on English spelling orthography. They make creative use of many digraphs, trigraphs, and even quadrographs to indicate certain consonant and vowel qualities. Some linguists refer to this type of writing as folk writing (not her own term, but see Hinton [2001c:246]), but we prefer *transphonic*, as it calls attention to intent. Table 13.2 presents an overview of domains where some of the writing systems are used, and table 13.3 provides three examples of writing in the various systems.[12]

Some of the transphonic systems were also conceived with ease of teaching and learning in mind. Kiowa teacher and author Alecia Gonzales put a lot of time and care into developing her system (System I), which she has improved upon throughout her years of teaching Kiowa at the high school and college levels. She described the development of her system to us in this way:

Parker was a friend of my family, and he gave me a lot of materials and things off and on, and talked with me. So I was familiar with his system. But being a speech person, this was easier for me. And as I tried it on my nieces and nephews, and later on my grandchildren, they were my field study, my guinea pigs, and they just seemed to fall right into it. And I thought well, I think I'll try it. So as I went out there, I found out the sounds that are difficult for us, and how they could be noticeable, and recognized for the sound that they're supposed to represent.

These "difficult sounds" are the main issue that any Kiowa orthography must address, and transphonic writing systems, which are all based on English, can be complicated because Kiowa has a number of consonants not present in English. Particularly problematic for English-dominant speakers is the Kiowa four-way distinction in stops, featuring four distinctive phonemes within a single place of articulation: (1) voiceless, unaspirated; (2) voiceless, aspirated; (3) voiced, unaspirated; and (4) ejective consonants (see table 13.4). This range is distinguished in three different places of articulation (labial, alveolar, and velar), and there is one range of fricatives/affricates as well. This results in eight sounds that are not found, either contrastively or at all, in English. In addition, there are also six vowels and four diphthongs to represent, all of which are further distinguishable by length and/or nasalization. Vowels also bear phonemic tone.

The PMK system makes use of those letters of the English alphabet for which the corresponding phonemes are not present in Kiowa (c, f, j, v, q, and x) to represent these eight sounds without resorting to diacritics or any symbols not present on a regular keyboard (see table 13.4). McKenzie also used two digraphs, *ch* for the affricate /ts/ and *th* for the ejective /t'/.

Transphonic systems deal with the consonantal "discrepancy" in various ways. The majority make extensive use of digraphs or trigraphs to try to systematically represent Kiowa consonants not present in English. Some make use of the apostrophe, but to represent different qualities. Where one system uses it, as does the International Phonetic Alphabet (IPA), to mark the ejective consonants, another uses it to mark plosives.[13] Other systems use it to mark only a glottal stop.

Not all of these systems make all of the phonemic distinctions systematically (see table 13.4). Some conflate categories from the plosive gradient scale, for example, using one symbol, t, to represent three distinct phonemes: voiceless, unaspirated /t/, aspirated /tʰ/, and ejective /t'/. Linguistically, this is referred to as "underspecification," which can make it difficult for students to learn the language. Although it is certainly possible to internalize spelling rules and distinguish between homophones from context, under- and overspecification have been shown to be detrimental to language learning, especially in situations where language input is limited (Dauenhauer and Dauenhauer 1998). In combination with the reduced sensitivity to certain phonemic distinctions often existing in situations of language shift, spelling and even reading can become a

TABLE 13.4. Comparative Chart of Multiple Kiowa Orthography Systems.

PoA	IPA	PMK	SIL	Sys I	Sys II	Sys III	Sys IV
Stops							
Labial	p	f	p	**p', p**	p	p̱	**ph, bh, bp, bp'h, bph**
	pʰ	p	ph	**p, p'**	p	p	p
	b	b	b	b	**b, p**	b	b
	p'	v	p'	p'	p	p'	**p', ph, pbh, pbh'**
Alveolar	t	j	t	**t, td**	**t, d**	ṯ	**th, dt, dt'**
	tʰ	t	th	**t**	t	t̄	t
	d	d	d	d	d	d	d
	t'	th	t'	**th**	t	t'	**td', td**
Velar	k	c	k	**kh, k'**	k	k̲	**gk, gk'**
	kʰ	k	kh	**k, kh**	k	k̄	**k, kh**
	g	g	g	**g, kh**	g	g	g
	k'	q	k'	kx	k	k'	**kch, kch'**
Laryngeal	ʔ	-	'	'	'	'	'
Fricatives							
Alveolar	/s/	s	s	s	s	s	s
Alveolar-V	/z/	z	z	z	z	**s**	z
Laryngeal	/h/	h	h	h	h	h	**h, h'**
Affricates							
Alveolar	/ts/	ch	ts	**ts**	**ts**	ts	**tsh**
	/ts'/	x	ts'	**ts**	**ts**	t's	ts, ts'
Sonorants							
Labial	/m/	m	m	m	m	m	m
Alveolar	/n/	n	n	n	n	n	n
	/l/	l	l	l	**dl**	l	**dl, l**
Palatal	/j/	y	y	y	**e, y**	y	y
Vowels							
Front	/i/	i	ee	**ee, eh**	ee	**ee, eeh**	**ee, y**
	/e/	e	ay	ay	**ay, ai, aCe**	**aih, ai, aCe, ay**	**ay, ai, aCe**
	/a/	a	ah	**ah, ai**	ah	ah	**a, igh, ih', Cye, y**
Back	/u/	u	oo	**oo, ou**	oo	**ooh, ou**	**oo, wu**
	/o/	o	ow	**oe, oCe**	**o, oh, ow, oe, oCe**	oh	**o, oCe, oh**
	/ɔ/	au	aw	**au, aw**	au, aw	**aw, oh, auh**	**au, aw, ow**
Dipthongs	/ui/	ui	ooy	ooie	ooie	ooi	ooy
	/oi/	oi	owy	oye	oy	oy	oy
	/ai/	ai	ahy	ai	igh	ai	iCe
	/ɔi/	aui		oiye	oy	oy	auoy
Length		:, ā	*doubling*	-	-	-	-
Nasalization			n	**n, -**	**nh, -**	[ ]	**Vn, nV, nVe, n'V**

PoA = place of articulation; IPA = International Phonetic Alphabet; PMK = Parker McKenzie writing system; SIL = Summer Institute of Linguistics system.
Note: Representations of phonemes in current writing systems. Bolded graphs indicate under- or overspecification, based on a comparison of spelling conventions in that system with IPA from Watkins (1984). A *C* between vowels indicates any consonant, and a *V* preceding or following a consonant represents any vowel.

major challenge not only for language learners but increasingly also for speakers who may no longer be accustomed to speaking the endangered language.

In addition, phonemic vowel length and nasalization are not always shown systematically and are sometimes ignored. Kiowa is also a tonal language with three tones: high, low, and falling.[14] Most fluent speakers are highly aware of tonal distinctions connected with particular lexical items, and incorrect use is a serious impediment to conversation. However, not all classes explicitly teach this. As can be seen in the examples above, the PMK system makes use of the diacritics for tone in a similar way to IPA. Tone is not marked at all in the majority of the transphonic systems.

Kiowa Language Ideologies and Their Respective Discourses

There are structural and/or pedagogical complications with most of the current Kiowa writing systems, yet teachers and students are loyal to the systems they have chosen. Users of many of these systems do not hold that their system is better than any other but rather that their system works for them, although "working" is perhaps a relative term. The writing system should work not only for the individual but also for communication with others. Matters are further complicated by language ideologies enmeshed within larger public spheres of discourse (Eire 1998:16). When it comes to representations, symbolic and practical issues of power and authority ultimately cast shadows over decision-making processes. A standard orthography is not just a practical representation of a language but also an intrinsically political manifestation of group relations. The emphasis in recent decades on the importance of Native American languages as symbolic tools and badges of identity that encode and embody important cultural information has the potential for both empowerment and disenfranchisement (Kroskrity 2000b:8). Particularly in Native American communities, these issues also draw on questions of authority and authenticity. Following Eire, we suggest that the interwoven Foucauldian discourses of tradition, religion, pedagogy, and power underlie understandings of language in the public sphere, "impinging on . . . orthography choices" (1998:173). A number of ideologies spring from these quietly dynamic discourses, and we treat them singly as well as examine interactions between them.

Discourses on Tradition, Power, and Authority

Discourses on tradition underlie many aspects of Native American culture. Within the discourse on the tradition of a community, connections are often made between culture, language, and ideas of authenticity, sovereignty, and nationhood (see, e.g., Kroskrity 2000b; Pecos and Blum-Martinez 2001; Schieffelin and Doucet 1994). Language ideologies are found in the discourses on tradition of many American Indian communities. Within the Kiowa community some have expressed the idea that it is better to use oral methods to teach an oral language, while others feel that doing so is an excuse to avoid orthography issues altogether. What Dorian (1998) has termed "language purism" is also linked to the discourses of tradition, power, and authority: a number of elders have indicated reluctance to use Kiowa words for things of the "modern" world. For many elders this reluctance is connected with a disassociation of anything "modern" from Kiowa, from cars to television to the technology of writing itself.

According to some of the Kiowas with whom we have spoken, it would be just as well if Kiowa was spoken until it is spoken no more, and once it ceases to be spoken it would mean the end of Kiowa as it is understood right now. In the minds of some Kiowas, especially older speakers, Kiowa can never be anything but a spoken language. It is an attitude more complex than many of us realize. There are those who believe that something that occurs in one's life as natural as drinking water and breathing air is best left alone, that things that work are best left alone because tampering with them might cause something to go terribly wrong. Some would argue that we should formulate rules to protect the Kiowa language because of a secret fear that if someone meddles in something as important as language it might set off things that could turn against us.

There are also those within the community who dispute this, as evidenced by the continued attempts of other elders to write the language. Yet many Kiowa people we know agree that language change should be worked against at all costs. These types of conservatism are strengthened by a fear of accusations from peers that anyone who uses new words (or even older words that are less widely known) is trying to "change" the language; the authority to do so may be called into question. The invention of slang and other hybrid forms coined by children (who often fit English pronunciation and word formation rules to Kiowa lexemes) is sometimes seen as disrespectful or just "un-Kiowa." But as one elder from the community expressed to one of us, community values about the need to speak the language correctly should not keep people from learning the language:

> I guess if you mean by disrespect, I mean um, because I don't . . . I don't want to speak, because I want to speak it right. And so that's a measure, you're showing respect for the language, when you're afraid that you're going to not speak it right. There's that. But . . . and then on the other hand . . . if you really want to speak it, then you will try to learn it.

This dislike of change goes beyond a simple fear of change in endangered language; there is a very real fear of the dangers of "tampering" with a system that is "natural and real," of damaging what is already being lost. Many Kiowa elders have expressed regret that "Old Kiowa" is no longer spoken by anyone, that the language will never be what it once was. Ingrained in the psyche of many Kiowa people is the idea that Kiowa as a spoken language has already passed and that whatever is passed down will not be Kiowa at all, no matter how hard Kiowas themselves try to preserve and maintain it. Kiowa people seem divided about the idea that establishing a writing system will help curtail language shift and language change. This goes along with an overall disinclination or resistance to change how Kiowa has been acquired (i.e., as a spoken language), which is connected to ideas that "spoken Kiowa is the only true Kiowa." This idea, despite the widespread use of writing in previous generations by fluent speakers and teachers, is quite prevalent: some have almost always indicated preference for Kiowa orality over Kiowa literacy, seeing it as an either/or choice.

Elders' roles in society are changing, as Kiowa society has become more and more assimilated to white American culture. Respect for elders has always been an irreproachable facet of Kiowa culture, but danger of the possibility of a clash between traditional elder authority and the Western obsession with youth-oriented culture and rebel idolization remains. If a new writing system were to be taught to youth, care would need to be taken to continue to reassert the ultimate authority of the elders as language experts and to emphasize the supplementary character of writing as a language-learning tool (see Bennett et al. 1999:9). One way of involving elders is illustrated by Cowell (2002:35) in his discussion of the bilingual materials developed by the Northern Arapaho tribe, whose elders designed dialogues and stories for language learning.

Many language ideologies are connected with different power struggles both within the community and between the community and wider society. Language can be used to express identity and solidarity, but along with in-group identification come certain types of exclusion. People have different types of personal and political ties and varying expectations about who is authorized to speak about certain subjects that are bound up with ideas of authenticity. In connection with ideologies from the discourse of tradition, speakers of the language are perceived as more authentically Kiowa, just as people from tribes who have few remaining speakers are perceived as less authentically Indian. Speakers of the language are correspondingly attributed more authority, and those in authority justify their position on the basis of their status as speakers. This power structure is the reason why decisions regarding the language, including which orthography to use, can only be made by those with the proper (linguistic and cultural) authority to do so. As Walker (1969:149) noted, becoming embroiled in tribal politics, especially a particular faction, can be a major deterrent to agreement upon orthography and other literacy proposals. Politics in the Kiowa tribe is connected to various levels of organization, including one's connections of family, band, and religious affiliation within the tribe.[15] Issues of authority are often questioned in language use (and this goes doubly for language planning) in the community, particularly who speaks Kiowa (well), who doesn't, who is qualified to teach, who is old enough to be considered an elder, who is qualified to offer an opinion, and whose writing system is worthy of consideration. The legitimacy of opinions from tribal insiders as contrasted with that of "experts" from outside the community is a frequent underlying theme. Writing systems designed by Kiowa speakers as opposed to those designed by linguists are typically preferred. Parker McKenzie's association with the University of Oklahoma and his later distinction as a Ph.D. as well as his professional connections with the Bureau of Indian Affairs and his culturally mixed family history are mentioned as factors by community teachers who discount his system. Respect is supposed to be attributed to one; one is not supposed to claim legitimacy for oneself. This attitude is unfortunate in the context of language renewal, as those who are doing the work of promoting and teaching the languages are subject to unfavorable commentary and questioning of their authority as well.

In the past the professional language ideologies of academics have often been privileged over ideologies from within indigenous communities (see Rice and Saxon 2002). But times have changed, and it is now recognized that in any language renewal effort the community must have significant input. Top-down strategies do not tend to be effective in many Native American communities. It is important for a community to feel ownership in any decision-making process regarding the language, or the depth of dedication needed for any success in a language renewal program will not be there. Kroskrity (this volume) provides a useful discussion of assertion of agency by community members in language revitalization efforts. There is no one better than a community member to help determine which types of efforts are most affirming and appropriate, although complications resulting from differing voices present within a community can be daunting.

Another issue belonging to the discourses of power and authority is the question of intellectual property rights and who has the authority to decide how language materials should be used. In a tribe as full of accomplished artists, musicians, and leaders as the Kiowa tribe, creativity is clearly highly valued. Individual ownership of certain songs, artistic patterns, events, or deeds is remembered and passed down through the family. One must ask the owner's permission or that of the family before using their creative material; for example, there are restrictions on who may lead certain songs at events. In some cases, particular songs may only be led by descendants of the song's creators. These restrictions hold for material culture as well; in the past many artists avoided using the patterns or deeds of others in calendars; individually accomplished events were only depicted on individually owned articles such as teepees or shields (Greene 2005, personal communication). Certain stories are considered the property of those who first told them. This phenomenon is not unheard of among other groups. Among the Tlingit, assertions of ownership of stories have proved a barrier to material production (Dauenhauer and Dauenhauer 1998:91). Moore also notes that in Wasco-Wishram society words can become "objectualized" (1988:467) as things of value owned by descendants. This evidently also holds for language materials. Some teachers have stated that they have had to come up with their own materials because others wouldn't share their materials for language teaching. Others indicate that such disagreements could be chalked up to differences between dialects, although this has not yet been measured, and most would agree that Kiowa is a single speech community.[16]

Discourse on Religion

The Kiowa language is important in religious contexts for many Kiowa people; it is still used in Native American Church meetings (also known as peyote meetings), especially in song. There are four sets of peyote songs that each participant and drummer sing as the drum makes its round during the nocturnal ceremony. Peyote practitioners regularly sing these four sets using Kiowa words and phrases. The words denote powerful expressions of worship and praise to "the Maker of the Universe" and often invoke the spiritual essences of "Father Peyote" in special prayers for family, friends, and the world, among other prayer offerings. A view expressed by Kiowa peyote practitioners recently in services conducted in southwestern Oklahoma is that expressive Kiowa prayer is not devoid of meaning and richness, though an understanding of the language would amplify these qualities. In religious contexts, for many it would not be appropriate to commit these powerful phrases to paper. These sentiments recall similar ones from the pueblo of Cochiti, where leaders wish to avoid the "unwanted changes" in both religious as well as secular traditions that writing could potentially effect (Pecos and Blum-Martinez 2001:76). This language ideology is also clearly linked to the discourse on tradition.

A number of language learners have indicated that they wish to learn Kiowa in order to pray more effectively and more "deeply." Many people believe that the Kiowa language is a gift from God. Multiple people have explained to us that since Kiowa is such a "deep language," prayers in Kiowa are much more appropriate and meaningful. The hymnbook written at the Summer Institute of Linguistics by linguists and Kiowa people in the 1960s is an important resource that helps bolster pride and interest in the language. These hymns are sung nearly every week in some of the Baptist and Methodist churches in the community, although the fear that this will not long continue is strong, since few younger people know how to lead these hymns correctly.

Ideology about the sacredness of the language is sometimes also linked to traditionalist ideology that "maybe God didn't want Kiowa to be written" and even "maybe Kiowa shouldn't even be spoken at all; perhaps it is dying out because God wants it to." Although few language teachers subscribe to this belief, some people in the community feel this way. It is not surprising that as religious contexts are among the increasingly few domains where Kiowa is heard, people begin to have reservations about writing the language. Since sacred things are only to be shared in certain circumstances with certain people, the issue of control of information is at stake. As Hinton remarks, "Much ceremonial and religious information . . . is secret and if written down could get into the hands of people who have no right of access" (2001c:241). The Kiowa hymns are an obvious counterexample to this ideology; they are not only written but also freely copied and shared by the community. Of course, their nature as belonging to a public (and nontraditionally Kiowa) context of Christian religion puts them in a somewhat different category.

Discourse on Pedagogy

One common complaint is that "Kiowa is so complex, it's really just too difficult to be used daily." This language ideology is sometimes heard among frustrated language class absentees. This perceived complexity relates not only to Kiowa's grammatical structure but also to Kiowa sounds that are not found in English (ejectives, voiceless unaspirated consonants, and nasal vowels in particular) as well as to the necessity to master tones despite a general lack of understanding on the part of teachers about how the tone system works. The PMK system in particular is often associated in the community with being too complicated to use due to its use of replacement letters and tone marking. This "complexity" is sometimes given as a reason why children are not learning the language as well as the reason why there are so many different orthographies. One reason that is often not addressed is the fact that many classes (with the exception of the classes at OU) do not treat grammar but instead mostly focus on memorizing vocabulary lists and learning stock phrases.

One of the main ideological areas of conflict regarding orthography choice, which is embedded firmly within the discourse on pedagogy, is a belief in "maximum transfer" of literacy skills. Some believe that spelling Kiowa sounds using English letter combinations will ease learning Kiowa as a second language for those already literate in English. Many Kiowa educators profess to subscribe to this belief, and the orthographies they use illustrate this conviction to a large extent. On the other hand, many linguists' and educators' professional language ideologies have recently shifted, and currently the idea of maximum transfer is losing its popularity. Rather, transfer of the phonetic values for the graphs of one language onto another is now recognized as a potential source of confusion or interference. Coulmas notes that "where the phonology and other structures of a particular language differ very much from those of the major contact language, every feature that favors transferability frustrates faithful mapping" (1989:236–37), which can lead to orthography systems being judged "inadequate." Interference is, however, not unassailable. The idea that the real focus should remain on the readability of the language as opposed to extreme simplification is still a valid one (Gudschinsky 1973:122). The fact remains that only an orthography that is user-friendly, as defined by the user, will be a successful language-learning tool in the long run.

Searching for Practical Solutions: Heterographia as an Alternative to Standardization?

The relatively strong attachment to heterographia displayed in the Kiowa community is the result of the interplay of the underlying discourses and their embedded, often overlapping, and sometimes conflicting language ideologies. The combination of heterographia with a paucity of widespread knowledge in the community of how the phonetic inventory of Kiowa functions as a system makes effective language teaching difficult. The discord regarding how one should best represent various words has been functionally limiting in terms of cooperative renewal efforts. This continuing dissension even intensifies discussions about proper pronunciation of words that are older and less familiar today, perhaps found only in a written form of one of the orthographies that does not systematically distinguish between similar phonemes.

Is heterographia a viable, functional alternative to standardization? In the Kiowa situation it would seem that the answer to this question is "no, heterographia has not been working," not in terms of language maintenance, teaching, or renewal, or at least not very well. Kiowa functions as an index of identity for some Kiowa people, but it is not fulfilling an intratribal, intergenerational, communicative function. It is the confusion of failed communication that Bakhtin opines "a systematic linguistics must always suppress" (1987:428), since the overwhelming number of potential perceptions can undermine the project of interpersonal communication when it interferes with pronunciation and understanding. Yet the Kiowa debate over orthographies is not just about interpersonal communication but also about politics and representations. When there are many speakers of a language around, even the staunchest prescriptionist would agree that the manner of spelling is less vital to the perpetuation of the language. In fact, we have evidence of an exchange of letters between Parker McKenzie and Charlie Redbird, both of whom utilized a different writing system when writing to each other in Kiowa. This is a prime example of functional heterographia, because the two systems were mutually intelligible to the two writers (who were both also fluent speakers). But what if there are few fluent speakers?

While heterographia may seem tempting as a politically neutral and egalitarian alternative, it can be functionally disabling when trying to revitalize a language. When few speakers are available, heterographia can be confusing and discouraging for students. It is difficult enough to learn a language when speakers and materials are scarce without being required to re-create the spelling of a word each time it is encountered. Ease of reading is improved when there is a standard word image to which to attribute meaning as opposed to being required to sound out each word (Mattingly 1992). Yet an attempt at top-down standardization of an existing system would carry with it its own set of complications for cohesion in the Kiowa community. These factors must be weighed systematically before any official action is advocated.

Each Kiowa learning community (i.e., each community whose loyalty is to a different orthography) needs to carefully evaluate its situation and make an informed decision for itself. Albert White Hat (1999:3–5) reports that Lakota educators came together in the 1970s to work out a simple standardized alphabet and to facilitate sharing of teaching materials. It took almost ten years for Lakota educators to work out an alphabet that everyone could agree on, and in the meantime they kept track of what worked for them in the classroom and what worked less well. This type of grassroots, communally based method of determining needs is certainly a good model for assuring a higher success rate for collaborative efforts, boosting feelings of ownership, intracommunity cooperation, and pride of accomplishment, as opposed to a top-down approach based on academic or professional advice and prevailing pedagogical ideologies tied to language.

Many in the Kiowa community are coming to the realization that at some point in the near future differences need to be pushed aside if the goal of effective language teaching and more widespread use is to be achieved. Is another "new orthography" the answer? A focus on teaching Kiowa in schools using transphonic orthographies combined with lessons that focus on vocabulary lists and phrases has not been producing the desired results; children are not becoming communicatively competent. Whether this is due to the systems themselves or to difficulties with motivation or teaching methods is as yet unclear. Though pedagogical research shows that a straightforward writing system can aid students, the matters of motivation and of teaching methodologies need further examination. We see, however, division in the community as the primary problem to be addressed at this time, and heterographia adds to this division. One possible contribution would be the formation of a committee to test the current orthographies and work out a "unified" orthography that would eliminate the problems of the old ones and combine their strengths. In addition to reducing division in the community, writing could be a powerful tool for cohesion, as Bender (this volume) shows that the syllabary historically has been within the Cherokee community. A shared writing system would enable people living at a distance to keep in touch with each other. A newsletter would be a great sign of pride and even unity as well as an incentive to learn the language well enough to read and write for it. But these goals seem momentarily out of reach. During an interview one Kiowa elder phrased it in this way:

It probably will work in years to come, but as long as you have people in my generation, they're going to feel like, like I do, it's kind of um. Our people don't agree on things and uh [pause]. That and they're no different from anyone else. If you work at it, and um, the situation is, actually it's a grave situation right now, for everything. . . . If we realize that, that we need to, focus on one way to do it, that would be good. . . . Not if, if you see the interest isn't there. So their interest has to be there.

Self-Reflections on Revitalization and Research

Through our close association with the Kiowa people we have become more knowledgeable about their struggles, including the fact that speaking and writing Kiowa have not been at the top of the list as a tribal goal during past years. It is important that we as language professionals question our own motivations and goals as well, for we may not understand the priorities many Indian people set for themselves to live their daily lives in Indian Country. Nor are we affected by the tribal policies that conduct tribal support and social services for the aged and the young from year to year. Who are we to decide what a tribe needs to survive during these times? Is saving tribal languages a great priority for the tribe, or is it something that others desire for academic, political, or even personal reasons? In other words, if we take the opportunity to accompany the tribe to the realization of a standardized writing system, will it make their lives truly better when we ourselves know that most if not all Indian communities are among the most socially and economically wretched in this country? Will writing their language make Indians feel better about their lives? Or will writing their language make us feel better about their lives?

We think these are vital questions for any researcher, linguist, anthropologist, or otherwise to ask. What are the potential repercussions of the questions we ask, and how can the questions we ask help the communities where and with whom we work? Personally, we believe that language maintenance, renewal, and even sovereignty of choice can be useful to a people's social as well as economic well-being, as new sources of pride, and even new types of industry (see Bernard 1997). But we are idealistic academics, and clearly it is a community's right to decide these things for itself, even though this process is never easy or straightforward. Language professionals are there to observe, to advise, to enable, and to assist but not to determine. We must be aware of our own ideologies as well as those of the people with whom we collaborate. Language planning for the Kiowa tribe in the near future clearly needs to revolve around first finding out exactly where the interest does lie in the community and then bringing people together for discussion. The discourses on tradition, religion, power, and authority will continue to shape the space within which the dialogue must occur, and an awareness of these discourses and their overlapping language ideologies will be necessary, as well as a healthy dose of diplomacy, should negotiations for a single orthography be undertaken. The important matter for Kiowa language renewal is that the language is viewed as a shared resource as opposed to grounds for contestation.

Conclusion

In conclusion, a single agreed-upon writing system for Kiowa will probably not become a reality right away. Although for most Kiowa people the concept of Kiowa as a spoken language overrides the notion of writing Kiowa, the formal adoption of one orthography is largely supported by younger Kiowas. There are many tribal members who generally support writing Kiowa because they are closer to the urgency of language loss than others who may be speakers. This sometimes younger set, like us, understands the usefulness and power of the written word and that it can be a powerful tool to advance language learning and retention. They know because they are surrounded by the printed word on a daily basis at home, in the streets, in school, and in places of business. They are influenced by both the language ideologies of their elders and those of the society at large. It is this vital group of younger Kiowas who we believe will determine the future fate of Kiowa.

Whatever the community might decide, we hope to advocate a collaborative focus designed to bring the community together, however Kiowa is taught and learned. Our personal opinion is that a committee approach, designed around a focus on teaching efficiency, would be useful, but only if the community can collectively decide on this matter. Until that time it may be better to focus on strategies that can emphasize the things Kiowa speakers and language learners have in common, to bridge and rebuild. As one language teacher concluded during our interview, she would be glad to take part in meetings that advocated collaborative efforts, even for standardization, "because I think the more that we get together and compare, [the better,] not for differences but for likenesses that we can use to help one another in this rebuilding and stabilizing."

Notes

Chapter 2

1. One is from the Shiprock area and the other is from Ganado.

2. According to Young, Morgan, and Midgette, the distributive plural morpheme -*da* may occur with a limited number of Navajo basic stem nouns (clouds, mountains, lands) but "is not synonymous with the simple plurality attaching to English nouns. Distributive plurality carries the connotation 'each of 3+'" (1992:963). For example:

k'os	"cloud"	daa k'os	"clouds"
dził	"mountain"	daadził	"mountains"
kéyah	"land"	kédaayah	"lands"

3. Whether examples of English plurals actually serve as nouns (and not verbs) in Navajo is difficult to say. Whether the examples given here are not actually nominalized verbs in the minds of the speakers is equally difficult to know—it is possible that they are, since nominalized verbs in Navajo are also now being pluralized through the addition of -*da*. Example 4 illustrates this: *deeyíjeehigíída*, "the ones who are competing." Nominalized verbs commonly function as noun phrases in Navajo.

4. The verb stem in this example, -*jeeh*, literally translates to "three or more subjects run."

5. The iterative prefix *na*- is glossed as "usually" in this example and example 5 as well.

6. That child ideology should differ from that of adults within a speech community should not surprise us, given that there is a substantial literature on the development of social identity, especially among ethnic minority groups in this country (Atkinson, Morton, and Sue 1983; Cross 1978; Phinney 1989), which suggests that negative attitudes toward one's own group are typical of the first stage of children's identity development.

7. However, there has been at least one example of Navajo morphology added to an English verb in Navajo child language. There are probably more, although to my knowledge they have not been published, and I doubt that there are very many of them. In a study of Navajo child language done at Northern Arizona University by Susan Foster-Cohen (Foster et al. 1989), they found the example *nascruise*, which translates to "I cruise around." Thanks to an anonymous reviewer for pointing this out.

Chapter 4

Author's Note: The data analyzed here were collected while doing fieldwork supported by a National Science Foundation Pre-Doctoral Research Grant and a grant from the

UCLA Institute of American Cultures. Many thanks to Margaret Field, Paul Kroskrity, and three anonymous readers for the comments and critiques on earlier drafts of this chapter. All remaining errors are mine alone.

1. The portions of the Hopi courtroom interactions captured in the examples come from transcripts of audio recordings prepared by me and my Hopi consultants during my field visit to the Hopi reservation in 2000–2001. The audio recordings of these hearings are part of the court's public record (in lieu of a court stenographer) and are kept on file, in both analog and digital formats, with the Hopi Tribal Court. Speakers are identified by their first name or title. Note also the following conventions using a modified system developed by Jefferson and described in Sacks, Schegloff, and Jefferson (1974). A dash indicates that speech was suddenly cut off during or after the preceding word; a question mark indicates a marked rising pitch; a period indicates marked falling pitch; brackets mark the onset of portions of utterance that are spoken in overlap with other talk, and the overlapping portions of talk are placed immediately above or below each other on the page; parentheses that enclose utterances indicate doubt about the accuracy of enclosed materials, and parentheses that enclose question marks indicate that something was said at that point but it is not clear enough to transcribe; parentheses that enclose a period indicate a pause in speech; equal signs indicate speech that is linked to subsequent talk by the same speaker but that had to be split for transcript clarity; underlining indicates speech that is the primary focus of analysis; italicized speech indicates Hopi language.

Chapter 5

Authors' Note: We want to thank all the people who helped us think through this chapter and generously contributed their valuable insights. We want to particularly acknowledge Roseann Willink, Maureen Olson, Wilhelmina Phone, Matilda Martinez, Irvin Max Phone, Sam Montoya, Catherine Vigil, Virgie Bigbee, Clara Green, and Brenda McKenna for their wisdom and for their help over the past several years. We also thank Tom McElwain for sharing the Mingo rabbit tale with us. Work with the Jicarilla Apache Nation and with Nambé Pueblo is supported by grants from the National Science Foundation.

1. Although map and Internet searches will yield Hano, Arizona, as the name of the Tewa home in Arizona, "Tewa Village" is the name preferred by the Arizona Tewa. The Tewa live in the midst of the Hopi people and are regarded by many federal and state agencies as officially being members of the Hopi population. "Hano" is a Hopi name for the area where the Arizona Tewa live (Kroskrity 1993b:6–7).

Chapter 6

1. For a detailed insider's account of the Carnegie Project see Wahrhaftig (1998).

Chapter 7

Author's Note: This research is part of a larger fieldwork project on language socialization and revitalization in an endangered language context. The majority of this research was carried out from December 1997 to April 2000 and has been supported through grants and fellowships from the following: the Woodrow Wilson National Fellowship Foundation, the National Institute for General and Medical Sciences, the Wenner-Gren Foundation for Anthropological Research, the Social and Behavioral Sciences Research Institute (University of Arizona), the Northern Research Institute (Whitehorse, Yukon Territory), the Departments of Anthropology and Linguistics at the University of Arizona, and the Department of Anthropology at the University of Michigan. I would also like to thank the following individuals for their encouraging and careful comments on this chapter: Gerald Carr, Margaret Field, Paul Kroskrity, and an anonymous reviewer. All errors are my own.

1. In the 1940s Aboriginal children had several educational options: day schools, residential schools, and territorial public schools. However, most Aboriginal students attended a residential school up until the 1960s and 1970s due to concerns about integration (Coates 1991:203–6). The last residential school closed in 1975. By this time public schools had become the primary educational institution, with some exceptions. One such exception was the Kluane First Nation–run school during the 1970s; it closed when the student population dropped to zero (Nadasdy 2003).

2. In government documents these interested parties are referred to as "stakeholders."

3. This self-determinism is a central concept behind the move toward land claims and First Nations self-governance, which is more of the devolution of programs and services from federal ministerial control to the First Nations governmental entities.

4. See Burnaby (1999) regarding the role of anthropologists in the development of Canadian policies concerning Aboriginal peoples and Aboriginal languages.

5. As Paul Nadasdy notes, elders are not respected authorities "because they have special knowledge, powers, or wealth . . . but because they have learned to live respectfully themselves" (2003:103).

6. It is important to note that it is much easier for someone such as an elder who has experienced language socialization in the heritage language to naturalize the language acquisition process and assume that the language is already inside of him or her.

7. This phrase traces back to the planning stages of the conference, where it was agreed upon as the conference theme (Gardner et al. 1997:21). It is not a mantra vocalized by First Nations citizens locally; it is more centrally a part of official institutional discourse.

Chapter 8

Author's Note: I am deeply indebted to the San Juan Paiute people for their friendship, interpretive help, and willingness to try new things. This research could not have taken place without their active collaboration. I especially want to acknowledge Evelyn James and Mabel Lehi, who have devoted considerable effort to our mutual projects. I would also like to thank Helen Lehi, Roseanne Whiskers, Cecilia Whiskers, Johnny Lehi, and Grace

Lehi for their various contributions. An earlier version of this chapter was presented at the 2001 American Anthropological Association annual meeting in the "Language Ideologies in Native American Cultures: Multiplicity and Change" session.

1. For more information on Angel Whiskers' and Blue Lee's participation in the deposition and trial and on Paiute cross-cultural communication issues see Bunte and Franklin (1994).

2. Although English words are sometimes borrowed into the Paiute speech and Paiute words may be borrowed into English talk, there is not a separate mixed code. The relative frequency of Paiute versus English in interaction between caregivers and children varies depending on a number of factors. For example, adults speak more Paiute to children when the adults are already having an interaction in Paiute among themselves (see example 1) than when the interaction can be perceived as focused on the children (see example 3). Of course, the English and Paiute abilities of the adult are also relevant—Kwis and Tsanna always speak Paiute, whereas some other adults always speak English. However, a lack of real fluency does not necessarily prevent the speaker from using English (see the discussion surrounding example 4).

3. Over the last twelve years or so most non-English speakers have been so thoroughly exposed to English that they now understand a great deal of what is said in English.

4. The orthography used here was developed for Kaibab Paiute by me and the late Kaibab elder Lucille Jake. It has been used for educational and other purposes by members of the Paiute Indian Tribe of Utah, by Kaibab, and by the San Juan. It is the official orthography of the San Juan Southern Paiute Tribe. Most characters have their International Phonetic Alphabet values. The following are exceptions or are otherwise worthy of special mention. The apostrophe is the glottal stop. The letter x is the spirantized version of k and stands for a (usually) voiceless velar fricative. The glide is y. A short apical trill or flap is represented by r and is the spirantized version of t. The digraph ng stands for a velar nasal. Before k, however, the velar nasal is written simply as n. The digraphs ts, ch, and sh are pronounced as they would be in English—ts, $tʃ$, and $ʃ$. The high back unrounded vowel ʉ is similar to the i in Russian. The sound $ø$ that in Southern Ute and San Juan Paiute replaces Kaibab and other Southern Paiute open o is a midfront rounded vowel often pronounced with noticeable retroflex approximant r coloring (pronounced very similarly to the er in "writer"). Long vowels are phonemic and are written as double vowels—aa. Three or more identical vowels in a row signal stylistic lengthening. A voiceless vowel is written with a small circle under the vowel—ạ. Voiceless vowels are frequently dropped at the end of words. An acute accent on a vowel ($í$) indicates word stress.

5. As noted above, San Juan Paiutes have told me that it is a common experience to hear instructions from a parent coming on the wind. Although I was never explicitly told this by Kaibab Paiutes, it was probably because I did not ask. I do know that the Wind is an important personified being for both the Kaibab and the San Juan Paiutes. This is probably a widespread phenomenon. The Navajo portray the Wind as a beneficent deity who helps people by whispering in their ears (McNeely 1988; Witherspoon 1977). In addition, a woman came up to me after a talk I gave at a SCAAN (Southern California Applied Anthropology Network) meeting in December 2004 to tell me that her grandmother, a

member of a Mexican tribe, used to tell her the same thing that the Paiute elders had told me—that the parents' words would come to them on the wind.

6. In the transcribed examples italics are used to indicate that the original was spoken in English rather than in Paiute. Numbers enclosed in parentheses designate the number of seconds of a pause: (2) is a two-second pause, while a very brief pause is noted by (.o). Latching between speakers is designated by an equal sign. Overlapping speech is designated by double slashes. Square brackets are used to present either contextual information or a morpheme breakdown. Three spaced periods indicate that I skipped some interaction at that point.

7. The following abbreviations are used in the examples and texts: 1, 2, 3—personal pronouns; anim—animate; cont—continuative; dim—diminutive; fut—future; hab—habitual; incl—inclusive; iter—iterative; inv—invisible (alternates with visible, a characteristic of demonstratives and pronouns); mom—momentaneous; neg—negative; nom—nominative case; npst—narrative past; obl—oblique case; part—participle; perf—perfective; pl—plural; pres—present; redup—reduplicative; quot—quotative (found frequently in both formal and informal narratives); s—singular; sub—subordinate suffix; vis—visible.

8. /l/s are found in San Juan Southern Paiute only in songs, names, and baby talk. As baby talk, /l/s can be used both by caregivers when speaking to small children and by small children.

9. The simple imperative form in Paiute does not have the same abruptness and force of the simple unsoftened English imperative. The Paiute imperative form seems to be inherently softened by employing case markers ergatively (Bunte 1980). When native Paiute speakers use the English imperative, they typically use it the same way they use their Paiute imperative (i.e., without softeners) and, therefore, sound less polite and much more forceful to native English speakers than they probably intend.

10. When I began fieldwork with the San Juan Paiutes in 1980, there were still Paiute speakers below the age of thirty who did not speak or understand English.

11. The Navajo-speaking man did not leave the workshop, and it is difficult to determine what effect, if any, the other man's statement had on him—he seemed to just ignore it.

12. For more information on the San Juan Southern Paiute language situation and language programs see Bunte and Franklin (2001) and Hinton and Hale (2001b).

13. This is "carrot" borrowed from English but incorporated into the Paiute phonological system. Since it appears to be fully incorporated, I have not italicized it.

14. It was suggested to me that her use of English might have been triggered more by the English-speaking context. Although this indeed might have been a factor, it is important to note that there was a great deal of Paiute speaking among community members during the workshop, and everything that the presenters said was translated into Paiute. In addition, the commentary on this exchange was entirely in Paiute.

Chapter 9

Author's Note: This chapter is a syncretic product that combines aspects of papers I presented at sessions at the annual meetings of the American Anthropological Association in 1999 and in 2002 and combines these with a reworking of some data segments first published in Kroskrity (1999). I want to thank Laura Ahearn, Jan Blommaert, Tom Csordas, and Jane H. Hill for comments on earlier versions of the papers on which this chapter was based. I also want to thank Margaret Field, Pamela Bunte, and an anonymous reviewer for useful comments on earlier drafts of this chapter. Of course, I assume all responsibility for any shortcomings in the following presentation.

1. My use of the term *embodiment* is a deliberate attempt to invoke the perspective of embodiment theory (Csordas 1990) and other "person-centered" anthropological perspectives (e.g., Hollan 2001) that provide a focus on individuals and their subjective experience of their worlds. Hollan effectively reviews recent work in this area and organizes it as methodological and theoretical responses to three questions: what do people say, what do they do, and what do they embody? Some hybridization of such person-centered approaches along with language ideological approaches seems, in my view, to be a critical linkage to both individual and other intragroup variation, which we know to be an important aspect of language ideological (and all linguistic and sociocultural) change. In this brief treatment I can only hint at the productivity of such a connection; any attempt to carefully explicate the phenomenological connection between embodiment/incorporation and language ideologies must await another venue. I also want to take this opportunity to thank William Bright and two anonymous reviewers for their suggestions for revision of this chapter. I take full responsibility for any remaining shortcomings.

2. The notion of "turnings" directs analytical attention to moments of change and transformation in biographical materials. Given my interest here, I am restricting these turnings to the kinds of events that are appropriate for lingual life histories (Kroskrity 1993a). Mandelbaum defines "turnings" as "when the person takes on a new set of roles, enters into fresh relations with a new set of people, and acquires a new self-conception" (1973:181).

3. I borrow the phrase "meditations in an emergency" from the New York school poet Frank O'Hara (1957). I am indebted to the late Kenneth Koch for introducing O'Hara's work to me. Writing at the present time, there is really a double emergency. The first emergency is the general pattern of language extinction, which threatens to take as many as 90 percent of the world's "small" languages, especially indigenous languages that lack state support. The second emergency, as of this writing in April 2003, is the destabilization of regional and world peace due to the U.S.–Iraq war.

4. Some younger speakers have knowledge of their ancestral language's grammar and vocabulary, but they often know more than they can say, and this makes it unlikely that they will be able to pass this passive knowledge of the language to the next generation. There are reasons for the relatively high number of self-reported speakers in census and other survey data. Two important reasons are the availability of courses both in and outside of schools, which greatly increases the number of people with some knowledge of the language, and the increased prestige of Native languages for younger speakers, many of whom have adopted the language as an emblem of Mono identity. Western Mono is not alone in experiencing a rebirth of local interest in ancestral languages by Native groups. Indeed, this is happening elsewhere in the state and all over the United States more generally.

5. This "Andersonian" model, which tends to equate linguistic unity and national identity, operates as both a folk and an academic model for understanding language and identity relationships. The folk model is clearly related to homologous European folk models. The academic model, as Michael Silverstein (1996) has argued, has provided many graphic examples of how the language ideology of Euro-American scholars—here the Andersonian model that represents an uncritical adoption of a folk model—has falsified the linguistic diversity of Native North American speech communities. I share with Silverstein and other linguistic anthropological colleagues a great sense of ambivalence about the work of Benedict Anderson (1983). On the positive side, we applaud his acknowledgment of the role of language in the constructivist project of creating communities, national and otherwise, through linguistic products and practices. But on the negative side, we reject his claim that nations-in-the-making must be monolingual communities that "naturally" share a common language. Indeed, this Andersonian precondition appears to be more a product of European and Euro-American language ideologies than of a substantiated finding.

Also regarding the use of "iconization" here, I use this concept in the sense of Irvine and Gal as a productive semiotic process involved in the formation of language ideologies in which "linguistic features that index social groups . . . appear to be iconic representations of them, as if a linguistic feature somehow depicted or displayed a social group's inherent nature or essence" (2000:37).

6. Unless otherwise indicated, the Mono orthography used in this article is the revised version of Bethel et al. (1984) currently used by the Mono Language Project. It uses the Roman alphabet but adds three symbols: a high, central, unrounded vowel (i); a back-velar g; and a glottal stop. Also regarding the name "bread-eaters," it is appropriate to point out, as an anonymous reviewer has suggested, that distinguishing groups by naming a distinctive food is a semiproductive linguistic practice among Numic groups. For example, the Western Mono called the Eastern Mono of the Mono Lake area "brine fly larvae eaters" (kwizabi-dikati'; fly:larvae-eater) for this distinctive item of their diet.

7. This word is reproduced from a poster used to advertise the Annual Mono Indian Days celebration in the summer of 1997. It is not written in the Mono Language Project Orthography (where it would be rendered Niimmi).

8. Rosalie Bethel gives special credit to Singing Jack, Susan Johnson, Lucy Kinsman, Minnie McDonald, Bill Sherman, and Chiefs Willie and Sam Pimono for her Mono education.

9. For those unfamiliar with the basic story "Coyote Races the Little Mole," a brief schematic description follows. The story begins with Coyote waking up in early spring after a long hibernation-type sleep. He decides to walk in the countryside and marches off to explore it. After awhile he tires and naps. While doing so he is disturbed by a sound that turns out to be the tunneling of a mole. The two characters meet and talk briefly. Coyote challenges Mole to a race. Mole agrees on the condition that he can run his course underground. They agree on these terms and return home, arranging to race the following morning. While he is home Mole mobilizes his supporters to witness the event. The following day Mole and Coyote race in the predetermined manner. After a difficult start in

which Coyote trips over protruding tree roots, he then runs very well and appears to have victory in hand as he approaches the finish line. But just as he approaches, a mole pops up out of his burrow and crosses the finish line. Mole and his supporters celebrate. Coyote feels ashamed about his improbable loss.

10. Gloss abbreviations used in the examples are: COMPL—completive aspect; DIM—diminutive; EMPH—emphatic particle; FUT—future tense; HAB—habitual; IMP—imperative; INCL—inclusive pronouns; LOC—locative; NEG—negative; NOM—nominalizer; OBL—oblique case marker; PAS—passive voice; PROG—progressive aspect; SUB—subordinate clause marker; TNS—unmarked tense-aspect suffix (a default choice).

11. Though this discussion is more of a suggestion about the important linkages of agency and language ideologies rather than a more fully developed contribution to theory refinement, my remarks assume the need for considerable typological refinement of the analytical categories used to identify the various types and loci of agency. By highlighting three related dimensions (awareness, transformation, and consequentiality), I am focusing on the theoretical intersection of some recent research on agency and language ideology. In the present analysis I only adumbrate the outlines of a typology that correlates "robust" agency with discursive consciousness and (partially) successful attempts to transform selves and sociocultural systems. The opposite end would pair petite agency with practical consciousness and cultural reproduction. My concern here is to develop analytical categories of agency that can be helpful in understanding language ideological change. This hybridized interest may produce a sense of what is focally important that is different from research focused more on nonlinguistic agency. Clearly, a more complete confrontation would require a greatly expanded treatment, which is beyond the scope of this chapter.

12. I am indebted to Margaret Field for suggesting the importance of the literature regarding the awareness of levels of discourse organization.

Chapter 10

1. The number of Mayan languages spoken in Guatemala has been at the center of much ideological debate. The dividing line between what constitutes a language versus a dialect varies depending on the linguistic and sociopolitical criteria used to assess them. Maya linguists from the nongovernmental organization Oxlajuuj Keej Maya' Ajtz'iib' (OKMA) would argue that there are as few as nineteen languages, while others argue for as many as twenty-one. See England (2003) for a summary of the languages/dialects in dispute. Here I have chosen to adopt the official number published by the ALMG (Oxlajuuj Keej Maya' Ajtz'iib' 1993:5).

2. "Culture of violence" was a phrase newspaper columnists often used to depict Guatemalan society during my field stay in 1998–99. See Oglesby (2007) for a critique of how this phrase was paradoxically used in postwar era discourses to reify state violence and erase the historical agency of Mayas' oppositional organizing.

3. Pan-Mayas additionally work toward reviving Mayan forms of religious practice and reforming bilingual education to better represent the plurilingual and multiethnic com-

position of Guatemala. See Richards and Richards (1996) for a brief history of Mayan language educational policies.

4. Shaming routines are culturally salient affective language socialization practices in highland Maya households. Utterances such as "¿No tenés vergüenza?" (Have you no shame?) stress that shame and embarrassment are emotions one should feel if one acts inappropriately in a social setting. Discursive forms range from indirect strategies (formulaic and nonformulaic declarative statements that highlight the child's behavior, telling stories about the child's actions while the child is present, invoking/creating pejorative nicknames) to direct ones that challenge and confront the child with evidence of his or her inappropriate behavior. An example of an indirect strategy, one that would take place in a multiparty exchange, would be of a caregiver commenting about a child's excessive crying to another: "Ahorita contratar para el mejor chillón" (Hire [him or her] for [being] the best crybaby).

5. Analyses are based on ethnographic data collected during sixteen months of fieldwork in two communities, San Juan Comalapa and San Antonio Aguas Calientes, over the course of three visits: July–September 1994, March 1998–March 1999, and August 1999.

6. Gal (2005) recently noted a terminological shift from the semiotic process of "iconization" in Irvine and Gal (2000) to "rhematization." Gal writes that the new term more precisely resembles the spirit of "Peirce's notion of 'rheme' as an indexical sign that its interpretant takes to be an icon" (2005:35).

7. See Annis (1987) and Brown (1998b) for a more in-depth history of San Antonio Aguas Calientes bilingualism.

8. The study of language ideology is not the only area of interest of scholars working within this third paradigm. I single it out here solely for the sake of clarity and to show a potential thread of continuity between the three paradigms.

9. Also see Dorian (1989), Kulick (1992), Hornberger (1997), and Paulston (1997) in addition to the other edited collections cited.

10. In the Maya canon the gender division is construed as separate and complementary. In actual practice, however, this is rarely the case (Rosenbaum 1993; Watanabe 2000).

11. See Berkley (2001) for an analysis of competing language ideologies linked to the discourse genre tsikbal (respectful conversation) within the context of Yucatec Maya adult literacy classes that also emphasized linguistic revitalization.

12. The very title of the parable, with its alternate dialectal expression for "sit" (katz'uye'), reflects a Pan-Maya compromise made to acknowledge localist linguistic allegiances to regional varieties while at the same time promoting standard forms. Man kach'oke' was not an appropriate title for Comalapenses because the expression denotes the more specific semantic meaning "mount" (as in "Mount the horse!").

13. Transcripts are organized in columns (from left to right) and sequentially (from top to bottom). Information indicated within each line number co-occurs and includes the pseudonym of the social actor, his or her utterance with supersegmentable features (verbal behavior), and any "action" (nonverbal behavior). Actions include what participants do (activities). The English gloss appears in the far right-hand column.

I use Spanish orthography and diacritic system (á, é, í, ó, ú, ü, ñ) with some minor modifications to indicate spoken words. I also follow the ALMG's standard orthography for Kaqchikel and K'ichee' (e.g., /a/ versus /ä/ indicates a tense and lax vowel, respectively, in Kaqchikel; /e/ and /ee/ indicate a short and long vowel, respectively, in K'ichee'). An apostrophe indicates a glottal stop. A name/role followed by a semicolon indicates the participant. A period indicates a falling intonation contour. A question mark indicates a rising intonation contour. A comma indicates a rising-falling intonation contour. An inverse question mark indicates a falling-rising intonation contour. A bracket indicates overlapping talk. An equal sign marks latched talk by two different speakers or continued talk by the same speaker. A dash indicates a self-cutoff or interruption; a speaker interrupts or cuts off his or her own talk. A period inserted between parentheses indicates a micropause. The word "pause" in parentheses indicates a pause timed in tenths of seconds in talk or activity. A colon indicates sound stretches. Prolonged sounds are marked with many colons. Italicized words indicate slightly increased volume. Words in all caps indicate very loud volume. Talk inserted between two degree signs is significantly softer than surrounding speech. Enclosed items between single parenthesis indicate talk difficult to discern on the original tape.

14. This phrase was often invoked in political discourses by the right-wing party, FRG, headed by the ex-dictator Efraín Ríos Montt.

15. The 1989 United Nations Convention on the Rights of the Child represents this worldwide phenomenon as it identifies a series of "children at risk" who require protection (Scheper-Hughes and Sargent 1998:1). This list includes abused children, refugee children, mentally or physically disabled children, *linguistic/religious minority children*, child labor, children using narcotic drugs, sexually abused children, children in trafficking, children in war, and child criminals. In the Guatemalan case Maya children make up a linguistic majority.

Chapter 11

1. The 1990 U.S. Census counted 2,284 Shoshoni speakers and ranked the language eighteenth in the number of speakers for American Indian languages, but these figures are not accurate, since only 12 percent of the population in any one area was questioned concerning language use. The 2000 U.S. Census reported 2,724 speakers, ranking Shoshoni seventeenth in the number of speakers. This is an increase of 440 speakers.

2. The language purists can also be academics, such as professional linguists. In his article "Our Ideologies and Theirs" (1998) James Collins discusses how he negatively criticized the kind of language being taught in community-based Tolowa language classes by tribal language activist Loren Bommelyn, well knowing that he put their funding at risk. His experience brings up the question of who gets to define what "good" or "fluent" speech is in any particular language: academics, fluent speakers, semispeakers, community language activists, a language board or academy, teachers of the language? I think this is a question not many communities have seriously addressed in any adequate fashion. In some

sense, whoever produces the most publications available to the public wins, since availability translates into familiarity, and this is what a standardized language needs to have credibility among its promoters and potential users. The only resistance to the Shoshoni Language Project has come in the form of disapproval of the orthography we have chosen to use for Northern Shoshoni by promoters of the Miller orthography.

3. There are currently three different orthographies used for Shoshoni: the Miller orthography (Crum and Dayley 1993; Miller 1972), the Tidzump orthography (Tidzump 1970), and the Shoshoni Language Project orthography (Gould and Loether 2002).

4. Paul Kroskrity (personal communication, 2004) has suggested that this may explain a reticence on the part of young speakers of Shoshoni to be creative with the language, instead preferring to repeat what has been said before.

Chapter 12

1. I use the designation "Native American" to refer to the Aboriginal peoples of North America in particular and also to coincide with the terminology established for this volume by the editors. However, I will use Aboriginal, Aboriginal First Nations, First Nations, as well as other derivatives to indicate the usage particular to the Canadian context.

2. Edward P. Dozier was a fluent speaker of Santa Clara Tewa, a regional variant of Rio Grande Tewa, who performed doctoral research on the Arizona Tewa community of First Mesa on the Hopi Reservation for his anthropology dissertation at UCLA. His research and writing were done during the late 1940s and early 1950s, a time when theory of "acculturation" prevailed. In Kroskrity's (2000b) representation of Dozier, his professional socialization to "acculturation" theory proved more telling in his ability to recognize language and identity processes than did his primary socialization to the Tewa language. See Kroskrity (2000b) for more details.

3. I have obtained permission from the chief of Tobique First Nation to use the name of the community in articles I write and submit for publication.

4. I use "interdiscursivity" to identify the process "to historicize linguistic practice and ideology on the one hand and, on the other, to understand them as a site for social and political processes in which history and temporality are the center of contestation" (Inuoe 2004:5).

5. See note 1.

6. I asked the teacher how she would like to be represented in this paper (and other publications), and she stated that "Native language teacher" is her preference.

7. *Giving Thanks: A Native American Good Morning Message* by Jake Swamp, 1997 reprint edition. There may have been an earlier 1995 edition. I have not been able to confirm the earlier date.

8. I asked the elder how she would like to be represented in this publication (as well as others), and she stated that "consulting elder" was her preferred title.

9. A Maliseet notion of "speaker" is defined by a wide range of criteria used by members of the community, and they all depend on context. Sometimes the greeting exchange

is enough to satisfy some speakers in some contexts, while communicative competence across discursive contexts is expected for other claims to "speaker" status. In short, a "speaker" is contextually defined.

Chapter 13

Authors' Note: The research for this work was partially funded by an NSF EPSCoR scholarship for 2004–6. Additional assistance was provided by the Morris E. Opler Memorial Scholarship in 2005 from the Department of Anthropology at the University of Oklahoma. We are very grateful to a number of people for their input and critiques to earlier drafts of this paper. The organizers, discussants, and participants of the 2005 AAA Session on New Writing Systems, especially Alexander King, Leanne Hinton, and Eve Danziger, provided a stimulating backdrop and important critiques. The editors of this book, Paul Kroskrity and Margaret Field, have been extraordinarily helpful, as have Mary Linn and Sean O'Neill. Thanks are also due to Daniel Harbour and Jason Jackson for their insightful remarks on later versions of the paper. Amber would like to thank Elke Karan from the Summer Institute of Linguistics, whose class on writing systems at the University of North Dakota in the summer of 2005 provided a thorough and enjoyable introduction to the issues of writing system development. We would especially like to thank our friends at the Carnegie Adult Learning Center Kiowa Language Group and all of the language teachers who have provided thoughtful critiques and viewpoints. Their help has been invaluable.

1. We are using "discourse" in the sense that Eire (1998:172) does, drawing upon both Pennycock's (1994) vision of discourse as "ways of understanding" and from Foucault's (1972) discussion of "discursive formations."

2. The authors are greatly indebted to Sean O'Neill, who suggested this term in the midst of a discussion during class in the fall of 2005. We have since expanded upon the concept, helping put it into a larger framework. Our use of heterographia is quite different from the use of the term in the field of comparative literature, where it denotes the condition of a literature composed of different languages and written genres (Herron 1998; Lock 2002).

3. An important note here is that "standardization" in common usage is a complex matter involving several different types of processes. We are not referring to the codification of a language variety to be the official "standard" of a nation or state, supported in the educational system and media. Instead, we focus on the question of producing a unified, accurate orthography for practical purposes of language teaching and communication. Despite this selective focus on our part, it is possible that the conflation of notions of standardization involving official sanction of one regional or social variety as the "standard" play into people's feelings about orthographic standardization as well.

4. The Master-Apprentice approach focuses on learning a language within real-life contexts. Simulating a natural initial language (L1) learning context, a student works one on one with a fluent speaker and communicates using only the target language and gestures.

5. The system the instructor uses is represented as System V in table 13.2 and will be

discussed in more detail during the treatment of the ideological construct of the complexity of the Kiowa language below.

6. While nearly all Native American language instructors at OU are fluent speakers, this is not always true for many programs due to certification constraints. In some cases, using competent second language learners as teachers actually has pedagogical advantages. All language courses at OU require alphabets and written exercises for instruction.

7. One example is the Tenadooah family reunion, held every summer since the old patriarch Tenadooah started it. Based on Kiowa ritual prayer, the reunion brings together Tenadooahs to offer prayers and ritual cedar smoking in a tipi. The family leader of the reunion has indicated interest in making spoken Kiowa here an expected goal.

8. Plans are under way for development of these materials; in fact, at least two different dictionaries are currently being compiled by different sources using different orthographies.

9. While his system is highly systematic, the proliferation of unusual symbols and a high degree of specificity make it difficult for speakers, teachers, and language learners to use.

10. He conveyed many times in his association with Palmer that he thought his method was sound because it had a practical application that was "straight out of the teepee." He was disappointed with Harrington for not including his writing system in the monograph *Popular Account of the Kiowa Indian Language*. Harrington's monograph was published in 1948 by the School of American Research, University of New Mexico Press.

11. These originally composed hymns are a great source of pride in the community.

12. These are, of course, not the only systems out there, merely the main ones with which we have come into contact. In fact, if one "Googles" Kiowa on the Internet, one of the first sites to come up has been crafted by a Finnish ecologist who proposes an alternative system, an "unofficial practical orthography" that is not used by anyone in the Kiowa community, as far as we know (http://www.uusikaupunki.fi/olsalmi/kiowa.html, accessed May 2, 2005).

13. The term "plosive" is used inconsistently. It has been used to refer to "released stops" (Bickford and Floyd 2003:23). The general usage of the term is reserved for "stops that use only an egressive, or outward-moving, pulmonic airstream" (Ladefoged 1993:130). It seems that this alternate usage is what is being indicated.

14. Although Watkins treats tone at the word level in her *Grammar of Kiowa* (1984), there has been no analysis of intonation at the phrasal level except for minor discussion in Sivertson (1956).

15. See Lassiter, Ellis, and Kotay (1999) for details on the cultural importance of distinctions between practicing Christians and traditional religions among the Kiowa community. The rift is showing indications of narrowing.

16. Little actual documentation has been done on perceptual differences between dialects in Kiowa, although there may not be enough quality information to carry out this type of research at this point. Some in the community note that dialectical differences do exist.

References

Aberle, David. 1966. *The Peyote Religion among the Navajo*. Chicago: Aldine.

Abeyta, Marie. 1984. *Tewa Tuukannin Tanin: A Tewa Reader*. San Juan Pueblo, NM: San Juan Bilingual Program.

Aboriginal Language Services. 1991. *Voices of the Talking Circle: Yukon Aboriginal Languages Conference*. Whitehorse, YT: Yukon Executive Council Office.

———. 1995. *Working Together to Pass It On*. Whitehorse, YT: Yukon Executive Council Office.

———. 2004a. *Evaluation Report: Hope for the Future: A Call for Strategic Action. Five Year Report 1998–2003*. Whitehorse, YT: Yukon Executive Council Office.

———. 2004b. *We Are Our Language: Sharing the Gift of Language: Profile of Yukon First Nation Languages*. Whitehorse, YT: Yukon Executive Council Office.

Abu-Lughod, Lila. 1991. "Writing against Culture." In *Recapturing Anthropology: Working in the Present*. Ed. Richard G. Fox. Santa Fe: School of American Research Press. 137–62.

Adley-SantaMaria, Bernadette. 1997. "White Mountain Apache Language: Issues in Language Shift, Textbook Development, and Native Speaker–University Collaboration." In Reyhner, *Teaching Indigenous Languages*, 129–43.

Administration for Children and Families: Kiowa Tribe of Oklahoma. 2003. Summary Program Description. http://www.acf.hhs.gov/programs/opre/strengthen/imple_prom/reports/imp_of_pro2/imp_of_pro2_ki_tribe.html#foot21.a. Accessed 2007.

Agha, Asif. 2005. "Introduction: Semiosis across Encounters." *Linguistic Anthropology* 15(1): 1–5.

Ahearn, Laura. 2001. "Language and Agency." *Annual Review of Anthropology* 30:109–37.

Althusser, Louis. 1969. *For Marx*. Trans. Ben Brewster. New York: Pantheon.

Amith, Jonathan. 2005. "The Impracticality of Practical Orthography." Paper presented at the annual meeting of the American Anthropological Association, December 4. Washington, D.C.

Amsterdam, Anthony G., and Jerome Bruner. 2000. *Minding the Law*. Cambridge, MA: Harvard University Press.

Anderson, Benedict. 1983. *Imagined Communities: Reflections on the Origins and Spread of Nationalism*. London: Verso.

Anderson, Jeffrey. 1998. "Ethnolinguistic Dimensions of Northern Arapaho Language Shift." *Anthropological Linguistics* 40(1): 43–108.

———. 2001. *The Four Hills of Life: Northern Arapaho Knowledge and Life Movement*.

Anthropology of North American Indians Series. Ed. Raymond J. DeMallie and Douglas R. Parks. Lincoln: University of Nebraska Press.

——. 2003. *One Hundred Years of Old Man Sage: An Arapaho Life Story*. Anthropology of North American Indians Series. Ed. Raymond J. DeMallie and Douglas R. Parks. Lincoln: University of Nebraska Press.

Anisfeld, M., and W. E. Lambert. 1961. "Social and Psychological Variables in Learning Hebrew." *Journal of Abnormal and Social Psychology* 63:524–29.

Annis, Sheldon. 1987. *God and Production in a Guatemalan Town*. Austin: University of Texas Press.

Anonby, S. L. 1997. "Reversing Language Shift: Can Kwak'wala Be Revived?" Master's thesis, University of North Dakota.

Appadurai, Arjun. 1996. *Modernity at Large: Cultural Dimensions of Globalization*. Minneapolis: University of Minnesota Press.

Atkins, J. D. C. 1973. "The English Language in Indian Schools." In *Americanizing the American Indians*. Ed. Francis Paul Prucha. Cambridge, MA: Harvard University Press. 197–206. (Orig. pub. 1887.)

Atkinson, D., G. Morten, and D. Sue. 1983. *Counseling American Minorities*. Dubuque, IA: Wm. C. Brown Co.

Atkinson, J. Maxwell, and Paul Drew. 1979. *Order in Court*. London: Macmillan Press.

Augsburger, Deborah. 2004. "Language Socialization and Shift in an Isthmus Zapotec Community of Mexico." Ph.D. diss., University of Pennsylvania.

Axelrod, M., J. Gómez de García, J. Lachler, and M. Sandoval. 1999. "Jicarilla Apache Language Preschool Immersion Program." In *Mid-America Linguistics Conference Papers*. Columbia: University of Missouri. 373–75.

Axelrod, Melissa, Jordan Lachler, and Jule Gómez de García. 2001. *The Native Languages of New Mexico: A Census Report*. Distributed to all Pueblos and Reservations in New Mexico. Albuquerque, NM.

Bacon, Herbert L., et al. 1982. "The Effectiveness of Bilingual Instruction with Cherokee Indian Students." *Journal of American Indian Education*, no. 21. http://jaie.asu.edu/v21V21S2eff.html. Accessed September 12, 2006.

Bakhtin, Mikhail. 1929. *Problemy tvorchestva Dostoevskogo* (Problems of Dostoevsky's Work). Leningrad: Priboj.

——. 1963. *Problemy poetiki Dostoevskogo*. Moscow: Sovetskij pisatel'. Trans. and ed. Caryl Emerson as *Problems of Dostoevsky's Poetics*. Minneapolis: University of Minnesota Press, 1984.

——. 1987. *The Dialogic Imagination*. Ed. and trans. Michael Holquist and Caryl Emerson. Austin: University of Texas Press.

Baldwin, Daryl. 2003. "Miami Project Initiatives: Dictionary and Completed Projects." *Myaamia Project Messenger* 2(Fall): 2–5. http://www.units.muohio.edu/myaamiaproject/newsletter/documents/Fa1103MyaamiaNews.pdf.

Balibar, Etienne. 1991. "Racism and Nationalism." In *Race, Nation, Class: Ambiguous Identities*. Ed. Etienne Balibar and Immanuel Wallerstein. London: Verso. 37–67.

Baraby, Anne-Marie. 2003. "The Process of Spelling Standardization of Innuaimun (Montagnais)." Trans. Marguerite MacKenzie. In Burnaby and Reyhner, *Indigenous Languages across the Community*, 199–212.

Barsh, Russel L. 1999. "Putting the Tribe in Tribal Courts: Possible? Desirable?" *Kansas Journal of Law and Public Policy* 8:74–97.

Barth, Fredrik. 1969. *Ethnic Groups and Boundaries: The Social Organization of Culture Difference*. Boston: Little, Brown and Company.

Basso, Keith H. 1979. *Portraits of "the Whiteman": Linguistic Play and Cultural Symbols among the Western Apache*. New York: Cambridge University Press.

——. 1988. "Speaking with Names: Language and Landscape among the Western Apache." *Cultural Anthropology* 3(2): 99–130.

——. 1990. *Western Apache Language and Culture*. Tucson: University of Arizona Press.

——. 1998. *Wisdom Sits in Places: Language and Landscape among the Western Apache*. Albuquerque: University of New Mexico Press.

Batchelder, Ann. 2000. "Teaching Dine Language and Culture in Navajo Schools." In *Learn in Beauty: Indigenous Education for a New Century*. Ed. Jon Reyhner, Joseph Martin, Louise Lockard, and W. Sakiestewa Gilbert. Flagstaff: Northern Arizona University Press. 1–8.

Bauman, James J. 1980. *A Guide to Issues in Indian Language Retention*. Washington, D.C.: Center for Applied Linguistics.

Bauman, Richard. 1975. "Verbal Art as Performance." *American Anthropologist* 77:290–311.

——. 1986. *Story, Performance, and Event*. Cambridge: Cambridge University Press.

——. 1992. "Contextualization, Tradition, and the Dialogue of Genres: Icelandic Legends of the Kraftaskald." In *Rethinking Context*. Ed. A. Duranti and C. Goodwin. Cambridge: Cambridge University Press. 125–45.

——. 2005. "Commentary: Indirect Indexicality, Identity, Performance: Dialogic Observations." *Linguistic Anthropology* 15(1): 145–50.

Bauman, Richard, and Charles Briggs. 1990. "Poetics and Performance as Critical Perspectives on Language and Social Life." *Annual Review of Anthropology* 19:59–88.

——. 2000. "Language Philosophy as Language Ideology: John Locke and Johann Gottfried Herder." In Kroskrity, *Regimes of Language*, 139–204.

Begay, Jimmie C. 2005. "Tse Nitsaa Deez'áhi Diné Bi'ólta'—Rock Point Community School." http://www.sidecanyon.com/rpcs.htm#Academic. Accessed 2007.

Bender, Margaret. 2002a. "From 'Easy Phonetics' to the Syllabary: An Orthographic Division of Labor in Cherokee Language Education." *Anthropology and Education Quarterly* 33(1): 90–117.

——. 2002b. *Signs of Cherokee Culture: Sequoyah's Syllabary in Eastern Cherokee Life*. Chapel Hill: University of North Carolina Press.

Bennett, Ruth, Pam Mattz, Silish Jackson, and Harold Campbell. 1999. "The Place of Writing in Preserving an Oral Language." In *Revitalizing Indigenous Languages*. Ed. Jon Reyhner, Gina Cantoni, Robert N. St. Clair, and Evangeline Parsons Yazzie. Flagstaff: Northern Arizona University Press. 84–102.

Berkley, Anthony R. 2001. "Respecting Maya Language Revitalization." *Linguistics and Education* 12(3): 345–66.

Bernard, H. Russell. 1992. "Preserving Linguistic Diversity." *Human Organization* 51(1): 82–89.

——. 1997. "Language Preservation and Publishing." In *Indigenous Literacies in the Americas: Language Planning from the Bottom Up.* Ed. Nancy H. Hornberger. New York: Mouton de Gruyter. 139–56.

Bethel, Rosalie, Paul V. Kroskrity, Christopher Loether, and Gregory A. Reinhardt. 1984. *A Practical Dictionary of Western Mono.* North Fork, CA: Sierra Mono Museum.

Biava, Christina. 1990. "Native American Languages and Literacy: Issues of Orthography Choice and Bilingual Education." *Kansas Working Papers in Linguistics* 15(2): 45–59.

Bickford, Anita, and Rick Floyd. 2003. *Tools for Analyzing the World's Languages: Articulatory Phonetics.* Dallas: SIL International.

Bielenburg, Brian. 1999. "Cultural Effects of Writing Indigenous Languages." In *Revitalizing Indigenous Languages.* Ed. Jon Reyhner, Gina Cantoni, Robert N. St. Clair, and Evangeline Parsons Yazzie. Flagstaff: Northern Arizona University Press. 103–12.

Biolsi, Thomas. 2001. *Deadliest Enemies: Law and the Making of Race Relations on and off Rosebud Reservation.* Berkeley: University of California Press.

Blommaert, Jan. 1999. *Language Ideological Debates.* Berlin: Mouton de Gruyter.

Blommaert, Jan, James Collins, and Stef Slembrouck. 2005. "Spaces of Multilingualism." *Language and Communication* 25:197–216.

Blommaert, Jan, and Jef Verschueren. 1998. "The Role of Language in European Nationalist Ideologies." In Schieffelin, Woolard, and Kroskrity, *Language Ideologies,* 189–210.

Bloomfield, Leonard. 1933. *Language.* New York: Henry Holt.

——. 1944. "Secondary and Tertiary Responses to Language." *Language* 20:44–55.

Boas, Franz. 1911 [1966]. *Introduction to the Handbook of American Indian Languages.* Lincoln: University of Nebraska Press.

Bourdieu, Pierre. 1977. *Outline of a Theory of Practice.* New York: Cambridge University Press.

——. 1990. *The Logic of Practice.* Trans. Richard Nice. Stanford, CA: Stanford University Press.

——. 1997. *Language and Symbolic Power.* Ed. John B. Thompson, trans. Gino Raymond and Matthew Adamson. Cambridge, MA: Harvard University Press.

Boyden, Jo. 1997. "Childhood and the Policy Makers: A Comparative Perspective on the Globalization of Childhood." In *Constructing and Reconstructing Childhood: Contemporary Issues in the Sociological Study of Childhood.* Ed. Allison James and Alan Prout. London: Falmer Press. 184–215.

Brandt, Elizabeth A. 1970. "Sandia Pueblo, New Mexico: A Linguistic and Ethnolinguistic Investigation." Ph.D. diss., Southern Methodist University, Dallas.

——. 1981. "Native American Attitudes toward Literacy and Recording in the Southwest." In "Native Languages of the Americas." Special issue, *Journal of the Linguistic Association of the Southwest* 4(2): 185–96.

Briggs, Charles. 1998. "You're a Liar—You're Just Like a Woman." In Schieffelin, Woolard, and Kroskrity, *Language Ideologies,* 229–55.

Bright, William. 1994. "Native North American Languages." In *Portrait of the Peoples*. Ed. Duane Champagne. Canton, MI: Visible Ink Press. 397–440.

Brown, H. Douglas. 1994. *Teaching by Principles: An Interactive Approach to Language Pedagogy*. Upper Saddle River, NJ: Prentice Hall Regents.

Brown, Robert McKenna. 1998a. "A Brief Cultural History of the Highlands." In Garzon et al., *The Life of Our Language*, 44–61.

——. 1998b. "Case Study Two: San Antonio Aguas Calientes and the Quinizilapa Valley." In Garzon et al., *The Life of Our Language*, 101–28.

——. 1998c. "Mayan Language Revitalization in Guatemala." In Garzon et al., *The Life of Our Language*, 155–70.

Brown, Roger, and A. Gilman. 1960. "The Pronouns of Power and Solidarity." In *Style in Language*. Ed. Thomas Sebeok. Cambridge, MA: MIT Press. 253–76.

Bucholtz, Mary, and Kira Hall. 2004a. "Language and Identity." In Duranti, *Companion to Linguistic Anthropology*, 369–94.

——. 2004b. "Theorizing Identity in Language and Sexuality Research." *Language in Society* 33:501–47.

Bunte, Pamela A. 1980. "Birdpeople: A Southern Paiute Coyote Tale." In *Coyote Stories*. Ed. M. B. Kendall. International Journal of American Linguistics, Native American Texts series. Chicago: University of Chicago Press. 111–18.

——. 2000. "'Your Mom's Words Come to You on the Wind': Myth, Language Socialization, and Language Ideology." Paper presented at the annual meeting of the American Anthropological Association, San Francisco, November 16.

Bunte, Pamela A., and Robert Franklin. 1987. *From the Sands to the Mountain: A Study of Change and Persistence in a Southern Paiute Community*. Lincoln: University of Nebraska Press.

——. 1994. "You Can't Get There from Here: Taking Southern Paiute Testimony as Intercultural Communication." *Anthropological Linguistics* 34:19–44.

——. 2001. "Language Revitalization in the San Juan Paiute Community and the Role of a Paiute Constitution." In Hinton and Hale, *The Green Book*, 255–62.

Burnaby, Barbara. 1997. "Personal Thoughts on Indigenous Language Stabilization." In *Teaching Indigenous Languages*. Ed. John Reyhner. Flagstaff: Northern Arizona University Press. 292–300.

——. 1999. "Policy on Aboriginal Languages in Canada: Notes on Status Planning." In *Theorizing the Americanist Tradition*. Ed. Lisa Philips Valentine and Regna Darnell. Toronto, ON: University of Toronto Press. 299–314.

Burnaby, Barbara, and Jon Reyhner, eds. 2003. *Indigenous Languages across the Community*. Flagstaff: Northern Arizona University Press.

Burns, Allan F. 1993. *Maya in Exile*. Philadelphia: Temple University Press.

Campbell, Lyle. 1997. *American Indian Languages: The Historical Linguistics of Native America*. New York: Oxford University Press.

Canfield, Kip. 1980. "A Note on Navajo–English Code-Mixing." *Anthropological Linguistics* 22(5): 218–20.

Carlo, María S., and James M. Royer. 1999. "Cross-Language Transfer of Reading Skills." In *Literacy: An International Handbook*. Ed. Daniel A. Wagner, Richard L. Venezky, and Brian V. Street. Boulder, CO: Westview Press. 148–54.

Carter, Bob, and Alison Sealey. 2000. "Language, Structure and Agency: What Can Realist Social Theory Offer to Sociolinguistics?" *Journal of Sociolinguistics* 4(1): 3–20.

Casagrande, Joseph. 1954. "Comanche Linguistic Acculturation." *International Journal of American Linguistics* 20:140–51, 217–37, 21:8–25.

Champagne, Duane, and Carole Goldberg. 2005. "Changing the Subject: Individual versus Collective Interests in Indian Country Research." *Wicazo Sa Review* 20:49–69.

Chavez, Will. 2007. "Cherokee Speaker's Bureau Holds First Meeting." http://www.chero keephoenix.org/News/News.aspx?StoryID=2550. Accessed August 15, 2007.

Cherokee Nation. 2002. *Ga-du-gi: A Vision for Working Together to Revitalize the Cherokee Language*. Tahlequah, Oklahoma: Cherokee Nation Culture Resource Center.

Christ, Charlotte. 1999. " 'Bilingual Navajo': The Non-Standard Variety of Navajo Is Not as Bad as It Sounds." Paper presented at the Athabaskan Language Conference, University of New Mexico, Albuquerque.

Clifford, James. 1986. "On Ethnographic Allegory." In *Writing Culture*. Ed. J. Clifford and G. E. Marcus. Berkeley: University of California Press. 98–121.

Coates, Ken S. 1991. *Best Left as Indians*. Montreal: McGill–Queen's University Press.

Coffey, Wallace, and Rebecca Tsosie. 2001. "Rethinking the Tribal Sovereignty Doctrine: Cultural Sovereignty and the Collective Future of Indian Nations." *Stanford Law and Policy Review* 12:191–210.

Cojtí Cuxil, Demetrio. 1990. "Lingüistica e idiomas mayas en Guatemala." In *Lecturas sobre la lingüistica maya*. Ed. Nora C. England and Stephen R. Elliot. Antigua, Guatemala: CIRMA. 1–25.

——. 1996. "The Politics of Maya Revindication." In Fischer and Brown, *Maya Cultural Activism*, 19–50.

Collins, James. 1992. "Our Ideologies and Theirs." *Pragmatics* 2(3): 405–15.

——. 1998. "Our Ideologies and Theirs." In Schieffelin, Woolard, and Kroskrity, *Language Ideologies*, 256–70.

——. 2003. "Reclaiming Traditions, Remaking Community: Politics, Language, and Place among the Tolowa of Northwest California." In *Language and Social Identity*. Ed. Richard K. Blot. Westport, CT: Praeger. 225–41.

Comaroff, Jean, and John L. Comaroff. 1997. *Of Revelation and Revolution*, vol. 2. Chicago: University of Chicago Press.

Conley, John M., and William M. O'Barr. 1990. *Rules versus Relationships*. Chicago: University of Chicago Press.

——. 1998. *Just Words: Law, Language, and Power*. Chicago: University of Chicago Press.

Cooter, Robert D., and Wolfgang Fikenschter. 1998. "Indian Common Law: The Role of Custom in American Indian Tribal Courts." *American Journal of Comparative Law* 46:287.

Coulmas, Florian. 1989. *The Writing Systems of the World*. Oxford: Blackwell.

Cowell, A. 2002. "Bilingual Curriculum among the Northern Arapaho." *American Indian Quarterly* 26(1): 24–43.

Crago, M., B. Annahatak, and L. Ningiuruvik. 1993. "Changing Patterns of Language-Socialization in Inuit Homes." *Anthropology and Education Quarterly* 24:205–23.

Crawford, J. 1992. *Language Loyalties: A Source Book on the Official English Controversy.* Chicago: University of Chicago Press.

——. 1995. "Endangered Native American Languages: What Is to Be Done—and Why?" *Bilingual Research Journal* 19:17–38.

——. 1997. *Best Evidence: Research Foundations for the Bilingual Education Act.* Washington, D.C.: National Clearinghouse for Bilingual Education.

Creamer, Mary H. 1974. "Ranking in Navajo Nouns. (Dine Bizaad Nanil'iih)." *Navajo Language Review* 1:29–38. Center for Applied Linguistics, Arlington, VA.

Crook, Rena, Leanne Hinton, and Nancy Stinson. 1976. "Literacy and Linguistics: The Havasupai Writing System." In *Proceedings of the 1976 Hokan-Yuman Languages Workshop.* Ed. James E. Redden. San Diego: University of California. 1–16.

Cross, W. 1978. "The Thomas and Cross Models of Psychological Nigrescence: A Literature Review." *Journal of Black Psychology* 4:13–31.

Cruikshank, Julie. 1990. *Life Lived like a Story: Life Stories of Three Yukon Native Elders.* Lincoln: University of Nebraska Press.

Crum, Beverly, and Jon Dayley. 1993. *Western Shoshoni Grammar.* Occasional Papers and Monographs in Cultural Anthropology and Linguistics, vol. 1. Boise, ID: Boise State University, Department of Anthropology.

Crystal, David. 2000. *Language Death.* Cambridge: Cambridge University Press.

Csordas, Thomas J. 1990. "Embodiment as a Paradigm for Anthropology." *Ethos* 18:5–47.

Daly, Gail Ellen. 2002. "'Dreaming' a Language Back to Life." *Canku Ota—A Newsletter Celebrating Native America* 58. http://www.turtletrack.org/Issues02/C004062002/CO _04062002_Dreaming_Language.htm. Accessed 2007.

Dauenhauer, Nora Marks, and Richard Dauenhauer. 1998. "Technical, Emotional, and Ideological Issues in Reversing Language Shift: Examples from Southeast Alaska." In Grenoble and Whaley, *Endangered Languages,* 57–98.

Deloria, Philip J. 2004. *Indians in Unexpected Places.* Lawrence: University Press of Kansas.

Deloria, Vine, Jr. 1985. "Out of Chaos." *Parabola: The Magazine of Myth and Tradition* 3:14–22.

——. 1997. "Anthros, Indians, and Planetary Reality." In *Indians and Anthropologists.* Ed. Thomas Biolsi and Larry J. Zimmerman. Tucson: University of Arizona Press. 209–21.

Deyhle, D. 1986. "Success and Failure: A Micro-Ethnographic Comparison of Navajo and Anglo Students' Perceptions of Testing." *Curriculum Inquiry* 16(4): 364–89.

Dombrowski, Kirk. 2001. *Against Culture: Development, Politics, and Religion in Indian Alaska.* Lincoln: University of Nebraska Press.

——. 2002. "The Praxis of Indigenism and Native Timber Politics." *American Anthropologist* 104(4): 1062–73.

——. 2005. "The Politics of Native Culture." In *A Companion to the Anthropology of American Indians.* Ed. Thomas Biolsi. London: Blackwell Publishers. 360–82.

Donaldson, Laure. 1998. "Writing the Talking Stick: Alphabetic Literacy as Colonial Technology and Postcolonial Appropriation." *American Indian Quarterly* 22(1–2): 46–62.

Dorian, Nancy C. 1981. *Language Death*. Philadelphia: University of Pennsylvania Press.

——, ed. 1989. *Investigating Obsolescence: Studies in Language Contraction and Death*. Cambridge: Cambridge University Press.

——. 1994a. "Comment: Choices and Values in Language Shift and Its Study." *International Journal of the Sociology of Language* 110:113–224.

——. 1994b. "Purism v. Compromise in Language Revitalization and Language Revival." *Language in Society* 23:479–94.

——. 1998. "Western Language Ideologies and Small Language Prospects." In Grenoble and Whaley, *Endangered Languages*, 3–21.

Dorsey, George A., and Alfred L. Kroeber. 1997. *Traditions of the Arapaho*. Lincoln: University of Nebraska Press. (Orig. pub. 1903.)

Dozier, Edward. 1949. "Tentative Description and Classification of Tewa Verb Structure." M.A. thesis, University of New Mexico, Albuquerque.

Drapeau, Lynn. 1998. "Aboriginal Languages: Current Status." In *Language in Canada*. Ed. John Edwards. Cambridge: Cambridge University Press. 144–59.

Dreadfulwater, Andrew. 1998. "We'll Have Feathers in Our Hats, but We Won't Be No Indians." In *A Good Cherokee, a Good Anthropologist: Papers in Honor of Robert K. Thomas*. Ed. S. Pavlik. Los Angeles: American Indian Studies Center, University of California, Los Angeles. 351–54.

Drew, Paul. 1992. "Contested Evidence in a Courtroom Cross-Examination: The Case of a Trial for Rape." In *Talk at Work: Social Interaction in Institutional Settings*. Ed. Paul Drew and John Heritage. Cambridge: Cambridge University Press. 470–520.

Duranti, Alessandro. 2003. "Language as Culture in U.S. Anthropology: Three Paradigms." *Current Anthropology* 44(3): 323–47.

——. 2004a. "Agency in Language." In Duranti, *Companion to Linguistic Anthropology*, 451–73.

——, ed. 2004b. *Companion to Linguistic Anthropology*. Malden, MA: Basil Blackwell.

Duranti, Alessandro, and Charles Goodwin. 1992. *Rethinking Context*. Cambridge: Cambridge University Press.

Dyc, Gloria. 2002. "Language Learning in the American Southwestern Borderlands: Navajo Speakers and Their Transition to Academic English Literacy." *Bilingual Research Journal* 26(3): 611–30.

Edmo, Ronald Snake. 2002. *Spirit Rider: A Collection of Contemporary Poetry in the Shoshoni Language*. Pocatello: Idaho State University Press.

Eggan, Fred. 1950. *Social Organization of the Western Pueblos*. Chicago: University of Chicago Press.

Eire, Christina. 1998. "Authority and Discourse: Towards a Model for Orthography Selection." *Written Language and Literacy* 1(2): 171–224.

——. 2002. "Language Maintenance at the Micro Level: Among Ex-Refugee Communities." In *Language Endangerment and Language Maintenance*. Ed. David Bradley and Maya Bradley. London: Routledge. 230–53.

Elkin, Henry. 1940. "The Northern Arapaho of Wyoming." In *Acculturation in Seven American Indian Tribes*. Ed. Ralph Linton. New York: D. Appleton–Century Co. 207–58.

England, Nora. 1992. "Doing Mayan Linguistics in Guatemala." *Language* 68:29–35.

——. 1996. "The Role of Language Standardization in Revitalization." In Fischer and Brown, *Maya Cultural Activism*, 178–94.

——. 1998. "Mayan Efforts toward Language Preservation." In Grenoble and Whaley, *Endangered Languages*, 99–116.

——. 2003. "Mayan Language Revival and Revitalization Politics: Linguists and Linguistic Ideologies." *American Anthropologist* 105(4): 733–43.

Errington, J. 1998a. "Indonesian('s) Development: On the State of a Language of State." In Schieffelin, Woolard, and Kroskrity, *Language Ideologies*, 271–84.

——. 1998b. *Shifting Languages: Interaction and Identity in Javanese Indonesia*. Cambridge: Cambridge University Press.

——. 2001. "Colonial Linguistics." *Annual Review of Anthropology* 30:19–40.

——. 2003. "Getting Language Rights: The Rhetorics of Language Endangerment and Loss." *American Anthropologist* 105(4): 723–32.

Fabian, Johannes. 1980. *Time and the Other: How Anthropology Makes Its Object*. New York: Columbia University Press.

Faltz, Leonard M. 1998. *The Navajo Verb: A Grammar for Students and Scholars*. Albuquerque: University of New Mexico Press.

Fernald, Theodore, and Paul Platero, eds. 2000. *The Athabaskan Languages: Perspectives on a Native American Language Family*. Oxford: Oxford University Press.

Fettes, Mark. 1997. "Stabilizing What? An Ecological Approach to Language Renewal." A revised and expanded version of a paper presented at the Fourth Stabilizing Indigenous Language Symposium, Flagstaff, AZ, May 2–3.

Field, Margaret. 1993. "On the Internalization of Language and Its Use: Some Functional Motivations for Other-Correction in Children's Discourse." *Pragmatics* 4(2): 203–20.

——. 1998. "Maintenance of Indigenous Ways of Speaking despite Language Shift: Language Socialization in a Navajo Preschool." Ph.D. diss., Department of Linguistics, University of California, Santa Barbara.

——. 2001. "Triadic Directives in Navajo Language Socialization." *Language in Society* 30(2): 249–64.

Fillerup, Michael. 2000. "Racing against Time: A Report on the Leupp Navajo Immersion Project." *Learn in Beauty: Indigenous Education for a New Century*. Ed. Jon Reyhner, Joseph Martin, Louise Lockard, and W. Sakiestewa Gilbert. Flagstaff: Northern Arizona University Press. 21–34.

Fillmore, Charles. 1985. "Frames and the Semantics of Understanding." *Quaderni di Semantica* 62:222–53.

Fischer, Edward F. 1992. "Creating Political Space for Cultural Pluralism: The Guatemalan Case." Paper presented at the annual meeting of the American Anthropological Association, San Francisco.

——. 1999. "Cultural Logic and Maya Identity." *Current Anthropology* 40(4): 473–99.

Fischer, Edward F., and Robert McKenna Brown, eds. 1996. *Maya Cultural Activism in Guatemala*. Austin: University of Texas Press.

Fishman, Joshua. 1972. "Domains and Relationships between Micro and Macro Sociolinguistics." In *Directions in Sociolinguistics: The Ethnography of Communication*. Ed. John J. Gumperz and Del Hymes. New York: Holt, Rinehart and Winston. 435–53.

———. 1980. "Bilingualism and Biculturalism as Individual and Societal Phenomena." *Journal of Multilingual and Multicultural Development* 1:3–7.

———. 1991. *Reversing Language Shift: Theoretical and Empirical Foundations of Assistance to Threatened Languages*. Clevedon, UK: Multilingual Matters, Ltd.

———. 2002. "Commentary: What a Difference 40 Years Make!" *Journal of Linguistic Anthropology* 12(2): 144–49.

Five County Cherokee Organization. 1968. "First Cherokee Picket Line Surprises Village Guests." *Indian Voices* (Winter): 13–15.

Foster, Susan, Gloria Singer, Lucy Benally, Theresa Boone, and Ann Beck. 1989. "Describing the Language of Navajo Children." *Journal of Navajo Education* 7(1): 13–17.

Foucault, Michel. 1972. *The Archaeology of Knowledge*. New York: Pantheon Books.

———. 1984. *The Foucault Reader*. Ed. Paul Rabinow. New York: Pantheon Books.

———. 1986. "Of Other Spaces." *Diacritics* 16(1): 22–27.

Fowler, Loretta. 1982. *Arapahoe Politics, 1851–1878: Symbols in Crises of Authority*. Lincoln: University of Nebraska Press.

Francis, Norbert, and Jon Reyhner. 2002. *Language and Literacy Teaching for Indigenous Education: A Bilingual Approach*. Clevedon, UK: Multilingual Matters, Ltd.

Franciscan Fathers. 1910. *An Ethnologic Dictionary of the Navaho Language*. St. Michaels, AZ: St. Michael's Press.

Franklin, Robert, and Pamela A. Bunte. 1996. "Animals and Humans, Sex and Death: Towards a Symbolic Analysis of Southern Numic Rituals." *Journal of California and Great Basin Anthropology* 18(2): 178–203.

Frawley, William, Kenneth Hill, and Pamela Munro. 2002a. "Making a Dictionary: Ten Issues." In Frawley, Hill, and Munro, *Making Dictionaries*, 1–22.

———, eds. 2002b. *Making Dictionaries: Preserving Indigenous Languages of the Americas*. Berkeley: University of California Press.

French, Brigittine M. 2001. "Language Ideologies and Collective Identities in Post-Conflict Guatemala." Ph.D. diss., Department of Anthropology, University of Iowa.

———. 2003. "The Politics of Mayan Linguistics in Guatemala: Native Speakers, Expert Analysts, and the Nation." *Pragmatics* 13(4): 483–98.

Friedman, Jonathan. 2003. "Globalizing Languages: Ideologies and Realities of the Contemporary Global System." *American Anthropologist* 105(4): 744–52.

Friedrich, Paul. 1989. "Language, Ideology, and Political Economy." *American Anthropologist* 91(2): 295–312.

Fuchs, Estelle, and Robert J. Havighurst. 1972. *To Live on This Earth: American Indian Education*. Garden City, NY: Anchor Press/Doubleday.

Gal, Susan. 1979. *Language Shift: Social Dimensions of Linguistic Change in Bilingual Austria*. New York: Academic Press.

——. 1989. "Language and Political Economy." *Annual Review of Anthropology* 18:345–67.

——. 1992. "Multiplicity and Contention among Ideologies." *Pragmatics* 2:445–50.

——. 1993. "Diversity and Contestation in Language Ideologies: German Speakers in Hungary." *Language in Society* 22:337–59.

——. 1998. "Multiplicity and Contention among Language Ideologies: A Commentary." In Schieffelin, Woolard, and Kroskrity, *Language Ideologies*, 317–31.

——. 2005. "Language Ideologies Compared: Metaphors of Public/Private." *Journal of Linguistic Ideology* 15(1): 23–37.

Gal, Susan, and Judith T. Irvine. 1995. "The Boundaries of Languages and Disciplines: How Ideologies Construct Difference." *Social Research* 62(4): 967–1001.

Gal, Susan, and Kathryn Woolard. 2001. *Languages and Publics: The Making of Authority.* Manchester, UK: St. Jerome Publishing.

Gardiner, M. 1992. *The Dialogics of Critique: M. M. Bakhtin and the Theory of Ideology.* London: Routledge.

Gardner and Associates. 1993. *Walking the Talk: Implementation Evaluation of the Canada-Yukon Funding Agreement on the Development and Enhancement of Aboriginal Languages, 1988/89–1992/93.* Whitehorse, YT: Queen's Printer.

——. 1997. *We Are Our Language: An Evaluation of the Implementation and Impact of the Canada-Yukon Cooperation and Funding Agreement on the Development and Enhancement of Aboriginal Languages 1993–1998.* Whitehorse, YT: Queen's Printer.

Garzon, Susan. 1998a. "Case Study Three: San Juan Comalapa." In Garzon et al., *The Life of Our Language,* 129–54.

——. 1998b. "Conclusions." In Garzon et al., *The Life of Our Language,* 189–99.

——. 1998c. "Indigenous Groups and Language Contact Relations." In Garzon et al., *The Life of Our Language,* 9–43.

Garzon, Susan, R. McKenna Brown, Julia Becker Richards, and Wuqu' Ajpub' (Arnulfo Simón), eds. 1998. *The Life of Our Language.* Austin: University of Texas Press.

Gaskins, Suzanne. 1999. "Children's Daily Lives in a Mayan Village: A Case Study of Culturally Constructed Roles and Activities." In *Children's Engagement in the World.* Ed. Artin Göncü. Cambridge: Cambridge University Press. 25–61.

Giddens, Anthony. 1979. *Central Problems in Social Theory.* Berkeley: University of California Press.

——. 1984. *The Constitution of Society.* Berkeley: University of California Press.

——. 1987. *The Constitution of Society: Outline of the Theory of Structuration.* Berkeley: University of California Press.

Gleick, James. 2000. *Faster: The Acceleration of Just about Everything.* New York: Vintage.

Goddard, Ives, ed. 1996. *Languages.* Vol. 17 of *Handbook of North American Indians.* Washington, D.C.: Smithsonian Institution Press.

Goddard, P. E. 1911. *Jicarilla Texts.* Anthropological Papers, 8. American Museum of Natural History, New York.

Goffman, Erving. 1974. *Frame Analysis: An Essay on the Organization of Experience.* New York: Harper and Row.

Golla, Victor. 2000. "Language Histories and Communicative Strategies in Aboriginal

California and Oregon." In O. Miyaoka, *Languages of the North Pacific Rim*, vol. 5. Osaka, Japan: Gakuin University.

Gómez de García, J., M. Axelrod, and J. Lachler. 2002. "'If You Play with Fire . . .': Literary Production in Jicarilla Apache." In *Proceedings of the 2002 Foundation for Endangered Languages Conference*. Ed. R. M. Brown. Bath, UK: Foundation for Endangered Languages. 51–58.

Gómez de García, J., M. Olson, and M. Axelrod. 2002. "The Importance of Women's Literacy in Language Stabilization Projects." In Burnaby and Reyhner, *Indigenous Languages across the Community*, 137–50.

Gonzales, Alecia. 2000. *Thaum Khoiye Tdoen Gyah*. Chickasha: University of Science and Arts of Oklahoma Press.

Gonzalez, Norma. 2000. *I Am My Language: Discourses of Women and Children in the Borderlands*. Tucson: University of Arizona Press.

Goode, Ron W. 1992. *Cultural Traditions Endangered*. Clovis, CA: Eagle Eye Enterprises.

Goody, Jack. 1971. "The Fission of Domestic Groups among the LaDagaba." In *The Developmental Cycle in Domestic Groups*. Cambridge: Cambridge University Press. 53–91.

Goossen, Irvy W. 1995–98. *Dine Bizaad: Speak, Read, Write Navajo*. Vols. 1–3. Flagstaff, AZ: Salina Bookshelf.

Gould, Drusilla. 1986. *Shoshoni Language Dictionary*. Fort Hall, ID: Shoshone-Bannock Tribes, Inc.

Gould, Drusilla, and Christopher Loether. 2002. *An Introduction to the Shoshoni Language: Dammen Daigwape*. Salt Lake City: University of Utah Press.

Government of Yukon. 1993. *Umbrella Final Agreement between the Government of Canada and the Council for Yukon Indians*. Whitehorse, YT: Queen's Printer.

——. 1996. *People to People, Nation to Nation: Highlights from the Report of the Royal Commission on Aboriginal Peoples*. Ottawa: Minister of Supply and Services Canada.

Gramsci, Antonio. 1971. *Selections from the Prison Notebooks*. London: Lawrence and Wishart.

Greene, Candace. 2005. "Winter Counts and Coup Counts: Pictorial Art as Native History." Lecture presented at the University of Oklahoma.

Greenhouse, Carol, Elizabeth Mertz, and Kay B. Warren, eds. 2002. *Ethnography in Unstable Places: Everyday Lives in Contexts of Dramatic Political Change*. Durham, NC: Duke University Press.

Grenoble, Lenore A., and Lindsay J. Whaley, eds. 1998. *Endangered Languages: Current Issues and Future Prospects*. Cambridge: Cambridge University Press.

Greymorning, Steve. 1997. "Going beyond Words: The Arapaho Immersion Program." In Reyhner, *Teaching Indigenous Languages*, 22–30.

Grillo, Ralph. 1989. *Dominant Languages: Language and Hierarchy in Britain and France*. Cambridge: Cambridge University Press.

Grimes, Barbara F., ed. 2005. "Ethnologue: Languages of the World." http://www.ethnologue.com/. Accessed 2007.

Grinevald, Colette. 1998. "Language Endangerment in South America: A Programmatic Approach." In Grenoble and Whaley, *Endangered Languages*, 124–60.

Gross, Feliks. 1949. "Nomadism of the Arapaho Indians of Wyoming and Conflict between Economics and Idea System." *Ethnos* 14:65–88.

——. 1951. "Language and Value Changes among the Arapaho." *International Journal of American Linguistics* 17:10–17.

Gudschinsky, Sarah. 1973. *A Manual of Literacy for Preliterate Peoples.* Ukarumpa, Papua New Guinea: Summer Institute of Linguistics.

Gulick, John. 1958. "Language and Passive Resistance among the Eastern Cherokees." *Ethnohistory* 5:60–81.

——. 1960. *Cherokees at the Crossroads.* Chapel Hill: University of North Carolina Press.

Gumperz, John. 1972. "The Speech Community." In *Language and Social Context.* Ed. P. Giglioli. 219–31.

——. 1982. *Discourse Strategies.* Cambridge: Cambridge University Press.

Haile, Fr. Bernard, OFM. 1941. *Learning Navajo,* vol. 1. St. Michaels, AZ: St. Michael's Press.

Hale, Ken. 1973. "A Note on Subject-Object Inversion in Navajo." In *Issues in Linguistics: Papers in Honor of Henry and Renee Kahane.* Ed. B. Kachru et al. Chicago: University of Chicago Press. 300–309.

——. 1992. "On Endangered Languages and the Safeguarding of Diversity." *Language* 68:1–3.

——. 2001. "Linguistic Aspects of Language Teaching and Learning in Immersion Contexts." In Hinton and Hale, *The Green Book,* 227–35.

Hale, Kenneth, Michael Krauss, Lucille Watahomigie, Akira Yamamoto, Colette Craig, Laverne Jeanne, and Nora England. 1992. "Endangered Languages." *Language* 68(1): 1–43.

Halpern, K. S., and S. McGreevy. 1997. "Foreword." In *Washington Matthews: Studies of Navajo Culture.* Ed. K. S. Halpern and S. McGreevy. Albuquerque: University of New Mexico Press.

Haraway, Donna J. 1990. *Simians, Cyborgs, and Women: The Reinvention of Nature.* New York: Routledge.

Harnum, Betty. 1998. "Language in the Northwest Territories and the Yukon Territory." In *Language in Canada.* Ed. John Edwards. Cambridge: Cambridge University Press.

Harrington, J. P. 1910a. "A Brief Description of the Tewa Language." *American Anthropologist* 12(4): 497–504.

——. 1910b. "On Phonetic and Lexical Resemblances between Kiowa and Tanoan." *American Anthropologist* 12(1): 119–23.

——. 1910c. "An Introductory Paper in the Tiwa Language, Dialect of Taos." *American Anthropologist* 12(4): 11–48.

——. 1928. *Vocabulary of the Kiowa Language.* Bureau of American Ethnology, Bulletin 84. Washington, D.C.: Government Printing Office.

Harshav, Benjamin. 1993. *Language in Time of Revolution.* Berkeley: University of California Press.

Harvey, David. 1990. "Between Space and Time: Reflections on the Geographical Imagination." *Annals of the Association of American Geographers* 80(3): 418–34.

Haviland, John B. 1996. "Projections, Transpositions, and Relativity." In *Rethinking Linguistic Relativity*. Ed. John J. Gumperz and Steve C. Levinson. Cambridge: Cambridge University Press. 271–323.

Heizer, Robert F. 1974. *The Destruction of California Indians*. Lincoln: University of Nebraska Press.

Heller, Monica, and Marilyn Martin-Jones, eds. 2001. *Voices of Authority: Education and Linguistic Difference*. Westport, CT: Ablex.

Hensel, Chase. 1996. *Telling Our Selves: Ethnicity and Discourse in Southwestern Alaska*. New York: Oxford University Press.

Henze, Rosemary, and Kathryn A. Davis. 1999. "Authenticity and Identity: Lessons from Indigenous Language Education." *Anthropology & Education Quarterly* 30(1): 3–21.

Herron, Tom. 1998. "Encountering Ourselves: *The Field Day Anthology of Irish Writing* as Communicative Space/Act or, Into the Inter: The Heterographia of *The Field Day Anthology*." In *Irish Encounters: Literature, History and Culture*. Ed. Alan Marshall and Neil Sammells. Bath, UK: Sulis Press. 180–89.

Hilger, Sister M. Inez. 1952. *Arapaho Child Life and Its Cultural Background*. Bureau of American Ethnology, Bulletin 148. Smithsonian Institution, Washington, D.C.

Hill, Jane H. 1983. "Language Death in Uto-Aztecan." *International Journal of American Linguistics* 49(3): 258–76.

———. 1993. "Structure and Practice in Language Shift." In *Progression and Regression in Language: Sociocultural, Neuropsychological, and Linguistics Perspectives*. Ed. K. Hyltenstam and A. Viberg. Cambridge: Cambridge University Press. 68–93.

———. 1995. "The Voices of Don Gabriel: Responsibility and Self in a Modern Mexicano Narrative." In *The Dialogic Emergence of Culture*. Ed. D. Tedlock and B. Mannheim. Urbana: University of Illinois Press. 97–147.

———. 1998. "'Today There Is No Respect': Nostalgia, 'Respect,' and Oppositional Discourse in Mexicano (Nahuatl) Language Ideology." In Schieffelin, Woolard, and Kroskrity, *Language Ideologies*, 68–86.

———. 1999. "Syncretism." *Journal of Linguistic Anthropology* 9(1–2): 244–46.

———. 2002. "'Expert Rhetorics' in Advocacy for Endangered Languages: Who Is Listening, and What Do They Hear?" *Journal of Linguistic Anthropology* 12(2): 119–21.

———. 2005. "Intertextuality as Source and Evidence for Indirect Indexical Meanings." *Linguistic Anthropology* 15(1): 113–24.

Hill, Jane, and Kenneth Hill. 1984. *Speaking Mexicano: Dynamics of Syncretic Language in Central Mexico*. Tucson: University of Arizona Press.

Hill, Robert M., and John Monaghan. 1987. *Continuities in Highland Maya Social Organization: Ethnohistory in Sacapulas, Guatemala*. Philadelphia: University of Pennsylvania Press.

Hill, W. W. 1948. "Navajo Trading and Trading Ritual: A Study of Cultural Dynamics." *Southwestern Journal of Anthropology* 4:371–96.

Hinton, Leanne. 1994. *Flutes of Fire*. Berkeley, CA: Heydey Books.

——. 2001a. "Introduction to Revitalization of National Indigenous Languages." In Hinton and Hale, *The Green Book*, 101–4.

——. 2001b. "Language Revitalization: An Overview." In Hinton and Hale, *The Green Book*, 3–18.

——. 2001c. "New Writing Systems." In Hinton and Hale, *The Green Book*, 239–50.

——. 2002. "Commentary: Internal and External Language Advocacy." *Journal of Linguistic Anthropology* 12:150–56.

Hinton, Leanne, and Jocelyn Ahlers. 1999. "The Issue of 'Authenticity' in California Language Restoration." *Anthropology and Education Quarterly* 30(1): 56–67.

Hinton, Leanne, and Ken Hale, eds. 2001a. *The Green Book of Language Revitalization in Practice*. New York: Academic Press.

——. 2001b. "An Introduction to Paiute." In Hinton and Hale, *The Green Book*, 251–52.

Hinton, Leanne, Matt Vera, and Nancy Steele. 2002. *How to Keep Your Language Alive: A Commonsense Approach to One-on-One Language Learning*. Berkeley, CA: Heyday Books.

Hirsch, Susan F. 1996. *Pronouncing and Persevering: Gender and the Discourses of Disputing in an African Islamic Court*. Chicago: University of Chicago Press.

Hofling, Charles Andrew. 1996. "Indigenous Linguistic Revitalization and Outsider Interaction: The Itzaj Maya Case." *Human Organization* 55(1): 108–16.

Hoijer, Harry. 1938a. *Chiricahua and Mescalero Apache Texts: With Ethnological Notes by Morris Edward Opler*. Chicago: University of Chicago Press.

——. 1938b. "The Southern Athapaskan Languages." *American Anthropologist* 40:75–87.

Hollan, Douglas. 2001. "Developments in Person-Centered Ethnography." In *The Psychology of Cultural Experience*. Ed. Carmella C. Moore and Holly F. Mathews. Cambridge: Cambridge University Press. 48–67.

Holm, Agnes, and Wayne Holm. 1995. "Navajo Language Education: Retrospect and Prospects." *Bilingual Research Journal* 19(1): 141–67.

Holm, Agnes, Wayne Holm, and Bernard Spolsky. 1971. *English Loan Words in the Speech of Six-Year-Old Navajo Children*. Navajo Reading Study Progress Report, no. 16. University of New Mexico.

Hopi Language Assessment Project. 1997. On file with the Hopi Tribal Cultural Preservation Office, Kykostmovi, AZ.

Hornberger, Nancy H., ed. 1997. *Indigenous Literacies in the Americas: Language Planning from the Bottom Up*. New York: Mouton de Gruyter.

——. 1998. "Language Policy, Language Education, Language Rights: Indigenous, Immigrant, and International Perspectives." *Language in Society* 27(4): 439–58.

House, Deborah. 2002. *Language Shift among the Navajos: Identity Politics and Cultural Continuity*. Tucson: University of Arizona Press.

Huffines, Marion. 1989. "Case Usage among the Pennsylvania German Sectarians and Nonsectarians." In Dorian, *Investigating Obsolescence*, 211–27.

Hymes, Dell. 1972. "Models of the Interaction of Language and Social Life." In *Directions in Sociolinguistics: The Ethnography of Communication*. Ed. John J. Gumperz and Del Hymes. New York: Holt, Rinehart and Winston. 35–71.

——. 1979. "Sapir, Competence, Voices." In *Individual Differences in Language Ability and Behavior.* Ed. C. J. Fillmore, D. Kempler, and W. S.-Y. Wang. New York: Academic Press. 33–46.

——. 1981. *"In Vain I Tried to Tell You": Essays in Native American Ethnopoetics.* Philadelphia: University of Pennsylvania Press.

Indian Affairs and Northern Development. 1993. *Umbrella Final Agreement between the Government of Canada, the Council for Yukon Indians and the Government of the Yukon.* Ottawa: Minister of Supply and Services Canada.

Indian and Northern Affairs Canada. 1997. *First Nations in Canada.* Ottawa: Minister of Public Works and Government Services Canada.

Inoue, Miyako. 2004. "Introduction: Temporality and Historicity in and through Linguistic Ideology." In "The History of Ideology and the Ideology of History." Ed. Miyako Inoue. Special issue, *Linguistic Anthropology* 14(1): 1–5.

Irvine, Judith. 1989. "When Talk Isn't Cheap: Language and Political Economy." *American Ethnologist* 16:248–67.

——. 2004. "Say When: Temporalities in Language Ideology." *Linguistic Anthropology* 14(1): 99–109.

Irvine, Judith, and Susan Gal. 2000. "Language Ideology and Linguistic Differentiation." In Kroskrity, *Regimes of Language,* 35–83.

Joh, Elizabeth E. 2000. "Custom, Tribal Court Practice, and Popular Justice." *American Indian Law Review* 25:117–32.

Johnstone, Barbara. 1996. *The Linguistic Individual.* New York: Oxford University Press.

Jung, Dagmar. 1999. "The Dynamics of Polysynthetic Morphology: Person and Number Marking in Athabaskan." Ph.D. diss., Department of Linguistics, University of New Mexico.

Karp, Ivan. 1986. "Agency and Social Theory: A Review of Anthony Giddens." *American Ethnologist* 13:131–37.

Kipp, Darrel R. 2000. *Encouragement, Guidance, Insights, and Lessons Learned for Native Language Activists Developing Their Own Tribal Language Programs.* Browning, MT: Piegan Institute.

Klaiman, M. H. 1989. "Inverse Voice and Head-Marking in Tanoan Languages." *Papers from the Regional Meetings, Chicago Linguistic Society* 25(1): 258–71.

——. 1993. "The Relationship of Inverse Voice and Head-Marking in Arizona Tewa and Other Tanoan Languages." *Studies in Language* 17(2): 343–70.

Kotay, Ralph, L. Eric Lassiter, and Chris Wendt. 2002. *Kiowa Hymns.* Lincoln: University of Nebraska Press.

Kracht, Benjamin. 2005. "Kiowa." In *Encyclopedia of North American Indians.* Boston: Houghton Mifflin.

Krauss, Michael. 1996. "Status of Native American Language Endangerment." In *Stabilizing Indigenous Languages.* Ed. J. Reyhner. Flagstaff: Northern Arizona University. http://www.ncela.gwu.edu/pubs/stabilize/i-needs/status.htm. Accessed July 4, 2007.

——. 1998. "The Condition of Native North American Languages: The Need for Realistic Assessment and Action." *International Journal of the Sociology of Language* 132:9–21.

Kroeber, Alfred L. 1916. "Arapaho Dialects." *University of California Publications in American Archaeology and Ethnology* 12(3): 71–138. Berkeley: University of California Press.

———. 1916–20. Field Notes. Manuscripts 2622, 2560. National Anthropological Archives, Smithsonian Institution, Washington, D.C.

———. 1947. *Cultural and Natural Areas of North America.* Berkeley: University of California Press.

Kroskrity, Paul V. 1982. "Language Contact and Linguistic Diffusion: The Arizona Tewa Speech Community." In *Bilingualism and Language Contact: Spanish, English, and Native American Languages.* Ed. F. Barkin, E. Brandt, and J. Ornstein-Galicia. New York: Teacher's College Press. 51–73.

———. 1984. "Negation and Subordination in Arizona Tewa: Discourse Pragmatics Influencing Syntax." *International Journal of American Linguistics* 50(1): 94–104.

———. 1985a. "Areal-Historical Influences on Tewa Possession." *International Journal of American Linguistics* 51(4): 486–89.

———. 1985b. "A Holistic Understanding of Arizona Tewa Passives." *Language* 61(2): 306–28.

———. 1992a. "Arizona Tewa Kiva Speech as a Manifestation of Linguistic Ideology." *Pragmatics* 2(3): 297–309.

———. 1992b. "Arizona Tewa Public Announcements: Form, Function, and Linguistic Ideology." *Anthropological Linguistics* 3(1–4): 104–16.

———. 1993a. "Aspects of Syntactic and Semantic Variation within the Arizona Tewa Speech Community." *Anthropological Linguistics* 35(1–4): 250–73.

———. 1993b. *Language, History, and Identity: Ethnolinguistic Studies of the Arizona Tewa.* Tucson: University of Arizona Press.

———. 1997. "Discursive Convergence with an Evidential Particle." In *The Life of Language: Papers in Linguistics in Honor of William Bright.* Ed. J. H. Hill, P. J. Mistry, and L. Campbell. Berlin: Mouton de Gruyter. 25–34.

———. 1998. "Arizona Tewa Kiva Speech as a Manifestation of a Dominant Language Ideology." In Schieffelin, Woolard, and Kroskrity, *Language Ideologies,* 103–22.

———. 1999. "Language Ideologies, Language Shift, and the Imagination of a Western Mono Community: The Recontextualization of a Coyote Story." In *Language and Ideology.* Ed. Jef Verschueren. Antwerp, Belgium: International Pragmatics Association. 270–89.

———. 2000a. "Language Ideologies in the Expression and Representation of Arizona Tewa Ethnic Identity." In Kroskrity, *Regimes of Language,* 329–59.

———. 2000b. "Regimenting Languages: Language Ideological Perspectives." In Kroskrity, *Regimes of Language,* 1–34.

———, ed. 2000c. *Regimes of Language: Ideologies, Polities, and Identities.* Santa Fe: School of American Research Press.

———. 2002. "Language Renewal and the Technologies of Literacy and Post-Literacy." In Frawley, Hill, and Munro, *Making Dictionaries,* 171–92.

———. 2004. "Language Ideologies." In Duranti, *Companion to Linguistic Anthropology,* 496–517.

Kroskrity, Paul V., Rosalie Bethel, and Jennifer F. Reynolds. 2002. *Taitaduhaan: Western Mono Ways of Speaking*. CD ROM. Norman: University of Oklahoma Press.

Kroskrity, Paul V., and Gregory A. Reinhardt. 1984. "Spanish and English Loanwords in Western Mono." *Journal of California and Great Basin Anthropology, Papers in Linguistics* 4:107–38.

Kulick, Don. 1992. *Language Shift and Cultural Reproduction*. Cambridge: Cambridge University Press.

——. 1998. "Anger, Gender, Language Shift, and the Politics of Revelation in a Papua New Guinean village." In Schieffelin, Woolard, and Kroskrity, *Language Ideologies*, 87–102.

Kwachka, Patricia, and Charlotte Basham. 1990. "Literacy Acts and Cultural Artifacts." *Journal of Pragmatics* 14:413–29.

Labov, William. 1978. "Sociolinguistics." In *Survey of Linguistic Science*. Ed. W. O. Dingwall. Stanford, CT: Greylock Publishing.

Ladefoged, Peter. 1993. *A Course in Phonetics*. 3rd ed. Fort Worth, TX: Harcourt Brace.

Lakoff, George. 1987. *Women, Fire, and Dangerous Things*. Chicago: University of Chicago Press.

Lamb, Sydney. 1957. "Mono Grammar." Ph.D. diss., Department of Linguistics, University of California, Berkeley.

Lambert, W. E. 2003. "A Social Psychology of Bilingualism." In *Sociolinguistics: The Essential Readings*. Ed. C. B. Paulston and G. R. Tucker. Malden, MA: Basil Blackwell.

Langness, Lew L., and Gelya Frank. 1981. *Lives: An Anthropological Approach to Biography*. Novato, CA: Chandler & Sharp.

Larsen, Soren C. 2003. "Promoting Aboriginal Territoriality through Interethnic Alliances: The Case of the Cheslatta T'en in Northern British Columbia." *Human Organization* 62(1): 74–84.

Lassiter, L. Eric, Clyde Ellis, and Ralph Kotay. 1999. *The Jesus Road: Kiowas, Christianity, and Indian Hymns*. Lincoln: University of Nebraska Press.

Lawrence, Denise L., and Setha M. Low. 1990. "The Built Environment and Spatial Form." *Annual Review of Anthropology* 19:453–505.

Laylin, Laura. 1988. "The Prefix in Isletan Tiwa: A Functional Approach." Ph.D. diss., American University.

Leap, William L. 1988. "Indian Language Renewal." *Human Organization* 47(4): 283–91.

——. 1993. *American Indian English*. Salt Lake City: University of Utah Press.

Lee, Gaylen. 1998. *Walking Where We Lived: Memoirs of a Mono Indian Family*. Norman: University of Oklahoma Press.

Lefebvre, Henri. 1991. *The Production of Space*. Oxford: Oxford University Press.

Lefler, Lisa J. 1996. "Mentorship as an Intervention Strategy in Relapse Reduction among Native American Youth." Ph.D. diss., University of Tennessee.

Leonard, Wesley. 2006. "Language Development in a Revitalization Setting: The Role of Teaching." Paper presented at the annual meeting of the Society for the Study of Indigenous Languages of the Americas, Albuquerque, NM.

Levy, Jerrold. 1992. *Orayvi Revisited: Social Stratification in an "Egalitarian Society."* Santa Fe: School of American Research Press.

Levy, Jerrold, and Stephen Kunitz. 1974. *Indian Drinking: Navajo Practices and Anglo-American Theories.* New York: John Wiley and Sons.

Liljeblad, Sven S. 1972. *The Idaho Indians in Transition, 1805–1960.* Pocatello: Idaho State University Museum Press.

Limón, José E. 1991. "Representations, Ethnicity, and the Precursory Ethnography: Notes of a Native Anthropologist." In *Recapturing Anthropology: Working in the Present.* Ed. Richard G. Fox. Santa Fe: School of American Research Press. 115–35.

Linn, Mary S., Tessie Naranjo, Sheilah Nicholas, Inée Slaughter, Akira Yamamoto, and Ofelia Zepeda. 2003. "Awakening the Languages: Challenges of Enduring Language Programs; Field Reports from Fifteen Programs from Arizona, New Mexico and Oklahoma." In Burnaby and Reyhner, *Indigenous Languages across the Community.*

Little, Walter E. 2004. "Outside of Social Movements: Dilemmas of Indigenous Handicraft Vendors in Guatemala." *American Ethnologist* 31(1): 43–59.

Lock, Charles. 2002. "Otherwise than Speaking: On Heterographia." *Literary Research/Recherche Littéraire* 19(37–38): 407–11.

Loether, Christopher. 1991. "Verbal Art among the Western Mono." Ph.D. diss., UCLA.

——. 1993. "Niimina Ahubiya: Western Mono Song Genres." *Journal of California and Great Basin Anthropology* 15:48–57.

——. 1997. "Yokuts and English Loanwords in Western Mono." In *The Life of Language: Papers in Linguistics in Honor of William Bright.* Ed. J. H. Hill, P. J. Mistry, and L. Campbell. Berlin: Mouton de Gruyter. 101–22.

Lucy, John. 1992. *Language Diversity and Thought: A Reformulation of the Linguistic Relativity Hypothesis.* Cambridge: Cambridge University Press.

Luykx, Aurolyn. 2004. "The Future of Quechua and the Quechua of the Future." *International Journal of American Linguistics* 167:147–58.

Lyons, Scott Richard. 2000. "Rhetorical Sovereignty: What Do American Indians Want from Writing?" *College Composition and Communication* 51(3): 447–68.

Madumulla, Joshua, Elena Bertoncini, and Jan Blommaert. 1999. "Politics, Ideology and Poetic Form: The Literary Debate in Tanzania." In *Language Ideological Debates.* Ed. Jan Blommaert. Berlin: Mouton de Gruyter. 307–42.

Mandelbaum, David G. 1973. "The Study of Life History: Gandhi." *Current Anthropology* 14:177–206.

Manz, Beatriz. 2004. *Paradise in Ashes: A Guatemalan Journey of Courage, Terror, and Hope.* Berkeley: University of California Press.

Martin, Laura. 1986. "'Eskimo Words for Snow': A Case Study in the Genesis and Decay of an Anthropological Example." *American Anthropologist* 88:418–23.

Martinez, Esther. 1982. *San Juan Pueblo Tewa Dictionary.* San Juan Pueblo, NM: SJP Bilingual Program.

Mateo Toledo, B'alam Q'ug'. 2000. "Un pueblo con dos idiomas? El caso Q'anjob'al." Paper presented at the Latin American Studies Association's Twenty-second International Congress, Miami, FL, March 16–18.

Matoesian, Gregory. 2001. *Law and the Language of Identity.* Oxford: Oxford University Press.

Mattingly, I. G. 1992. "Linguistic Awareness and Orthographic Form." In *Orthography, Phonology, Morphology and Meaning*. Ed. R. Frost and L. Katz. Amsterdam: North-Holland. 11–26.

Maxwell, Judith. 1996. "Prescriptive Grammar and Kaqchikel Revitalization." In Fischer and Brown, *Maya Cultural Activism*, 195–207.

McCarty, Theresa. 1993. "Federal Language Policy and American Indian Education." *Bilingual Research Journal* 17(1–2): 13–34.

McCarty, Theresa L., Lucille J. Watahomigie, Akira Yamamoto, and Ofelia Zepeda. 2001. "Indigenous Educators as Change Agents." In Hinton and Hale, *The Green Book*, 371–83.

McClellan, Catharine. 2001. *My Old People Say: An Ethnographic Survey of Southern Yukon Territory*. 2 vols. Ottawa: National Museum of Man. (Orig. pub. 1975.)

McKenna, Cora, Evelyn O. Anaya Hatch, Brenda McKenna, and Quella Musgrave. In preparation. *Dictionary of Nambé Tewa*. Ed. Evan Ashworth, Melissa Axelrod, and Susan Buescher.

McKenzie, Parker. N.d. "Essential Elements of the Kiowa Language." Manuscript.

McLaughlin, D. 1989. "The Sociolinguistics of Navajo Literacy." *Anthropology and Education Quarterly* 20(4): 275–90.

———. 1992. *When Literacy Empowers: Navajo Language in Print*. Albuquerque: University of New Mexico Press.

McNeely, James. 1988. *Holy Wind in Navajo Philosophy*. Tucson: University of Arizona Press.

Meek, Barbra A. 2001. "Kaska Language Socialization, Acquisition and Shift." Ph.D. diss., University of Arizona.

———. 2007. "Respecting the Language of Elders: Ideological Shift and Linguistic Discontinuity in a Northern Athapascan Community." *Journal of Linguistic Anthropology* 17(1): 23–43.

Menchú, Rigoberta. 1984. *I, Rigoberta Menchú*. London: Verso.

Mersol, Stanley Alfonse. 1977. "A Sociolinguistic-Conceptual-Cultural-Ethnographic Jicarilla Apache–English Dictionary: The Dulce Springs Dialect." Ph.D. diss., University of California, Irvine.

Mertz, Elizabeth. 1989. "Sociolinguistic Creativity: Cape Breton's Gaelic Linguistic 'Tip.'" In Dorian, *Investigating Obsolescence*, 103–16.

———. 1998. "Linguistic Ideology and Praxis in U.S. Law School Classrooms." In Schieffelin, Woolard, and Kroskrity, *Language Ideologies*, 149–62.

Messing, Jacqueline. 2007. "Multiple Ideologies, Competing Discourses and Language Shift in Tlaxcala, Mexico." *Language in Society* 36(4): 555–77.

Metcalfe, Betty, with assistance from Leslie Gardner and Gladys Netro. 1997. *We Are Our Language: The Story of the Yukon Aboriginal Language Services Program 1993–1997*. Whitehorse, YT: Aboriginal Language Services.

Michelson, Truman. 1912. *Preliminary Report on the Linguistic Classification of Algonquian Tribes*. Bureau of American Ethnology, Twenty-eighth Annual Report (1906–7). Washington, D.C.

Miller, Bruce G. 2002. *The Problem of Justice: Tradition and Law in the Coast Salish World*. Lincoln: University of Nebraska Press.

——. 2005. "Tribal or Native Law." In *A Companion to the Anthropology of American Indians*. Ed. Thomas Biolsi. London: Blackwell Publishers. 95–111.

Miller, Wick R. 1970. "Western Shoshoni Dialects." In *Languages and Cultures of Western North America: Essays in Honor of Sven S. Liljeblad*. Ed. Earl H. Swanson, Jr. Pocatello: Idaho State University Press.

——. 1972. *Newe Natekwinnappeh: Shoshoni Stories and Dictionary*. University of Utah Anthropological Papers, no. 94. Salt Lake City: University of Utah Press.

——. 1983. "Uto-Aztecan Languages." In *Southwest*. Ed. Alfonso Ortiz. Vol. 10 of *Handbook of North American Indians*. Washington, D.C.: Smithsonian Institution Press. 113–24.

Mithun, Marianne. 1999. *The Languages of Native North America*. Cambridge: Cambridge University Press.

Montejo, Victor. 1987. *Testimony: Death of a Guatemalan Village*. Willamantic, CT: Curbstone Press.

——. 2005. "Maya Ways of Knowing." In *Mayan Intellectual Renaissance: Identity, Representation, and Leadership*. Austin: University of Texas Press. 139–57.

Moore, Patrick, ed. 1999. *Dene Gudeji: Kaska Narratives*. Whitehorse, YT: Queen's Printer.

——. 2002. "Point of View in Kaska Historical Narratives." Ph.D. diss., Indiana University, Bloomington.

Moore, Robert E. 1988. "Lexicalization versus Lexical Loss in Wasco-Wishram Language Obsolescence." *International Journal of American Linguistics* 54(4): 453–68.

Munn, Nancy. 1992. "The Cultural Anthropology of Time: A Critical Essay." *Annual Review of Anthropology* 21:93–123.

Nadasdy, Paul. 2003. *Hunters and Bureaucrats: Power, Knowledge and Aboriginal-State Relations in the Southwest Yukon*. Vancouver: University of British Columbia Press.

Nagata, Shuichi. 1970. *Modern Transformations of Moenkopi Pueblo*. Urbana: University of Illinois Press.

National Clearinghouse for Bilingual Education. 1999. Native Speakers of Indigenous Languages in the United States. http://www.ncbe.gwu.edu/askncbe/faqs/20natlang.htm. Accessed 2007.

Nettle, Daniel, and Suzanne Romaine. 2000. *Vanishing Voices: The Extinction of the World's Languages*. Oxford: Oxford University Press.

Nevins, M. Eleanor. 2004. "Learning to Listen: Confronting Two Meanings of Language Loss in the Contemporary White Mountain Apache Speech Community." *Journal of Linguistic Anthropology* 14(2): 269–88.

O'Barr, William M. 1982. *Linguistic Evidence: Language, Power and Strategy in the Courtroom*. New York: Academic Press.

Ochs, Elinor. 1986. "Introduction." In *Language Socialization across Cultures*. Ed. Bambi Schieffelin and Elinor Ochs. Cambridge: Cambridge University Press. 1–16.

——. 1988. *Culture and Language Development*. Cambridge: Cambridge University Press.

——. 1996. "Linguistic Resources for Socializing Humanity." In *Rethinking Linguistic*

Relativity. Ed. J. Gumperz and S. Levinson. Cambridge: Cambridge University Press. 407–38.

Oficina de Derechos Humanos del Arzobispado de Guatemala. 1998. *Guatemala nunca más*. Vols. 1–4. Guatemala City: Informe Proyecto Interdiocesano de Recuperación de la Memoria Histórica.

Oglesby, Elizabeth. 2007. "Educating Citizens in Postwar Guatemala: Historical Memory, Genocide, and the Culture of Peace." *Radical History Review* 97(1): 77–98.

O'Hara, Frank. 1957. *Meditations in an Emergency*. New York: Grove.

Ong, Walter. 1982. *Orality and Literacy: The Technologizing of the Word*. London: Routledge.

Ortner, Sherry B. 1996. "Toward a Feminist, Minority, Postcolonial, Subaltern, etc., Theory of Practice." In *Making Gender: The Politics and Erotics of Culture*. Boston: Beacon. 1–20.

Otzoy, Irma. 1996. "Maya Clothing and Identity." In Fischer and Brown, *Maya Cultural Activism*, 141–55.

Oxlajuuj Keej Maya' Ajtz'iib'. 1993. *Maya' Chii': Los idiomas mayas de Guatemala*. Guatemala City: Cholsamaj.

Paddlety, David. 1998. *Conversational Kiowa*. Chickasha: University of Science and Arts of Oklahoma Press.

Pakal B'alam. 1994. *Rutzi'ib'axik ri Kaqchikel: Manual de redacción kaqchikel*. Guatemala City: Cholsamaj.

Palmer, Gus. 2003. *Telling Stories the Kiowa Way*. Tucson: University of Arizona Press.

Parsons-Yazzie, Evangeline. 1995. "Navajo-Speaking Parents' Perceptions of Reasons for Navajo Language Attrition." *Journal of Navajo Education* 13(1): 29–38.

———. 1996. "Perceptions of Selected Navajo Elders Regarding Navajo Language Attrition." *Journal of Navajo Education* 13(2): 51–57.

Patrick, Donna. 2001. "Languages of State and Social Categorization in an Arctic Quebec Community." In *Voices of Authority: Education and Linguistic Difference*. Ed. Monica Heller and Marilyn Martin-Jones. Westport, CT: Ablex. 297–314.

———. 2003. *Language, Politics and Social Interaction in an Inuit Community*. Berlin: Mouton de Gruyter.

Paulston, Christina Bratt. 1997. "Language Policies and Language Rights." *Annual Review of Anthropology* 26:73–85.

Pecos, Regis, and Rebecca Blum-Martinez. 2001. "The Key to Cultural Survival: Language Planning and Revitalization in the Pueblo de Cochiti." In Hinton and Hale, *The Green Book*, 75–82.

Pennycock, Allan. 1994. "Incommensurable Discourses?" *Applied Linguistics* 15(2): 115–38.

Perley, Bernard C. 2002. "Language, Culture and Landscape: Protecting Aboriginal 'Deep Time' for Tomorrow." http://projects.gsd.harvard.edu/heritage. Accessed 2007.

———. 2006. "Aboriginality at Large: Varieties of Resistance in Maliseet Language Instruction." *Identities: Global Studies in Culture and Power* 13(2): 187–208.

Philips, Susan. 1983. *The Invisible Culture: Communication in Classroom and Community on the Warm Springs Indian Reservation*. Research on Teaching Monograph series. New York: Longman.

——. 1989. "Warm Springs 'Indian Time': How the Regulation of Participation Affects the Progression of Events." In *Explorations in the Ethnography of Speaking*. Ed. R. Bauman and J. Scherzer. Cambridge: Cambridge University Press. 92–109.

——. 1992. "Evidentiary Standards for American Trials: Just the Facts." In *Responsibility and Evidence in Oral Discourse*. Ed. Jane H. Hill and Judith T. Irvine. Cambridge: Cambridge University Press.

——. 1998a. "Ideologies in Institutions of Power: A Commentary." In Schieffelin, Woolard, and Kroskrity, *Language Ideologies*, 211–28.

——. 1998b. *Ideology in the Language of Judges*. Oxford: Oxford University Press.

——. 2002. "Constructing a Tongan Nation State through Language Ideology in the Courtroom." In Kroskrity, *Regimes of Language*.

Phillipson, Robert. 1992. *Linguistic Imperialism*. Oxford: Oxford University Press.

Phinney, Jean. 1989. "Stages of Ethnic Identity Development in Minority Group Adolescents." *Journal of Early Adolescence* 9(1–2): 34–49.

Phone, Wilhelmina, Maureen Olson, and Matilda Martinez. 2007. *Abáachi Mizaa Łáo Ilkee' Shijai: Dictionary of Jicarilla Apache*. Ed. Melissa Axelrod, Jule Gómez de García, and Jordan Lachler, with Sean Burke. Albuquerque: University of New Mexico Press.

Pickering, Kathleen. 2004. "Decolonizing Time Regimes: Lakota Conceptions of Work, Economy, and Society." *American Anthropologist* 106(1): 85–97.

Pike, Kenneth. 1947. "The Formation of Practical Alphabets." In *Phonemics: A Technique for Reducing Languages to Writing*. Ann Arbor: University of Michigan Press.

Platero, Paul. 1992. "Navajo Headstart Language Study." Ms. on file, Navajo Division of Education, Window Rock, AZ.

——. 2001. "Navajo Head Start Language Study." In Hinton and Hale, *The Green Book*, 87–100.

Pommersheim, Frank. 1995a. *Braid of Feathers: American Indian Law and Contemporary Tribal Life*. Berkeley: University of California Press.

——. 1995b. "Tribal Courts: Providers of Justice and Protectors of Sovereignty." *Judicature* 79:97.

Porter, Robert B. 1997. "Strengthening Tribal Sovereignty through Peacemaking: How the Anglo-American Legal Tradition Destroys Indigenous Societies." *Columbia Human Rights Law Review* 20:235–304.

Prucha, F. P. 1973. *Americanizing the American Indian: Writings by Friends of the Indian, 1800–1900*. Cambridge, MA: Harvard University Press.

Pullum, Geoffrey K. 1991. *The Great Eskimo Vocabulary Hoax and Other Irreverent Essays on the Study of Language*. Chicago: University of Chicago Press.

Pye, Clifton. 1992. "Language Loss among the Chilcotin." *International Journal of the Sociology of Language* 93:75–86.

Rampton, Ben. 1995. *Crossing: Language and Ethnicity among Adolescents*. London: Longman Publishing.

Recovery of Historical Memory Project. 1999. *Guatemala Never Again!* Maryknoll, NY: Orbis Books.

Reed, Eric. 1944. "Navajo Monolingualism." *American Anthropologist* 46:147–49.

Reyhner, Jon, ed. 1997. *Teaching Indigenous Languages*. Flagstaff: Northern Arizona University Press.

Reyhner, Jon, and Jeanne Eder. 1992. *American Indian Education: A History*. Norman: University of Oklahoma Press.

Reynolds, Jennifer Fiona. 1997. "Creating Complementary Research Agendas out of Competing Canons: Doing Linguistic Anthropology in Guatemala." Paper presented at the 119th annual meeting of the American Ethnological Society, Seattle, March 6–9.

———. 2002. "Maya Children's Practices of the Imagination: (Dis)Playing Childhood and Politics in Guatemala." Ph.D. diss., Department of Anthropology, University of California, Los Angeles.

Rice, Keren, and Leslie Saxon. 2002. "Issues of Standardization and Community in Aboriginal Language Lexicography." In Frawley, Hill, and Munro, *Making Dictionaries*, 125–54.

Richards, Julia Becker. 1998. "Case Study One: San Marcos La Laguna." In Garzon et al., *The Life of Our Language*, 62–100.

Richards, Julia Becker, and Michael Richards. 1996. "Maya Education: A Historical and Contemporary Analysis of Mayan Language Education Policy." In Fischer and Brown, *Maya Cultural Activism*, 208–22.

Richland, Justin B. 2005. "'What Are You Going to Do with the Village's Knowledge?' Talking Tradition, Talking Law in Hopi Tribal Court." *Law and Society Review* 39(2): 235–72.

———. 2007. "Pragmatic Paradoxes and the Ironies of Indigeneity at the Edge of Hopi Sovereignty." *American Ethnologist* 34(3): 540–57.

———. In press. "Arguing with Tradition." In *The Language of Law in Hopi Tribal Court*. Chicago: University of Chicago Press.

Riles, Annelise. 2000. *The Network inside Out*. Ann Arbor: University of Michigan Press.

Rogoff, Barbara. 2003. *The Cultural Nature of Human Development*. Oxford: Oxford University Press.

Romaine, Suzanne. 1989. *Bilingualism*. Cambridge: Blackwell.

Rosaldo, Renato. 1988. "Ideology, Place, and People without Culture." *Cultural Anthropology* 3:77–87.

Rosenbaum, Brenda. 1993. *With Our Heads Bowed: The Dynamics of Gender in a Maya Community*. Albany: Institute for Mesoamerican Studies, State University of New York.

Rosier, Paul, and Wayne Holm. 1980. *The Rock Point Experience: A Longitudinal Study of a Navajo School Program (Saad Naaki Bee Na'nitin)*. Washington, D.C.: Center for Applied Linguistics.

Rumsey, Alan. 1990. "Wording, Meaning, and Linguistic Ideology." *American Anthropologist* 92:346–61.

Russell, Evalu Ware. 1991. *A Kiowa Language Sampler*. Richardson, TX: Various Indian Peoples Publishing Co.

Salzmann, Zdenek. 1998. *Language, Culture, and Society: An Introduction to Linguistic Anthropology*. Boulder, CO: Westview Press.

Sapir, Edward. 1934. "The Emergence of a Concept of Personality in a Study of Cultures." *Journal of Social Psychology* 5:408–15.

——. 1949a. *Language: An Introduction to the Study of Speech*. New York: Harcourt Brace. (Orig. pub. 1921.)

——. 1949b. "The Social Organization of the West Coast Tribes." In *Edward Sapir: Selected Writings in Language, Culture and Personality*. Ed. David Mandelbaum. Berkeley: University of California Press. 468–88.

——. 1994. "The Patterning of Culture." In *The Psychology of Culture*. Ed. Judith Irvine. Berlin: Mouton de Gruyter. 103–23.

Schaafsma, Curtis. 2002. *Apaches de Navajo: Seventeenth-Century Navajos in the Chama Valley of New Mexico*. Salt Lake City: University of Utah Press.

Schaengold, Charlotte. 2004. "Bilingual Navajo: Mixed Codes, Bilingualism, and Language Maintenance." Ph.D. diss., Department of Linguistics, Ohio State University.

Scheper-Hughes, Nancy, and Carolyn Sargent, eds. 1998. *Small Wars: The Cultural Politics of Childhood*. Berkeley: University of California Press.

Schieffelin, Bambi B. 1990. *The Give and Take of Everyday Life: Language Socialization of Kaluli Children*. Cambridge: Cambridge University Press.

Schieffelin, Bambi, and Rachelle Charlier Doucet. 1994. "The 'Real' Haitian Creole: Ideology, Metalinguistics, and Orthographic Choice." *American Ethnologist* 21(1): 176–200.

Schieffelin, Bambi B., and Elinor Ochs. 1979. *Language Socialization across Cultures*. Cambridge: Cambridge University Press.

Schieffelin, Bambi B., Kathryn A. Woolard, and Paul V. Kroskrity, eds. 1998. *Language Ideologies: Practice and Theory*. New York: Oxford University Press.

Schiffman, Harold. 1996. *Linguistic Culture and Language Policy*. London: Routledge.

Schmidt, Annette. 1985. *Young People's Dyirbal: An Example of Language Death from Australia*. Cambridge: Cambridge University Press.

Scollon, Ron, and Suzanne Scollon. 1981. *Narrative, Literacy and Face in Interethnic Communication*. Norwood, NJ: Ablex.

——. 1995. *Intercultural Communication: A Discourse Approach*. Malden, MA: Blackwell.

Sherzer, Joel. 1976. *An Areal-Typological Study of American Indian Languages North of Mexico*. Amsterdam: North-Holland.

Silentman, Irene. 1995. "Revaluing Indigenous Language Resources through Language Planning." *Bilingual Research Journal* 19(1): 179–82.

Silver, Shirley, and Wick R. Miller. 1997. *American Indian Languages: Cultural and Social Contexts*. Tucson: University of Arizona Press.

Silverstein, Michael. 1979. "Language Structure and Linguistic Ideology." In *The Elements: A Parasession on Linguistic Units and Levels*. Ed. P. R. Clyne et al. Chicago: Chicago Linguistic Society. 193–247.

——. 1981. *The Limits of Awareness*. Working Papers in Sociolinguistics, no. 84. Austin: Southwest Educational Development Laboratory.

——. 1985. "Language and the Culture of Gender." In *Semiotic Mediation*. Ed. Elizabeth Mertz and Richard Parmentier. New York: Academic Press. 219–59.

———. 1993. "Metapragmatic Discourse and Metapragmatic Function." In *Reflexive Language*. Ed. John Lucy. Cambridge: Cambridge University Press.

———. 1996. "Encountering Language and the Languages of Encounter in North American Ethnohistory." *Journal of Linguistic Anthropology* 6:126–44.

———. 1998a. "Contemporary Transformations of Local Linguistic Communities." *Annual Review of Anthropology* 27:401–26.

———. 1998b. "The Uses and Utility of Ideology." In Schieffelin, Woolard, and Kroskrity, *Language Ideologies*, 123–48.

———. 2003a. "Indexical Order and the Dialectics of Sociolinguistic Life." *Language and Communication* 23(3–4): 193–229.

———. 2003b. "The Whens and Wheres—as Well as Hows—of Ethnolinguistic Recognition." *Public Culture* 31(3): 531–57.

———. 2004. " 'Cultural' Concepts and the Language-Culture Nexus." *Current Anthropology* 45(5): 621–52.

Sims, Christine. 2001. "Native Language Planning: A Pilot Process in the Acoma Pueblo Community." In Hinton and Hale, *The Green Book*, 75–82.

Sis Ib'oy, Nickte'. 2000. "Dos pueblos con un idioma: El caso K'ichee'-Achi'." Paper presented at the Latin American Studies Association's Twenty-second International Congress, Miami, March 16–18.

Sivertson, Eva. 1956. "Pitch Problems in Kiowa." *International Journal of American Linguistics* 22:117–30.

Smith, Carol A. 1990. "Conclusion: History and Revolution in Guatemala." In *Guatemalan Indians and the State: 1540–1988*. Ed. Carol A. Smith. Austin: University of Texas Press. 258–85.

Smith, Linda Tuhiwai. 1999. *Decolonizing Methodologies: Research and Indigenous Peoples*. London: Zed Books.

Smith, Michael French. 1982. "Bloody Time and Bloody Scarcity: Capitalism, Authority, and the Transformation of Temporal Experience in a Papua New Guinea Village." *American Ethnologist* 9(3): 503–18.

Snider, Keith. 2001. "Linguistic Factors in Orthography Design." In *Research in African Linguistics: Focus on Cameroon*. Ed. N. Mutaka and S. Chumbow. Cologne, Germany: Rüdiger Köppe Verlag. 323–32.

Speirs, Anna. 1974. "Classificatory Verb Stems in Tewa." *Studies in Linguistics* 24:45–64.

Speirs, Randall. 1968. "Some Aspects of the Structure of Rio Grande Tewa." Ph.D. diss., State University of New York.

———. 1972. "Number in Tewa." In *Studies in Linguistics in Honor of George L. Trager*. Ed. M. Estellie Smith. Janua Linguarum, series maior, 52. The Hague: Mouton. 479–86.

Spicer, Edward H. 1954. "Spanish-Indian Acculturation in the Southwest." *American Anthropologist* 56(4): 663–78.

Spier, Robert F. G. 1978. "Monache." In *California*. Ed. R. F. Heizer. Vol. 8 of *Handbook of North American Indians*. Washington, D.C.: Smithsonian Institution Press. 426–36.

Spitulnik, Deborah. 1998a. "The Language of the City: Town Bemba as Urban Hybridity." *Journal of Linguistic Anthropology* 8(1): 30–59.

——. 1998b. "Mediating Unity and Diversity: The Production of Language Ideologies in Zambian Broadcasting." In Schieffelin, Woolard, and Kroskrity, *Language Ideologies*, 163–88.

Spolsky, Bernard. 1978. "American Indian Bilingual Education." In *Case Studies in Bilingual Education*. Ed. B. Spolsky and R. Cooper. Cambridge, MA: Newbury House. 332–61.

Spolsky, Bernard, and P. Irvine. 1982. "Sociolinguistic Aspects of the Acceptance of Literacy in the Vernacular." In *Bilingualism and Language Contact: Spanish, English, and Native American Languages*. Ed. F. Barkin, E. Brandt, and J. Ornstein-Galicia. New York: Teacher's College Press. 73–79.

Starkloff, Carl F. 1974. *The People of the Center: American Indian Religion and Christianity*. New York: Seabury Press.

Stephens, Sharon. 1995. "Children and the Politics of Culture in 'Late Capitalism.' " In *Children and the Politics of Culture*. Ed. Sharon Stephens. Princeton, NJ: Princeton University Press. 3–48.

Stiles, Dawn B. 1997. "Four Successful Indigenous Language Programs." In Reyhner, *Teaching Indigenous Languages*, 148–262.

Sullivan, David. 1998. *Conversational Kiowa: A Study Guide*. Chickasha: University of Science and Arts of Oklahoma Press.

Sun Rhodes, Dennis. 1993. "My Home: A Communal American Indian Home." *Native Peoples Magazine* 6(3): 40–47.

Swamp, Jake. 1997. *Giving Thanks: A Native American Good Morning Message*. Reprinted. New York: Lee and Low Books.

Swanson, Earl H., Jr., ed. 1970. *Languages and Cultures of Western North America: Essays in Honor of Sven S. Liljeblad*. Pocatello: Idaho State University Press.

Swigart, Leigh. 2000. "The Limits of Legitimacy: Language Ideology and Shift in Contemporary Senegal." *Journal of Linguistic Anthropology* 10:90–130.

Szasz, Margaret. 1974. *Education and the American Indian: The Road to Self-Determination since 1928*. Albuquerque: University of New Mexico Press.

——. 1988. *Indian Education in the American Colonies, 1607–1783*. Albuquerque: University of New Mexico Press.

Tax, Sol. 1937. "The *Municipios* of the Midwestern Highlands of Guatemala." *American Anthropologist* 39(3): 423–44.

Tax, Sol, and Robert K. Thomas. 1969. "An Experiment in Cross-Cultural Education, 1962–1967." In U.S. Congress, Senate, *Hearings before a Special Subcommittee on Indian Education*, 940–58.

Taylor, Charles. 1989. *Sources of the Self*. Cambridge, MA: Harvard University Press.

Tedlock, D., and B. Mannheim, eds. 1995. *The Dialogic Emergence of Culture*. Urbana: University of Illinois Press.

Thomason, Sarah. 2001. *Language Contact*. Washington, D.C.: Georgetown University Press.

Thompson, Charles D., Jr. 2001. *Maya Identities and the Violence of Place*. Burlington, VT: Ashgate Publishing Ltd.

Thompson, E. P. 1967. "Time, Work and Discipline in Industrial Capitalism." *Past and Present* 38:56–97.

Tidzump, Malinda. 1970. *Shoshone Thesaurus*. Grand Forks: Summer Institute of Linguistics, University of North Dakota.

Titiev, Mischa. 1944. *Old Oraibi: A Study of the Hopi Indians of Third Mesa*. Harvard University, Peabody Museum of American Archaeology and Ethnology Papers, vol. 22(1).

Tlen, Daniel L. 1986. *Speaking Out: Consultations and Survey of Yukon Native Languages: Planning, Visibility and Growth*. Council for Yukon Indians and Government of Yukon. Whitehorse, YT: Queen's Printer.

Toll, Oliver W. 1914. "Report on the Visit of Arapaho Indians to Estes Park." Manuscript from the Collections of the Colorado Historical Society.

——. 1962. *Arapaho Names and Trails: A Report of a 1914 Pack Trip*. Published by the author.

Trager, Felicia. 1968. "Picuris Pueblo: A Language Salvage Study." Ph.D. diss., State University of New York at Buffalo.

Trechter, Sara. 1999. "Contextualizing the Exotic Few: Gender Dichotomies in Lakhota." In *Reinventing Identities: The Gendered Self in Discourse*. Ed. M. Bucholtz, A. C. Liang, and L. A. Sutton. New York: Oxford University Press. 101–19.

——. 2001. "White between the Lines: Ethnic Positioning in Lakhota Discourse." *Journal of Linguistic Anthropology* 11:22–35.

——. 2006. *Gendered Voices in Lakhota*. New York: Oxford University Press.

Trudel, François. 1992. "La politique des gouvernements du Canada et du Québec en matière de langues autochtones." In *Les langues autochtones du Québec*. Ed. Jacques Maurais. Quebec City: Conseil supérieur de la langue française.

Tsosie, Rebecca. 2002. "Symposium: Cultural Sovereignty: Native Rights in the 21st Century." *Arizona State Law Journal* 34:1–14.

Urban, Greg. 1991. *A Discourse-Centered Approach to Culture: Native South American Myths and Rituals*. Austin: University of Texas Press.

U.S. Census. 2002. PHC-T-18, American Indian and Alaska Native Tribes in the United States, Table 1: "American Indian and Alaska Native Alone or Alone and in Combination Population by Tribe for the United States." www.census.gov/population/cen2000/phc-t18/tab001.pdf.

U.S. Congress. 1868. *Report of Indian Peace Commissioners*. January 14. 40th Cong., 2nd sess.

U.S. Congress. Senate. 1969. *Hearings before a Special Subcommittee on Indian Education of the Senate Committee on Labor and Public Welfare, on the Study of the Education of Indian Children*. 90th Cong., 1st and 2nd sess., pt. 2. Washington, D.C.: Government Printing Office.

Valencia-Webber, Gloria. 1994. "Tribal Courts: Custom and Innovative Law." *New Mexico Law Review* 24:225–32.

Valentine, Lisa. 1994. "Performing Native Identities." In *Papers of the Algonquian Conference*, vol. 25. Ottawa, ON: National Museums of Canada. 482–92.

——. 1995. *Making It Their Own: Severn Ojibwe Communicative Practices*. Toronto, ON: University of Toronto Press.

Vicenti, Carey. 1981. *Jicarilla Apache Dictionary*. Albuquerque, NM: Native American Materials Development Center, Ramah Navajo School Board.

Vincenti, C. N. 1995. "The Reemergence of Tribal Society and Traditional Justice Systems." *Judicature* 79(3): 134–41.

Vizenor, Gerald. 1994. *Manifest Manners*. Lincoln: University of Nebraska Press.

Voegelin, C. F., F. M. Voegelin, and W. Schutz. 1967. "The Language Situation in Arizona as Part of the Southwest Culture Area." In *Studies in Southwestern Ethnolinguistics*. Ed. D. Hymes and W. Bittle. The Hague: Mouton. 403–51.

Vogt, Evon Z., and Malcolm Arth. 1970. *People of Rimrock: A Study of Values in Five Cultures*. New York: Athenaeum.

Voloshinov, V. N. 1962. *Thought and Language*. Ed. and trans. Eugenia Hanfmann and Gertrude Vakar. New York: Wiley.

——. 1973. *Marxism and the Philosophy of Language*. New York: Seminar Press.

Vygotsky, Lev. 1986. *Thought and Language*. Cambridge, MA: MIT Press.

Wachacha, Herbert, and Yvonne Wachacha. 1981. "Tradition and Change: Traditions Kept by the Snowbird Cherokees of Graham County." In *The Cherokee Perspective*. Ed. L. French and J. Hornbuckle. Boone, NC: Appalachian Consortium Press. 58–62.

Wahrhaftig, Albert L. 1969a. "The Cherokee People Today." In U.S. Congress, Senate, *Hearings before a Special Subcommittee on Indian Education*, 795–883.

——. 1969b. "The Tribal Cherokee Population of Eastern Oklahoma: Report of a Demographic Survey of Cherokee Settlements in the Cherokee Nation." In U.S. Congress, Senate, *Hearings before a Special Subcommittee on Indian Education*, 897–939.

——. 1998. "Looking back to Tahlequah: Robert K. Thomas' Role among the Oklahoma Cherokee, 1963–1967." In *A Good Cherokee, a Good Anthropologist: Papers in Honor of Robert K. Thomas*. Ed. S. Pavlik. Los Angeles: American Indian Studies Center, University of California, Los Angeles. 93–104.

Wald, Benji. 1981. "English in Los Angeles: Searching for a Speech Community." In *Style and Variables in English*. Ed. T. Shopen and J. Williams. Cambridge: Winthrop.

Waldman, C. 1999. *Encyclopedia of Native American Tribes*. New York: Checkmark.

——. 2000. *Atlas of the North American Indian*. New York: Checkmark.

Walker, Willard. 1969. "Notes on Native Writing Systems and the Design of Native Literacy Programs." *Anthropological Linguistics* 11(5): 148–66.

Wallerstein, Immanuel. 1991. "The Construction of Peoplehood: Racism, Nationalism, Ethnicity." In *Race, Nation, Class: Ambiguous Identities*. Ed. Etienne Balibar and Immanuel Wallerstein. London: Verso. 71–85.

Warren, Kay B. 1992. "Transforming Memories and Histories: The Meanings of Ethnic Resurgence for Mayan Indians." In *Americas: New Interpretive Essays*. Ed. Alfred Stepan. New York: Oxford University Press. 189–219.

——. 1998. *Indigenous Movements and Their Critics: Pan-Maya Activism in Guatemala*. Princeton, NJ: Princeton University Press.

Warrior, Robert, and Paul Chaat Smith. 1996. *Like a Hurricane: The Indian Movement from Alcatraz to Wounded Knee.* New York: New Press.

Watanabe, John M. 2000. "Maya and Anthropologists in the Highlands of Guatemala since the 1960s." In *Ethnology.* Ed. John D. Monaghan and Barbara W. Edmonson. Vol. 6 of *Supplement to the Handbook of Middle American Indians.* Austin: University of Texas Press. 224–47.

Watchman, D. 1994. "Johnson O'Malley Act Promotes Native American Education." *Forum* 17(6): 1–2.

Watkins, Laurel. 1984. *A Grammar of Kiowa.* Lincoln: University of Nebraska Press.

Wellmeier, Nancy J. 1998. *Ritual, Identity, and the Mayan Diaspora.* New York: Garland Publishing, Inc.

White Hat, Albert, Sr. 1999. *Introduction to Reading and Writing the Lakota Language.* Salt Lake City: University of Utah Press.

Whiteley, Peter. 1992. "Hopitutungwni: Hopi Names as Literature." In *On the Translation of Native American Literatures.* Ed. Brian Swann. Washington, D.C.: Smithsonian Institution Press. 208–27.

———. 1998. *Rethinking Hopi Ethnography.* Washington, D.C.: Smithsonian Institution Press.

———. 2003. "Do 'Language Rights' Serve Indigenous Interests? Some Hopi and Other Queries." *American Anthropologist* 105(4): 712–22.

Whorf, Benjamin Lee. 1956. *Language, Thought, and Reality.* Cambridge, MA: MIT Press.

Wiget, Andrew. 1987. "Telling the Tale: A Performance Analysis of a Hopi Coyote Story." In *Recovering the Word.* Ed. B. Swann and A. Krupat. Berkeley: University of California Press. 297–336.

Williams, Brackette. 1993. "The Impact of the Precepts of Nationalism on the Concept of Culture: Making Grasshoppers of Naked Apes." *Cultural Critique* (Spring): 143–91.

Williams, Raymond. 1977. *Marxism and Literature.* Oxford: Oxford University Press.

Wilson, Alan, and Rita Vigil Martine. 1996. *Apache.* Guilford, CT: Audio-Forum.

Witherspoon, Gary. 1977. *Language and Art in the Navajo Universe.* Ann Arbor: University of Michigan Press.

———. 1980. "Language in Culture and Culture in Language." *International Journal of American Linguistics* 46(1): 1–13.

Woolard, Kathryn A. 1985. "Language Variation and Cultural Hegemony." *American Ethnologist* 12(4): 738–48.

———. 1989. "Language Convergence and Language Death as Social Processes." In Dorian, *Investigating Obsolescence,* 355–67.

———. 1998. "Language Ideology as a Field of Inquiry." In Schieffelin, Woolard, and Kroskrity, *Language Ideologies,* 51–67.

Woolard, Kathryn A., and Bambi B. Schieffelin. 1994. "Language Ideology." *Annual Review of Anthropology* 23:55–82.

Yamane, Linda. 2001. "New Life for a Lost Language." In Hinton and Hale, *The Green Book,* 429–32.

Young, Robert. 1968. *The Role of the Navajo in the Southwestern Drama*. Gallup, NM: Gallup Independent.

——. 2000. *The Navajo Verb System: An Overview*. Albuquerque: University of New Mexico Press.

Young, Robert W., E. Jelinek, and L. Saxon. 1996. *Athabaskan Language Studies: Essays in Honor of Robert W. Young*. Albuquerque: University of New Mexico Press.

Young, Robert, and William Morgan. 1984. *A Colloquial Navajo Dictionary*. New York: Hippocrene Books.

——. 1987. *The Navajo Language: A Grammar and Colloquial Dictionary*. Albuquerque: University of New Mexico Press.

Young, Robert, William Morgan, and Sally Midgette. 1992. *Analytical Lexicon of Navajo*. Albuquerque: University of New Mexico Press.

Zaharlick, Amy. 1974. "Pronominal Reference in Picuris." *Studies in Linguistics* 25:79–88.

——. 1977. "Picuris Syntax." Ph.D. diss., American University.

——. 1980. "An Outline of Picuris Syntax." *Annals of the New York Academy of Sciences* 345:147–63.

——. 1981. "A Preliminary Examination of Tone in Picuris." In "Native Languages of the Americas." Special issue, *Journal of the Linguistic Association of the Southwest* 4(2): 123–29.

——. 1982. "Tanoan Studies: Passive Sentences in Picuris." *Ohio State University, Working Papers in Linguistics* 26:34–48.

Zepeda, Ofelia, and Jane H. Hill. 1991. "The Condition of Native American Languages in the United States." In *Endangered Languages*. Ed. R. H. Robins and M. Uhlenbeck. New York: Berg. 135–55.

Zion, James W. 1987. "Searching for Indian Common Law." In *Indigenous Law and the State*. Ed. Bradford Morse and Gordon Woodman. Dordrecht, the Netherlands: Foris Publications. 121–48.

About the Contributors

Jeffrey D. Anderson (Ph.D., University of Chicago) is associate professor of anthropology at Colby College. His research has focused on the language, culture, and history of the Northern Arapaho tribe. He is author of *The Four Hills of Life: Northern Arapaho Knowledge and Life Movement* (2001), *One Hundred Years of Old Man Sage: An Arapaho Life Story* (2003), and various articles. His topical interests include creativity, language shift, ethnoepistemology, ethnopoetics, age grade systems, human rights, ethnohistory, and comparative human development. He is currently working on a book about Arapaho women's quillwork art.

Melissa Axelrod (Ph.D., University of Colorado) is professor of linguistics at the University of New Mexico in Albuquerque. Her research focuses on morphology, semantics, and sociolinguistic issues in Native American languages. Along with colleagues Jule Gómez de García, Jordan Lachler, and Sean Burke, she is the editor of *Abáachi Mizaa Łáo Iłkee' Shijai: Dictionary of Jicarilla Apache* (2007). She also served as editor of the *Dictionary of Koyukon Athabaskan* (2000) and is the author of *The Semantics of Time: Aspectual Categorization in Koyukon Athabaskan* (1993). She is currently working on two NSF-funded projects, one to produce a dictionary, grammar, and pedagogical materials for Nambé Tewa in collaboration with language specialists at Nambé Pueblo in New Mexico and the second to produce an electronic archive of oral history and linguistic documentation with an Ixil Mayan woman's cooperative, the Grupo de Mujeres por la Paz, in highland Guatemala.

Margaret Bender received her Ph.D. in anthropology from the University of Chicago and currently teaches anthropology and linguistics at Wake Forest University. Her 2002 book, *Signs of Cherokee Culture: Sequoyah's Syllabary in Eastern Cherokee Life*, explored the religious, social, and political implications of reading and writing in the Cherokee language. *Signs* received the James Mooney Award from the Southern Anthropological Society in 2004. More recently (2004), she edited a volume entitled *Linguistic Diversity in the South: Changing Codes, Practices and Ideology.* Bender's research and teaching interests also include educational anthropology, gender studies, and Native American studies. She is currently working on a comparison of attitudes toward and practices related to fatherhood and masculinity in two Oklahoma Indian communities and on linguistic analyses of Cherokee medicinal and religious texts.

Pamela A. Bunte is a professor of anthropology and linguistics at California State University, Long Beach, where she was chair of the Department of Anthropology from 1989 to 1995. She received an M.A. in French in 1974 and her Ph.D. in anthropology in 1979 from Indiana University. Her dissertation research was with the Kaibab Paiutes. She later began working with the San Juan Paiute community in 1980 on a dictionary. Her research interests include verbal art, language socialization, intercultural communication, language maintenance and revitalization, and language ideology. She worked with the San Juan Paiute tribe on their successful federal recognition case, and this research produced *From the Sands to the Mountain: Change and Persistence in a Southern Paiute Community.* She has continued to work with the San Juan Paiute Tribe on land claims and other applied projects. She also recently completed a five-year project working on the federal recognition of the Little Shell Chippewas of Montana. Her current project is to finish writing a book, "Words on the Wind," which combines many of her aforementioned research interests. In addition, she is working to complete the dictionary of San Juan Paiute that she started in 1980.

Margaret C. Field is associate professor and chair of American Indian studies at San Diego State University. She received her Ph.D. in linguistics from the University of California, Santa Barbara. Her research interests include American Indian languages, language socialization, language ideology, and multimedia applications to language maintenance, among other things. Her current research focuses on the relationship between language ideology and the development of lexical dialects in the Kumeyaay community of Baja, California.

Jule Gómez de García (Ph.D., University of Colorado) is an associate professor at California State University, San Marcos, where she teaches linguistics in the Department of Liberal Studies. She is an expert in the area of language documentation and revitalization who has done research and linguistic consultation with the Oklahoma Kickapoo and, in collaboration with Dr. Melissa Axelrod, with the Mescalero, Plains, and Jicarilla Apache communities. Along with colleagues Axelrod, Jordan Lachler, and Sean Burke she is an editor of *Abáachi Mizaa Łáo Iłkee' Shijai: Dictionary of Jicarilla Apache* (2007). She is currently working with the Grupo de Mujeres por la Paz, an Ixil Maya women's cooperative in Guatemala, to produce a multimedia archive of Ixil conversations, narratives, and oral histories.

Paul V. Kroskrity is a professor of anthropology at UCLA, where he served as the chair of the Interdepartmental Program in American Indian Studies from 1985 to 2007. He received his B.A. from Columbia College, Columbia University, and earned his Ph.D. in anthropology from Indiana University in 1977. His involvement with Native American communities began with his dissertation research in 1973 on the Arizona Tewas. This developed into more than two decades of research involvement on Arizona Tewa grammar, sociolinguistics, verbal art, and language ideology. This research resulted in numerous articles and books on these topics, including *Language, History and Identity: Ethnolinguistic Studies of the Arizona Tewa* (1993), the edited collection *Regimes of Language: Ideologies, Polities, and Identities* (2000), and the coedited volume *Language Ideologies: Practice and Theory* (1998). In addition, he has also worked with members of the Western Mono communities of North Fork and Auberry in central California. This research has focused on lexicography, language contact, verbal art, and language revitalization and has continued since 1980, when the UCLA Mono Language Project began. In addition to numerous articles, this community-based research has produced *A Practical Dictionary of Western Mono and Taitaduhaan: Western Mono Ways of Speaking* (CD-ROM, 2003). His current research projects are concerned with dictionary making and producing edited collections of representative verbal art for both of these communities.

Jordan Lachler is the Haida language program director for the Sealaska Heritage Institute in Ketchikan, Alaska. He received his Ph.D. in linguistics from the University of New Mexico in 2006, writing a grammar of Laguna Keres for his dissertation. His work involves the practical application of linguistic documentation and multimedia technologies in the day-to-day process of language revitalization in the Haida community. He is one of the coeditors of the recently published *Dictionary of Jicarilla*

Apache (2007) and is a coauthor of *A Handbook of the Cherokee Verb* (2003). He travels widely in the United States and Canada, providing training on language technology and curriculum development for Native language communities. He is also currently working on a project to document Oroha, an endangered language from the Solomon Islands.

Christopher Loether received his Ph.D. in anthropological linguistics from the University of California Los Angeles in 1991. He has taught at Idaho State University since 1989. His specialties include the Uto-Aztecan languages, Semitic languages, Celtic languages, sociolinguistics, and the study of endangered languages. He became interested in Welsh when he lived in Britain as a child and has been studying the Welsh language movement since 1990. He has been studying Western Mono since 1979, Shoshone since 1989, and Owens Valley Paiute since 2000. He is currently working on a Geographic Information Systems map of Shoshone dialects in time and space.

Barbra A. Meek is a Comanche citizen and an assistant professor of anthropology and a faculty affiliate of Native American studies at the University of Michigan. After completing her undergraduate degrees at the University of Akron in Akron, Ohio, she pursued a joint Ph.D. in linguistics and anthropology from the University of Arizona, Tucson. Her forthcoming book, *We Are Our Language: An Ethnography of Language Revitalization in a Northern Athabaskan Community, Yukon Territory, Canada,* describes the social and linguistic circumstances affecting and complicating Kaska language revitalization (a Northern Athabaskan language spoken in the Yukon Territory and British Columbia, Canada). She frames language revitalization as a sociolinguistic phenomenon and investigates its complexity through the interrelatedness of changing practices, emerging language ideologies, and the role of disjunctures in everyday life. In addition to this work she has also co-organized Kaska language revitalization workshops and coproduced Kaska language materials. Her current research project focuses on the ways in which the speech of American Indian peoples is portrayed across various public domains and the role such representations play in socialization.

Amber A. Neely received her B.A. in anthropology and German from the University of Notre Dame and her M.S. in anthropology and linguistics from the University of Amsterdam in 2004. She is pursuing her Ph.D. in anthropology at the University of Oklahoma. She worked with Dr.

Mary Linn on the Euchee Dictionary Project from 2005 to 2007 and is assistant teaching the course Language across Cultures. Her research interests include language ideologies, sociolinguistics, language variation, Native American languages, language change and obsolescence, language revitalization movements, lexicography, and the study and description of endangered languages. Her current research involves the process of language change and obsolescence, both structural and ideological aspects, in the Kiowa community. She is also currently working with a grassroots Kiowa community organization in Carnegie, Oklahoma, toward their goals of language teaching and revitalization.

Gus Palmer, Jr., is an associate professor in the Department of Anthropology and the Native American Studies Program at the University of Oklahoma. He is a linguistic anthropologist whose main area of concentration is on the Kiowa language. He is presently working on a Kiowa dictionary with other Kiowa speakers in Oklahoma. A fluent speaker of Kiowa, Palmer teaches and has been teaching Kiowa since 1992. He spent several summers working with the Pawnee Nation language revitalization and preservation program, producing curriculum and updating original South Band and Skiri digital sound recordings for use by tribal members. Palmer has written a book, *Telling Stories the Kiowa Way* (2003), and also poems and fiction in several anthologies and literary magazines.

Bernard C. Perley received his Ph.D. in anthropology from Harvard University and currently teaches linguistic anthropology and American Indian studies in the Department of Anthropology at the University of Wisconsin–Milwaukee. His research interests include language endangerment, language politics, repatriation, and American Indian sovereignty and self-determination. He returned to his community to examine the many factors contributing to the endangerment of the Maliseet language at Tobique First Nation in New Brunswick, Canada. While acknowledging the historical contexts of Aboriginal language endangerment, he is actively promoting Maliseet language maintenance and revitalization through the incorporation of language, oral traditions, and landscape as everyday practices of Aboriginal self-determination.

Jennifer F. Reynolds is an assistant professor in the Department of Anthropology at the University of South Carolina. She is a linguistic anthropologist who examines the relationship(s) between discursive practices and language ideologies as they are manifest in everyday life—from quotidian child language socialization routines, peers' and youths' playful ways with words, verbal art and narrative, immigrant practices of interpretation and translation in the United States, and counterhegemonic discourses promoted by social movements organized around issues of indigenous language revitalization and maintenance. She has worked extensively with young people, here and abroad, from Maya children in Guatemala to Samoan and Mexican immigrant children and youth in the United States. She explores how children experience and interpret the multiple dimensions of social inequality that shape their lives and pathways.

Justin B. Richland is assistant professor of criminology, law, and society at the University of California, Irvine. He received his Ph.D. in anthropology from UCLA in 2004 and his J.D. from UC Berkeley in 1996. His research considers the pragmatics and metapragmatics of law and cultural identity in the discourses of contemporary Hopi jurisprudence. This has resulted in publications that have appeared in various outlets, including *American Ethnologist*, *Law and Society Review*, and *Discourse and Society*. His book *Arguing with Tradition: The Language of Law in Hopi Tribal Court* is forthcoming from the University of Chicago Press. He is also justice pro tempore of the Hopi Appellate Court.

Index

CPSIA information can be obtained at www.ICGtesting.com
Printed in the USA
LVOW091207180911

246766LV00004B/2/P